The Proverbial
Charles Dickens

Dickens' Universe

Charlotte Rotkin
General Editor

Vol. 4

PETER LANG
New York • Washington, D.C./Baltimore
Bern • Frankfurt am Main • Berlin • Vienna • Paris

George B. Bryan
& Wolfgang Mieder

The Proverbial
Charles Dickens

An Index to Proverbs
in the Works
of Charles Dickens

PETER LANG
New York • Washington, D.C./Baltimore
Bern • Frankfurt am Main • Berlin • Vienna • Paris

Library of Congress Cataloging-in-Publication Data

Bryan, George B.
The proverbial Charles Dickens: an index to proverbs in the works
of Charles Dickens / George B. Bryan and Wolfgang Mieder.
p. cm. — (Dickens' universe; 4)
Includes bibliographical references.
1. Dickens, Charles, 1812–1870—Indexes. 2. Proverbs, English—Indexes.
I. Mieder, Wolfgang. II. Title. III. Series: Dickens' universe; vol. 4.
PR4580.B78   823'.8—DC21   97-13446
ISBN 0-8204-3837-5
ISSN 1054-8777

Die Deutsche Bibliothek-CIP-Einheitsaufnahme

Bryan, George B.:
The proverbial Charles Dickens: an index to proverbs in the works
of Charles Dickens / George B. Bryan and Wolfgang Mieder. –New York;
Washington, D.C./Baltimore; Bern; Frankfurt am Main;
Berlin; Vienna; Paris: Lang.
(Dickens' universe; 4)
ISBN 0-8204-3837-5

Cover design by James F. Brisson.

The paper in this book meets the guidelines for permanence and durability
of the Committee on Production Guidelines for Book Longevity
of the Council of Library Resources.

∞

© 1997 Peter Lang Publishing, Inc., New York

Printed in the United States of America.

CONTENTS

PREFACE

This book on the proverbial language of Charles Dickens was begun a good year ago by my dear colleague and special friend Prof. George B. Bryan and me with much excitement and vigor. We had previously joined forces to publish similar volumes on Bernard Shaw, Winston S. Churchill, Eugene O'Neill, and Harry S. Truman. But as we joyfully worked along on this vast Dickensian project, and as we could envision the end of our labors, George Bryan was suddenly and unexpectedly taken from my side by a massive heart attack on September 19, 1996. Shocked and deeply saddened by this tragic event, it has fallen upon me to conclude this book by myself. It has been a painful task, since fond memories of my friend kept entering my mind which in turn filled me with such grief and sadness that I could at times not work on the book's completion. Alas, I knew that George would want me to finish it, and I have now accomplished this task. Doubtlessly the book would be more perfect if George could have put the finishing touches on it as well, but I hope that I have brought our book to its conclusion in such a fashion that George would have been proud of it as well.

For me personally this book on Charles Dickens brings to an end my scholarly partnership with Prof. George B. Bryan. Together we managed to write some useful volumes, and I will always treasure our joint accomplishments. We had many other projects on the "back burner," and we had hoped to have the time and pleasure to complete them. Some of them I intend to execute during the years that I might still have left to work, and my dear friend George will doubtlessly look over my shoulder and encourage me with his unforgotten gentle smile, his vast knowledge imparted onto me over the years, and his rigorous and untiring work ethics which made us such a perfect research team.

December 1996   Wolfgang Mieder

HOW TO USE THIS BOOK

The work consists of an introductory essay on Dickens's use of proverbs, a list of the editions of his works consulted, and a Key-word Index, which is the heart of the book.

Proverbs are arranged in the Key-word Index according to the most significant word, usually a noun, in the text. Each entry is preceded by the year of writing or utterance and followed by the page number. The precise reference to the particular work from Dickens is then added in small print. Examples of the same proverb are listed chronologically, which demonstrates the range of the years of its use. On a separate line after each different proverb is a citation of lexicographical sources in major proverb and quotation dictionaries that provide additional historical information.

CHARLES DICKENS AND THE PROVERB

> I had (and have all my life) observed that conventional
> phrases are a sort of fireworks, easily let off, and liable
> to take a great variety of shapes and colours not at all
> suggested by their original form.
>
> *The Personal History of David Copperfield.* 1850. The
> Oxford Illustrated Dickens, Vol. II. Oxford: Oxford Univer-
> sity Press, 1948, p. 590.

The vast scholarship on Charles Dickens (1812-1870) has rather
tangentially dealt with his rich proverbial language. While a few scholars
have commented in passing on Dickens's predilection for the use of
metaphorical language, no detailed study has ever been undertaken to
register and interpret the contextual function of the numerous proverbs,
proverbial expressions, proverbial comparisons, and wellerisms in his
voluminous works. James S. Stevens has included a few traditional texts
in his *Quotations and References in Charles Dickens* (Boston: The
Christopher Publishing House, 1929), the same is true in the case of
Fred Levit, *A Dickens Glossary* (New York: Garland Publishing, 1990),
and the newer compilation of *The Sayings of Charles Dickens* (London:
Gerald Duckworth, 1995), edited by Cedric Charles Dickens and Alan
S. Watts, also includes but fifteen proverbial texts. At least some
elements of folk speech are also registered in George Newlin's *Every
Thing in Dickens: Ideas and Subjects Discussed by Charles Dickens in
His Complete Works* (Westport, Connecticut: Greenwood Press, 1996).[1]

---

[1]See also "A Sampler of Quotations," in Michael and Mollie
Hardwick, *The Charles Dickens Companion* (London: John Murray,
1965), pp. 173-228; "Familiar Sayings" and "Wellerisms," in Arthur L.
Hayward, *The Dickens Encyclopaedia* (Hamden, Connecticut: Archon
Books, 1968), pp. 171-174; "Quotations," in M. and M. Hardwick, *The
Charles Dickens Encyclopedia* (New York: Charles Scribner's Sons,
1973), pp. 239-521; "Neologisms" and "Archaisms," in Knud Sørensen,
Charles Dickens: Linguistic Innovator (Aarhus: Arkona, 1985), pp. 115-
171; and Nicolas Bentley, Michael Slater, and Nina Burgis, *The Dickens*

It certainly is not an overstatement to claim that paremiologists, folklorists, linguists, and literary historians have for the most part either missed or ignored the rich treasure of folk speech in Dickens's novels.[2]

It must come as sort of a surprise to learn that the most inclusive statement on Dickens's use of proverbial language is to be found in a comprehensive analysis of idiomatic language in English literature by the German literary critic and paremiologist Wolfgang Schmidt-Hidding, whose book *Englische Idiomatik in Stillehre und Literatur* (München: Max Hueber, 1962) has, unfortunately, not been acknowledged by Anglo-American scholars. While Schmidt-Hidding only dedicates a ten-page chapter to Dickens, he nevertheless points out by a series of convincing examples that Dickens uses proverbial rhetoric for the purposes of characterization, humor, punning, *leitmotif*, metaphorization, and dramatization.[3] Independently of Schmidt-Hidding's findings, the British linguist G.L. Brook comments with at least some depth on Dickens's use of similes, metaphors and catch phrases in his important book on *The Language of Dickens* (London: Andre Deutsch, 1970), noting in particular that "catch phrases can be recognized by such characteristics as vividness of imagery and obscurity. They are features of class dialect and they are often used in repartee by Cockneys. They may occur only once in a particular novel, but they give the impression of being quotations from a large and constantly changing stock of vernacular idiom."[4] The third scholar to have made some general comments on Dickens's proverbial language is the Danish linguist Knud Sørensen in his significant study entitled *Charles Dickens: Linguistic Innovator* (Aarhus: Arkona, 1985). He observes that Dickens enjoys using proverbial comparisons as "formulation[s] that make oblique

---

Index (Oxford: Oxford University Press, 1988).

[2]For a list of studies dealing primarily with the appearance of wellerisms in the works of Charles Dickens see Wolfgang Mieder and George B. Bryan, *Proverbs in World Literature: A Bibliography* (New York: Peter Lang, 1996), pp. 89-90 (nos. 856-867).

[3]See the chapter on "Charles Dickens (1812-1870)," pp. 60-69.

[4]Brook, p. 101; see also pp. 30-35 for similes and metaphors; and pp. 101-103 for catch-phrases.

reference to a state of things" and that "some idioms are regularly associated with individual characters as their signature tunes [i.e., as *leitmotifs*]."[5] And there is also a ten-page treatise on the function of six proverbs in several Dickens novels in the introductory chapter on "Short Sentences from Long Novels" in Rebecca Hogan's dissertation on the proverbs in the works of Leo Tolstoy and Anthony Trollope. She stresses in particular that Dickens cites proverbs as part of the "general consciousness" of the times and places in which the characters of his novels live, and she is quick to point out that while Dickens employs some proverbs in their traditional wording, he is also "given to playing games with pious proverbial wisdom."[6]

Of considerable importance are three additional studies that deal with the proverbial rhetoric in specific works by Charles Dickens. In his analysis of "The Language of *Martin Chuzzlewit*" (1980), Patrick J. McCarthy draws special attention to Dickens's interest in the "rearranging of language" which can also be observed in his "creativity and freshness and ability to manipulate clichés."[7] As will be discussed later and as can be seen from the many textual examples in the Key-word Index, Dickens does indeed delight in the innovative play and intentional manipulation of fixed expressions. Ian Ousby in his essay on "Figurative Language in *Hard Times*" (1981) emphasizes the aspect of "plain speaking"[8] in Dickens's repetitive employment of figurative language

---

[5]Sørensen, p. 32; see also pp. 33, 50-51, and 85-86. Compare also Knud Sørensen, "Charles Dickens: Linguistic Innovator," *English Studies*, 65 (1984), 237-247 (esp. p. 246).

[6]Rebecca S.H. Hogan, *The Wisdom of Many, the Wit of One: The Narrative Function of the Proverb in Tolstoy's "Anna Karenina" and Trollope's "Orley Farm"* (Diss. University of Colorado at Boulder, 1984), p. 26 (the section concerning Dickens on pp. 18-28; the entire introductory chapter on pp. 1-68).

[7]Patrick J. McCarthy, "The Language of *Martin Chuzzlewit*," *Studies in English Literature*, 20 (1980), p. 642 and p. 644 (the entire article on pp. 637-649).

[8]Ian Ousby, "Figurative Language in *Hard Times*," *Durham University Journal*, 74 (1981), 106 (the entire article on pp. 103-109).

and also comments on the didactic nature of proverbial metaphors. In his more recent investigation on "Locution and Authority in *Martin Chuzzlewit*" (1993), R.S. Edgecombe emphasizes once again that Dickens does not consider proverbial wisdom to be sacrosanct. Instead he quite often questions proverbs' claim to authority by "pulling them [i.e., the proverbs] this way and that to shake out the humbug that has gathered in their folds."[9] Edgecombe argues correctly that Dickens "rephrases and updates proverbs—to penetrate to the reality behind the utterance,"[10] but that is not to mean that he does not quite frequently also employ proverbs in their traditional wording as fitting statements of a basic truth.

While Dickens obviously knew many proverbs and traditional phrases as a person who was keenly interested in the linguistic richness of his native language, he also made an effort to collect specific slang expressions to add to the linguistic realism of his novels. For example, in a letter to Mark Lemon dated 20 February 1854, Dickens makes the following request:

> Will you note down and send me any slang terms among tumblers and Circus-people, that you can call to mind? I have noted some—I want them in my new story [i.e., *Hard Times*]—but it is very probable that you will recall several which I have not got.[11]

Dickens's interest in and use of slang was noticed by early reviewers of his novels. In his June 1839 review of *Oliver Twist*, Richard Ford quite appropriately stated that "Boz is regius professor of slang, that expression of the mother-wit, the low humour of the lower classes, their

---

[9] R.S. Edgecombe, "Locution and Authority in *Martin Chuzzlewit*," *English Studies*, 74 (1993), 143 (the entire article on pp. 143-153).

[10] Edgecombe, p. 150.

[11] *The Letters of Charles Dickens*: Volume Seven: 1853-1855. Eds. Graham Storey, Kathleen Tillotson, and Angus Easson (Oxford: The Clarendon Press, 1993), p. 279.

Sanskrit, their hitherto unknown tongue."[12] Clearly this use of slang or of colloquial language in general adds a high degree of realism to the verbal character of Dickens's novels. He always "tried to make his characters use appropriate language,"[13] and slang expressions serve to mark social class as well as professions and groups of people.[14] By the time Dickens also adds class idiolects of fools, idiots, prisoners, etc., and regional dialects in the form of Cockney, Cant, and the speech of East Anglia or Lancashire, his language and style are replete with fascinating communicative phenomena. Yet while much has been written about his diverse linguistic skills,[15] most scholars interested in his

---

[12]Richard Ford, "*Oliver Twist*," *Quarterly Review* (June 1839), 92 (the entire review on pp. 83-102. We owe this reference to Steven Michael, "Criminal Slang in *Oliver Twist*: Dickens's Survival Code," *Style*, 27 (1993), 41 (the entire article on pp. 41-62).

[13]Brook, p. 99.

[14]See Norman Page, *Speech in the English Novel* (London: Longman, 1973), pp. 81-86. See also the many examples in Karl Westendorpf, *Das Prinzip der Verwendung des Slang bei Dickens* (Diss. University of Greiswald, 1923; Greifswald: Hans Adler, 1923), esp. pp. 18-24.

[15]See Randolph Quirk, *Charles Dickens and Appropriate Language* (Durham: University of Durham, 1959); Robert Bruce Glenn, *Linguistic Class-Indicators in the Speech of Dickens' Characters* (Diss. University of Michigan, 1961); R. Quirk, "Some Observations on the Language of Dickens," *Review of English Literature*, 2 ((1961), 19-28; Brook, pp. 54-93 (class dialects), pp. 117-137 (regional dialects), and pp. 138-167 (idiolects); Norman Page, "Convention and Consistency in Dickens' Cockney Dialect," *English Studies*, 51 (1970), 339-344; Harvey Peter Sucksmith, *The Narrative Art of Charles Dickens: The Rhetoric of Sympathy and Irony in His Novels* (Oxford: Clarendon Press, 1970), pp. 60-61; Page, pp. 60-61, 133-134, and 158-159; Randolph Quirk, "Charles Dickens, Linguist," in R. Quirk, *The Linguist and the English Language* (London: Edward Arnold, 1974), pp. 1-36; Sørensen, p. 17; Bärbel Czennia, "Der fremde Dia-/Soziolekt: 'Cockney', 'Cant' und andere Sondersprachen in Übersetzungen zu Romanen von Charles Dickens," in Fred Lönker (ed.), *Die literarische Übersetzung als Medium der Fremderfahrung* (Berlin: Erich Schmidt, 1992), pp. 107-

"languages"[16] have ignored the important role which proverbial patterns play in all of this.

Dickens's "use of language for individualisation and for typification; his use of it structurally; and his use of it experimental-ly"[17] clearly reflect his own deep-rooted interest in linguistic realism. This can be seen from the many essays on various aspects of philology and language which he as editor of the journals *Household Words* (1850-1859) and *All the Year Round* (1859-1870) accepted for publication.[18] In addition, he was also clearly interested in folklore, making repeated use of ballads, fairy tales, and legends in his novels.[19] And yet, such promising articles like Arnold Kettle's "Dickens and the Popular Tradition" (1961) and Katharine Briggs's "The Folklore of Charles Dickens" (1970) do not even mention his frequent use of proverbial speech.[20] These scholars obviously did not register Dickens's interest

---

125; and Patricia Ingham, *Dickens, Women and Language* (Toronto: University of Toronto Press, 1992), esp. pp. 4-5.

[16]See the revealing study by Nicholas Guy Linfield, *The Languages of Charles Dickens* (Diss. University of Texas at Austin, 1969).

[17]Quirk, "Observations on the Language of Dickens," p. 20.

[18]See Dorothy Deering, "Dickens's Armory for the Mind: The English Language Studies in *Household Words* and *All the Year Round*," *Dickens Studies Newsletter*, 8 (1977), 11-17.

[19]See Shirley Grob, "Dickens and Some Motifs of the Fairy Tale," *Texas Studies in Literature and Language*, 5 (1964), 567-579; Michael C. Kotzin, *Dickens and the Fairy Tale* (Bowling Green, Ohio: Bowling Green University Popular Press, 1972); Harry Stone, *Dickens and the Invisible World: Fairy Tales, Fantasy, Novel-Making* (Bloomington, Indiana: Indiana University Press, 1979); and Jacqueline Simpson, "Urban Legends in *The Pickwick Papers*," *Journal of American Folklore*, 96 (1983), 462-470.

[20]Arnold Kettle, "Dickens and the Popular Tradition," *Zeitschrift für Anglistik und Amerikanistik*, 9 (1961), 229-252; and Katharine M. Briggs, "The Folklore of Charles Dickens," *Journal of the Folklore*

in certain proverbial phrases which he, as and interested linguist and folklorist, saw fit to explain within his narrative context. Here is an example of his explanation of the phrase "A Whitechapel shave":

> My heart beat high; for, in those four male personages, although complexionless and eyebrowless, I beheld four subjects of the Family P. Saley. Blue-bearded though they were, and bereft of the youthful smoothness of cheek which is imparted by what is termed in Albion a "Whitechapel shave" (and which is, in fact, whitening, judiciously applied for the jaws with the palm of the hand). I recognised them.[21]

Another example is the proverbial chapter title "Making a night of it," which Dickens explains in the following manner: "[...] and they had likewise agreed that, on the evening aforesaid, they would 'make a night of it'—an expressive term, implying the borrowing of several hours from to-morrow morning, adding them to the night before, and manufacturing a compound night of the whole."[22] But there is also the interesting proverbial title of Dickens's story *Tom Tiddler's Ground* (1861), which almost by necessity begins with the following folkloristic explanation which in turn permits the repeated use of the phrase as a *leitmotif*:

> "And why Tom Tiddler's ground?" asked the Traveller. "Because he scatters halfpence to Tramps and such-like," returned the Landlord, "and of course they pick 'em up. And this being done on his own land (which it *is* his own land, you observe, and were his family's before him), why it is but regarding the halfpence as gold and silver, and turning the ownership of the

---

Institute, 7 (1970), 3-20.

[21]Charles Dickens, *The Uncommercial Traveller and Reprinted Pieces Etc.* 1850-1860. The Oxford Illustrated Dickens, Vol. XXI (Oxford: Oxford University Press, 1958), p. 278.

[22]Charles Dickens, *Sketches by Boz.* 1833-40. The Oxford Illustrated Dickens. Vol. XII (Oxford: Oxford University Press, 1957), p. 267 (the entire chapter on pp. 266-271).

property a bit round your finger, and there you have the
name of the children's game complete. And it's appropriate too," said the Landlord, with his favourite action
of stooping a little, to look across the table out of
window at vacancy, under the window-blind which was
half drawn down.[23]

The expression thus means any place where money, etc., is picked up
readily, but one wonders which modern reader understands the phrase
without Dickens's explanation when he used it much earlier in 1839 in
The Life and Adventures of Nicholas Nickleby in the following fashion:
"'I am here, my soul's delight, upon Tom Tiddler's ground, picking up
the demnition [*sic*] gold and silver'."[24] Of course, there are other
proverbial expressions which Dickens employs and which present a
major problem to the modern reader. This is the case, for example, with
the phrase "to be brought up by hand" which appears several times in
Great Expectations (1861), and which in its obscure figurative way states
that Pip was brought up on the bottle and not breast-fed. This phrase is
by now an archaism at best, and it is good to have two short explanatory
essays detailing its origin and meaning.[25] Obviously there would be
many other proverbial texts in the Key-word Index that deserve similar
historical and etymological explanations.[26]

---

[23]Charles Dickens, *Christmas Stories*. 1871. The Oxford Illustrated
Dickens, Vol. XI (Oxford: Oxford University Press, 1956), p. 289.

[24]Charles Dickens, *The Life and Adventures of Nicholas Nickleby*.
1839. The Oxford Illustrated Dickens, Vol. VI (Oxford: Oxford
University Press, 1950), p. 428.

[25]See Charles Paris, "A Boy Brought up 'By Hand'," *Nineteenth-
Century Fiction*, 17 (1962), 286-288; and C.J.P. Beatty, "Charles
Dickens's *Great Expectations* (1860-1) and the Probable Source of the
Expression 'Brought up by Hand'," *Notes and Queries*, 38, old series
236 (1991), 315.

[26]In addition to the standard proverb dictionaries listed at the
beginning of the Key-word Index and which contain some explanatory
comments, see the many references in Wolfgang Mieder, *Investigations
of Proverbs, Proverbial Expressions, Quotations and Clichés: A*

One more textual reference might serve to illustrate Charles Dickens's own interest in linguistic and phraseological matters. It is generally known that he travelled twice to the United States, and his impressions, both positive and negative, were put to paper first in several letters and later in *American Notes* (1842) and *The Life and Adventures of Martin Chuzzlewit* (1844). In a letter written in America on 24 February 1842 to his friend John Forster in England Dickens amuses himself with a description of the steamer that brought him to America by using several "Americanisms":

> The daily difference in her rolling, as she burns the coals out, is something absolutely fearful. Add to all this, that by day and night she is full of fire and people, that she has no boats, and that the struggling of that enormous machinery in a heavy sea seems as though it would rend her into fragments—and you may have a pretty considerable damned good sort of a feeble notion that it don't fit nohow; and that it a'nt calculated to make you smart, overmuch; and that you don't feel 'special bright; and by no means first rate; and not at all tonguey (or disposed for conversation); and that however rowdy you may be by natur', it does you up com-plete-ly, and that's a fact; and makes you quake considerable, and disposed toe damn the engine!—All of which phrases, I beg to add, are pure Americanisms of the first water.[27]

Bibliography of Explanatory Essays which Appeared in "Notes and Queries" (1849-1983) (Bern: Peter Lang, 1984); and W. Mieder, *International Proverb Scholarship: An Annotated Bibliograohy*, 3 vols. (New York: Garland Publishing, 1982, 1990, and 1993).

[27]*The Letters of Charles Dickens*: Volume Three: 1842-1843. Eds. Madeline House, Graham Storey, and Kathleen Tillotson (Oxford: The Clarendon Press, 1974), p. 90.

Louise Pound in particular has commented on how Dickens showed much interest in English as it was spoken in the United States,[28] and it should thus not be surprising that even the phrase of "the almighty dollar"[29] appears in *American Notes*. And in a letter of 27 May 1844 to Edwin Landseer Dickens makes yet another interesting use of an expression that he picked up in the States: "I have let my house with such delicious promptitude, or, as the Americans would say, 'with sich everlass'in slickness and al'mity sprydom,' that we turn out to-night! in favour of a widow lady, who keeps it all the time we are away."[30] Finally, there is also a reference to yet another American expression in a letter to John Leech of 9 July 1849: "I am still of [the] opinion that Broadstairs [shower-bath] beats all watering places into what the Americans call 'sky-blue fits'."[31]

It should be noted that Charles Dickens makes frequent use of proverbial language in his numerous letters, which he described to his wife Catherine Hogarth on 9 November 1835 as having "brevity and matter-of-fact style."[32] But even in the shortest of them, he includes

---

[28]See Louise Pound, "The American Dialect of Charles Dickens," *Amercian Speech*, 22 (1947), 124-130; also Brook, pp. 130-137; and Sørensen, pp. 47-49.

[29]Charles Dickens, *American Notes and Pictures from Italy*. 1842 and 1846. The Oxford Illustrated Dickens, Vol. XIX (Oxford: Oxford University Press, 1957), p. 27. For the origin and history of this expression see Rex Forrest, "Irving and 'The Almighty Dollar'," *American Speech*, 15 (1940), 443-440. Washington Irving coined the phrase in 1836, and Dickens met him in America.

[30]*The Letters of Charles Dickens*: Volume Four: 1844-1846. Ed. Kathleen Tillotson (Oxford: The Clarendon Press, 1977), p. 131.

[31]*The Letters of Charles Dickens*: Volume Five: 1847-1849. Eds. Graham Storey and K.J. Fielding (Oxford: The Clarendon Press, 1981), p. 568.

[32]*The Letters of Charles Dickens*: Volume One: 1820-1839. Eds. Madeline House and Graham Storey (Oxford: The Clarendon Press, 1965), p. 91.

proverbs or proverbial phrases at strategic locations in order to add some expressiveness and colloquial color to his often rather mundane epistles occupied with everyday problems and frustrations. This becomes quite obvious in the following short excerpts:

> To Samuel Rogers, 14 November 1839:
> Did you ever "move"? We have taken a house near the Regents Park, intending to occupy it between this [date of the letter] and Christmas, and the consequent trials have already begun. There is an old proverb that three removes are as bad as a fire. I don't know how that may be, but I know that one is worse. (I, p. 602)[33]

> To Henry Austin, 1 May 1842:
> I am very sorry to hear that business is so flat, but the Proverb says it never rains but it pours; and it may be remarked with equal Truth upon the other side, that it never *don't* rain, but it holds up very much indeed. You will be busy again, long before we come home, I have no doubt. (III, p. 231)

> To Clarkson Stanfield, 25 May 1843:
> I am beating my head against the door, with grief and frenzy—and shall continue to do so, until I receive your answer. (III, p. 496)

> To Mrs. Gore, 7 September 1852:
> So you want a godchild. May I never have the opportunity of giving you one! But *if* I have—if my cup (I mean my quiver) be not yet full—then shall you hear again from the undersigned Camel that his back is broken by

---

[33]There is no need to repeat all the bibliographical information for each individual letter. This is all included in the section on "Dickens Editions Consulted" and also in the "Key-word Index," where all the proverb references are catalogued. The roman number in parentheses refers to the volume number of *The Letters of Charles Dickens*, and the arabic number indicates the page on which the reference is to be found.

the addition of the last overbalancing straw.[34] (VI, p. 756)

Quite revealing are also those proverbial passages from Dickens's letters, in which the author comments on his busy life as a serial writer working under extreme time pressure:

> To Thomas Beard, 15 November 1842:
> I am working away upon my new book, like—like a brick. I don't know why it is, but that popular simile *seems* a good one. (III, p. 372)

> To Emile de la Rue, 20 August 1846:
> My troubles are not greater, thank God, than they usually are, when I am plunging neck and heels into a new Book. It is always an anxious and worrying time. Mais il faut manger. (IV, p. 608)

> To Lady Kay-Shuttleworth, 4 July 1850:
> But my work (which is particularly hard just now) obliges me to avoid all public meetings, and almost all other interruptions of my attention, except long country walks and fresh air. If I were to permit anything to interfere with these relaxations just now, I fear the old

---

[34]For this Biblical proverb see Georg Aicher, *Kamel und Nadelöhr: Eine kritisch-exegetische Studie über Mt. 19,24 und Parallelen* (Münster: Aschendorff, 1908); Paul S. Minear, "'The Needle's Eye': A Study in Form Criticism," *Journal of Biblical Literature*, 61 (1942), 157-169; Eduard Koelwel, "Kamel und Nadelöhr," *Sprachpflege*, 6 (1957), 184-185; R.F. Fleissner, "Camel through a Needle's Eye," *American Notes and Queries*, 10 (1971-1972), 9 and 154-155; Karl Oberhuber, "Nochmals 'Kamel' und Nadelöhr," in Hermann M. Ölberg, Gernot Schmidt, and Heinz Bothien (eds.), *Sprachwissenschaftliche Forschungen. Festschrift für Johann Knobloch* (Innsbruck: Institut für Sprachwissenschaft der Universität Innsbruck, 1985), pp. 271-275; and Jes. P. Asmussen, "'Kamel'—'Nadelöhr'. Matth. 19:24, Mark. 10:25, Luk. 18:25," in Rüdiger Schmitt and Prods Oktor Skjaervo (eds.), *Studia Grammatica Iranica. Festschrift für Helmut Humbach* (München: R. Kitzinger, 1986), pp. 1-10.

spelling-book would "come true", and Jack would be but a dull boy. (VI, p. 124)

To Mrs. Gaskell, 27 January 1852:
I am very busy, and write shortly—not from choice but because needs must when *You*-don't-know-who drives. (VI, p. 583)

Many of these examples show how much Dickens enjoyed merely alluding to proverbs, always assuming, of course, that the receivers of his letters would recognize such traditional proverbs as "The last straw breaks the camel's back," "All work and no play, makes Jack a dull boy," and "Needs must when the devil drives." All of this is an indication that Dickens was a very conscious user of proverbial language. This can also be seen quite clearly from those instances where he begins a letter with a proverbial observation that sets the tone for the following comments:

To Thomas Mitton, 30 August 1841:
I was up and down—here and there—torn to pieces—until dinner time on Saturday, which was after you left town. (II, p. 372)

To Clarkson Stanfield, 5 February 1854:
Unless it should rain cats, dogs, pitchforks, and Cochin China poultry,—the Train which leaves Fenchurch Street at 12 on Tuesday and arrives at Blackwall at quarter past 12 is my means of going down. (VII, 267)

Even more often Dickens concludes a letter with a metaphorical proverb or an allusion to it, thus driving home a point with a piece of wisdom which would be difficult to argue against:

To Henry Bicknell, 28 November 1850:
We all hope to hear, shortly, that Mrs. Bicknell has recovered [from] that other little accident [the birth of their sixth child], which (as you and I know) *will* occasionally happen in well-regulated families. (VI, p. 219)

To Miss Emmely Gotschalk, 2 May 1853:

I shall never forget you and will always be interested in you. But this is a world of action, where everyone has a duty to fulfill, a part to play. And, my dear girl, if you sit down by the wayside to think and grieve, those who are dearest to you will be swept on in their better course, until they are lost and gone. It will be a poor comfort to you when you grow old, to think how you might have borne them company and done them good. Many a child grows into a giant and acorns into oaks. (VII, p. 74)

But there are also several very short letters in the form of a note of few lines which employ a proverb or two in a didactic or humorous fashion. They indicate clearly how much Dickens liked to play with language and how freely he manipulated so-called fixed expressions. To him they were ready-made linguistic wares that could be adapted in any way or shape that he saw fit:

To John Forster, 11 January 1838:
You don't feel disposed, do you, to muffle yourself up, and start off with me for a good brisk walk over Hampstead Heath? I knows a good 'ous there where we can have red hot chop for dinner, and a glass of good wine. All work and no play makes Jack a dull boy. *I* am as dull as a Codfish. (I, p. 353)

To Dr. F.H.F. Quin, 3 November 1854:
What *are* you a doin' on? Didn't I tell you in my note yes'day that Thursday was my only other engaged day. Blow'd if you an't enough to make a cove go an knock his ed agen the wall that aggerarvation you are. (VII, p. 458)

To Peter Cunningham, 12 September 1855:
We must put our shoulders to the wheel and come forward ... throwing ourselves into the tide, and a going with the stream. (VII, p. 700)

To George Dolby, 28 September 1856:
I don't care much for the weather and am off to the Foundling [Hospital], and (unless it should rain Tiger

cats and Newfoundland dogs), to Hampstead afterwards.
(VIII, p. 193)

To Bernhard Tauchnitz, 18 April 1856:
Leipzig is at present among my castles in the air, mes
Châteaux en Espagne, but perhaps Germany and I may
make a personal acquaintance yet.[35] (VIII, p. 93)

Such short epistulatory notes are true gems by a master proverbialist,
who never tired of citing complete and traditional proverbs or of alluding
to them in a playful manner that added much humor and irony to his
concise statements.[36] When one proverbial phrase is not enough, a
second metaphor quickly comes to mind, and it is this amassment of folk
expressions that can also be observed in his novels and speeches.

Turning next to how Dickens made use of proverbial rhetoric in
his speeches, it will become obvious that he expended quite a bit of
rhetorical energy in elaborating on proverbs to entertain the audience
with humorous reflections on their traditional wisdom. This certainly was
the case in the introductory paragraph of a speech that he delivered on
18 February 1842 in New York at a dinner presided over by Washington
Irving and attended by nearly eight hundred distinguished guests:

---

[35]For this proverbial expression see Alfred Morel-Fatio, "'Châteaux
en Espagne'," in Henri Omont (ed.), *Mélanges offerts à M. Emile Picot*
(Paris: Damascène Morgand, 1913; rpt. Genève: Slatkine, 1969), vol.
1, pp. 335-342; Arthur Langfors, "Châteaux en Brie et—en Espagne,"
Neuphilologische Mitteilungen, 16 (1914), 107-110; Roland M. Smith,
"Chaucer's 'Castle in Spain' (HF 1117)," *Modern Language Notes*, 60
(1945), 39-40; Axel Nelson, "'Châteaux en Espagne' dans le latin
médiéval," *Eranos*, 49 (1951), 159-169; and Stuart A. Gallacher,
"'Castles in Spain'," *Journal of American Folklore*, 76 (1963), 324-329.

[36]See James R. Kincaid, *Dickens and the Rhetoric of Laughter*
(Oxford: Clarendon Press, 1971); Sylvia B. Manning, *Dickens as Satirist*
(New Haven, Connecticut: Yale University Press, 1971); and D.S.
Racadio, *The Comic, the Grotesque, and the Uncanny in Charles
Dickens* (Diss. University of East Anglia, 1990).

> Gentlemen,—I don't know how to thank you—I really
> don't know how. You would naturally suppose that my
> former experience would have given me this power, and
> that the difficulties in my way would have been dimin-
> ished; but I assure you the fact is exactly the reverse,
> and I have completely baulked the ancient proverb that
> 'a rolling stone gathers no moss'; and in my progress to
> this city I have collected such a weight of obligations
> and acknowledgment—I have picked up such an enor-
> mous mass of fresh moss at every point, and was so
> struck by the brilliant scenes of Monday night, that I
> thought I could never by any possibility grow any
> bigger. I have made, continually, new accumulations to
> such an extent that I am compelled to stand still, and can
> roll no more![37]

In another speech delivered on 5 October 1843 in Manchester, Dickens
argued convincingly for the support of schools and education by
disagreeing with the wisdom of a well-known proverb. This splendidly
innovative rhetorical procedure must have attracted the attention of the
audience:

> How often have we heard from a large class of men
> wise in their generation, who would really seem to be
> born and bred for no other purpose than to pass into
> currency counterfeit and mischievous scraps of wisdom,
> as it is the sole pursuit of some other criminals to utter
> base coin—how often have we heard from them, as an
> all-convincing argument, that 'a little learning is a
> dangerous thing'? Why, a little hanging was considered

---

[37]*The Works of Charles Dickens: The Speeches* Ed. Richard H.
Shepherd. New National Edition, Vol. II (New York: Hearst's Interna-
tional Library Company, n.d.), p. 383. For a discussion of the meaning
of this proverb see George A. Lundberg, "The Semantics of Proverbs,"
ETC: A Review of General Semantics, 15 (1958), 215-217; and Barbara
Kirshenblatt-Gimblett, "Toward a Theory of Proverb Meaning,"
Proverbium, no. 22 (1973), 821-827; also in Wolfgang Mieder and Alan
Dundes (eds.), *The Wisdom of Many: Essays on the Proverb* (New York:
Garland Publishing, 1981), pp. 111-121.

a very dangerous thing, according to the same authorities, with this difference, that, because a little hanging was dangerous, we had a great deal of it; and, because a little learning was dangerous, we were to have none at all. Why, when I hear such cruel absurdities gravely reiterated, I do sometimes begin to doubt whether the parrots of society are not more pernicious to its interests than its birds of prey.[38]

While this argumentative way of using a proverb was based on serious convictions to change people's minds about the lack of support for education, Dickens begins a third speech on 5 November 1857 in London with a rather humorous play on words with a standard proverb:

I must now solicit your attention for a few minutes to the cause of your assembling together—the main and real object of the evening's gathering; for I suppose we are all agreed that the motto of these tables is not 'Let us eat and drink, for to-morrow we die'; but 'Let us eat and drink, for to-morrow we live.' It is because a great and good work is to live to-morrow, and to-morrow, and to-morrow, and to live a greater and better life with every succeeding to-morrow, that we eat and drink here at all.[39]

But what sounds as an enjoyable pun at the beginning of the speech is in fact only the introduction to yet another plea for more interest in good schools. Dickens, the social realist and reform-minded activist, does not do small talk, not even with proverbs. His speeches always have a goal and purpose in mind, and their proverbial rhetoric is subservient to these social commitments.

---

[38]*The Works of Charles Dickens: The Speeches.* Ed. Richard H. Shepherd. New National edition, Vol. II (New York: Hearst's International Library Company, n.d.), p. 390.

[39]*The Works of Charles Dickens: The Speeches.* Ed. Richard H. Shepherd. New National Edition, Vol. II (New York: Hearst's International Library Company, n.d.), pp. 470-471.

In some of the essays which Charles Dickens wrote for his journal *Household Words*, he continued his preoccupation with schools and education. In a piece entitled "Mr. Bendigo Buster on Our National Defences Against Education" from 28 December 1850, Dickens and his co-author Henry Morley employed several proverbs in their satirical comments:

> The country, certainly, is not in any immediate danger of education, thank Heaven, but forewarned is fore-armed.
> Britain, I warn you! Don't open your eyes when you are asked to look at yonder German school. You have other irons in the fire. Besides, the British are fine fellows, men of the right quality, and want no teaching. What says the comedian? 'Les gens de qualité savent tout, sans avoir jamais rien appris.' (People of quality know everything without ever learning anything.) England is of the true quality, [...].[40]

But there is also a wonderfully humorous paragraph in the essay "First Fruits" which Dickens published together with George Augustus Sala on 15 May 1852. While they translate the French proverb, they also delight in alluding playfully to the proverb "A bird in the hand is worth two in the bush":

> That it is *"le premier pas qui coûte"*—that the first step is the great point—is as much a household word to us, and is as familiar to our mouths as that the descent of Avernus is unaccompanied by difficulty, or that one member of the feathered creation held in the hand is worth two of the same species in the bush. And, if we might be permitted to add to the first quoted morsel of proverbial philosophy a humble rider of our own, we

---

[40]*Charles Dickens' Uncollected Writings from* Household Words *1850-1859*, 2 vols. Ed. Harry Stone (Bloomington, Indiana: Indiana University Press, 1968), vol. 1, p. 202.

would say that we *never* forget the first step, the first ascent, the first stumble, the first fall.[41]

Clearly Dickens wants his readers to notice that he is playing with "proverbial philosophy," and he insists rather often in his novels in particular on identifying proverbs as such by means of an introductory formular.[42] Such emphasis sets the proverbial utterance apart from the rest of the narration or dialogue, making it a particularly noteworthy statement couched in metaphorical and traditional language:

> The four Miss Willises, then settled in our parish thirteen years ago. It is a melancholy reflection that the old adage, "time and tide wait for no man," applies with equal force to the fairer portion of the creation; and willingly would we conceal the fact, that even thirteen years ago the Miss Willises were far from juvenile. (*Sketches by Boz*, p. 13)[43]

> There must always be two parties to a quarrel, says the old adage. (*Oliver Twist*, p. 104)

---

[41]*Charles Dickens' Uncollected Writings from* Household Words *1850-1859*, 2 vols. Ed. Harry Stone (Bloomington, Indiana: Indiana University Press, 1968), vol. 2, p. 410.

[42]For such introductory formulas see Carl Schulze, "Ausdücke für Sprichwort," *Zeitschrift für deutsches Altertum und deutsche Literatur*, 8 (1851), 376-384; J. Alan Pfeffer, "The Identification of Proverbs in Goethe," *Modern Language Notes*, 69 (1954), 596-598; and Wolfgang Mieder, *Das Sprichwort im Werke Jeremias Gotthelfs: Eine volkskundlich-literarische Untersuchung* (Bern: Peter Lang, 1972), pp. 34-42.

[43]For the textual examples from the novels only the shortened title and the page number are cited. The complete bibliographical information is given in the list of "Dickens Editions Consulted" and also in the "Key-word Index" where the proverbial statement is cited. In rows of examples, the contextual references are arranged chronologically according to the publication of the novels.

[...] for your popular rumour, unlike the rolling stone of the proverb, is one which gathers a deal of moss in its wanderings up and down, [...]. (*The Old Curiosity Shop*, p. 355)

[...] others had been desperate from the beginning, and comforted themselves with the homely proverb, that, being hanged at all, they might as well be hanged for a sheep as a lamb. (*Barnaby Rudge*, p. 402)

There is a most remarkably long-headed, flowing-bearded, and patriarchal proverb, which observes that it is the duty of a man to be just before he is generous. Be just now, and you can be generous presently. (*Martin Chuzzlewit*, p. 221)

And Mrs. Hominy not only talked, as the saying is, like a book, but actually did talk her own books, word for word. (*Martin Chuzzlewit*, p. 541)

[...], notwithstanding the proverb, that constant dropping will wear away a stone, [...]. (*Great Expectations*, p. 253)

By drawing attention to the fact that he is using a proverb, Dickens felt that he did not necessarily have to cite the proverb completely. He certainly felt that he could break the rigid structure of the traditional proverb in order to integrate it more effectively into his narrative flow. However, there are many examples of proverbs cited in their entirety and without any introductory formulas. In this case the reader will usually have no difficulty in recognizing the traditional proverb as a piece of folk wisdom:

Well, we shall see. "Honesty is the best policy," is it? We'll try that too. (*Nicholas Nickleby*, p. 368)

"Where's the good of putting things off? Strike while the iron's hot; that's what I say." (*Barnaby Rudge*, p. 336)

"You and me know what we know, don't we? Let sleeping dogs lie—who wants to rouse 'em? I don't."[44] (*David Copperfield*, p. 578)

"Let me see!" he would say. "I saved five pounds out of the brickmaker's affair; so, if I have a good rattle to London and back in a post-chaise, and put that down at four pounds, I shall have saved one. And it's a very good thing to save one, let me tell you: a penny saved, is a penny got!" (*Bleak House*, p. 114)

They made him out to be the Royal Arms, the Union-Jack, Magna Charta, John Bull, Habeas Corpus, the Bill of Rights, An Englishman's house is his castle, Church and State, and God save the Queen, all put together.[45] (*Hard Times*, p. 43)

"Observe me well, gentlemen, it's true. That which glitters is not always gold: but what I am going to tell, is true."[46] (*The Uncommercial Traveller*, p. 625)

"Bear in mind then, that Brag is a good dog, but that Holdfast is a better. Bear that in mind, will you?" (*Great Expectations*, p. 130)

---

[44]For this medieval proverb see Heiner Gillmeister, "Chaucer's 'Kan Ke Dort' (Troilus,II,1752), and the 'Sleeping Dogs' of the Trouvères," *English Studes*, 59 (1978), 310-323.

[45]See Archer Taylor, "The Road to 'An Englishman's House ...'," *Romance Philology*, 19 (1965-1966), 279-285.

[46]For this European proverb see Archer Taylor, "'All Is not Gold that Glitters' and *Rolandslied*, 1956," *Romance Philology*, 11 (1958), 370-371; A. Taylor, "'All Is not Gold that Glitters' and Hypothetical Reconstructions," *Saga och Sed*, No volume given (1959, printed 1960), 129-132; and Gyula Paczolay, "Magyar proverbiumok europai rokon-saga: A 'Nem minden arany, ami fénylik' példajan," *Ethnographia*, 97 (1986), 334-360.

There are also numerous Biblical proverbs which Dickens cites without alteration, since people of his time might have considered these texts to be especially didactic and moralistic:

"He that is without sin among you, let him throw the first stone at her." (*The Life of Our Lord*, p. 64) [John 8:7]

"Thou shalt love thy neighbour as thyself." (*The Life of Our Lord*, p. 68) [Matthew 19:19]

"Render unto Caesar the things that are Caesar's."[47] (*The Life of Our Lord*, p. 77) [Matthew 22:21]

"Pride shall have a fall, and it always was and will be so!" (*Dombey and Son*, p. 829) [Proverbs 16:8]

Yet there are also instances where Dickens only alludes to such Biblical proverbs.[48] The chapter title "Reaping the Whirlwind" (*Little Dorrit*, p. 711) is a shortened version of "They that sow the wind shall reap the whirlwind" (Hosea 8:7), and the reference to "the parable of the camel and the needle's eye" (*Little Dorrit*, p. 394) brings to mind the longer

---

[47]For this Biblical proverb see J. Denney, "Caesar and God," *The Expositor*, 5th series, 3 (1896), 61-69; Martin Rist, "Caesar or God (Mark 12:13-17)? A Study in 'Formgeschichte'," *Journal of Religion*, 16 (1936), 317-331; Ivar Benum, "Gud og keiseren. Mark 12,13-17," *Norsk teologisk tidsskrift*, 42 (1941), 65-96; and Terence G. White, "'Render unto Caesar the Things that are Caesar's, and unto God the Things that are God's' (Mark 12,17)," *The Hibbert Journal*, 44 (1945-1946), 263-270.

[48]For the role of the Bible in Dickens's works see George S. Larson, *Religion in the Novels of Charles Dickens* (Diss. University of Massachusetts, 1969); Jane Vogel, *Allegory in Dickens* (University, Alabama: University of Alabama Press, 1977), esp. pp. 32-33, 42-43, and 74-75; Dennis Walder, *Dickens and Religion* (London: George Allen & Unwin, 1981); and Janet L. Larson, *Dickens and the Broken Scripture* (Athens, Georgia: University of Georgia Press, 1985), esp. pp. 190-191 and 313-315.

proverb "It is easier for a camel to go through the eye of the needle, than for a rich man to enter into the kingdom of God" (Matthew 19:24).

Something quite similar can be observed in the way Dickens integrates numerous Shakespeare quotations into his works. He quotes Shakespeare more often than any other literary author,[49] and many of these references from Shakespeare were already proverbial in Dickens's time. Hamlet's famous exclamation "To be or not to be"[50] is found as "[...] to answer it, or not to answer it, as the event might prove" (*Christmas Stories*, p. 602) and also in a different variation as an expression of Dickens's indecisiveness concerning a second trip to America. On 24 September 1867 he writes to W.H. Wills: "I send you, enclosed, a plain statement of the American questions, deduced from a mass of notes and figures. Give me your opinion on it. To go, or not to go?"[51] Some other proverbial reminiscenses to Shakespeare play a role in the following texts:

> There cannot be a better practical illustration of the wise saw and ancient instance, that there may be too much of a good thing [...]. (*Sketches by Boz*, p. 563) [*As You Like It*, II, 7, 156]

---

[49]See especially Valerie L. Gager, *Shakespeare and Dickens: The Dynamics of Influence* (Cambridge: Cambridge University Press, 1996), with a "Catalogue of Dickens's References to Shakespeare" on pp. 251-369. Of value is also the earlier study by Robert F. Fleissner, *Dickens and Shakespeare (A Study in Historic Contrasts)* (New York: Haskell House, 1965).

[50]For a discussion of this quotation turned proverb see Wolfgang Mieder, "'Sein oder Nichtsein'—und kein Ende. Zum Weiterleben des Hamlet-Zitats in unserer Zeit," *Der Sprachdienst*, 23 (1979), 81-85; also in W. Mieder, *Sprichwort, Redensart, Zitat: Tradierte Formelsprache in der Moderne* (Bern: Peter Lang, 1985), pp. 125-130.

[51]*The Letters of Charles Dickens*, ed. Walter Dexter. Vol. III: 1858-1870. The Nonesuch Dickens (London: The Nonesuch Press, 1938), p. 553. For other Dickens quotations from Hamlet's soliloquy, notably also the proverbial expression "There's the rub," see the "Key-word Index" as well as Gager, pp. 284-286; and Fleissner, p. 230.

"Love at first sight! [...] But the course of it doesn't run smooth." (*Christmas Stories*, p. 702) [*A Midsummer Night's Dream*, I, 1, 134]

My salad-days...being gone...no coming event cast its shadow before. (*The Uncommercial Traveller*, p. 309) [*Antony and Cleopatra*, I, 5, 73]

"One keeps a secret better than two." (*Great Expectations*, p. 402) [*Romeo and Juliet*, II, 4, 208]

[...] taking his hat down from its peg to suit the action to the word [...]. (*Christmas Stories*, p. 545) [*Hamlet*, III, 2, 20]

OBENREIZER: As Shakespeare says, "Discretion is the better part of valour!" (*No Thoroughfare*, IV, ii, pp. 212-213) [*1 Henry IV*, V, 4, 122]

While the last example draws special attention to Shakespeare with an introductory formula, many of the other Shakespearean quotations will usually not be noticed as such. They have long become proverbial in their own right.

There can be no doubt, however, that Charles Dickens is far more fascinated by folk proverbs than obscure or proverbial Shakespeare quotations. This can be seen in partiuclar by his effective way of citing proverbs in their traditional wording and then adding a rather humorous comment to them. This practice undermines the didactic aspect of the proverbs and serves as proof that Dickens knows very well that the folk does not always use proverbs as a moral statement. The mere fact that they are cited so often invites this type of ironic opposition to their underlying wisdom,[52] and it is to be assumed that Dickens's readers enjoyed these rhetorical twists then and still do today:

---

[52]For a discussion of questioning proverbial wisdom today see Wolfgang Mieder, *Proverbs Are Never Out of Season: Popular Wisdom in the Modern Age* (New York: Oxford University Press, 1993).

"He will talk about business, and won't give away his time for nothing. He's very right. Time is money, time is money."

"He was one of us who made that saying. I should think," said Ralph. "Time is money, and very good money too, to those who reckon interest by it. Time *is* money! Yes, and time costs money; it's rather an expensive article to some people we could name, or I forget my trade." (*Nicholas Nickleby*, p. 612)

"Tush man!" said Joe, "I'm not so young as that. Needs must when the devil drives; and the devil that drives me is an empty pocket and an unhappy home. For the present, good-bye." (*Barnaby Rudge*, p. 237)

"This," he said, in allusion to the party, not the wine, "is a Mingling that repays one for much disappointment and vexation. Let us be merry." Here he took a captain's biscuit, "It is a poor heart that never rejoices; and our hearts are not poor. No!" (*Martin Chuzzlewit*, p. 83)

"Half a loaf's better than no bread, and the same remark holds good with crumbs. There's a few." (*Dombey and Son*, p. 131)

"My dear friend Copperfield," said Mr. Micawber, "accidents will occur in the best-regulated families; and in families not regulated by that pervading influence which sanctifies while it enhances the—a—I would say, in short, by the influence of Woman, in the lofty character of Wife, they may be expected with confidence, and must be borne with philosophy." (*David Copperfield*, p. 413)

"She's worth her weight in gold," says the trooper.
"In gold?" says Mr. Bagnet. "I'll tell you what. The old girl's weight—is twelve stone six. Would I take that weight—in any metal—*for* the old girl? No. Why not? Because the old girl's metal is far more precious—than

the preciousest metal. And she's *all* metal!" (*Bleak House*, p. 478)

It should be noted at this place that there exists a folk tradition of adding humorous comments to proverbs and proverbial expressions in a typically triadic structural pattern, as for example in "'Everyone to his own taste,' as the farmer said, when he kissed the cow" or "'Like will to like,' as the devil said to the collier." Normally these sayings consist of three parts: a statement (quite often a proverb, proverbial expression, quotation, exclamation, etc.), a speaker who makes the remark, and a phrase or clause that places the utterance in a new light or an incompatible setting. Charles Dickens made much use of these traditional structures, and he placed many of them in the mouth of his character Samuel Weller in *The Posthumous Papers of the Pickwick Club* (1837). In fact, scholars have decided to name these unique sayings "wellerisms" in direct association with Sam Weller's frequent use of them.[53] After Dickens had popularized such humorous, ironic, and satirical sayings as elements of a literary work, there followed a wave of imitations both in Great Britain and the United States. This has resulted in an impressive literature on wellerisms that have been collected from the nineteenth and twentieth centuries,[54] and it should be noted that the wellerism is the one sub-genre of proverbial folk speech which has been paid attention to most by Dickens scholars.[55] What they did not notice, however, is that

---

[53]See Archer Taylor, "Wellerisms," in A. Taylor, *The Proverb* (Cambridge, Massachusetts: Harvard University Press, 1931; rpt. Hatboro, Pennyslvania: Folklore Associates, 1962; rpt. again with an introduction and bibliography by Wolfgang Mieder, Bern: Peter Lang, 1985), pp. 201-220.

[54]See Wolfgang Mieder and Stewart A. Kingsbury (eds.), *A Dictionary of Wellerisms* (New York: Oxford University Press, 1994). This collection contains 1516 texts with annotations as well as a comprehensive bibliography (pp. 157-166).

[55]See especially M. Maass, "39 Old Similes aus den *Pickwick Papers* von Charles Dickens," *Archiv für das Studium der neueren Sprachen und Literaturen*, 41 (1867), 207-215; Charles Kent, *Wellerisms from "Pickwick" and "Master Humphrey's Clock"* (London: George Redway, 1886); William H. Bailey, "Wellerisms and Wit," *The Dickensian*, 1

Dickens used wellerisms already in his letters prior to writing *Pickwick Papers*. Thus a letter of spring 1934 to H.W. Kolle begins with the following statement: "I am beyond measure distressed at your having had to wait for your coat. 'Appearances are afinst me, I know' as the man said when he murdered his brother, but it really is not my fault that it has not been returned."[56] Other epistolary appearances of wellerisms have also not been registered before, as for example this next statement in a letter of 27 February 1842 to John Forster: "I have in my portmanteau a petition for an international copyright law, signed by all the best American writers with Washington Irving at their head. They have requested me to hand it to Clay for presentation, and to back it with any remarks I may think proper to offer. So 'Hoo-roar for the principle, as the money-lender said, ven he wouldn't renoo the bill'."[57] As the following examples will make obvious, the wellerisms in the novels give Charles Dickens the social critic an opportunity to make ironic, detached, and entertaining comments on sociopolitical issues and conflicts of the day:

(1905), 31-34; Gwenllian Williams, "Sam Weller," *Trivium*, 1 (1966), 88-101; Marie Teresa McGowan, *Pickwick and the Pirates: A Study of Some Early Imitations, Dramatisations [sic] and Plagiarisms of "Pickwick Papers"* (Diss. University of London, 1975), esp. pp. 284-296; Florence Baer, "Wellerisms in *The Pickwick Papers*," *Folklore* (London), 94 (1983), 173-183; George B. Bryan and Wolfgang Mieder, "'As Sam Weller Said, When Finding Himself on the Stage': Wellerisms in Dramatizations of Charles Dickens' *Pickwick Papers*," *Proverbium: Yearbook of International Proverb Scholarship*, 11 (1994), 57-76.

[56] *The Letters of Charles Dickens*: Volume One: 1820-1839. Eds. Madeline House and Graham Storey (Oxford: The Clarendon Press, 1965), p. 39.

[57] The Letters of Charles Dickens. Volume Three: 1842-1843. Eds. Madeline House, Graham Storey, and Kathleen Tillotson (Oxford: The Clarendon Press, 1974), p. 92. It should be noted, however, that Dickens is actually citing this wellerism from his own *Pickwick Papers* (p. 489). See also the discussion of this text in Garrett Stewart, *Dickens and the Trials of Imagination* (Cambridge, Massachusetts: Harvard University Press, 1974), p. 41, with sporadic comments on other wellerisms on pp. 48, 68-79, 104, 203-204, 218, 227, and 244.

"Then the next question is, what the devil do you want with me, as the man said wen he see the ghost?" (*Pickwick Papers*, p. 125)

"That's the pint," interposed Sam; "out vith it, as the father said to the child, wen he swallowed a farden." (*Pickwick Papers*, p. 154)

"He wants you particklar; and no one else'll do, as the Devil's private secretary said ven he fetched avay Doctor Faustus," replied Mr. Weller. (*Pickwick Papers*, 193)

"Think, sir!" replied Mr. Weller; "why, I think, he's the wictim o' connubiality, as Blue Beard's domestic chaplain said, with a tear of pity, ven he buried him." (*Pickwick Papers*, p. 273)

"That's what I call a self-evident proposition, as the dog's-meat man said, when the housemaid told him he warn't a gentleman." (*Pickwick Papers*, p. 299)

"Vell, sir," rejoined Sam, after a short pause, "I think I see your drift; and if I do see your drift, it's my 'pinion that you're a comin' it a great deal too strong, as the mail-coachman said to the snow-storm, ven it overtook him." (*Pickwick Papers*, p. 599)

It is exactly in his use of "language as play"[58] which makes Sam Weller such a memorable character as a most prolific employer of at times humorous, grotesque and also macabre wellerisms.

But there are also plenty of additional proverbs and proverbial expressions in the *Pickwick Papers*, which has made this novel a special

---

[58]See James E. Marlow, "Pickwick's Writing: Propriety and Language," *ELH*, 52 (1985), 960 (the entire article on pp. 939-963).

challenge for translators.[59] A particularly vexing problem would be the following paragraph from that novel with its amassment of proverbs, proverbial expressions, and idioms:

"Come along, then," said he of the green coat, lugging Mr. Pickwick after him by main force, and talking the whole way. "Here, No. 924, take your fare, and take yourself off—respectable gentleman,—know him well—none of your nonsense—this way, sir,—where's your friends?—all a mistake, I see—never mind—accidents will happen—best regulated famil- ies—never say die—down upon your luck—pull him up—put that in his pipe—like the flavour—damned rascals." And with a lengthened string of similar broken sentences, delivered with extraordinary volubility, the stranger led the way to the travellers' waiting-room, whither he was closely followed by Mr. Pickwick and his disciples. (*Pickwick Papers*, p. 9)

Similar amassments can be found especially in those cases, where Dickens strings several proverbial comparisons together to create a vivid if not grotesque imagery.[60] His works are replete with comparisons, metaphors, and similes,[61] of which the following examples might serve as a representative illustration:

"You're as slow as a tortoise, and more thick-headed than a rhinoceros," returned his obliging client with an impatient gesture. (*The Old Curiosity Shop*, p. 383)

---

[59]See Maria Boquera Matarredona, "La traducción al español de paremias en *The Pickwick Papers*: refranes y proverbios," *Paremia*, no. 3 (1994), 89-96.

[60]See Robert Barnard, *Imagery and Theme in the Novels of Dickens* (Oslo: Universitetsforlaget, 1974); and Nancy K. Hill, *A Reformer's Art: Dickens' Picturesque and Grotesque Imagery* (Athens, Ohio: Ohio University Press, 1981).

[61]See Walter Rehfeld, *Der Vergleich bei Charles Dickens* (Greifs- wald: Hans Adler, 1923), pp.10-13; and Brook, pp. 30-35.

> He was but a poor man himself, said Peggotty, but as
> good as gold and as true as steel—those were her
> similes. (*David Copperfield*, p. 33)

> "He is uncommonly improving to look at, and I am not
> at all so. He is as sweet as honey, and I am as dull as
> ditch-water. He provides the pitch, and I handle it, and
> it sticks to me." (*Little Dorrit*, p. 802)

Of course, Dickens will also string two common proverbs together for
a double didactic effect, as for example in the statement "'My advice is,
never do to-morrow what you can do to-day. Procrastination is the thief
of time'" (*David Copperfield*, p. 174).

Yet such direct citations of traditional proverbs are well balanced
with Dickens's intentional variations of these fixed phrases. His purpose
of employing proverbs is only at times didactic and moralistic. He
actually seems to prefer to play with the wording and the structure of
standard proverbs, always creating innovative variations and allusions,
and thereby entertaining his readers with his humorous or satirical puns.
He is indeed a "liberated" proverbialist, who uses them with utmost
linguistic freedom to add metaphorical language to his own narrative and
colorful spice to the language of his characters. Most readers will be able
to recognize the underlying proverbs without too much difficulty, and the
juxtaposition of traditional proverb and authorial innovation results in a
stylistic peculiarity which makes Dickens's prose so rich in metaphorical
language. By overcoming the direct didacticism of many proverbs,
Dickens is able to communicate his social criticism and his desire to
improve the lot of his fellow citizens in a language which is not tiring in
its social message but rather refreshingly colorful and often humorous.
It is this "proverbial realism" which make some of the following
passages so appealing to readers of Dickens's novels still today:

> "Roving stones gather no moss, Joe," said Gabriel.
> "Nor mile-stones much," replied Joe. "I'm little better
> than one here, and see as much of the world." (*Barnaby
> Rudge*, p. 24)

> "But that wasn't my fault," said Jonas.
> "Yes, it was; you know it was."

"Any trick is fair in love," said Jonas. "She may have thought I liked her best, but you didn't."
"I did!" (*Martin Chuzzlewit*, p. 336)

"Beautiful Truth!" exclaimed the Chorus, looking upward. "How is your name profaned by vicious persons! You don't live in a well, my holy principle, but on the lips of false mankind." (*Martin Chuzzlewit*, p. 668; the proverb alluded to is "Truth lies at the bottom of the well")

I did not allow my resolution, with respect to the Parliamentary Debates, to cool. It was one of the irons I began to beat immediately, and one of the irons I kept hot, and hammered at, with perseverance I may honestly admire. (*David Copperfield*, p. 545)

"He doesn't impose upon me the necessity of rolling myself up like a hedgehog with my points outward. I expand, I open, I turn my silver lining outward like Milton's cloud, and it's more agreeable to both of us." (*Bleak House*, p. 251)

"And I tell you again, darling, that Mrs. General, if I may reverse a common proverb and adapt it to her, is a cat in gloves who *will* catch mice. That woman, I am quite sure and confident, will be our mother-in-law." (*Little Dorrit*, p. 590)

Of course, at times Dickens takes his game with proverbs a bit too far, and the modern reader in particular might not be able to reconstruct the traditional saying alluded to in the passage. This might well be the case with the following passage: "'What,' he asked of Mr. Pecksniff, happening to catch his eye in its descent; for until now it had been piously upraised, with something of that expression which the poetry of ages has attributed to a domestic bird, when breathing its last amid the ravages of an electric storm: 'What are their names'?" (*Martin Chuzzlewit*, p. 158). The proverb allusion "Like a dying duck in a thunderstorm" will surely not come to everyone's mind immediately.[62] R.S. Edgecombe has appropriately referred to "Dickens's riddling way with proverbs,"[63] something that can also be observed in his letters. Note, for example, the beginning of Dickens's letter of 23 September 1854 to Thomas Beard: "Catherine is at last persuaded that October really *is* the finest month in the year at the seaside—though she is not yet quite converted to that other axiom concerning the salutary effects of going to bed at 8 o'Clock."[64] It takes a considerable jolt of the "proverbial" mind to realize that the axiom mentioned here alludes to the proverb "Early to bed and early to rise, makes a man healthy, wealthy, and wise."[65] In a second "play" with this proverb, Dickens is a bit more obvious with his allusion, thus enabling his readers to recall the traditional saying: "At length it became high time to remember the first clause of that great discovery made by the ancient philosopher, for securing health, riches, and wisdom; the infallibility of which has been for generations verified by the enormous fortunes constantly amassed by chimney-sweepers and other persons who get up early and go to bed betimes" (*Martin Chuzzlewit*, p. 83). What a wonderfully ironic reaction to an early medical proverb dating back to 1496 which, under the craftsmanship of Dickens, becomes a social criticism against the unfair

---

[62]For historical references of the proverbial comparison see F.P. Wilson, *The Oxford Dictionary of English Proverbs*, 3rd ed. (Oxford: Oxford University Press, 1970), p. 210.

[63]Edgecombe, p. 144.

[64]*The Letters of Charles Dickens*: Volume Seven: 1853-1855. Eds. Graham Storey, Kathleen Tillotson, and Angus Easson (Oxford: The Clarendon Press, 1993), p. 418.

[65]For this proverb see Wilson, p. 211; Wolfgang Mieder, Stewart A. Kingsbury, and Kelsie B. Harder (eds.), *A Dictionary of American Proverbs* (New York: Oxford University Press, 1992), p. 42; W. Mieder, "'An Apple a Day Keeps the Doctor Away': Traditional and Modern Aspects of English Medical Proverbs," *Proverbium: Yearbook of International Proverb Scholarship*, 8 (1991), 77-106 (esp. pp. 85-92); and W. Mieder, "'Early to Bed and Early to Rise': From Proverb to Benjamin Franklin and Back," in W. Mieder, *Proverbs Are Never Out of Season*, pp. 98-134.

distribution of wealth. After all, it does seem unfair that those people who get up early and work hard do not appear to be getting rich, leave alone receive a decent pay for their labors.

The final point in these introductory remarks on Charles Dickens's repeated use of proverbial rhetoric relates to his often commented upon inclination towards repetition in general. He attached certain "habitual phrases" to particular characters, and such statements become "the 'signature tune' by which a character may be recogniz-ed."[66] As was explained earlier, in the case of Sam Weller, these habitual phrases become a whole series of wellerisms. Since this work appeared in installments, readers were literally waiting for the wellerisms of the next issue. But Dickens can also delight in cramming a proverbial expression repeatedly into one short paragraph. Here are two examples based on the phrases "to be brand-new" and "to hold one's tongue":

> Mr. and Mrs. Veneering were bran-new people in a bran-new house in a bran-new quarter of London. Everything about the Veneerings was spick and span new. All their furniture was new, all their friends were new, all their servants were new, their plate was new, their carriage was new, their harness was new, their horses were new, their pictures were new, they them-selves were new, they were as newly married as was lawfully compatible with their having a bran-new baby, [...] (*Our Mutual Friend*, p. 6)

> "Hold your tongue!" said Mr. Boffin. "You oughtn't to like it in any case. There! I didn't mean to be rude, but you put me out so, and after all I'm master. I didn't intend to tell you to hold your tongue. I beg your pardon. Don't hold your tongue. Only, don't contra-dict." (*Our Mutual Friend*, p. 473)

This third and last example is a particularly telling one and centers around the proverbial expression "To have a skeleton in the cupboard (closet)" in the meaning of a secret source of shame or pain to a family

---

[66]Brook, pp. 143-144. See also Sheila M Foor, *Dickens' Rhetoric* (New York: Peter Lang, 1993), p. 17.

or person. In the following passage, Dickens succeeds in personifying the proverbial phrase and has it partake as a third party in the marriage quarrel between Mr. and Mrs. Alfred Lammle. The repetitive use of the "phrasal person" adds much to the humor of the situation and the authorial wisdom expressed in this short dialogue at the breakfast table:

"It seems to me," said Mrs. Lammle, "that you have had no money at all ever since we have been married."

"What seems to you," said Mr. Lammle, "to have been the case, may possibly have been the case. It doesn't matter."

Was it the speciality of Mr. and Mrs. Lammle, or does it ever obtain with other loving couples? In these matrimonial dialogues they never addressed each other, but always some invisible presence that appeared to take station about midway between them. Perhaps the skeleton in the cupboard comes out to be talked to, on such domestic occasions?

"I have never seen any money in the house," said Mrs. Lammle to the skeleton, "except my own annuity. That I swear."

"You needn't take the trouble of swearing," said Mr. Lammle to the skeleton; "once more, it doesn't matter. You never turned your annuity to so good an account."

"Good an account! In what way?" asked Mrs. Lammle.

"In the way of getting credit, and living well," said Mr. Lammle.

Perhaps the skeleton laughed scornfully on being intrusted with this question and this answer; certainly Mrs. Lammle did, and Mr. Lammle did.

"And what is to happen next?" asked Mrs. Lammle of the skeleton.

"Smash is to happen next," said Mr. Lammle to the same authority.

After this, Mrs. Lammle looked disdainfully at the skeleton—but without carrying the look on to Mr. Lammle—and drooped her eyes. After that, Mr. Lammle did exactly the same thing, and drooped *his* eyes. A servant then entering with toast, the skeleton retired into the closet, and shut itself up. (*Our Mutual Friend*, pp. 556-557)

One thing is for certain though, Charles Dickens as the author of this passage and of volumes of letters, essays, speeches, and novels (also a few plays and poems) does not need to hide in a closet when it comes to judging his ability to integrate proverbial language into his texts. He is doubtlessly a master craftsman in the traditional and innovative use of proverbial rhetoric, equalling in these linguistic and folkloric aspects the literary achievements of his models William Shakespeare and Miguel de Cervantes Saavedra.[67] From them he learned a great deal about the effective use of proverbial rhetoric, but he also stood very much on his own two feet regarding his careful attention to the linguistic realism of the people of his time and area. For an author with a commitment to the realistic depiction of social and political problems of the nineteenth century, proverbs and proverbial expressions as fixed phrases of human behavior had to enter his prose by necessity. They play a major role in his particular style and rhetoric, and it is surprising indeed that so little attention has thus far been paid to this major linguistic and folkloric aspect of his works. The Key-word Index of this book with its many proverbs, proverbial expressions, proverbial comparisons, and wellerisms will now enable scholars and students to undertake detailed contextualized studies of the use and function of these fixed phrases in individual novels. They will doubtlessly find that these elements of folk speech do not only add metaphorical color to the prose but rather that they function as intrinsic parts of the entire meaning and message of the novels. Charles Dickens knew this only too well, and in 1850, in the middle of his remarkable career as one of the greatest British writers, he quite appropriately stated that "conventional phrases are a sort of fireworks, easily let off, and liable to take a great variety

---

[67]See above all Charles George Smith, *Shakespeare's Proverb Lore* (Cambridge, Massachusetts: Harvard University Press, 1963); Robert William Dent, *Shakespeare's Proverbial Language: An Index* (Berkeley, California: University of California Press, 1981); Juan Sune Benages, *Fraseologia de Cervantes: Colleción de frases, refranes, proverbios, aforismos, adagios, expressiones y modos adverbiales que se leen en las obras cervantinas, recopilados y ordenados* (Barcelona: Editorial Lux, 1929); and Maria Cecilia Colombi, *Los refranes en el Quijote: texto y contexto* (Potomac, Maryland: Scripta Humanistica, 1989). For additional references see Mieder and Bryan, *Proverbs in World Literature*, pp. 244-253 (Shakespeare, nos. 2253-2358), and pp. 65-69 (Cervantes, nos. 617-653).

of shapes and colours not at all suggested by their original form" (*David Copperfield*, p. 590). These proverbial fireworks, as expressions of wit and wisdom, are indeed a major part of the language and message of an author who cared deeply about the human comedy and tragedy of his time.

DICKENS EDITIONS CONSULTED

The proverbial texts registered in the Key-word Index were excerpted from the 22,022 pages that comprise Charles Dickens's complete published writings included in the following list.

Novels:

The Posthumous Papers of the Pickwick Club. 1837. The Oxford Illustrated Dickens, Vol. I. Oxford: Oxford University Press, 1948. 801 pp.

The Personal History of David Copperfield. 1850. The Oxford Illustrated Dickens, Vol. II. Oxford: Oxford University Press, 1948. 877 pp.

Bleak House. 1853. The Oxford Illustrated Dickens, Vol. III. Oxford: Oxford University Press, 1948. 880 pp.

A Tale of Two Cities. 1859. The Oxford Illustrated Dickens, Vol. IV. Oxford: Oxford University Press, 1948. 358 pp.

The Adventures of Oliver Twist. 1838. The Oxford Illustrated Dickens, Vol. V. Oxford: Oxford University Press, 1948. 415 pp.

The Life and Adventures of Nicholas Nickleby. 1839. The Oxford Illustrated Dickens, Vol. VI. Oxford: Oxford University Press, 1950. 831 pp.

Dealings with the Firm of Dombey and Son. 1848. The Oxford Illustrated Dickens, Vol. VII. Oxford: Oxford University Press, 1950. 878 pp.

The Old Curiosity Shop. 1841. The Oxford Illustrated Dickens, Vol. VIII. Oxford: Oxford University Press, 1951. 555 pp.

The Life and Adventures of Martin Chuzzlewit. 1844. The Oxford Illustrated Dickens, Vol. IX. Oxford: Oxford University Press, 1951. 839 pp.

Our Mutual Friend. 1865. The Oxford Illustrated Dickens, Vol. X. Oxford: Oxford University Press, 1952. 822 pp.

Christmas Stories. 1871. The Oxford Illustrated Dickens, Vol. XI. Oxford: Oxford University Press, 1956. 758 pp.

Sketches by Boz. 1833-40. The Oxford Illustrated Dickens, Vol. XII. Oxford: Oxford University Press, 1957. 688 pp.

Great Expectations. 1861. The Oxford Illustrated Dickens, Vol. XIII. Oxford: Oxford University Press, 1953. 460 pp.

Little Dorrit. 1857. The Oxford Illustrated Dickens, Vol. XIV. Oxford: Oxford University Press, 1953. 826 pp.

Barnaby Rudge: A Tale of the Riots of 'Eighty. 1841. The Oxford Illustrated Dickens, Vol. XV. Oxford: Oxford University Press, 1954. 634 pp.

Christmas Books. 1843-49. The Oxford Illustrated Dickens, Vol. XVI. Oxford: Oxford University Press, 1954. 398 pp.

Hard Times for These Times. 1854. The Oxford Illustrated Dickens, Vol. XVII. Oxford: Oxford University Press, 1955. 299 pp.

The Mystery of Edwin Drood. 1870. The Oxford Illustrated Dickens, Vol. XVIII. Oxford: Oxford University Press, 1956. 278 pp.

American Notes and Pictures from Italy. 1842, 1846. The Oxford Illustrated Dickens, Vol. XIX. Oxford: Oxford University Press, 1957. 433 pp.

Master Humphrey's Clock and A Child's History of England. 1840-41, 1852-54. The Oxford Illustrated Dickens, Vol. XX. Oxford: Oxford University Press, 1958. 531 pp.

The Uncommercial Traveller and Reprinted Pieces Etc. 1850-1860. The Oxford Illustrated Dickens, Vol. XXI. Oxford: Oxford University Press, 1958. 756 pp.

Other Literary Works:

Complete Plays and Selected Poems of Charles Dickens. London: Vision Press, 1970. 245 pp.

Charles Dickens' Uncollected Writings from Household Words *1850-1859,* 2 vols. Ed. Harry Stone. Bloomington: Indiana University Press, 1968. 666 pp.

Dickens' Working Notes for His Novels. Ed. Harry Stone. Chicago, Il.: University of Chicago Press, 1987. xxiv + 393 pp.

The Life of Our Lord: Written for His Children... New York: Simon and Schuster, 1934. 128 pp.

Letters:

The Letters of Charles Dickens: Volume One: 1820-1839. Eds. Madeline House and Graham Storey. Oxford: The Clarendon Press, 1965. 744 pp.

The Letters of Charles Dickens: Volume Two: 1840-1841. Eds. Madeline House and Graham Storey. Oxford: The Clarendon Press, 1969. 547 pp.

The Letters of Charles Dickens: Volume Three: 1842-1843. Eds. Madeline House, Graham Storey, and Kathleen Tillotson. Oxford: The Clarendon Press, 1974. 692 pp.

The Letters of Charles Dickens: Volume Four: 1844-1846. Ed. Kathleen Tillotson. Oxford: The Clarendon Press, 1977. 771 pp.

The Letters of Charles Dickens: Volume Five: 1847-1849. Eds. Graham Storey and K. J. Fielding. Oxford: The Clarendon Press, 1981. 753 pp.

The Letters of Charles Dickens: Volume Six: 1850-1852. Eds. Madeline House, Graham Storey, and Kathleen Tillotson. Oxford: The Clarendon Press, 1988. 909 pp.

The Letters of Charles Dickens: Volume Seven: 1853-1855. Eds. Graham Storey, Kathleen Tillotson, and Angus Easson. Oxford: The Clarendon Press, 1993. 975 pp.

The Letters of Charles Dickens: Volume Eight: 1856-1858. Eds. Graham Storey and Kathleen Tillotson. Oxford: The Clarendon Press, 1995. pp. 807.

The Letters of Charles Dickens. Ed. Walter Dexter. Vol. III: 1858-1870. The Nonesuch Dickens. London: The Nonesuch Press, 1938. 854 pp.

Speeches:

The Works of Charles Dickens: The Speeches. Ed. Richard H. Shepherd. New National Edition, Vol. II. New York: Hearst's International Library Company, n. d. 221 pp.

KEY-WORD INDEX

The abbreviated citations in the Key-word Index refer to the following standard proverb collections of the English language:

APP: Taylor, Archer, and Bartlett Jere Whiting. *A Dictionary of American Proverbs and Proverbial Phrases, 1820-1880*. Cambridge, Massachusetts: Harvard University Press, 1958.

ODEP: Wilson, F.P. *The Oxford Dictionary of English Proverbs*, 3rd ed. Oxford: Clarendon Press, 1970.

EAP: Whiting, Barlett Jere. *Early American Proverbs and Proverbial Phrases*. Cambridge, Massachusetts: Harvard University Press, 1977.

CODP: Simpson, John A. *The Concise Oxford Dictionary of Proverbs*. Oxford: Oxford University Press, 1982.

MP: Whiting, Bartlett Jere. *Modern Proverbs and Proverbial Sayings*. Cambridge, Massachusetts: Harvard University Press, 1989.

DAP: Mieder, Wolfgang, Stewart A. Kingsbury, and Kelsie B. Harder. *A Dictionary of American Proverbs*. New York: Oxford University Press, 1992.

For those proverbial texts that could not be verified in the aforementioned reference works, the following eleven dictionaries were consulted to locate at least one citation. They are cited by the authors' last names:

Bartlett: Bartlett, John. *Familiar Quotations*, ed. Justin Kaplan. 16th ed. Boston: Little, Brown and Company, 1992.

Boatner: Boatner, Maxine Tull, and John Edward Gates. *A Dictionary of American Idioms*. Woodbury, New York: Barron's Educational Series, 1975.

Brewer: *Brewer's Dictionary of Phrase and Fable*, ed. Ivor H. Evans. Centenary edition. New York: Harper & Row, 1970.

Craig: Craig, Doris. *Catch Phrases, Clichés and Idioms: A Dictionary of Familiar Expressions*. Jefferson, North Carolina: McFarland & Company, 1990.

Partridge: Partridge, Eric. *A Dictionary of Slang and Unconventional English*, 7th ed. New York: Macmillan Publishing Company, 1970.

Sommer: Sommer, Elyse and Mike. *Similes Dictionary*. Detroit, Michigan: Gale Research Company, 1988.

Spears: Spears, Richard A. *NTC's American Idioms Dictionary*. Lincolnwood, Illinois: National Textbook Company, 1987.

Stevenson: Stevenson, Burton. *The Home Book of Proverbs, Maxims, and Famous Phrases*. New York: The Macmillan Company, 1948.

Urdang: Urdang, Laurence. *Idioms and Phrases Index*. 3 vols. Detroit, Michigan: Gale Research Company, 1983.

Wilkinson: Wilkinson, P.R. *Thesaurus of Traditional English Metaphors*. London: Routledge, 1992.

Wilstach: Wilstach, Frank J. *A Dictionary of Similes*. Boston: Little, Brown, and Company, 1916.

A

A B C

1850 ...you can't work up A, B, C into chairs and tables. (p. 193)

1850 Here's a pretty coil indeed, about teaching little ragamuffins their A B C! (p. 199)

"Mr. Bendigo Buster on Our National Defences Against Education." [with Henry Morley]. *Charles Dickens' Uncollected Writings from* Household Words *1850-1859*, 2 vols. Ed. Harry Stone. Bloomington: Indiana University Press, 1968.

1860 He...could read the depths of my nature better than his ABC.... (p. 355)

The Uncommercial Traveller and Reprinted Pieces Etc. 1850-1860. The Oxford Illustrated Dickens, Vol. XXI. Oxford: Oxford University Press, 1958.

APP 1; EAP 1; MP 1.

A to Z

1850-56 Peace be with all the Wedgingtons from A to Z. (p. 460)

The Uncommercial Traveller and Reprinted Pieces Etc. 1850-1860. The Oxford Illustrated Dickens, Vol. XXI. Oxford: Oxford University Press, 1958.

1854 ...the mill of knowledge, as per...tabular statements A to Z.... (p. 56)

Hard Times for These Times. 1854. The Oxford Illustrated Dickens, Vol. XVII. Oxford: Oxford University Press, 1955.

1865 'If there is a word in the dictionary under any letter from A to Z....' (p. 20)

Our Mutual Friend. 1865. The Oxford Illustrated Dickens, Vol. X. Oxford: Oxford University Press, 1952.

APP 1; EAP 1; MP 1.

To be **above-board**

1833-36 '...all fair and above board....' (p. 112)

Sketches by Boz. 1833-40. The Oxford Illustrated Dickens, Vol. XII. Oxford: Oxford University Press, 1957.

1857 "You're acting all fair and above-board by me," he said.... (p. 690)

Christmas Stories. 1871. The Oxford Illustrated Dickens, Vol. XI. Oxford: Oxford University Press, 1956.

MP 59.

Accidents will happen in the best-regulated families.

1837 '...accidents will happen—best regulated families—never say die—...put that in his pipe....' (p. 9)

The Posthumous Papers of the Pickwick Club. 1837. The Oxford Illustrated Dickens, Vol. I. Oxford: Oxford University Press, 1948.

1839 ...lay this to the account of one of those accidents which are inevitable in all-regulated...families. (p. 606)
The Letters of Charles Dickens: Volume One: 1820-1839. Eds. Madeline House and Graham Storey. Oxford: The Clarendon Press, 1965.

1846 ...emergency that will sometimes arise in the best regulated families (p. 57)
Dickens' Working Notes for His Novels. Ed. Harry Stone. Chicago, Ill.: University of Chicago Press, 1987.

1850 ...that other little accident which...*will* occasionally happen in well-regulated families. (p. 219)
The Letters of Charles Dickens: Volume Six: 1850-1852. Eds. Madeline House, Graham Storey, and Kathleen Tillotson. Oxford: The Clarendon Press, 1988.

1850 'My dear friend Copperfield, ...accidents will occur in the best-regulated families....' (p. 413)
The Personal History of David Copperfield. 1850. The Oxford Illustrated Dickens, Vol. II. Oxford: Oxford University Press, 1948.
APP 2; ODEP 2; EAP 2; CODP 1; MP 3; DAP 4.

There is no **accounting** for tastes.

1865 'There is no accounting...there is no accounting for tastes, Mary Anne.' (p. 710)
Our Mutual Friend. 1865. The Oxford Illustrated Dickens, Vol. X. Oxford: Oxford University Press, 1952.
APP 2; ODEP 2; EAP 2; CODP 1; MP 3; DAP 5.

May our **acquaintance** be a long one.

1837 'Werry glad to see you, indeed, and hope our acquaintance may be a long one, as the gen'l'm'n said to the fi' pun' note.' (p. 350)
The Posthumous Papers of the Pickwick Club. 1837. The Oxford Illustrated Dickens, Vol. I. Oxford: Oxford University Press, 1948.
DOW 113.

Suit the **action** to the word and the word to the action.

1867 ...taking his hat down from its peg to suit the action to the word.... (p. 545)
Christmas Stories. 1871. The Oxford Illustrated Dickens, Vol. XI. Oxford: Oxford University Press, 1956.
DAP 7; BARTLETT 196:22.

Not to know someone from **Adam**

1844 'I don't know this man from Adam....' (p. 607)
The Life and Adventures of Martin Chuzzlewit. 1844. The Oxford Illustrated Dickens, Vol. IX. Oxford: Oxford University Press, 1951.
1860 "...I don't know you from Adam." (p. 259)
Christmas Stories. 1871. The Oxford Illustrated Dickens, Vol. XI. Oxford: Oxford University Press, 1956.
EAP 4; MP 4.

To be much **ado** about nothing

1843 We took him to Drury Lane to see Much Ado About Nothing. (p. 452)
The Letters of Charles Dickens: Volume Three: 1842-1843. Eds. Madeline House, Graham Storey, and Kathleen Tillotson. Oxford: The Clarendon Press, 1974.
ODEP 549; EAP 4; MP 6.

To hear something of **advantage**

1850 This is the place for X. Y. Z. to hear something of advantage in. (p. 133)
"The Old Lady in Threadneedle Street." [with W. H. Wills]. *Charles Dickens' Uncollected Writings from* Household Words *1850-1859*, 2 vols. Ed. Harry Stone. Bloomington: Indiana University Press, 1968.

Adversity is a good teacher.

1849 '...how true the saying is, that adversity is a good teacher.' (p. 358)
Christmas Books. 1843-49. The Oxford Illustrated Dickens, Vol. XVI. Oxford: Oxford University Press, 1954.
STEVENSON 18:10.

Adversity acquaints a man with strange bed-fellows.

1837 Chapter XLII: Illustrative...of the old Proverb, that Adversity brings a Man acquainted with strange Bed-fellows. (p. 586)
The Posthumous Papers of the Pickwick Club. 1837. The Oxford Illustrated Dickens, Vol. I. Oxford: Oxford University Press, 1948.
ODEP 535; CODP 2; DAP 9. William Shakespeare, *The Tempest*, II, 2, 40

I'm **agreeable** to do it.

1840-41 'Well, I'm agreeable to do it,' said Sam, 'but not if you go cuttin' away like that, as the bull turned round and mildly observed to the drover ven they wos a goadin' him into the butcher's door.' (p. 78)

Master Humphrey's Clock and A Child's History of England. 1840-41, 1852-54. The Oxford Illustrated Dickens, Vol. XX. Oxford: Oxford University Press, 1958.

To vanish into **air**

1836 SQUIRE: ...your love for Edmunds had vanished into air.... (*The Village Coquettes*, II, i, p. 71)
Complete Plays and Selected Poems of Charles Dickens. London: Vision Press, 1970.
EAP 6; MP 7.

To give oneself **airs**

1853 '...I was an accomplished girl, who had any right to give herself airs,' said Caddy. (p. 196)
Bleak House. 1853. The Oxford Illustrated Dickens, Vol. III. Oxford: Oxford University Press, 1948.
APP 5; EAP 6.

Alive and kicking

1850-56 ...that unhappy landed interest...is always found to be alive—and kicking. (p. 600)
The Uncommercial Traveller and Reprinted Pieces Etc. 1850-1860. The Oxford Illustrated Dickens, Vol. XXI. Oxford: Oxford University Press, 1958.
APP 5; MP 8.

Alive and well

1865 ...please God I am alive and well. (p. 413)
The Letters of Charles Dickens, ed. Walter Dexter. Vol. III: 1858-1870. The Nonesuch Dickens. London: The Nonesuch Press, 1938.
SPEARS 6.

All in good time.

1844 'All in good time. All in good time!' (p. 126)
1844 ...to adopt that worthy man's phraseology, 'all in good time.' (p. 126)
The Life and Adventures of Martin Chuzzlewit. 1844. The Oxford Illustrated Dickens, Vol. IX. Oxford: Oxford University Press, 1951.
1850 'All in good time!' (p. 753)
The Personal History of David Copperfield. 1850. The Oxford Illustrated Dickens, Vol. II. Oxford: Oxford University Press, 1948.
EAP 7; MP 8.

All is fair in love and war.

1844 'Any trick is fair in love,' said Jonas. (p. 336)
The Life and Adventures of Martin Chuzzlewit. 1844. The Oxford Illustrated Dickens, Vol. IX. Oxford: Oxford University Press, 1951.
1850 'All stratagems are fair in love, sir.' (p. 573)
The Personal History of David Copperfield. 1850. The Oxford Illustrated Dickens, Vol. II. Oxford: Oxford University Press, 1948.
APP 5; MP 8; DAP 14; BARTLETT 482:13.

All is for the best.

1841 ...I console myself...with the reflection that "it's all for the best". (p. 423)
The Letters of Charles Dickens: Volume Two: 1840-1841. Eds. Madeline House and Graham Storey. Oxford: The Clarendon Press, 1969.
APP 26; CODP 13; DAP 48; STEVENSON 173:2.

It's **all** for my own good.

1837 'It's all for my own good; vich is the reflection vith wich the penitent schoolboy comforted his feelin's ven they flogged him,' rejoined the old gentleman. (p. 734)
The Posthumous Papers of the Pickwick Club. 1837. The Oxford Illustrated Dickens, Vol. I. Oxford: Oxford University Press, 1948.
DOW 53.

All's well that ends well.

1848 All's well that ends well.... (p. 388)
The Letters of Charles Dickens: Volume Five: 1847-1849. Eds. Graham Storey and K. J. Fielding. Oxford: The Clarendon Press, 1981.
APP 6; ODEP 879; EAP 7; CODP 244; MP 9; DAP 14.

The **almighty dollar**

1842 ...the almighty dollar sinks into something comparatively insignificant.... (p. 27)
American Notes and Pictures from Italy. 1842, 1846. The Oxford Illustrated Dickens, Vol. XIX. Oxford: Oxford University Press, 1957.
URDANG, *IDIOMS* 28; STEVENSON 617:2.

Animal, vegetable, or mineral

1846 The Baby's head was...a test and touchstone for every description of matter,—animal, vegetable, and mineral. (p. 231)

Christmas Books. 1843-49. The Oxford Illustrated Dickens, Vol. XVI. Oxford: Oxford University Press, 1954.

Anything for a quiet life.

1837 '...anything for a quiet life, as the man said wen he took the sitivation at the lighthouse.' (p. 611)
The Posthumous Papers of the Pickwick Club. 1837. The Oxford Illustrated Dickens, Vol. I. Oxford: Oxford University Press, 1948.
ODEP 15; MP 12; DAP 21; DOW 73.

In case **anything** turns up

1850 ...'in case anything turns up,' which was his favourite expression. (p. 163)
1850 'That he may be ready, in case of anything turning up.' (p. 171)
The Personal History of David Copperfield. 1850. The Oxford Illustrated Dickens, Vol. II. Oxford: Oxford University Press, 1948.
URDANG, *IDIOMS* 1565.

Appearances are against me.

1834 "Appearances are against me, I know" [*sic*] as the man said when he murdered his brother.... (p. 39)
The Letters of Charles Dickens: Volume One: 1820-1839. Eds. Madeline House and Graham Storey. Oxford: The Clarendon Press, 1965.

Appearances are deceptive.

1840-41 But appearances are often deceptive when they least seem so.... (p. 58)
Master Humphrey's Clock and A Child's History of England. 1840-41, 1852-54. The Oxford Illustrated Dickens, Vol. XX. Oxford: Oxford University Press, 1958.
APP 7; EAP 10; CODP 5; MP 13; DAP 22.

To be in **apple-pie order**

1865 'Apple-pie order!' said Mr. Boffin.... (p. 180)
Our Mutual Friend. 1865. The Oxford Illustrated Dickens, Vol. X. Oxford: Oxford University Press, 1952.
APP 8; ODEP 17; MP 16.

To be tied to someone's **apron-strings**

1841 '...he's old enough to make it, and to snap your apron-strings.' (p. 365)

Barnaby Rudge: A Tale of the Riots of 'Eighty. 1841. The Oxford Illustrated Dickens, Vol. XV. Oxford: Oxford University Press, 1954.

1845 '...I should be ashamed...to pin myself to a woman's apron-strings!' (p. 99)

Christmas Books. 1843-49. The Oxford Illustrated Dickens, Vol. XVI. Oxford: Oxford University Press, 1954.

APP 9; ODEP 18; EAP 12; MP 16.

Art improves nature.

1841 '...art improves natur'—that's my motto.' (p. 298)

Barnaby Rudge: A Tale of the Riots of 'Eighty. 1841. The Oxford Illustrated Dickens, Vol. XV. Oxford: Oxford University Press, 1954.

ODEP 19; DAP 27.

Art is long; life is short.

1844 '...art is long and time is short.' (p. 81)

The Life and Adventures of Martin Chuzzlewit. 1844. The Oxford Illustrated Dickens, Vol. IX. Oxford: Oxford University Press, 1951.

ODEP 19; EAP 13; CODP 6; MP 20; DAP 28.

B

To be a **babe** in the woods

1842 The babes in the wood had a rich and cruel uncle. (p. 281)

The Letters of Charles Dickens: Volume Three: 1842-1843. Eds. Madeline House, Graham Storey, and Kathleen Tillotson. Oxford: The Clarendon Press, 1974.

1850 '...for a pair of babes in the wood as you are!' (p. 639)

The Personal History of David Copperfield. 1850. The Oxford Illustrated Dickens, Vol. II. Oxford: Oxford University Press, 1948.

APP 12; EAP 16; MP 23.

Backwards and forwards

1841 '...as long as our people go backwards and forwards, to and fro, up and down....' (p. 186)

1841 '...you go a-trying to provoke three great neck-or-nothing chaps, that could keep on running over us, back'ards and for'ards...?' (p. 262)

Barnaby Rudge: A Tale of the Riots of 'Eighty. 1841. The Oxford Illustrated Dickens, Vol. XV. Oxford: Oxford University Press, 1954.

URDANG, *IDIOMS* 73.

To go from **bad** to worse

1861 Herbert and I went on from bad to worse.... (p. 272)
Great Expectations. 1861. The Oxford Illustrated Dickens, Vol. XIII. Oxford: Oxford University Press, 1953.
EAP 18; MP 26.

Bag and baggage

1842 ...I was obliged to pack up bag and baggage.... (p. 208)
The Letters of Charles Dickens: Volume Three: 1842-1843. Eds. Madeline House, Graham Storey, and Kathleen Tillotson. Oxford: The Clarendon Press, 1974.
1844 ...I "think" of leaving England...bag and baggage.... (p. 3)
1844 I...mean to decamp, bag and baggage.... (p. 68)
1844 Bag and baggage...I am coming to Italy.... (p. 81)
1844 I shall start for Rome...picking up bag and baggage.... (p. 191)
1846 I hope to reach there, bag and baggage.... (p. 644)
The Letters of Charles Dickens: Volume Four: 1844-1846. Ed. Kathleen Tillotson. Oxford: The Clarendon Press, 1977.
1858 ...I moved my old bones, bag and baggage, up to London. (p. 600)
"A House to Let." [with Wilkie Collins]. *Charles Dickens' Uncollected Writings from Household Words 1850-1859*, 2 vols. Ed. Harry Stone. Bloomington: Indiana University Press, 1968.
1865 '...the sooner you are gone, bag and baggage, the better....' (p. 595)
Our Mutual Friend. 1865. The Oxford Illustrated Dickens, Vol. X. Oxford: Oxford University Press, 1952.
APP 14; EAP 18; MP 27; BARTLETT 191:12.

A baker's dozen

1861 'And she's out now, making it a baker's dozen.' (p. 6)
Great Expectations. 1861. The Oxford Illustrated Dickens, Vol. XIII. Oxford: Oxford University Press, 1953.
APP 15; EAP 19; MP 27.

As **bald** as a Dutch cheese

1850-56 ...enforcing the benevolent moral, "Better to be bald as a Dutch cheese than come to this...." (p. 415)
The Uncommercial Traveller and Reprinted Pieces Etc. 1850-1860. The Oxford Illustrated Dickens, Vol. XXI. Oxford: Oxford University Press, 1958.
PARTRIDGE 250.

As **bald** as a friar

1850 'You'd be as bald as a friar on the top of your head....' (p. 331)
The Personal History of David Copperfield. 1850. The Oxford Illustrated Dickens, Vol. II. Oxford: Oxford University Press, 1948.

As **bald** as a Mussulman

1848 ...a waxen effigy, bald as a Mussulman in the morning.... (p. 170)
Dealings with the Firm of Dombey and Son. 1848. The Oxford Illustrated Dickens, Vol. VII. Oxford: Oxford University Press, 1950.

There is a **balm** in Gilead.

1851 ...although Olivia...had...tried...to break my heart, there was "balm in Gilead." (pp. 217-218)
"My Mahogany Friend." [with Mary Boyle]. *Charles Dickens' Uncollected Writings from Household Words 1850-1859*, 2 vols. Ed. Harry Stone. Bloomington: Indiana University Press, 1968.
ODEP 28; EAP 19; MP 29.

Barkis is willin'.

1849 Barkis is willin [*sic*] (p. 161)
Dickens' Working Notes for His Novels. Ed. Harry Stone. Chicago, Ill.: University of Chicago Press, 1987.
1850 '...you'd recollect to say that Barkis was willin'; would you?' (p. 65.)
1850 'That Barkis was willing,' I replied.... (p. 65)
1850 'Ye—es. Barkis is willin'.' (p. 65)
1850 ...saying, with profound gravity, 'Barkis is willin'.' (p. 65)
1850 'Barkis is willing.' (p. 65)
1850 '"Barkis is willin'," says you.' (p. 108)
1850 'Barkis is willin'!' (p. 445)
The Personal History of David Copperfield. 1850. The Oxford Illustrated Dickens, Vol. II. Oxford: Oxford University Press, 1948.
MP 31; BARTLETT 470:21.

To **be** or not to be; that is the question.

1840 To be or not to be? (p. 127)
The Letters of Charles Dickens: Volume Two: 1840-1841. Eds. Madeline House and Graham Storey. Oxford: The Clarendon Press, 1969.
1867 ...to answer it, or not to answer it, as the event might prove. (p. 602)

Christmas Stories. 1871. The Oxford Illustrated Dickens, Vol. XI. Oxford: Oxford University Press, 1956.

1867 To go, or not to go? (p. 553)

The Letters of Charles Dickens, ed. Walter Dexter. Vol. III: 1858-1870. The Nonesuch Dickens. London: The Nonesuch Press, 1938.

DAP 39; BARTLETT, 196:10.

Be-all and end-all

1848 ...he...was the be-all and end-all of this business. (p. 310)

Dealings with the Firm of Dombey and Son. 1848. The Oxford Illustrated Dickens, Vol. VII. Oxford: Oxford University Press, 1950.

URDANG, *IDIOMS* 101.

Bear and forbear.

1847 ...the power of knowledge...is, to bear and forbear.... (p. 411)

Address at the opening of the Glasgow Athenaeum, 28 Dec. 1847. *The Works of Charles Dickens: The Speeches.* Ed. Richard H. Shepherd. New National Edition, Vol. II. New York: Hearst's International Library Company, n. d.

APP 20; ODEP 34; EAP 312; CODP 10; DAP 40.

To beat someone hollow

1835 .. there is every probability of our beating them hollow. (p. 91)

The Letters of Charles Dickens: Volume One: 1820-1839. Eds. Madeline House and Graham Storey. Oxford: The Clarendon Press, 1965.

1836 FLAM: ...they're beating us hollow.... (*The Village Coquettes*, I, iii, p. 63)

Complete Plays and Selected Poems of Charles Dickens. London: Vision Press, 1970.

APP 186; EAP 215; MP 312.

Beauty cannot enter the house of anguish.

1850 They say Ideal Beauty cannot enter | The house of anguish. (p. 239)

Complete Plays and Selected Poems of Charles Dickens. London: Vision Press, 1970.

To be at someone's beck and call

1839 '...she is not at his beck and call....' (p. 696)

The Life and Adventures of Nicholas Nickleby. 1839. The Oxford Illustrated Dickens, Vol. VI. Oxford: Oxford University Press, 1950.

URDANG, *IDIOMS* 107.

Early to **bed**, early to rise makes a man healthy, wealthy, and wise.

1844 ...that great discovery made by the ancient philosopher, for securing health, riches, and wisdom; the infallibility of which has for generations been verified by the enormous fortunes constantly amassed by chimney-sweepers and other persons who get up early and go to bed betimes. (p. 83)

The Life and Adventures of Martin Chuzzlewit. 1844. The Oxford Illustrated Dickens, Vol. IX. Oxford: Oxford University Press, 1951.

1854 ...though she is not yet quite converted to that other axiom concerning the salutary effects of going to bed at 8 o'Clock. (p. 418)

The Letters of Charles Dickens: Volume Seven: 1853-1855. Eds. Graham Storey, Kathleen Tillotson, and Angus Easson. Oxford: The Clarendon Press, 1993.

1859 ...the paper's being called, SURE TO BE HEALTHY, WEALTHY, AND WISE. (p. 98)

The Letters of Charles Dickens, ed. Walter Dexter. Vol. III: 1858-1870. The Nonesuch Dickens. London: The Nonesuch Press, 1938.

APP 21; ODEP 211; EAP 24; CODP 62; MP 37; DAP 42.

Make your **bed**; so lie upon it.

1853 '"You have made your bed. Now, lie upon it."' (p. 750)

1853 '...my best amends was to lie upon the bed I had made....' (p. 751)

Bleak House. 1853. The Oxford Illustrated Dickens, Vol. III. Oxford: Oxford University Press, 1948.

ODEP 502; CODP 143; MP 37; DAP 42.

To get out of **bed** backwards

1844 'We got out of bed back'ards, I think, for we're as cross as two sticks.' (p. 465)

The Life and Adventures of Martin Chuzzlewit. 1844. The Oxford Illustrated Dickens, Vol. IX. Oxford: Oxford University Press, 1951.

APP 21; ODEP 678; EAP 24; MP 38.

Bedlam broke loose.

1846 'Bedlam broke loose!' said Tackleton.... (p. 187)

Christmas Books. 1843-49. The Oxford Illustrated Dickens, Vol. XVI. Oxford: Oxford University Press, 1954.

APP 180; MP 304.

To be all **beer and skittles**

1837 '...it's a regular holiday to them—all porter and skittles.' (p. 576)
The Posthumous Papers of the Pickwick Club. 1837. The Oxford Illustrated Dickens, Vol.
I. Oxford: Oxford University Press, 1948.

To be small **beer**

1838 TOM: ...I have very often felt as if I wasn't the small beer I was
taken for. (*The Lamplighter*, I, i, p. 119)
Complete Plays and Selected Poems of Charles Dickens. London: Vision Press, 1970.
APP 23; ODEP 744; EAP 26; MP 40.

Beg, borrow, or steal

1865 'I feel that I can't beg it, borrow it, or steal it....' (p. 320)
1865 'Beg money, borrow money, or steal money.' (p. 558)
Our Mutual Friend. 1865. The Oxford Illustrated Dickens, Vol. X. Oxford: Oxford
University Press, 1952.
STEVENSON 148:2.

To be the **beginning** of the end

1853 '...it was the beginning of the end!' (p. 96)
Bleak House. 1853. The Oxford Illustrated Dickens, Vol. III. Oxford: Oxford University
Press, 1948.
URDANG, *IDIOMS* 111.

To begin at the **beginning**

1846 ...if I am to tell a story I must begin at the beginning.... (p. 159)
Christmas Books. 1843-49. The Oxford Illustrated Dickens, Vol. XVI. Oxford: Oxford
University Press, 1954.
1850 To begin my life with the beginning of my life, I record.... (p. 1)
The Personal History of David Copperfield. 1850. The Oxford Illustrated Dickens, Vol.
II. Oxford: Oxford University Press, 1948.
STEVENSON 151:3.

To have a **bellyful** of something

1853 ...the National Sparkler will be prepared to give Lithers a
bellyfull.... (p. 12)
The Letters of Charles Dickens: Volume Seven: 1853-1855. Eds. Graham Storey, Kathleen
Tillotson, and Angus Easson. Oxford: The Clarendon Press, 1993.
APP 25; ODEP 46; EAP 28; MP 43.

It is better to **bend** than to break.

1841 'I have broken where I should have bent....' (p. 605)
Barnaby Rudge: A Tale of the Riots of 'Eighty. 1841. The Oxford Illustrated Dickens, Vol. XV. Oxford: Oxford University Press, 1954.
ODEP 52; EAP 28; MP 43.

To give someone the **benefit** of the doubt

1854 I have given...the benefit of the doubt.... (p. 309)
The Letters of Charles Dickens: Volume Seven: 1853-1855. Eds. Graham Storey, Kathleen Tillotson, and Angus Easson. Oxford: The Clarendon Press, 1993.
APP 25; MP 44.

To make the **best** of a bad bargain

1833-36 ...the only thing to be done is, just to make the best of a bad bargain.... (p. 120)
Sketches by Boz. 1833-40. The Oxford Illustrated Dickens, Vol. XII. Oxford: Oxford University Press, 1957.
APP 26; ODEP 48; EAP 29; MP 44.

To make the **best** of something

1854 'What I ha' getn, I mun mak th' best on.' (p. 142)
Hard Times for These Times. 1854. The Oxford Illustrated Dickens, Vol. XVII. Oxford: Oxford University Press, 1955.
1859 'Make the best of it, my dear sir,' said Stryver.... (p. 141)
A Tale of Two Cities. 1859. The Oxford Illustrated Dickens, Vol. IV. Oxford: Oxford University Press, 1948.
URDANG, *IDIOMS* 117.

For **better** or for worse

1842 ...I would take her to my heart for better or worse.... (p. 156)
The Letters of Charles Dickens: Volume Three: 1842-1843. Eds. Madeline House, Graham Storey, and Kathleen Tillotson. Oxford: The Clarendon Press, 1974.
URDANG, *IDIOMS* 118.

To be a **bigwig**

1854 He was a fine specimen of the British Bigwig.... (p. 501)
"On Her Majesty's Service." [with E. C. Grenville Murray]. *Charles Dickens' Uncollected Writings from* Household Words *1850-1859*, 2 vols. Ed. Harry Stone. Bloomington: Indiana University Press, 1968.
1864 ...don't let solemn big-wigs stare them out of countenance...of which said solemn big-wigs I have ever had the one opinion.... (p. 429)

Christmas Stories. 1871. The Oxford Illustrated Dickens, Vol. XI. Oxford: Oxford University Press, 1956.
WILKINSON 263.

To have a clear **bill** of health

1841 We have a clear bill of health here. (p. 825)
The Letters of Charles Dickens: Volume Seven: 1853-1855. Eds. Graham Storey, Kathleen Tillotson, and Angus Easson. Oxford: The Clarendon Press, 1993.
URDANG, *IDIOMS* 248.

Billingsgate

1850 ...nothing...calculated to sustain the ancient reputation of Billingsgate. (p. 114)
"A Popular Delusion." [with W. H. Wills]. *Charles Dickens' Uncollected Writings from Household Words 1850-1859*, 2 vols. Ed. Harry Stone. Bloomington: Indiana University Press, 1968.
ODEP 59; EAP 30.

A **bird** in the hand is worth two in the bush.

1839 '...we'll take it now; there being no time like the present, and no two birds in the hand worth one in the bush....' (p. 477)
The Life and Adventures of Nicholas Nickleby. 1839. The Oxford Illustrated Dickens, Vol. VI. Oxford: Oxford University Press, 1950.
1852 ...one member of the feathered creation held in the hand is worth two of the same species in the bush. (p. 410)
"First Fruits." [with George Augustus Sala]. *Charles Dickens' Uncollected Writings from Household Words 1850-1859*, 2 vols. Ed. Harry Stone. Bloomington: Indiana University Press, 1968.
1853 ...it is well remarked by Poor Richard that a bird in the Handbook is worth two in the bush. (p. 102)
The Letters of Charles Dickens: Volume Seven: 1853-1855. Eds. Graham Storey, Kathleen Tillotson, and Angus Easson. Oxford: The Clarendon Press, 1993.
1870 Chapter IX: Birds in the Bush (p. 80)
The Mystery of Edwin Drood. 1870. The Oxford Illustrated Dickens, Vol. XVIII. Oxford: Oxford University Press, 1956.
APP 27; ODEP 59; EAP 31; CODP 19; MP 47; DAP 51.

A little **bird** told me.

1857 'A certain bird...has been whispering among the lawyers....' (p. 703)

Little Dorrit. 1857. The Oxford Illustrated Dickens, Vol. XIV. Oxford: Oxford University Press, 1953.
APP 27; ODEP 60; EAP 32; MP 50.

The **bird** has flown.

1861 'There's some of the birds flown from the cages.' (p. 111)
Great Expectations. 1861. The Oxford Illustrated Dickens, Vol. XIII. Oxford: Oxford University Press, 1953.
ODEP 61; EAP 31; MP 47.

The **bird** that can and won't must be made to sing.

1846 'The bird that can sing and won't sing must be made to sing, they say,' grumbled Tackleton. (pp. 186-187)
Christmas Books. 1843-49. The Oxford Illustrated Dickens, Vol. XVI. Oxford: Oxford University Press, 1954.
ODEP 469; EAP 31; CODP 20; MP 49; DAP 52.

The early **bird** catches the worm.

1850 Send me a "Yes" or a "No" by the Early Bird who brings this. (p. 51)
The Letters of Charles Dickens: Volume Six: 1850-1852. Eds. Madeline House, Graham Storey, and Kathleen Tillotson. Oxford: The Clarendon Press, 1988.
1868 ...the early Christians, those early birds who *didn't* catch the worm.... (p. 680)
The Letters of Charles Dickens, ed. Walter Dexter. Vol. III: 1858-1870. The Nonesuch Dickens. London: The Nonesuch Press, 1938.
APP 28; ODEP 211; CODP 62; MP 49; DAP 52.

To sing like a **bird**

1839 'Then she can...sing like a little bird.' (p. 670)
The Life and Adventures of Nicholas Nickleby. 1839. The Oxford Illustrated Dickens, Vol. VI. Oxford: Oxford University Press, 1950.
STEVENSON 2165:4.

To get a **bird's-eye view**

1841 I have...taken a bird's-eye view of it.... (p. 267)
The Letters of Charles Dickens: Volume Two: 1840-1841. Eds. Madeline House and Graham Storey. Oxford: The Clarendon Press, 1969.
1842 There is a...bird's-eye view.... (p. 117)
American Notes and Pictures from Italy. 1842, 1846. The Oxford Illustrated Dickens, Vol. XIX. Oxford: Oxford University Press, 1957.

1846 A Bird's-eye glimpse of Miss Tux's dwelling place (p. 61)
Dickens' Working Notes for His Novels. Ed. Harry Stone. Chicago, Ill.: University of Chicago Press, 1987.

1850 Our traveller's first proceeding, was, to...gratify his fancy with a bird's-eye-view of the unimpeachable Registry. (p. 174)
"The Doom of English Wills: Cathedral Number Two." [with W. H. Wills]. *Charles Dickens' Uncollected Writings from* Household Words *1850-1859*, 2 vols. Ed. Harry Stone. Bloomington: Indiana University Press, 1968.

1862 Nothing...is left for me but to...take a bird's-eye view.... (p. 506)
Address to the Newsvendors' Benevolent and Protective Association, London, 20 May 1862. *The Works of Charles Dickens: The Speeches.* Ed. Richard H. Shepherd. New National Edition, Vol. II. New York: Hearst's International Library Company, n. d.

EAP 33.

Birds of a feather flock together.

1844 '...they are but birds of one feather.' (p. 42)
The Life and Adventures of Martin Chuzzlewit. 1844. The Oxford Illustrated Dickens, Vol. IX. Oxford: Oxford University Press, 1951.

1852-54 The witnesses were that atrocious Oates and two other birds of the same feather. (p. 511)
Master Humphrey's Clock and A Child's History of England. 1840-41, 1852-54. The Oxford Illustrated Dickens, Vol. XX. Oxford: Oxford University Press, 1958.

APP 28; ODEP 60; EAP 31; CODP 20; MP 49; DAP 52.

To kill two **birds** with one stone

1834 ...I will kill two Birds with one stone.... (p. 38)
The Letters of Charles Dickens: Volume One: 1820-1839. Eds. Madeline House and Graham Storey. Oxford: The Clarendon Press, 1965.

1844 ...it was their custom...to kill two birds with one stone.... (p. 119)
The Life and Adventures of Martin Chuzzlewit. 1844. The Oxford Illustrated Dickens, Vol. IX. Oxford: Oxford University Press, 1951.

1848 ...and so killed a brace of birds with one stone, dead as door-nails. (p. 342)
Dealings with the Firm of Dombey and Son. 1848. The Oxford Illustrated Dickens, Vol. VII. Oxford: Oxford University Press, 1950.

1850 Could we kill the French and American birds with one stone? (p. 23)
The Letters of Charles Dickens: Volume Six: 1850-1852. Eds. Madeline House, Graham Storey, and Kathleen Tillotson. Oxford: The Clarendon Press, 1988.

ODEP 423; EAP 33; MP 51.

Bit by bit

1867 ...I have to...hammer it out bit by bit.... (p. 548)
The Letters of Charles Dickens, ed. Walter Dexter. Vol. III: 1858-1870. The Nonesuch Dickens. London: The Nonesuch Press, 1938.
URDANG, *IDIOMS* 128.

To draw a **bit** of blood

1844 I...am more indebted...than I can express, for your great interest...in the matter of my small "bit of blood"—to use a sporting phrase. (p. 61)
The Letters of Charles Dickens: Volume Four: 1844-1846. Ed. Kathleen Tillotson. Oxford: The Clarendon Press, 1977.
URDANG, *IDIOMS* 137.

As **black** as jet; jet-black

1841 Their Scotch bonnets, ornamented with plumes of jet black feathers, Mr. Grinder carried.... (p. 133)
The Old Curiosity Shop. 1841. The Oxford Illustrated Dickens, Vol. VIII. Oxford: Oxford University Press, 1951.
1844 She had...jet black hair.... (p. 27)
The Life and Adventures of Martin Chuzzlewit. 1844. The Oxford Illustrated Dickens, Vol. IX. Oxford: Oxford University Press, 1951.
1850 'Why it's as black as jet!' (p. 103)
1850 Such a concentration...flashed in her jet-black eyes.... (p. 470)
The Personal History of David Copperfield. 1850. The Oxford Illustrated Dickens, Vol. II. Oxford: Oxford University Press, 1948.
1857 ...with his jet-black beads of eyes inquisitively sharp.... (p. 274)
1857 He had a quantity of hair and moustache—jet black.... (p. 344)
Little Dorrit. 1857. The Oxford Illustrated Dickens, Vol. XIV. Oxford: Oxford University Press, 1953.
1860 ...all this must be wholly swallowed up in the blackness of the jet-black country. (p. 252)
The Uncommercial Traveller and Reprinted Pieces Etc. 1850-1860. The Oxford Illustrated Dickens, Vol. XXI. Oxford: Oxford University Press, 1958.
APP 204; EAP 239; MP 343.

As **black** as pitch; pitch-black

1852-54 ...he lay through many a pitch-black night.... (p. 268)
Master Humphrey's Clock and A Child's History of England. 1840-41, 1852-54. The Oxford Illustrated Dickens, Vol. XX. Oxford: Oxford University Press, 1958.
APP 287; ODEP 63; EAP 340; MP 497.

Black and blue

1839 '...you'll pinch my arm black and blue.' (p. 534)
The Life and Adventures of Nicholas Nickleby. 1839. The Oxford Illustrated Dickens, Vol.
VI. Oxford: Oxford University Press, 1950.
1844 'One of them will be black and blue tomorrow....' (p. 334)
1844 '...that one beats 'em black and blue.' (p. 462)
The Life and Adventures of Martin Chuzzlewit. 1844. The Oxford Illustrated Dickens, Vol.
IX. Oxford: Oxford University Press, 1951.
1854 You are now in the Black and Blue stage. (p. 317)
The Letters of Charles Dickens: Volume Seven: 1853-1855. Eds. Graham Storey, Kathleen
Tillotson, and Angus Easson. Oxford: The Clarendon Press, 1993.
1860 ...he must have slapped them black and blue.... (p. 286)
Christmas Stories. 1871. The Oxford Illustrated Dickens, Vol. XI. Oxford: Oxford
University Press, 1956.
APP 30; ODEP 36.

To be written down in **black and white**

1841 'Here's a new brother, regularly put down in black and white....'
(p. 293)
Barnaby Rudge: A Tale of the Riots of 'Eighty. 1841. The Oxford Illustrated Dickens, Vol.
XV. Oxford: Oxford University Press, 1954.
1847 ...we could fix it in black and white.... (p. 143)
The Letters of Charles Dickens: Volume Five: 1847-1849. Eds. Graham Storey and K. J.
Fielding. Oxford: The Clarendon Press, 1981.
1854 Black and white (p. 251)
Dickens' Working Notes for His Novels. Ed. Harry Stone. Chicago, Ill.: University of
Chicago Press, 1987.
1862 Let us have it down in black and white.... (p. 348)
Christmas Stories. 1871. The Oxford Illustrated Dickens, Vol. XI. Oxford: Oxford
University Press, 1956.
1867 ...some little lapse he had made—...without having set down in
black and white some questionable indication.... (pp. 548-549)
Address to the Printers' Readers, London, 17 Sept. 1867. *The Works of Charles Dickens:
The Speeches*. Ed. Richard H. Shepherd. New National Edition, Vol. II. New York:
Hearst's International Library Company, n. d.
1870 ...presenting in black and white...the mysterious inscription.... (p.
112)
The Mystery of Edwin Drood. 1870. The Oxford Illustrated Dickens, Vol. XVIII. Oxford:
Oxford University Press, 1956.
APP 30; ODEP 63; EAP 34; MP 54.

There is a **black sheep** in every flock.

1842 ...I should have lived and died..."a black sheep...." (p. 158)

The Letters of Charles Dickens: Volume Three: 1842-1843. Eds. Madeline House, Graham Storey, and Kathleen Tillotson. Oxford: The Clarendon Press, 1974.
ODEP 65; EAP 387; MP 555; DAP 534.

To be a wet **blanket**

1857 ...the Circumlocution Office...tossed the business in a wet blanket. (p. 120)
Little Dorrit. 1857. The Oxford Illustrated Dickens, Vol. XIV. Oxford: Oxford University Press, 1953.

To be in full **blast**

1844 ...you were, as your American friends say, "in full blast...." (p. 232)
The Letters of Charles Dickens: Volume Four: 1844-1846. Ed. Kathleen Tillotson. Oxford: The Clarendon Press, 1977.
1847 There is a violin...and an Italian box of music...both in full blast. (p. 163)
The Letters of Charles Dickens: Volume Five: 1847-1849. Eds. Graham Storey and K. J. Fielding. Oxford: The Clarendon Press, 1981.
URDANG, *IDIOMS* 500.

As **blind** as a brickbat

1850 '...the Old Scholar...is as blind as a brickbat....' (p. 619)
The Personal History of David Copperfield. 1850. The Oxford Illustrated Dickens, Vol. II. Oxford: Oxford University Press, 1948.

As **blind** as a stone; stone-blind

1833-36 '...I don't think anybody but a man as was stone-blind would mistake Fixem for one....' (p. 27)
Sketches by Boz. 1833-40. The Oxford Illustrated Dickens, Vol. XII. Oxford: Oxford University Press, 1957.
1841 ...he might have been stone blind. (p. 285)
Barnaby Rudge: A Tale of the Riots of 'Eighty. 1841. The Oxford Illustrated Dickens, Vol. XV. Oxford: Oxford University Press, 1954.
1853 ...to be...stone blind and dumb! (p. 220)
Bleak House. 1853. The Oxford Illustrated Dickens, Vol. III. Oxford: Oxford University Press, 1948.
1857 ...blind alleys that are stone-blind. (p. 57)
Little Dorrit. 1857. The Oxford Illustrated Dickens, Vol. XIV. Oxford: Oxford University Press, 1953.
1860 MRS. DIBBLE: ...he be stone-blind. (p. 229)
1860 MR. DIBBLE: ...I be stone-blind. (p. 229)

The Uncommercial Traveller and Reprinted Pieces Etc. 1850-1860. The Oxford Illustrated Dickens, Vol. XXI. Oxford: Oxford University Press, 1958.
APP 355; MP 596.

Blindman's buff

1837 The evening concludes with a glorious game of blind-man's-buff....
(p. 222)
Sketches by Boz. 1833-40. The Oxford Illustrated Dickens, Vol. XII. Oxford: Oxford University Press, 1957.
1843 The clerk...ran home...to play at blindman's-buff. (p. 14)
1843 There was first a game at blind-man's buff. (p. 53)
Christmas Books. 1843-49. The Oxford Illustrated Dickens, Vol. XVI. Oxford: Oxford University Press, 1954.
1843 You are playing at blindmans [*sic*] buff.... (p. 456)
The Letters of Charles Dickens: Volume Three: 1842-1843. Eds. Madeline House, Graham Storey, and Kathleen Tillotson. Oxford: The Clarendon Press, 1974.
1860 ...they played at Blindman's Buff....The man below must be playing Blindman's Buff by himself to-night! (p. 142)
The Uncommercial Traveller and Reprinted Pieces Etc. 1850-1860. The Oxford Illustrated Dickens, Vol. XXI. Oxford: Oxford University Press, 1958.
1865 ...it was...cleared for blindman's buff. (p. 107)
Our Mutual Friend. 1865. The Oxford Illustrated Dickens, Vol. X. Oxford: Oxford University Press, 1952.
URDANG, *IDIOMS* 135.

To do something in cold **blood**

1848 ...'I'm sure you wouldn't injure a cove...in cold blood, would you?' (p. 731)
Dealings with the Firm of Dombey and Son. 1848. The Oxford Illustrated Dickens, Vol. VII. Oxford: Oxford University Press, 1950.
1853 '...you could never care for me in cool blood....' (p. 337)
Bleak House. 1853. The Oxford Illustrated Dickens, Vol. III. Oxford: Oxford University Press, 1948.
WILKINSON 304.

To make one's **blood** boil

1842 My blood so boiled as I thought of.... (p. 83)
The Letters of Charles Dickens: Volume Three: 1842-1843. Eds. Madeline House, Graham Storey, and Kathleen Tillotson. Oxford: The Clarendon Press, 1974.
1844 And no man knows....how my blood boils at the sight. (p. 82)
The Letters of Charles Dickens: Volume Four: 1844-1846. Ed. Kathleen Tillotson. Oxford: The Clarendon Press, 1977.

APP 34; WILKINSON 349.

To make one's **blood** run cold

1837 "...the bare thought of laying him in his grave without it makes my blood run cold!" (p. 373)
Sketches by Boz. 1833-40. The Oxford Illustrated Dickens, Vol. XII. Oxford: Oxford University Press, 1957.
1838 EMMA: ...it makes my blood run cold to hear you. (*The Lamplighter*, I, ii, p. 123)
Complete Plays and Selected Poems of Charles Dickens. London: Vision Press, 1970.
1839 'Her blood runs cold....' (p. 704)
1839 ...that would have made the blood of the stoutest man run cold in his veins.... (p. 724)
The Life and Adventures of Nicholas Nickleby. 1839. The Oxford Illustrated Dickens, Vol. VI. Oxford: Oxford University Press, 1950.
1848 'My uncle's child made people's blood run cold....' (p. 105)
1848 '...the lightest touch of your hand make my blood run cold....' (p. 761)
Dealings with the Firm of Dombey and Son. 1848. The Oxford Illustrated Dickens, Vol. VII. Oxford: Oxford University Press, 1950.
1861 ...my blood ran cold within me. (p. 305)
Great Expectations. 1861. The Oxford Illustrated Dickens, Vol. XIII. Oxford: Oxford University Press, 1953.
URDANG, *IDIOMS* 138.

To turn one's **blood** to gall

1842 ...the very suggestion of which turns my blood to gall.... (pp. 76-77)
The Letters of Charles Dickens: Volume Three: 1842-1843. Eds. Madeline House, Graham Storey, and Kathleen Tillotson. Oxford: The Clarendon Press, 1974.

You cannot get **blood** from a stone.

1850 'Blood cannot be obtained from a stone....' (p. 158)
The Personal History of David Copperfield. 1850. The Oxford Illustrated Dickens, Vol. II. Oxford: Oxford University Press, 1948.
APP 34; ODEP 869; EAP 36; CODP 21; MP 57; DAP 58.

As **blue** as the sky; sky-blue

1837 The Miss Maldertons were dressed in sky-blue satin.... (p. 357)
Sketches by Boz. 1833-40. The Oxford Illustrated Dickens, Vol. XII. Oxford: Oxford University Press, 1957.

1839 ...placing...a duplication of his thumb on a piece of sky-blue silk.... (p. 260)

The Life and Adventures of Nicholas Nickleby. 1839. The Oxford Illustrated Dickens, Vol. VI. Oxford: Oxford University Press, 1950.

1848 ...the baby...may not...wear a sky-blue fillet round his head.... (p. 240)

1848 ...here is Mrs. Blimber, with her sky-blue cap.... (p. 578)

Dealings with the Firm of Dombey and Son. 1848. The Oxford Illustrated Dickens, Vol. VII. Oxford: Oxford University Press, 1950.

1849 ...Broadstairs beats all watering places into what the Americans call "sky-blue fits". (p. 568)

The Letters of Charles Dickens: Volume Five: 1847-1849. Eds. Graham Storey and K. J. Fielding. Oxford: The Clarendon Press, 1981.

1850 '...I'd give him a sky-blue coat....' (p. 35)

1850 In a tight sky-blue suit that made his arms and legs like German sausages.... (p. 91)

1850 'That sky-blue suit you used to wear.' (p. 403)

The Personal History of David Copperfield. 1850. The Oxford Illustrated Dickens, Vol. II. Oxford: Oxford University Press, 1948.

1855 And he tucks her, in her little sky-blue mantle, under his arm.... (p. 117)

1855 The young gentleman...tucks her, in her little sky-blue mantle, under his arm.... (p. 120)

Christmas Stories. 1871. The Oxford Illustrated Dickens, Vol. XI. Oxford: Oxford University Press, 1956.

1861 I remember Mr. Hubble as a little curly sharp-edged person in sky-blue.... (p. 22)

Great Expectations. 1861. The Oxford Illustrated Dickens, Vol. XIII. Oxford: Oxford University Press, 1953.

WILKINSON 211.

Blue Beard

1860 ...he comes telling his keys like Blue Beard.... (p. 268)

The Uncommercial Traveller and Reprinted Pieces Etc. 1850-1860. The Oxford Illustrated Dickens, Vol. XXI. Oxford: Oxford University Press, 1958.

BREWER 125.

Blue Laws

1842 ...which sage body enacted...the renowned code of "Blue Laws. ..." (p. 73)

American Notes and Pictures from Italy. 1842, 1846. The Oxford Illustrated Dickens, Vol. XIX. Oxford: Oxford University Press, 1957.

URDANG, *IDIOMS* 141; STEVENSON 1368:1.

To get the **blues**

1846 I am horrified at the idea of getting the blues...again. (p. 628)
The Letters of Charles Dickens: Volume Four: 1844-1846. Ed. Kathleen Tillotson. Oxford: The Clarendon Press, 1977.
APP 35; EAP 37; MP 59.

To tread the **boards**

1839 '...first appearance on any boards....' (p. 306)
1839 '...she shall not appear on the London boards....' (p. 395)
The Life and Adventures of Nicholas Nickleby. 1839. The Oxford Illustrated Dickens, Vol. VI. Oxford: Oxford University Press, 1950.
WILKINSON 473.

To be in the same **boat**

1841 'You are in the same boat.' (p. 347)
Barnaby Rudge: A Tale of the Riots of 'Eighty. 1841. The Oxford Illustrated Dickens, Vol. XV. Oxford: Oxford University Press, 1954.

Bob swore!

1850 '"Bob swore!"—as the Englishman said for "Good night," when he first learnt French, and thought it so like English.' (p. 335)
The Personal History of David Copperfield. 1850. The Oxford Illustrated Dickens, Vol. II. Oxford: Oxford University Press, 1948.

Body and soul

1841 '...body and soul, you are lost.' (p. 129)
Barnaby Rudge: A Tale of the Riots of 'Eighty. 1841. The Oxford Illustrated Dickens, Vol. XV. Oxford: Oxford University Press, 1954.
1852 "Body and Soul", and Timbuctoo...are the two pieces I would rest my case on. (p. 647)
The Letters of Charles Dickens: Volume Six: 1850-1852. Eds. Madeline House, Graham Storey, and Kathleen Tillotson. Oxford: The Clarendon Press, 1988.
1858 ...it has a power over life and death, the body and the soul.... (p. 502)
Address to the Institutional Association of Lancashire and Cheshire, Manchester, 3 Dec. 1858. *The Works of Charles Dickens: The Speeches.* Ed. Richard H. Shepherd. New National Edition, Vol. II. New York: Hearst's International Library Company, n. d.
1861 ...she had the appearance of having dropped, body and soul.... (p. 56)

1861 '...so he has 'em, soul and body.' (p. 249)
Great Expectations. 1861. The Oxford Illustrated Dickens, Vol. XIII. Oxford: Oxford University Press, 1953.
URDANG, *IDIOMS* 145.

By the **body** of Caesar!

1845 By the body of Caesar, the scene was incredible! (p. 351)
The Letters of Charles Dickens: Volume Four: 1844-1846. Ed. Kathleen Tillotson. Oxford: The Clarendon Press, 1977.

To keep **body** and soul together

1857 '...and not more than able to keep body and soul together....' (p. 143)
1857 I was not bought, body and soul. (p. 670)
Little Dorrit. 1857. The Oxford Illustrated Dickens, Vol. XIV. Oxford: Oxford University Press, 1953.
EAP 38; MP 61.

(Not) to say **boh!** to a goose
1850 '...I'll be bound, as if you couldn't say boh! to a goose!' (p. 212)
The Personal History of David Copperfield. 1850. The Oxford Illustrated Dickens, Vol. II. Oxford: Oxford University Press, 1948.
APP 37; ODEP 701; MP 65.

As **bold** as brass

1839 '...he was as fierce as a lion and as bold as brass....' (p. 69)
The Life and Adventures of Nicholas Nickleby. 1839. The Oxford Illustrated Dickens, Vol. VI. Oxford: Oxford University Press, 1950.
1844 'Why, you're as bold as brass!' said Jonas.... (p. 446)
The Life and Adventures of Martin Chuzzlewit. 1844. The Oxford Illustrated Dickens, Vol. IX. Oxford: Oxford University Press, 1951.
1846 'But you're as bold as brass in general,' he said.... (p. 277)
Christmas Books. 1843-49. The Oxford Illustrated Dickens, Vol. XVI. Oxford: Oxford University Press, 1954.
1855 The young gentleman...walks into the house much bolder than Brass. (p. 120)
Christmas Stories. 1871. The Oxford Illustrated Dickens, Vol. XI. Oxford: Oxford University Press, 1956.
APP 41; MP 70.

To shoot one's **bolt**

1865 Having shot this bolt out with a great expenditure of force, Bella hysterically laughed.... (p. 597)
Our Mutual Friend. 1865. The Oxford Illustrated Dickens, Vol. X. Oxford: Oxford University Press, 1952.
ODEP 728; EAP 39; MP 62.

To pick a **bone** with someone

1831 ...I had anticipated...picking that bone that we have to discuss.... (p. 2)
The Letters of Charles Dickens: Volume One: 1820-1839. Eds. Madeline House and Graham Storey. Oxford: The Clarendon Press, 1965.
APP 37; ODEP 73; EAP 39; MP 63.

To feel something in one's **bones**

1841 '...I seem to hear it...in my wery bones.' (p. 403)
Barnaby Rudge: A Tale of the Riots of 'Eighty. 1841. The Oxford Illustrated Dickens, Vol. XV. Oxford: Oxford University Press, 1954.
APP 37; ODEP 253; EAP 40; MP 63.

As **bonny** as a rose

1854 'As bonny as a rose!' (p. 154)
Hard Times for These Times. 1854. The Oxford Illustrated Dickens, Vol. XVII. Oxford: Oxford University Press, 1955.

To talk like a **book**

1844 And Mrs. Hominy not only talked, as the saying is, like a book.... (p. 541)
The Life and Adventures of Martin Chuzzlewit. 1844. The Oxford Illustrated Dickens, Vol. IX. Oxford: Oxford University Press, 1951.
APP 38; EAP 40; MP 66.

To be in someone's good **books**

1850 ...to die in her good books, is to leave a far better inheritance.... (p. 124)
"The Old Lady in Threadneedle Street." [with W. H. Wills]. *Charles Dickens' Uncollected Writings from* Household Words *1850-1859,* 2 vols. Ed. Harry Stone. Bloomington: Indiana University Press, 1968.
EAP 40; MP 65.

To be from the **bottom** of one's soul

1842 ...I believe it from the bottom of my soul.... (p. 82)
The Letters of Charles Dickens: Volume Three: 1842-1843. Eds. Madeline House, Graham Storey, and Kathleen Tillotson. Oxford: The Clarendon Press, 1974.
URDANG, *IDIOMS* 156.

Within the sound of **Bow Bells** a cockney is born.

1848 Though the offices of Dombey and Son were...within hearing of Bow Bells.... (p. 33)
Dealings with the Firm of Dombey and Son. 1848. The Oxford Illustrated Dickens, Vol. VII. Oxford: Oxford University Press, 1950.
ODEP 76; EAP 79; MP 125.

To go to the **bow-wows** [*i.e.*, the dogs]

1839 'He has gone to the demnition bow-wows.' (p. 821)
The Life and Adventures of Nicholas Nickleby. 1839. The Oxford Illustrated Dickens, Vol. VI. Oxford: Oxford University Press, 1950.
PARTRIDGE 86 (CITING DICKENS); URDANG, *IDIOMS* 158.

Brag is a good dog, but Holdfast is better.

1861 '...Brag is a good dog, but...Holdfast is a better.' (p. 130)
Great Expectations. 1861. The Oxford Illustrated Dickens, Vol. XIII. Oxford: Oxford University Press, 1953.
APP 41; ODEP 80; CODP 24; MP 70; DAP 66.

To knock someone's **brains** out

1837 MRS. LIMBURY: Oh! he'll kick somebody's brains out.... (*Is She His Wife?*, I, p. 102)
1837 LIMBURY: But perhaps he'll kick my brains out.... (*Is She His Wife?*, I, p. 102)
Complete Plays and Selected Poems of Charles Dickens. London: Vision Press, 1970.
1841 ...the only congenial prospect left him, was to...get some obliging enemy to knock his brains out.... (p. 107)
Barnaby Rudge: A Tale of the Riots of 'Eighty. 1841. The Oxford Illustrated Dickens, Vol. XV. Oxford: Oxford University Press, 1954.
URDANG, *IDIOMS* 162.

To be **bran** new

1848 A bran-new Tavern....had taken for its sign The Railway Arms.... (p. 63)

1848 ...the happy schoolmaster put on a bran-new pair of gloves.... (p. 347-348)

Dealings with the Firm of Dombey and Son. 1848. The Oxford Illustrated Dickens, Vol. VII. Oxford: Oxford University Press, 1950.

1850 To conclude with a bran new phrase, "I am on the tip toe of expectation"! (p. 61)

The Letters of Charles Dickens: Volume Six: 1850-1852. Eds. Madeline House, Graham Storey, and Kathleen Tillotson. Oxford: The Clarendon Press, 1988.

1851 ...a bran new hat did (I hate bran new hats—mine was bran new too—they shine so).... (p. 225)

"My Mahogany Friend." [with Mary Boyle]. *Charles Dickens' Uncollected Writings from Household Words 1850-1859*, 2 vols. Ed. Harry Stone. Bloomington: Indiana University Press, 1968.

1859 ...I have not forgotten the old shop now bran new.... (p. 85)
1861 ...THEY must be bran new.... (p. 271)

The Letters of Charles Dickens, ed. Walter Dexter. Vol. III: 1858-1870. The Nonesuch Dickens. London: The Nonesuch Press, 1938.

1860 ...nearly all with bran-new tin cans.... (p. 222)

The Uncommercial Traveller and Reprinted Pieces Etc. 1850-1860. The Oxford Illustrated Dickens, Vol. XXI. Oxford: Oxford University Press, 1958.

1865 Mr. and Mrs. Veneering were bran-new people in a bran-new house in a bran-new quarter of London. (p. 6)

1865 ...they were as newly married as was lawfully compatible with their having a bran-new baby.... (p. 6)

1865 ...the boy looked at the bran-new pilgrims.... (p. 18)

Our Mutual Friend. 1865. The Oxford Illustrated Dickens, Vol. X. Oxford: Oxford University Press, 1952.

PARTRIDGE 88.

As **brazen** as alabaster

1838 '...they'll come back...as brazen as alabaster.' (p. 167)

The Adventures of Oliver Twist. 1838. The Oxford Illustrated Dickens, Vol. V. Oxford: Oxford University Press, 1948.

WILSTACH 31 (CITING DICKENS).

Bread and butter

1850 'She might whistle for her bread and butter....' (p. 462)

The Personal History of David Copperfield. 1850. The Oxford Illustrated Dickens, Vol. II. Oxford: Oxford University Press, 1948.

EAP 44; MP 71.

To make a clean **breast**

1841 '...I will make a clean breast.' (p. 500)
The Old Curiosity Shop. 1841. The Oxford Illustrated Dickens, Vol. VIII. Oxford: Oxford University Press, 1951.
1843 ...now is the time to...make a clean breast. (p. 513)
The Letters of Charles Dickens: Volume Three: 1842-1843. Eds. Madeline House, Graham Storey, and Kathleen Tillotson. Oxford: The Clarendon Press, 1974.
APP 42; ODEP 125.

To take one's **breath** away

1848 ...the increasing row of items rather took my breath away.... (p. 327)
The Letters of Charles Dickens: Volume Five: 1847-1849. Eds. Graham Storey and K. J. Fielding. Oxford: The Clarendon Press, 1981.
URDANG, *IDIOMS* 168.

To be a **brick**

1839 ...you have eaten and drunk too "like bricks [=with a good will] ...." (p. 542)
The Letters of Charles Dickens: Volume One: 1820-1839. Eds. Madeline House and Graham Storey. Oxford: The Clarendon Press, 1965.
1842 I am working away...like a brick. I don't know why it is, but that popular simile *seems* a good one. (p. 372)
The Letters of Charles Dickens: Volume Three: 1842-1843. Eds. Madeline House, Graham Storey, and Kathleen Tillotson. Oxford: The Clarendon Press, 1974.
1844 ...I should have shewn you...a...dog...barking, as the vulgar expression is, like Bricks. (pp. 71-72)
The Letters of Charles Dickens: Volume Four: 1844-1846. Ed. Kathleen Tillotson. Oxford: The Clarendon Press, 1977.
1850 Charley...has already distinguished himself like a Brick.... (p. 71)
The Letters of Charles Dickens: Volume Six: 1850-1852. Eds. Madeline House, Graham Storey, and Kathleen Tillotson. Oxford: The Clarendon Press, 1988.
PARTRIDGE 92.

As **bright** as a diamond

1843 ...her mental eyes are brighter than Diamonds. (p. 597)
The Letters of Charles Dickens: Volume Three: 1842-1843. Eds. Madeline House, Graham Storey, and Kathleen Tillotson. Oxford: The Clarendon Press, 1974.
APP 101.

As **bright** as a star

1850 "...you'll come out as bright as a star, and as sleek as this here Moke." (p. 120)

"A Popular Delusion." [with W. H. Wills]. *Charles Dickens' Uncollected Writings from Household Words 1850-1859*, 2 vols. Ed. Harry Stone. Bloomington: Indiana University Press, 1968.

APP 350; EAP 413; MP 591.

Britons never will be slaves.

1848 ...Britons, as I am informed, never never never—will—be—Slaves! (p. 396)

The Letters of Charles Dickens: Volume Five: 1847-1849. Eds. Graham Storey and K. J. Fielding. Oxford: The Clarendon Press, 1981.

STEVENSON 693:1.

A new **broom** sweeps clean.

1842 Mr. P. though no longer a new broom, sweeps clean still. (p. 91)

The Letters of Charles Dickens: Volume Three: 1842-1843. Eds. Madeline House, Graham Storey, and Kathleen Tillotson. Oxford: The Clarendon Press, 1974.

APP 44; ODEP 564; EAP 47; CODP 161; MP 75; DAP 72.

As **brown** as a berry

1841 There were...three young sturdy children, brown as berries. (p. 118)

The Old Curiosity Shop. 1841. The Oxford Illustrated Dickens, Vol. VIII. Oxford: Oxford University Press, 1951.

MP 44.

P'raps if vun of us wos to **brush**.

1837 'P'raps if vun of us wos to brush, without troubling the man, it 'ud be more agreeable for all parties, as the schoolmaster said wen the young gentleman objected to being flogged by the butler.' (p. 588)

The Posthumous Papers of the Pickwick Club. 1837. The Oxford Illustrated Dickens, Vol. I. Oxford: Oxford University Press, 1948.

DAP 13; DOW 15.

To be tarred with the same **brush**

1865 'They are both tarred with a dirty brush....' (p. 69)

Our Mutual Friend. 1865. The Oxford Illustrated Dickens, Vol. X. Oxford: Oxford University Press, 1952.

APP 353; ODEP 805; EAP 47; MP 76.

To kick the **bucket**

1840-41 ...'I think I'm a-goin' the wrong side o' the post, and that my foot's wery near the bucket....' (p. 88)
Master Humphrey's Clock and A Child's History of England. 1840-41, 1852-54. The Oxford Illustrated Dickens, Vol. XX. Oxford: Oxford University Press, 1958.
APP 45; ODEP 422; EAP 47; MP 77.

So much for **Buckingham**.

1833-36 . . .(...then slow and sneeringly)—"So much for Bu-u-u-uckingham!" (p. 119)
Sketches by Boz. 1833-40. The Oxford Illustrated Dickens, Vol. XII. Oxford: Oxford University Press, 1957.
STEVENSON 1095:3. Colley Cibber's alteration of Shakespeare's *Richard III*, IV, 3

To nip something in the **bud**

1846 ...short vocal snorts, which it checked in the bud.... (p. 161)
Christmas Books. 1843-49. The Oxford Illustrated Dickens, Vol. XVI. Oxford: Oxford University Press, 1954.
1864 Mr Boffin...nips their designs in the bud (p. 365)
Dickens' Working Notes for His Novels. Ed. Harry Stone. Chicago, Ill.: University of Chicago Press, 1987.
APP 45; ODEP 567; EAP 48; MP 77.

Like a **bull** in a china shop

1844 ...shaggy horses...who would have stood stock-still in a china-shop, with a complete dinner-service at each hoof. (p. 70)
The Life and Adventures of Martin Chuzzlewit. 1844. The Oxford Illustrated Dickens, Vol. IX. Oxford: Oxford University Press, 1951.
1848 ...suggesting a remembrance of the celebrated bull who got by mistake into a crockery shop.... (p. 289)
Dealings with the Firm of Dombey and Son. 1848. The Oxford Illustrated Dickens, Vol. VII. Oxford: Oxford University Press, 1950.
APP 46; ODEP 90; MP 79.

To hit the **bull's-eye**

1846 ...the ball had struck the bull's-eye.... (p. 580)
1846 I have seen them...never miss the bull's-eye. (p. 632)
The Letters of Charles Dickens: Volume Four: 1844-1846. Ed. Kathleen Tillotson. Oxford: The Clarendon Press, 1977.

MP 80.

Every **bullet** has its billet.

1837 It is an established axion, that 'every bullet has its billet.' (p. 254)
The Posthumous Papers of the Pickwick Club. 1837. The Oxford Illustrated Dickens, Vol. I. Oxford: Oxford University Press, 1948.
1843 ...every bullet has its billet.... (p. 499)
The Letters of Charles Dickens: Volume Three: 1842-1843. Eds. Madeline House, Graham Storey, and Kathleen Tillotson. Oxford: The Clarendon Press, 1974.
APP 47; ODEP 90; CODP 27; MP 80; DAP 74.

To be a reg'lar **Bunter**

1846 ...an American lady...looked like what we call in old England "a reg'lar Bunter...." (p. 634)
The Letters of Charles Dickens: Volume Four: 1844-1846. Ed. Kathleen Tillotson. Oxford: The Clarendon Press, 1977.
PARTRIDGE 110.

To beat about the **bush**

1839 'Why should I hint, and beat about the bush?' (p. 620)
The Life and Adventures of Nicholas Nickleby. 1839. The Oxford Illustrated Dickens, Vol. VI. Oxford: Oxford University Press, 1950.
1841 'Not to beat about the bush...what's to prevent your marrying her?' (p. 55)
The Old Curiosity Shop. 1841. The Oxford Illustrated Dickens, Vol. VIII. Oxford: Oxford University Press, 1951.
1842 ...let us not...beat about the bush.... (p. 243)
American Notes and Pictures from Italy. 1842, 1846. The Oxford Illustrated Dickens, Vol. XIX. Oxford: Oxford University Press, 1957.
1866 ...it is its principle...never...to beat about the bush until the bush is withered and dead.... (p. 535)
Address to the Dramatic, Equestrian, and Musical Fund, London, 14 Feb. 1866. *The Works of Charles Dickens: The Speeches*. Ed. Richard H. Shepherd. New National Edition, Vol. II. New York: Hearst's International Library Company, n. d.
APP 48; ODEP 36; EAP 50; MP 81.

Business before pleasure.

1837 'Business first, pleasure arterwards, as King Richard the Third said wen he stabbed the t'other king in the Tower, afore he smothered the babbies.' (p. 339)

The Posthumous Papers of the Pickwick Club. 1837. The Oxford Illustrated Dickens, Vol. I. Oxford: Oxford University Press, 1948.
APP 48; ODEP 93; EAP 51; CODP 28; MP 82; DAP 75; DOW 16.

Business is business.

1855 ...business *is* business.... (p. 773)
The Letters of Charles Dickens: Volume Seven: 1853-1855. Eds. Graham Storey, Kathleen Tillotson, and Angus Easson. Oxford: The Clarendon Press, 1993.
1870 '...business being business the world over.' (p. 123)
The Mystery of Edwin Drood. 1870. The Oxford Illustrated Dickens, Vol. XVIII. Oxford: Oxford University Press, 1956.
APP 48; ODEP 93; MP 82; DAP 75.

To look as if **butter** would not melt in one's mouth

1844 ...he looked at this moment as if butter wouldn't melt in his mouth. (p. 38)
The Life and Adventures of Martin Chuzzlewit. 1844. The Oxford Illustrated Dickens, Vol. IX. Oxford: Oxford University Press, 1951.
1850-56 "...butter wouldn't melt in his mouth!" (p. 499)
The Uncommercial Traveller and Reprinted Pieces Etc. 1850-1860. The Oxford Illustrated Dickens, Vol. XXI. Oxford: Oxford University Press, 1958.
APP 49; ODEP 177; MP 84.

Butterflies are free.

1853 'The butterflies are free.' (p. 75)
Bleak House. 1853. The Oxford Illustrated Dickens, Vol. III. Oxford: Oxford University Press, 1948.

(Not) to care a **button**

1854 '...I don't care a button what you do....' (p. 47)
Hard Times for These Times. 1854. The Oxford Illustrated Dickens, Vol. XVII. Oxford: Oxford University Press, 1955.
1861 ...it became sheer monomania in my master's daughter to care a button for me.... (p. 110)
Great Expectations. 1861. The Oxford Illustrated Dickens, Vol. XIII. Oxford: Oxford University Press, 1953.
APP 50; ODEP 102; EAP 52; MP 85.

By and by

1843 The new dialogue I will ask you by-and-bye [*sic*] to let me see. (p. 512)

The Letters of Charles Dickens: Volume Three: 1842-1843. Eds. Madeline House, Graham Storey, and Kathleen Tillotson. Oxford: The Clarendon Press, 1974.

1846 We can moot these by and by.... (p. 631)

The Letters of Charles Dickens: Volume Four: 1844-1846. Ed. Kathleen Tillotson. Oxford: The Clarendon Press, 1977.

1846-49 And bye and bye...he went out again.... (p. 61)

The Life of Our Lord: Written for His Children... New York: Simon and Schuster, 1934.

1851 GABBLEWIG: That you shall know by and by. (*Mr. Nightingale's Diary*, I, i, p. 155)

Complete Plays and Selected Poems of Charles Dickens. London: Vision Press, 1970.

1851 ...I shall take the liberty of asking your advice bye and bye.... (p. 374)

1851 It won't do so well bye and bye. (p. 450)

The Letters of Charles Dickens: Volume Six: 1850-1852. Eds. Madeline House, Graham Storey, and Kathleen Tillotson. Oxford: The Clarendon Press, 1988.

1853 We shall probably hear more from her...bye and bye. (p. 21)

The Letters of Charles Dickens: Volume Seven: 1853-1855. Eds. Graham Storey, Kathleen Tillotson, and Angus Easson. Oxford: The Clarendon Press, 1993.

1854 ...thou shalt fill each jar brim full by-and-by.... (p. 8)

1854 She was gone by-and-by.... (p. 80)

1854 '...it may be of more use by-and-by.' (p. 177)

1854 ...she trusted to become familiar with it by-and-by.... (p. 194)

Hard Times for These Times. 1854. The Oxford Illustrated Dickens, Vol. XVII. Oxford: Oxford University Press, 1955.

1854 ...you will have terrific botheration from it, close in around you bye and bye. (p. 400)

The Letters of Charles Dickens: Volume Seven: 1853-1855. Eds. Graham Storey, Kathleen Tillotson, and Angus Easson. Oxford: The Clarendon Press, 1993.

1858 ...you will judge for yourself about that, bye-and-bye. (p. 602)

"A House to Let." [with Wilkie Collins]. *Charles Dickens' Uncollected Writings from Household Words 1850-1859*, 2 vols. Ed. Harry Stone. Bloomington: Indiana University Press, 1968.

1862 ...I keep myself well-primed...to make selection easier by and bye. (p. 316)

The Letters of Charles Dickens, ed. Walter Dexter. Vol. III: 1858-1870. The Nonesuch Dickens. London: The Nonesuch Press, 1938.

1866 ...he should be examined in it by-and-by.... (p. 504)

1867 ...they must pass, by and by.... (p. 629)

Christmas Stories. 1871. The Oxford Illustrated Dickens, Vol. XI. Oxford: Oxford University Press, 1956.

URDANG, *IDIOMS* 193.

By the bye

1837 We have described him, by the bye, as having deeply-sunken eyes.... (p. 598)
The Posthumous Papers of the Pickwick Club. 1837. The Oxford Illustrated Dickens, Vol. I. Oxford: Oxford University Press, 1948.

1842 By the bye...will you get Sir John's permission...? (p. 189)

1842 ...by the bye, Washington had not a pleasant face.... (p. 193)

1842 By the bye, if you could only have seen the Prince...! (p. 217)
The Letters of Charles Dickens: Volume Three: 1842-1843. Eds. Madeline House, Graham Storey, and Kathleen Tillotson. Oxford: The Clarendon Press, 1974.

1845 I care for nothing but girls by the bye.... (p. 418)

1846 He knew Charley's present Master by the bye.... (p. 539)

1846 ...the first day being but half a one by the bye.... (p. 595)

1846 ...by the bye, there are only three remaining.... (p. 619)

1846 By the bye, I have stirred up my French.... (p. 644)
The Letters of Charles Dickens: Volume Four: 1844-1846. Ed. Kathleen Tillotson. Oxford: The Clarendon Press, 1977.

1847 Treating of bed, by the bye...I, have proposed ten o'Clock.... (p. 187)

1848 ...Waller was laid up in bed with gout, by the bye.... (p. 269)

1849 ...by the bye, I incidentally found.... (p. 493)
The Letters of Charles Dickens: Volume Five: 1847-1849. Eds. Graham Storey and K. J. Fielding. Oxford: The Clarendon Press, 1981.

1847 ...I cannot help feeling it, bye the bye.... (p. 410)
Address at the opening of the Glasgow Athenaeum, 28 Dec. 1847. *The Works of Charles Dickens: The Speeches.* Ed. Richard H. Shepherd. New National Edition, Vol. II. New York: Hearst's International Library Company, n. d.

1851 ...by the bye I have forgotten that.... (p. 429)

1851 By the bye, would you like to go to the Play? (p. 446)

1851 By the bye, I observe...that Carlyle...don't know what Mumbo Jumbo is. (p. 452)

1852 ...by the bye, I suppose the baths for the Infants are not to be Showery? (p. 574)

1852 And by the bye...tell me...what Hotel accommodations you want.... (p. 635)
The Letters of Charles Dickens: Volume Six: 1850-1852. Eds. Madeline House, Graham Storey, and Kathleen Tillotson. Oxford: The Clarendon Press, 1988.

1853 ...he made a speech...by the bye.... (p. 4)

1853 You remember his father, by the bye? (p. 148)

1853 Lady Walpole by the bye is living alone.... (p. 182)

1853 Due I suppose—by the bye? (p. 211)

1853 You don't say by the bye that you have bought the...pannier. (p. 217)

1855 I don't think I ever saw boys more closely stowed than at that eminent Grinder's bye the bye. (p. 508)

1855 I have not advanced an inch...by the bye. (p. 549)

1855 And bye the bye...I mislaid your letter.... (p. 585)

1855 ...by the bye, I think I have a capital name.... (p. 613)

The Letters of Charles Dickens: Volume Seven: 1853-1855. Eds. Graham Storey, Kathleen Tillotson, and Angus Easson. Oxford: The Clarendon Press, 1993.

1862 He is rather knocked up by the bye.... (p. 310)

1865 ...to the remarkable terror, by-the-bye, of the two big dogs.... (p. 416)

1865 ...which killed the original old Parr by-the-bye. (p. 419)

1867 ...Dolby and our man have been stamping tickets...by-the-bye, and keeping me awake. (p. 581)

1868 We have not been on fire again, by-the-bye.... (p. 595)

1868 ...appreciated here in Boston, by-the-bye, even more than Copperfield.... (p. 598)

1868 By-the-bye....I lost my old year's pocketbook.... (p. 601)

1868 ...on which head, by-the-bye, I notice.... (p. 605)

1868 ...the Mare shall roll in the lap of luxury (which is very much dried up by the bye).... (p. 656)

The Letters of Charles Dickens, ed. Walter Dexter. Vol. III: 1858-1870. The Nonesuch Dickens. London: The Nonesuch Press, 1938.

1865 ...which, by the bye, is quite in the Cheap Jack way again.... (p. 441)

Christmas Stories. 1871. The Oxford Illustrated Dickens, Vol. XI. Oxford: Oxford University Press, 1956.

1869 I can most truthfully assure you, by the bye, that.... (p. 576)

Address to the Birmingham and Midland Institute, Birmingham, 27 Sept. 1869. *The Works of Charles Dickens: The Speeches*. Ed. Richard H. Shepherd. New National Edition, Vol. II. New York: Hearst's International Library Company, n. d.

URDANG, *IDIOMS* 196.

Let **bygones** be bygones.

1844 'Bygones shall be bygones between us.' (p. 766)

The Life and Adventures of Martin Chuzzlewit. 1844. The Oxford Illustrated Dickens, Vol. IX. Oxford: Oxford University Press, 1951.

1853 'Bygones shall be bygones....' (p. 339)

1853 'Let bygones be bygones.' (p. 619)

Bleak House. 1853. The Oxford Illustrated Dickens, Vol. III. Oxford: Oxford University Press, 1948.

1857 'Any unpleasant bygones between us, are bygones, I hope.' (p. 808)

Little Dorrit. 1857. The Oxford Illustrated Dickens, Vol. XIV. Oxford: Oxford University Press, 1953.

1865 'Why can't you let bygones be bygones?' (p. 227)

Our Mutual Friend. 1865. The Oxford Illustrated Dickens, Vol. X. Oxford: Oxford University Press, 1952.

APP 51; ODEP 96; EAP 52; MP 86; DAP 78.

C

To be a **cackler**

1854 'He has his points as a Cackler....' ¶'A Cackler!' ¶'A speaker....' (p. 32)

Hard Times for These Times. 1854. The Oxford Illustrated Dickens, Vol. XVII. Oxford: Oxford University Press, 1955.

PARTRIDGE 119 (CITING DICKENS).

Render unto **Caesar** the things that are Caesar's.

1844 ...it contemplates...that moral sense which renders unto Caesar nothing that is his.... (p. 341)

The Life and Adventures of Martin Chuzzlewit. 1844. The Oxford Illustrated Dickens, Vol. IX. Oxford: Oxford University Press, 1951.

1846-49 "Render unto Caesar the things that are Caesar's." (p. 77)

The Life of Our Lord: Written for His Children... New York: Simon and Schuster, 1934.

ODEP 671; EAP 53; MP 88; DAP 79.

Caesar's wife must be above suspicion.

1853 'I feel myself as far above suspicion as Caesar's wife.' (p. 829)

Bleak House. 1853. The Oxford Illustrated Dickens, Vol. III. Oxford: Oxford University Press, 1948.

APP 52; ODEP 97; EAP 53; CODP 30; MP 87; DAP 79.

You can't have your **cake** and eat it too.

1853 ...a book, in spite of the old proverb, is a cake that you can eat and have.... (p. 479)

"In and Out of Jail." [with Henry Morley and W. H. Wills]. *Charles Dickens' Uncollected Writings from* Household Words *1850-1859*, 2 vols. Ed. Harry Stone. Bloomington: Indiana University Press, 1968.

APP 52; ODEP 215; EAP 53; CODP 109; MP 88; DAP 79.

To kill the fatted **calf**

1844 'You...will kill the fatted calf if you please!' (p. 87)
The Life and Adventures of Martin Chuzzlewit. 1844. The Oxford Illustrated Dickens, Vol.
IX. Oxford: Oxford University Press, 1951.
ODEP 422; EAP 54; MP 89.

As **calm** as coffins

1840-41 ...I would be calm as coffins. (p. 48)
Master Humphrey's Clock and A Child's History of England. 1840-41, 1852-54. The
Oxford Illustrated Dickens, Vol. XX. Oxford: Oxford University Press, 1958.

There is a **calm** after a storm.

1850 ...after all storms there is a calm. (p. 169)
"The Doom of English Wills." [with W. H. Wills]. *Charles Dickens' Uncollected Writings
from* Household Words *1850-1859*, 2 vols. Ed. Harry Stone. Bloomington: Indiana
University Press, 1968.
APP 54; ODEP 6; EAP 418; CODP 2; DAP 566.

It is easier for a **camel** to go through the eye of a needle....

1844 'Rich folks may ride on camels, but it ain't so easu for 'em to see
out of a needle's eye.' (p. 407)
The Life and Adventures of Martin Chuzzlewit. 1844. The Oxford Illustrated Dickens, Vol.
IX. Oxford: Oxford University Press, 1951.
1857 ...it was the last reading of the parable of the camel and the
needle's eye.... (p. 394)
Little Dorrit. 1857. The Oxford Illustrated Dickens, Vol. XIV. Oxford: Oxford University
Press, 1953.
APP 54; ODEP 559; EAP 54; MP 89; DAP 81.

(Not) to hold a **candle** to someone (-thing)

1844 '...there are hundreds of men not fit to hold a candle to me....' (p.
792)
The Life and Adventures of Martin Chuzzlewit. 1844. The Oxford Illustrated Dickens, Vol.
IX. Oxford: Oxford University Press, 1951.
APP 54; ODEP 377; EAP 55; MP 90.

To be **cap** in hand

1859 The fellow was brought in, cap in hand.... (p. 108)
A Tale of Two Cities. 1859. The Oxford Illustrated Dickens, Vol. IV. Oxford: Oxford
University Press, 1948.
URDANG, *IDIOMS* 210.

To set one's **cap** at someone

1837 "...one of the young ladies may set her cap at young Mr. Simpson...." (p. 277)
Sketches by Boz. 1833-40. The Oxford Illustrated Dickens, Vol. XII. Oxford: Oxford University Press, 1957.
1846 '...it might be a good speculation if I were to set my cap at Michael Warden....' (p. 308)
Christmas Books. 1843-49. The Oxford Illustrated Dickens, Vol. XVI. Oxford: Oxford University Press, 1954.
APP 55; ODEP 716; EAP 56; MP 91.

To be a sure **card**

1839 '...that's a sure card, a sure card.' (p. 301)
The Life and Adventures of Nicholas Nickleby. 1839. The Oxford Illustrated Dickens, Vol. VI. Oxford: Oxford University Press, 1950.
ODEP 789.

To be on the **cards**

1867 It is on the cards. (p. 535)
The Letters of Charles Dickens, ed. Walter Dexter. Vol. III: 1858-1870. The Nonesuch Dickens. London: The Nonesuch Press, 1938.
EAP 57; MP 92.

To be on the **carpet**

1849 Think of me...when chops are on the carpet (figuratively speaking).... (p. 479)
The Letters of Charles Dickens: Volume Five: 1847-1849. Eds. Graham Storey and K. J. Fielding. Oxford: The Clarendon Press, 1981.
EAP 58; MP 93.

Do not build your **castles** in the air.

1852 "My Castle...is in the Air....My Castle is in the Air!" (p. 39)
Christmas Stories. 1871. The Oxford Illustrated Dickens, Vol. XI. Oxford: Oxford University Press, 1956.
1855 A Castle in the Air (p. 299)
Dickens' Working Notes for His Novels. Ed. Harry Stone. Chicago, Ill.: University of Chicago Press, 1987.
1857 Chapter XIX: The Storming of the Castle in the Air (p. 637)
Little Dorrit. 1857. The Oxford Illustrated Dickens, Vol. XIV. Oxford: Oxford University Press, 1953.

1862 ...she had better attach her fernery to one of her châteaux in Spain, or one of her English castles in the air. (p. 298)

The Letters of Charles Dickens, ed. Walter Dexter. Vol. III: 1858-1870. The Nonesuch Dickens. London: The Nonesuch Press, 1938.

APP 57; ODEP 107; EAP 59; MP 94; DAP 85.

A **cat** has nine lives.

1850 'If he had as many lives as a cat...he'd bark at me...!' (p. 699)

The Personal History of David Copperfield. 1850. The Oxford Illustrated Dickens, Vol. II. Oxford: Oxford University Press, 1948.

APP 58; ODEP 108; EAP 61; MP 96; DAP 86.

A **cat** in gloves will not catch mice.

1857 '...Mrs. General, if I may reverse a common proverb and adapt it to her, is a cat in gloves who *will* catch mice.' (p. 590)

Little Dorrit. 1857. The Oxford Illustrated Dickens, Vol. XIV. Oxford: Oxford University Press, 1953.

ODEP 108; EAP 61; CODP 32; DAP 87.

To fight like **cat** and dog

1841 ...she and her husband lived like cat and dog.... (p. 170)

Barnaby Rudge: A Tale of the Riots of 'Eighty. 1841. The Oxford Illustrated Dickens, Vol. XV. Oxford: Oxford University Press, 1954.

APP 61; EAP 62; MP 100.

To make a **cat** talk French

1839 'It's enough to make a Tom cat talk French grammar....' (p. 135)

The Life and Adventures of Nicholas Nickleby. 1839. The Oxford Illustrated Dickens, Vol. VI. Oxford: Oxford University Press, 1950.

ODEP 8.

When the **cat** is away, the mice will play.

1853 ...when the Audit mice are away, the cats of that great public establishment will play. (p. 102)

The Letters of Charles Dickens: Volume Seven: 1853-1855. Eds. Graham Storey, Kathleen Tillotson, and Angus Easson. Oxford: The Clarendon Press, 1993.

ODEP 109; EAP 63; CODP 32; MP 102; DAP 87.

Cats will run their heads against milestones.

1837 'All them old cats *will* run their heads agin mile-stones,' observed Mr. Weller.... (p. 216)

The Posthumous Papers of the Pickwick Club. 1837. The Oxford Illustrated Dickens, Vol. I. Oxford: Oxford University Press, 1948.

To rain **cats and dogs**

1843 If the day be anything short of cats, dogs, and pitchforks, in its dampness.... (p. 444)

The Letters of Charles Dickens: Volume Three: 1842-1843. Eds. Madeline House, Graham Storey, and Kathleen Tillotson. Oxford: The Clarendon Press, 1974.

1854 Unless it should rain cats, dogs, pitchforks and Cochin China poultry, the Train...is my means of going down. (p. 267)

The Letters of Charles Dickens: Volume Seven: 1853-1855. Eds. Graham Storey, Kathleen Tillotson, and Angus Easson. Oxford: The Clarendon Press, 1993.

APP 62; ODEP 662; EAP 63; MP 102.

To be born with a **caul**

1850 I was born with a caul.... (p. 1)

The Personal History of David Copperfield. 1850. The Oxford Illustrated Dickens, Vol. II. Oxford: Oxford University Press, 1948.

ODEP 76.

Do not stand on **ceremony**.

1841 'Don't stand on ceremony.' (p. 255)

The Old Curiosity Shop. 1841. The Oxford Illustrated Dickens, Vol. VIII. Oxford: Oxford University Press, 1951.

URDANG, *IDIOMS* 225.

As **certain** as the existence of the sun

1850 It is as certain as the existence of the Sun. (p. 247)

The Letters of Charles Dickens: Volume Six: 1850-1852. Eds. Madeline House, Graham Storey, and Kathleen Tillotson. Oxford: The Clarendon Press, 1988.

As **certain** as the sun

1839 ...it is as certain...as the Sun is to rise tomorrow. (p. 532)

The Letters of Charles Dickens: Volume One: 1820-1839. Eds. Madeline House and Graham Storey. Oxford: The Clarendon Press, 1965.

1848 ...he is as certain to pervert...as the Sun is to rise tomorrow morning. (p. 313)

The Letters of Charles Dickens: Volume Five: 1847-1849. Eds. Graham Storey and K. J. Fielding. Oxford: The Clarendon Press, 1981.

APP 361; EAP 424; MP 605.

To walk the **chalks**

1847 ...that perfectly unintelligible ceremony which is called, in the vulgar, walking the chalks [=departing]. (p. 34)
The Letters of Charles Dickens: Volume Five: 1847-1849. Eds. Graham Storey and K. J. Fielding. Oxford: The Clarendon Press, 1981.
PARTRIDGE 138.

Change begets change.

1844 Change begets change. (p. 298)
The Life and Adventures of Martin Chuzzlewit. 1844. The Oxford Illustrated Dickens, Vol. IX. Oxford: Oxford University Press, 1951.
STEVENSON 314:10.

This is rayther a **change** for the vorse.

1837 'This is rayther a change for the vorse, Mr. Trotter, as the gen'l'm'n said, wen he got two doubtful shillin's and sixpenn'orth o' pocket pieces for a good half-crown.' (p. 640)
The Posthumous Papers of the Pickwick Club. 1837. The Oxford Illustrated Dickens, Vol. I. Oxford: Oxford University Press, 1948.
DOW 20.

Ve make no extra **charge** for the settin' down.

1837 '...ve make no extra charge for the settin' down, as the king remarked wen he blowed up his ministers. (p. 633)
The Posthumous Papers of the Pickwick Club. 1837. The Oxford Illustrated Dickens, Vol. I. Oxford: Oxford University Press, 1948.
APP 335; ODEP 116; MP 569; DOW 20.

As **cheap** as dirt; dirt-cheap

1836 FLAM: ...which would have been cheap, dirt-cheap, at double the money. (*The Village Coquettes*, II, iv, p. 87)
Complete Plays and Selected Poems of Charles Dickens. London: Vision Press, 1970.
1839 'It's dirt cheap.' (p. 396)
The Life and Adventures of Nicholas Nickleby. 1839. The Oxford Illustrated Dickens, Vol. VI. Oxford: Oxford University Press, 1950.
1850-56 "...you'll find it a bargain—dirt cheap." (p. 495)
The Uncommercial Traveller and Reprinted Pieces Etc. 1850-1860. The Oxford Illustrated Dickens, Vol. XXI. Oxford: Oxford University Press, 1958.

APP 102; EAP 109; MP 168.

To be a **Cheap Jack**

1860 ...he went about the country...like a glorified Cheap-Jack. (p. 70)
1860 Here, do I encounter...Cheap Jack and Dear Jill.... (p. 114)
The Uncommercial Traveller and Reprinted Pieces Etc. 1850-1860. The Oxford Illustrated Dickens, Vol. XXI. Oxford: Oxford University Press, 1958.
1865 I am a Cheap Jack.... (p. 435)
1865 ...my father was a Cheap Jack before me. (p. 436)
1865 The old couple...got to be...devoted to the Cheap Jack business.... (p. 436)
1865 ...here...is a working model of a used-up old Cheap Jack.... (p. 437)
1865 Bid for the working model of the old Cheap Jack.... (p. 437)
1865 ...an old woman...was married to the old Cheap Jack.... (p. 437)
1865 My father had been a lovely one...at the Cheap Jack work.... (p. 438)
1865 ...the Cheap Jack calling is the worst used. (p. 438)
1865 ...we are Cheap Jacks, and they are Dear Jacks. (p. 438)
1865 This is me, the Cheap Jack. (p. 439)
1865 These Dear Jacks soap the people shameful, but we Cheap Jacks don't. (p. 440)
1865 ...the Cheap Jack is treated ill in Great Britain.... (p. 40)
1865 ...which, by the bye, is quite in the Cheap Jack way again, and shows once more how the Cheap Jack customs pervade society. (p. 441)
1865 ..."Here's a wretch of a Cheap Jack been a beating his wife." (p. 443)
1865 The Cheap Jack business had been worse than ever.... (p. 443)
1865 ...I went on again in my Cheap Jack style. (p. 445)
1865 ...all my being looked up to the King of Cheap Jacks. (p. 446)
1865 In the Cheap Jack patter, we usually sound it [the word "melancholy"] lemonjolly, and it gets a laugh. (p. 449)
1865 "I am nothing but a Cheap Jack...." (p. 450)
1865 I shouldn't wish...to go partners with yourself in the Cheap Jack cart. (p. 452)
1865 ...and a boy being laid on for the Cheap Jack cart.... (p. 454)
1865 ...meaning me, the Cheap Jack in the sleeved waistcoat.... (p. 489)
Christmas Stories. 1871. The Oxford Illustrated Dickens, Vol. XI. Oxford: Oxford University Press, 1956.
URDANG, *IDIOMS* 232.

As **cheerful** as a bird

1853 '...you are to be as cheerful as a bird.' (p. 612)
Bleak House. 1853. The Oxford Illustrated Dickens, Vol. III. Oxford: Oxford University Press, 1948.
APP 35.

To be a **chicken**

1844 'Why, what a chicken you are!' (p. 651)
The Life and Adventures of Martin Chuzzlewit. 1844. The Oxford Illustrated Dickens, Vol. IX. Oxford: Oxford University Press, 1951.
ODEP 118; EAP 68; MP 109.

Train up a **child** in the way he should go....

1848 'Train up a fig-tree in the way it should go, and when you are old sit under the shade on it.' (p. 267)
Dealings with the Firm of Dombey and Son. 1848. The Oxford Illustrated Dickens, Vol. VII. Oxford: Oxford University Press, 1950.
APP 68; DAP 96.

To be **child's play**

1838 ...a consultation of great doctors...would be mere child's play. (p. 224)
The Adventures of Oliver Twist. 1838. The Oxford Illustrated Dickens, Vol. V. Oxford: Oxford University Press, 1948.
APP 68; EAP 70; MP 111.

To be a **chip** off the old block

1844 I suppose chip to mean chap, but it may include the custom-house officer's father and have some reference to the old block.... (p. 224)
The Letters of Charles Dickens: Volume Four: 1844-1846. Ed. Kathleen Tillotson. Oxford: The Clarendon Press, 1977.
APP 69; ODEP 121; EAP 72; MP 113.

Chit-chat

1841 ...as if he were discussing some pleasant chit-chat.... (p. 179)
Barnaby Rudge: A Tale of the Riots of 'Eighty. 1841. The Oxford Illustrated Dickens, Vol. XV. Oxford: Oxford University Press, 1954.
PARTRIDGE 149.

To howl like a **Christian**

1841 'The wind...is howling like a Christian....' (p. 250)
Barnaby Rudge: A Tale of the Riots of 'Eighty. 1841. The Oxford Illustrated Dickens, Vol. XV. Oxford: Oxford University Press, 1954.

Christmas comes but once a year.

1837-39 ...like Christmas...they come to us but once a year.... (p. 668)
Sketches by Boz. 1833-40. The Oxford Illustrated Dickens, Vol. XII. Oxford: Oxford University Press, 1957.
1854 ...Christmas comes but once a year.... (p. 73)
Christmas Stories. 1871. The Oxford Illustrated Dickens, Vol. XI. Oxford: Oxford University Press, 1956.
APP 69; ODEP 123; MP 114; DAP 99.

To run on **church-time**

1850 ...on account of the Railway Trains not running in church-time.... (p. 75)
1850 ...the Blackwall Trains don't run in church-time. (p. 75)
The Letters of Charles Dickens: Volume Six: 1850-1852. Eds. Madeline House, Graham Storey, and Kathleen Tillotson. Oxford: The Clarendon Press, 1988.

Circumstances alter cases.

1870 'But circumstances alter cases....' (p. 90)
The Mystery of Edwin Drood. 1870. The Oxford Illustrated Dickens, Vol. XVIII. Oxford: Oxford University Press, 1956.
APP 70; ODEP 124; EAP 73; MP 116; DAP 100.

As **clean** as a whistle

1865 '...you're as clean as a whistle after it.' (p. 180)
Our Mutual Friend. 1865. The Oxford Illustrated Dickens, Vol. X. Oxford: Oxford University Press, 1952.
APP 400; EAP 480; MP 680.

As **clear** as a bell

1841 '...they was as clear as a bell, and as good as a play.' (p. 502)
Barnaby Rudge: A Tale of the Riots of 'Eighty. 1841. The Oxford Illustrated Dickens, Vol. XV. Oxford: Oxford University Press, 1954.
APP 24; EAP 27; MP 42.

As **clear** as crystal

1853 ...a brook 'as clear as crystial' once ran down the middle of Holborn.... (p. 130)

Bleak House. 1853. The Oxford Illustrated Dickens, Vol. III. Oxford: Oxford University Press, 1948.

1870 'You are always training yourself to be...as clear as crystal....' (p. 166)

The Mystery of Edwin Drood. 1870. The Oxford Illustrated Dickens, Vol. XVIII. Oxford: Oxford University Press, 1956.

EAP 89; MP 142.

Cloak and dagger

1841 'With a cloak and dagger?' said Mr. Chester. (p. 184)

Barnaby Rudge: A Tale of the Riots of 'Eighty. 1841. The Oxford Illustrated Dickens, Vol. XV. Oxford: Oxford University Press, 1954.

1862 This letter...is to be regarded as...a cloak-and-dagger conspiracy. (p. 285)

The Letters of Charles Dickens, ed. Walter Dexter. Vol. III: 1858-1870. The Nonesuch Dickens. London: The Nonesuch Press, 1938.

URDANG, *IDIOMS* 250.

Every **cloud** has a silver lining.

1853 '...I turn my silver lining outward like Milton's cloud....' (p. 251)

Bleak House. 1853. The Oxford Illustrated Dickens, Vol. III. Oxford: Oxford University Press, 1948.

APP 73; ODEP 128; CODP 39; MP 121; DAP 104.

To be under a **cloud**

'...if one gentleman under a cloud, is not to put himself a little out of the way to assist another gentleman in the same condition....' (p. 587)

The Posthumous Papers of the Pickwick Club. 1837. The Oxford Illustrated Dickens, Vol. I. Oxford: Oxford University Press, 1948.

1862 Under a Cloud was one of the names on my list. (p. 284)

The Letters of Charles Dickens, ed. Walter Dexter. Vol. III: 1858-1870. The Nonesuch Dickens. London: The Nonesuch Press, 1938.

ODEP 128; EAP 175.

To be in the **clouds**

1851 Whether we shall come to terms or no, is yet in the clouds.... (p. 269)

The Letters of Charles Dickens: Volume Six: 1850-1852. Eds. Madeline House, Graham Storey, and Kathleen Tillotson. Oxford: The Clarendon Press, 1988.

APP 177; EAP 75.

To be in **clover**

1865 '...a man...might be in clover here.' (p. 188)
Our Mutual Friend. 1865. The Oxford Illustrated Dickens, Vol. X. Oxford: Oxford University Press, 1952.
APP 73; ODEP 129; EAP 75; MP 121.

To heap **coals** of fire upon someone's head

1841 '...I would...heap coals of fire upon his head.' (p. 497)
The Old Curiosity Shop. 1841. The Oxford Illustrated Dickens, Vol. VIII. Oxford: Oxford University Press, 1951.
1842 ...what coals of fire were heaped upon your head...! (p. 153)
The Letters of Charles Dickens: Volume Three: 1842-1843. Eds. Madeline House, Graham Storey, and Kathleen Tillotson. Oxford: The Clarendon Press, 1974.
1844 She had laid in several chaldrons of live coals, and was prepared to heap them on the heads of her enemies. (p. 826)
The Life and Adventures of Martin Chuzzlewit. 1844. The Oxford Illustrated Dickens, Vol. IX. Oxford: Oxford University Press, 1951.
1846 ...there's a shovelful of live coals for your head—does it burn? (p. 661)
The Letters of Charles Dickens: Volume Four: 1844-1846. Ed. Kathleen Tillotson. Oxford: The Clarendon Press, 1977.
1848 How few...suspected what a heap of fiery coals was piled upon his head! (p. 347)
Dealings with the Firm of Dombey and Son. 1848. The Oxford Illustrated Dickens, Vol. VII. Oxford: Oxford University Press, 1950.
1854 ...the Sherbornians will...cast quantities of live coals on their own heads. (p. 477)
The Letters of Charles Dickens: Volume Seven: 1853-1855. Eds. Graham Storey, Kathleen Tillotson, and Angus Easson. Oxford: The Clarendon Press, 1993.
APP 74; ODEP 129; EAP 77; MP 123.

The **coast** is clear.

1841 'Disperse, my lads, while the coast's clear....' (p. 423)
Barnaby Rudge: A Tale of the Riots of 'Eighty. 1841. The Oxford Illustrated Dickens, Vol. XV. Oxford: Oxford University Press, 1954.
1848 ...the coast was quite clear.... (p. 67)
Dealings with the Firm of Dombey and Son. 1848. The Oxford Illustrated Dickens, Vol. VII. Oxford: Oxford University Press, 1950.
APP 74; ODEP 129; EAP 77; MP 123.

To tell a **cock-and-bull** story

1853 '...this young hardened Heathen told us a story of a Cock, and of a Bull....' (p. 360)

Bleak House. 1853. The Oxford Illustrated Dickens, Vol. III. Oxford: Oxford University Press, 1948.

APP 75; ODEP 130; EAP 79; MP 125.

To beat **cock-fighting**

1837 '...if this don't beat cock-fightin', nothin' never vill, as the Lord Mayor said, ven the chief secretary o' state proposed his missis's health arter dinner.' (p. 549)

The Posthumous Papers of the Pickwick Club. 1837. The Oxford Illustrated Dickens, Vol. I. Oxford: Oxford University Press, 1948.

PARTRIDGE 165; DOW 23.

According to **Cocker**

1853 It would...be an unspeakable comfort to him...to know the Gospel according to Cocker.... (p. 485)

"In and Out of Jail." [with Henry Morley and W. H. Wills]. *Charles Dickens' Uncollected Writings from* Household Words *1850-1859*, 2 vols. Ed. Harry Stone. Bloomington: Indiana University Press, 1968.

1854 According to Cocker (p. 251)

Dickens' Working Notes for His Novels. Ed. Harry Stone. Chicago, Ill.: University of Chicago Press, 1987.

ODEP 131; MP 125.

To drink a **cocktail**

1842 There the stranger is initiated into the mysteries of...Cocktail.... (p. 60)

American Notes and Pictures from Italy. 1842, 1846. The Oxford Illustrated Dickens, Vol. XIX. Oxford: Oxford University Press, 1957.

PARTRIDGE 165.

Here's pretty **coil**.

1850 Here's a pretty coil indeed, about teaching little ragamuffins their A B C! (p. 199)

"Mr. Bendigo Buster on Our National Defences Against Education." [with Henry Morley]. *Charles Dickens' Uncollected Writings from* Household Words *1850-1859*, 2 vols. Ed. Harry Stone. Bloomington: Indiana University Press, 1968.

As **cold** as death

1861 ...he was as cold as death.... (p. 330)
Great Expectations. 1861. The Oxford Illustrated Dickens, Vol. XIII. Oxford: Oxford University Press, 1953.
APP 94; EAP 98; MP 157.

As **cold** as stone

1857 '...I introduce you to a lady...cold as the stone....' (p. 772)
Little Dorrit. 1857. The Oxford Illustrated Dickens, Vol. XIV. Oxford: Oxford University Press, 1953.
APP 355; EAP 416; MP 596.

To nail one's **colours** to the mast

1848 ...Mrs. Chick had nailed her colours to the mast.... (p. 46)
Dealings with the Firm of Dombey and Son. 1848. The Oxford Illustrated Dickens, Vol. VII. Oxford: Oxford University Press, 1950.
1851 ...I cannot bear to un-nail my colors from the Mast. (p. 303)
The Letters of Charles Dickens: Volume Six: 1850-1852. Eds. Madeline House, Graham Storey, and Kathleen Tillotson. Oxford: The Clarendon Press, 1988.
ODEP 553.

To pass with flying **colours**

1839 ...I hope to go out with flying colours.... (p. 561)
The Letters of Charles Dickens: Volume One: 1820-1839. Eds. Madeline House and Graham Storey. Oxford: The Clarendon Press, 1965.
EAP 80; MP 126.

To **come to** [=regain consciousness]

1857 ...he "came to," as the phrase goes.... (p. 699)
Christmas Stories. 1871. The Oxford Illustrated Dickens, Vol. XI. Oxford: Oxford University Press, 1956.
URDANG, *IDIOMS* 268.

To **come** up piping

1844 ...Cant..."comes up piping" [panting with exhaustion].... (p. 218)
The Letters of Charles Dickens: Volume Four: 1844-1846. Ed. Kathleen Tillotson. Oxford: The Clarendon Press, 1977.

Coming events cast their shadows before.

1843 Coming events cast their shadows before. (p. 551)
The Letters of Charles Dickens: Volume Three: 1842-1843. Eds. Madeline House, Graham Storey, and Kathleen Tillotson. Oxford: The Clarendon Press, 1974.
1853 ...casting the shadow of that virgin event before her full two centuries.... (p. 563)
Bleak House. 1853. The Oxford Illustrated Dickens, Vol. III. Oxford: Oxford University Press, 1948.
1860 My salad-days...being gone...no coming event cast its shadow before. (p. 309)
The Uncommercial Traveller and Reprinted Pieces Etc. 1850-1860. The Oxford Illustrated Dickens, Vol. XXI. Oxford: Oxford University Press, 1958.
APP 122; ODEP 136; CODP 40; MP 204; DAP 184.

You're a **comin'** it a great deal too strong.

1837 '...you're a comin' it a great deal too strong, as the mail-coachman said to the snow-storm, ven it overtook him.' (p. 599)
The Posthumous Papers of the Pickwick Club. 1837. The Oxford Illustrated Dickens, Vol. I. Oxford: Oxford University Press, 1948.
DOW 36.

We look **compact** and comfortable.

1837 '...we look compact and comfortable, as the father said ven he cut his little boy's head off, to cure him o' squintin'.' (p. 384)
The Posthumous Papers of the Pickwick Club. 1837. The Oxford Illustrated Dickens, Vol. I. Oxford: Oxford University Press, 1948.
DOW 25.

To jump to **conclusions**

1858 "...you jump instantly to the conclusion that...." (p. 608)
"A House to Let." [with Wilkie Collins]. *Charles Dickens' Uncollected Writings from Household Words 1850-1859*, 2 vols. Ed. Harry Stone. Bloomington: Indiana University Press, 1968.
MP 129.

That's vun **consolation**.

1837 '...I'm pretty tough, that's vun consolation, as the wery old turkey remarked wen the farmer said he wos afeerd he should be obliged to kill him for the London market.' (p. 451)
The Posthumous Papers of the Pickwick Club. 1837. The Oxford Illustrated Dickens, Vol. I. Oxford: Oxford University Press, 1948.
DOW 26.

As **constant** as death

1857 ...the smell...was as constant as Death to man.... (p. 805)
Little Dorrit. 1857. The Oxford Illustrated Dickens, Vol. XIV. Oxford: Oxford University Press, 1953.

As **constant** as the evergreen

1848 '...it is...constant as the evergreen.' (p. 367)
Dealings with the Firm of Dombey and Son. 1848. The Oxford Illustrated Dickens, Vol. VII. Oxford: Oxford University Press, 1950.

As **convivial** as a trout

1837 '...looks as conwivial as a live trout in a lime basket,' added Mr. Weller.... (p. 213)
The Posthumous Papers of the Pickwick Club. 1837. The Oxford Illustrated Dickens, Vol. I. Oxford: Oxford University Press, 1948.
WILSTACH 69 (CITING DICKENS).

As **cool** as a cucumber

1845 ...you were as cool as a Cucumber, and safer than the Bank.... (p. 428)
The Letters of Charles Dickens: Volume Four: 1844-1846. Ed. Kathleen Tillotson. Oxford: The Clarendon Press, 1977.
APP 86; ODEP 143; EAP 89; MP 143.

To turn the **corner**

1847 I...hope I am turning the corner. (p. 66)
The Letters of Charles Dickens: Volume Five: 1847-1849. Eds. Graham Storey and K. J. Fielding. Oxford: The Clarendon Press, 1981.
WILKINSON 203.

To tread on someone's **corns**

1860 ...a Platform composed of other people's corns, on which he had stumped his way.... (p. 206)
The Uncommercial Traveller and Reprinted Pieces Etc. 1850-1860. The Oxford Illustrated Dickens, Vol. XXI. Oxford: Oxford University Press, 1958.
EAP 84; MP 132.

As **correct** as arithmetic

1850 The tale itself is as correct as arithmetic. (p. 182)

"Chips: 'Household Words' and English Wills." [with W. H. Wills]. *Charles Dickens' Uncollected Writings from* Household Words *1850-1859*, 2 vols. Ed. Harry Stone. Bloomington: Indiana University Press, 1968.

To screw one's **courage** to the sticking place

1850 If she once screws her courage to the sticking place, I have no fear of her.... (p. 203)

The Letters of Charles Dickens: Volume Six: 1850-1852. Eds. Madeline House, Graham Storey, and Kathleen Tillotson. Oxford: The Clarendon Press, 1988.
APP 82; MP 133.

The **course** of true love never did run smooth.

1857 "Love at first sight!...But the course of it doesn't run smooth." (p. 702)

Christmas Stories. 1871. The Oxford Illustrated Dickens, Vol. XI. Oxford: Oxford University Press, 1956.
APP 82; ODEP 148; EAP 85; CODP 44; MP 134; DAP 390.

To send someone to **Coventry**

1850 '...the owners of all the names...seemed to send me to Coventry....' (p. 79)

The Personal History of David Copperfield. 1850. The Oxford Illustrated Dickens, Vol. II. Oxford: Oxford University Press, 1948.
1854 'You are the hand they have sent to Coventry...?' (p. 145)

Hard Times for These Times. 1854. The Oxford Illustrated Dickens, Vol. XVII. Oxford: Oxford University Press, 1955.
APP 82; ODEP 149; EAP 85; MP 134.

From the **cradle** to the grave

1854 '...people as has been broughten into bein heer, an' to piece out a livin'...'twixt their cradles and their graves.' (p. 149)

Hard Times for These Times. 1854. The Oxford Illustrated Dickens, Vol. XVII. Oxford: Oxford University Press, 1955.
1862 "Not from the cradle to the grave." (p. 364)

Christmas Stories. 1871. The Oxford Illustrated Dickens, Vol. XI. Oxford: Oxford University Press, 1956.
ODEP 57; BARTLETT 407:5, 559:4.

To get the **creeps**

1850 She was constantly complaining...of a visitation in her back which she called 'the creeps.' (p. 38)

The Personal History of David Copperfield. 1850. The Oxford Illustrated Dickens, Vol. II. Oxford: Oxford University Press, 1948.
PARTRIDGE 190.

To be an admirable **Crichton**

1852   ...his admirable Crichton qualities. (p. 418)
"First Fruits." [with George Augustus Sala]. *Charles Dickens' Uncollected Writings from Household Words 1850-1859*, 2 vols. Ed. Harry Stone. Bloomington: Indiana University Press, 1968.
STEVENSON 453:6.

As **cross** as two sticks

1844 'We got out of bed back'ards, I think, for we're as cross as two sticks.' (p. 465)
The Life and Adventures of Martin Chuzzlewit. 1844. The Oxford Illustrated Dickens, Vol. IX. Oxford: Oxford University Press, 1951.
ODEP 155; MP 594.

As **crusty** as a jackdaw

1857 ...he was as tough as an old yew-tree, and as crusty as an old jackdaw. (pp. 680-681)
Little Dorrit. 1857. The Oxford Illustrated Dickens, Vol. XIV. Oxford: Oxford University Press, 1953.

Great **cry** but little wool

1841 There's great cry there, Mr Willer, but very little wool. (p. 234)
Barnaby Rudge: A Tale of the Riots of 'Eighty. 1841. The Oxford Illustrated Dickens, Vol. XV. Oxford: Oxford University Press, 1954.
APP 86; ODEP 333; EAP 88; CODP 156; MP 142.

To have a good **cry**

1839 ...the poor soul...had what she termed 'a real good cry.' (p. 129)
The Life and Adventures of Nicholas Nickleby. 1839. The Oxford Illustrated Dickens, Vol. VI. Oxford: Oxford University Press, 1950.

As **cunning** as a weasel

1841 'I'm...as cunning as a weasel.' (p. 172)
The Old Curiosity Shop. 1841. The Oxford Illustrated Dickens, Vol. VIII. Oxford: Oxford University Press, 1951.
MP 674.

What cannot be **cured** must be endured.

1837 ...what couldn't be cured must be endured.... (p. 677)
The Posthumous Papers of the Pickwick Club. 1837. The Oxford Illustrated Dickens, Vol.
I. Oxford: Oxford University Press, 1948.
APP 87; ODEP 161; EAP 90; CODP 46; MP 144; DAP 131.

To ring up (down) the **curtain**

1854 ...he may desire to ring the curtain down upon them.... (p. 458)
Address on Administrative Reform, London, 27 June 1855.
1858 'All right,' said the actor of universal capabilities, 'ring up.' (p.
488)
Address to the General Theatrical Fund, London, 29 Mar. 1858.
1866 ...we should 'ring down' on these remarks. (p. 537)
Address to the Dramatic, Equestrian, and Musical Fund, London, 14 Feb. 1866. *The
Works of Charles Dickens: The Speeches.* Ed. Richard H. Shepherd. New National Edition,
Vol. II. New York: Hearst's International Library Company, n. d.
WILKINSON 472.

Cut and dried

1859 ...I saw the beast...(with my mind's eye)...delivering his cut-and-
dried speech.... (p. 118)
The Letters of Charles Dickens, ed. Walter Dexter. Vol. III: 1858-1870. The Nonesuch
Dickens. London: The Nonesuch Press, 1938.
APP 89; EAP 91; MP 145.

To **cut** someone (dead)

1837 'I can't let you cut an old friend in this way.' (p. 383)
The Posthumous Papers of the Pickwick Club. 1837. The Oxford Illustrated Dickens, Vol.
I. Oxford: Oxford University Press, 1948.
PARTRIDGE 201.

D

To be at **daggers'** points

1857 '...we may be at daggers' points....' (p. 769)
Little Dorrit. 1857. The Oxford Illustrated Dickens, Vol. XIV. Oxford: Oxford University
Press, 1953.
APP 90; ODEP 165; EAP 92; MP 147.

To look **daggers** at someone

1837 ...the old lady...looked carving knives as the hard-headed delinquent. (p. 69)
1837 ...Miss Bolo looked a small armoury of daggers.... (p. 503)
The Posthumous Papers of the Pickwick Club. 1837. The Oxford Illustrated Dickens, Vol. I. Oxford: Oxford University Press, 1948.

As **dark** as pitch; pitch-dark

1842 Ascend these pitch-dark stairs.... (p. 89)
American Notes and Pictures from Italy. 1842, 1846. The Oxford Illustrated Dickens, Vol. XIX. Oxford: Oxford University Press, 1957.
1848 'Think of the pitch-dark nights....' (p. 39)
1848 '...the stormy nights is so pitch dark,' said the Captain.... (p. 689)
Dealings with the Firm of Dombey and Son. 1848. The Oxford Illustrated Dickens, Vol. VII. Oxford: Oxford University Press, 1950.
APP 287; ODEP 63; EAP 340; MP 497.

As **dark** as the grave

1838 'It's as dark as the grave,' said the man.... (p. 192)
The Adventures of Oliver Twist. 1838. The Oxford Illustrated Dickens, Vol. V. Oxford: Oxford University Press, 1948.
APP 160; EAP 186; MP 269.

To be in the **dark**

1838 'Don't leave us in the dark,' said Kags.... (p. 385)
The Adventures of Oliver Twist. 1838. The Oxford Illustrated Dickens, Vol. V. Oxford: Oxford University Press, 1948.
1841 ...Barnaby himself was equally in the dark. (p. 361)
Barnaby Rudge: A Tale of the Riots of 'Eighty. 1841. The Oxford Illustrated Dickens, Vol. XV. Oxford: Oxford University Press, 1954.
1844 'Don't mind leaving me in the dark.' (p. 99)
The Life and Adventures of Martin Chuzzlewit. 1844. The Oxford Illustrated Dickens, Vol. IX. Oxford: Oxford University Press, 1951.
APP 91; EAP 93.

*Bis **dat** qui citò dat.*
1844 'Bis dat qui citò dat....' (p. 438)
The Life and Adventures of Martin Chuzzlewit. 1844. The Oxford Illustrated Dickens, Vol. IX. Oxford: Oxford University Press, 1951.
ODEP 304; EAP 175; CODP 92; MP 253; DAP 251.

Davy Jones

1859 I wouldn't...shiver my ould timbers and rouse me up with a monkey's tail (man-of-war metaphor), not to chuck a biscuit into Davy Jones's weather eye.... (p. 123)
The Letters of Charles Dickens, ed. Walter Dexter. Vol. III: 1858-1870. The Nonesuch Dickens. London: The Nonesuch Press, 1938.
1860 ...descending...in ghostly procession to Davy Jones's locker. (p. 181)
The Uncommercial Traveller and Reprinted Pieces Etc. 1850-1860. The Oxford Illustrated Dickens, Vol. XXI. Oxford: Oxford University Press, 1958.
APP 91; ODEP 169; EAP 94; MP 151.

The better the **day**, the better the deed.

1870 '...the better the day the better the deed....' (p. 110)
The Mystery of Edwin Drood. 1870. The Oxford Illustrated Dickens, Vol. XVIII. Oxford: Oxford University Press, 1956.
APP 93; ODEP 52; EAP 95; CODP 16; MP 153; DAP 136.

Until one's dying **day**

1833 ...I...ever should feel towards you till my dying day. (p. 25)
The Letters of Charles Dickens: Volume One: 1820-1839. Eds. Madeline House and Graham Storey. Oxford: The Clarendon Press, 1965.
URDANG, *IDIOMS* 391.

In all of one's born **days**

1838 BETSY: ...his mother...kissed that grumpy old face of his in all his born days. (*The Lamplighter*, I, iii, p. 133)
Complete Plays and Selected Poems of Charles Dickens. London: Vision Press, 1970.
URDANG, *IDIOMS* 325.

To have seen better **days**

1837 A very poor man, "who has seen better days," as the phrase goes, is a strange compound.... (p. 262)
Sketches by Boz. 1833-40. The Oxford Illustrated Dickens, Vol. XII. Oxford: Oxford University Press, 1957.
1860 It is...a neighbourhood which has seen better days.... (p. 29)
The Uncommercial Traveller and Reprinted Pieces Etc. 1850-1860. The Oxford Illustrated Dickens, Vol. XXI. Oxford: Oxford University Press, 1958.
URDANG, *IDIOMS* 324.

As **dead** as a doornail

1843 Old Marley was as dead as a door-nail. (p. 7)
1843 ...Marley was as dead as a door-nail. (p. 7)
Christmas Books. 1843-49. The Oxford Illustrated Dickens, Vol. XVI. Oxford: Oxford University Press, 1954.
1843 "He is as dead Sir as a door-nail. But we must all die...sooner or later...." (p. 550)
The Letters of Charles Dickens: Volume Three: 1842-1843. Eds. Madeline House, Graham Storey, and Kathleen Tillotson. Oxford: The Clarendon Press, 1974.
1844 ...I don't know what there is particularly dead about a door-nail.... (p. 85)
The Letters of Charles Dickens: Volume Four: 1844-1846. Ed. Kathleen Tillotson. Oxford: The Clarendon Press, 1977.
1848 ...and so killed a brace of birds with one stone, dead as door-nails. (p. 342)
Dealings with the Firm of Dombey and Son. 1848. The Oxford Illustrated Dickens, Vol. VII. Oxford: Oxford University Press, 1950.
APP 109; ODEP 170; EAP 119; MP 183.

As **dead** as a stone; stone-dead

1838 'Stone dead!' said one of the old women.... (p. 176)
The Adventures of Oliver Twist. 1838. The Oxford Illustrated Dickens, Vol. V. Oxford: Oxford University Press, 1948.
APP 355; ODEP 776; EAP 416; CODP 214; MP 596.

As **dead** as Adam

1854 ...he was picked up as Dead as Adam.... (p. 319)
The Letters of Charles Dickens: Volume Seven: 1853-1855. Eds. Graham Storey, Kathleen Tillotson, and Angus Easson. Oxford: The Clarendon Press, 1993.
APP 3; MP 4.

As **dead** as pharaoh

1853 'He's just as dead as Phairy!' (p. 139)
1853 '...he is indeed as dead as Pharaoh....' (p. 140)
Bleak House. 1853. The Oxford Illustrated Dickens, Vol. III. Oxford: Oxford University Press, 1948.
MP 485.

As **dead** as the Doges

1857 'He is as dead as the Doges!' (p. 502)

Little Dorrit. 1857. The Oxford Illustrated Dickens, Vol. XIV. Oxford: Oxford University Press, 1953.

Dead and buried

1847 ...the spectral shadow of a certain dead and buried opposition.... (p. 410)
Address at the opening of the Glasgow Athenaeum, 28 Dec. 1847. *The Works of Charles Dickens: The Speeches.* Ed. Richard H. Shepherd. New National Edition, Vol. II. New York: Hearst's International Library Company, n. d.
URDANG, *IDIOMS* 326.

Dead and gone

1837 "...he is dead and gone now!" (p. 442)
Sketches by Boz. 1833-40. The Oxford Illustrated Dickens, Vol. XII. Oxford: Oxford University Press, 1957.
1850-56 "...son of the dead and gone Fletcher...." (p. 371)
1860 ...indeed they were—dead and gone.... (p. 125)
The Uncommercial Traveller and Reprinted Pieces Etc. 1850-1860. The Oxford Illustrated Dickens, Vol. XXI. Oxford: Oxford University Press, 1958.
1859 ...he already considered the prisoner as good as dead and gone. (p. 62)
A Tale of Two Cities. 1859. The Oxford Illustrated Dickens, Vol. IV. Oxford: Oxford University Press, 1948.
1865 'I love my husband long dead and gone...I love my children dead and gone, in him...I love my young and hopeful days dead and gone, in him....' (p. 203)
Our Mutual Friend. 1865. The Oxford Illustrated Dickens, Vol. X. Oxford: Oxford University Press, 1952.
1870 'My dead and gone father and Pussy's dead and gone father must needs marry us together....' (p. 12)
The Mystery of Edwin Drood. 1870. The Oxford Illustrated Dickens, Vol. XVIII. Oxford: Oxford University Press, 1956.
URDANG, *IDIOMS* 326.

In the **dead** of the night

1860 ...how many over-laden vans...had to be dragged out...in the dead of the night.... (p. 182)
The Letters of Charles Dickens, ed. Walter Dexter. Vol. III: 1858-1870. The Nonesuch Dickens. London: The Nonesuch Press, 1938.
WILKINSON 322.

To wake the **dead**

1839 'Then just blo' away into that...fit to wakken the deead, will'ee' said the man.... (p. 53)
The Life and Adventures of Nicholas Nickleby. 1839. The Oxford Illustrated Dickens, Vol. VI. Oxford: Oxford University Press, 1950.
APP 94; EAP 97; MP 155.

As **deaf** as a flint

1844 'He's getting deafer than a flint,' said Pecksniff. (p. 477)
The Life and Adventures of Martin Chuzzlewit. 1844. The Oxford Illustrated Dickens, Vol. IX. Oxford: Oxford University Press, 1951.

As **deaf** as a post

1839 'Then you are...deaf...as deaf as a demnition post.' (p. 426)
The Life and Adventures of Nicholas Nickleby. 1839. The Oxford Illustrated Dickens, Vol. VI. Oxford: Oxford University Press, 1950.
APP 292; ODEP 172; EAP 344; MP 505.

As **deaf** as a stone; stone-deaf

1850 Still stone-deaf to the voice...Miss Betsey pursued her discourse. (p. 213)
The Personal History of David Copperfield. 1850. The Oxford Illustrated Dickens, Vol. II. Oxford: Oxford University Press, 1948.
1860 ...as if he were stone deaf. (p. 225)
The Uncommercial Traveller and Reprinted Pieces Etc. 1850-1860. The Oxford Illustrated Dickens, Vol. XXI. Oxford: Oxford University Press, 1958.
MP 596.

As **deaf** as an adder

1839 ...Ralph was deaf as an adder.... (p. 618)
The Life and Adventures of Nicholas Nickleby. 1839. The Oxford Illustrated Dickens, Vol. VI. Oxford: Oxford University Press, 1950.
1841 ...she was as deaf as any adder. (p. 540)
Barnaby Rudge: A Tale of the Riots of 'Eighty. 1841. The Oxford Illustrated Dickens, Vol. XV. Oxford: Oxford University Press, 1954.
ODEP 172; EAP 4; MP 6.

Deaf and dumb

1841 '...here's your deaf and dumb son.' (p. 328)
The Old Curiosity Shop. 1841. The Oxford Illustrated Dickens, Vol. VIII. Oxford: Oxford University Press, 1951.
1844 '...you are not deaf and dumb....' (p. 714)

The Life and Adventures of Martin Chuzzlewit. 1844. The Oxford Illustrated Dickens, Vol. IX. Oxford: Oxford University Press, 1951.

1852 Wonderful things have been done...for the Deaf and Dumb.... (p. 391)

"A Curious Dance Round a Curious Tree." [with W. H. Wills]. *Charles Dickens' Uncollected Writings from* Household Words *1850-1859,* 2 vols. Ed. Harry Stone. Bloomington: Indiana University Press, 1968.

1853 ...she is deaf and dumb. (p. 878)

Bleak House. 1853. The Oxford Illustrated Dickens, Vol. III. Oxford: Oxford University Press, 1948.

1865 ...the cruelty of his master towards a step-daughter who was deaf and dumb. (p. 447)

1865 ...I went with her...to the Deaf and Dumb establishment.... (p. 449)

Christmas Stories. 1871. The Oxford Illustrated Dickens, Vol. XI. Oxford: Oxford University Press, 1956.

1865 It may be said almost equally, of...the blind, and the deaf and dumb. (p. 527)

Toast at a banquet of the Newspaper Press Fund, London, 20 May, 1865. *The Works of Charles Dickens: The Speeches.* Ed. Richard H. Shepherd. New National Edition, Vol. II. New York: Hearst's International Library Company, n. d.

URDANG, *IDIOMS* 327.

To be a **Dear Jack** [Opposite to Cheap Jack, *q. v.*]

1865 ...the Dear Jacks beats us hollow. (p. 440)

Christmas Stories. 1871. The Oxford Illustrated Dickens, Vol. XI. Oxford: Oxford University Press, 1956.

To catch one's **death**

1837 TAPKINS: He'll catch his death of cold! (*Is She His Wife?*, I, p. 99)

Complete Plays and Selected Poems of Charles Dickens. London: Vision Press, 1970.

URDANG, *IDIOMS* 329.

The **descent** to Avernus is easy.

1852 ...the descent of Avernus is unaccompanied by difficulty.... (p. 410)

"First Fruits." [with George Augustus Sala]. *Charles Dickens' Uncollected Writings from* Household Words *1850-1859,* 2 vols. Ed. Harry Stone. Bloomington: Indiana University Press, 1968.

ODEP 177; MP 160; DAP 144.

To get one's just **deserts**

1846 ...the man should have his deserts. (p. 703)
The Letters of Charles Dickens: Volume Four: 1844-1846. Ed. Kathleen Tillotson. Oxford: The Clarendon Press, 1977.
URDANG, *IDIOMS* 334.

He whom the **devil** drives feels no lead at his heels.

1854 We were close at your heels last night, but you had vanished with a celerity worthy of...a better cause. (p. 479)
The Letters of Charles Dickens: Volume Seven: 1853-1855. Eds. Graham Storey, Kathleen Tillotson, and Angus Easson. Oxford: The Clarendon Press, 1993.
ODEP 180.

Needs must when the **devil** drives.

1839 'Needs must, you know, when somebody drives.' (p. 43)
The Life and Adventures of Nicholas Nickleby. 1839. The Oxford Illustrated Dickens, Vol. VI. Oxford: Oxford University Press, 1950.
1841 'Needs must when the devil drives; and the devil that drives me is an empty pocket and an unhappy home.' (p. 237)
Barnaby Rudge: A Tale of the Riots of 'Eighty. 1841. The Oxford Illustrated Dickens, Vol. XV. Oxford: Oxford University Press, 1954.
1852 ...needs must when *You*-don't-know who drives. (p. 583)
The Letters of Charles Dickens: Volume Six: 1850-1852. Eds. Madeline House, Graham Storey, and Kathleen Tillotson. Oxford: The Clarendon Press, 1988.
APP 260; ODEP 560; EAP 106; MP 444; DAP 426.

Shake the **Devil** from your shoulders although he is wearing your cloak.

1840 ...when one has the Devil on one's shoulders, it is best to shake him off, though he has one's cloak on. (p. 85)
The Letters of Charles Dickens: Volume Two: 1840-1841. Eds. Madeline House and Graham Storey. Oxford: The Clarendon Press, 1969.

The **devil** can quote Scripture for his own ends.

1844 ...the Devil (being a layman) quotes Scripture for his own ends? (p. 173)
The Life and Adventures of Martin Chuzzlewit. 1844. The Oxford Illustrated Dickens, Vol. IX. Oxford: Oxford University Press, 1951.
APP 98; ODEP 180; EAP 103; CODP 51; MP 161; DAP 146.

The **Devil** is not as black as he has been painted.

1860 ...is it quite as black as it has been lately painted? (p. 251)

The Uncommercial Traveller and Reprinted Pieces Etc. 1850-1860. The Oxford Illustrated Dickens, Vol. XXI. Oxford: Oxford University Press, 1958.
APP 99; ODEP 182; EAP 104; CODP 52; MP 162; DAP 147.

To go to the **Devil**

1836 ...he may just go to the Devil.... (p. 183)
The Letters of Charles Dickens: Volume One: 1820-1839. Eds. Madeline House and Graham Storey. Oxford: The Clarendon Press, 1965.
URDANG, *IDIOMS* 336.

To have the **devil** to pay

1839 ...there will be the devil to pay. (p. 503)
The Letters of Charles Dickens: Volume One: 1820-1839. Eds. Madeline House and Graham Storey. Oxford: The Clarendon Press, 1965.
1845 Here is the Devil to pay. (p. 415)
The Letters of Charles Dickens: Volume Four: 1844-1846. Ed. Kathleen Tillotson. Oxford: The Clarendon Press, 1977.
1851 Here is the Devil to pay.... (p. 543)
The Letters of Charles Dickens: Volume Six: 1850-1852. Eds. Madeline House, Graham Storey, and Kathleen Tillotson. Oxford: The Clarendon Press, 1988.
1869 Here is the Devil to pay! (p. 699)
The Letters of Charles Dickens, ed. Walter Dexter. Vol. III: 1858-1870. The Nonesuch Dickens. London: The Nonesuch Press, 1938.
APP 99; ODEP 184; EAP 105; MP 164.

To play the **Devil**

1836 Melbourne v Norton has played the devil with me. (p. 153)
The Letters of Charles Dickens: Volume One: 1820-1839. Eds. Madeline House and Graham Storey. Oxford: The Clarendon Press, 1965.
1841 That monstrosity of yesterday has played the very devil with me. (p. 224)
The Letters of Charles Dickens: Volume Two: 1840-1841. Eds. Madeline House and Graham Storey. Oxford: The Clarendon Press, 1969.
1850 ...gold and silver bide their time in cool retreats, not...anxious to play the Devil with our souls. (p. 130)
"The Old Lady in Threadneedle Street." [with W. H. Wills]. *Charles Dickens' Uncollected Writings from* Household Words *1850-1859*, 2 vols. Ed. Harry Stone. Bloomington: Indiana University Press, 1968.
1854 ....that Liqueur-case will have been playing the very Devil with your peace of mind. (p. 464)
The Letters of Charles Dickens: Volume Seven: 1853-1855. Eds. Graham Storey, Kathleen Tillotson, and Angus Easson. Oxford: The Clarendon Press, 1993.
PARTRIDGE 216.

To yell like a **devil**

1840-41 ...crowds made their way...yelling like devils let loose. (p. 72)
Master Humphrey's Clock and A Child's History of England. 1840-41, 1852-54. The Oxford Illustrated Dickens, Vol. XX. Oxford: Oxford University Press, 1958.

What the **devil** do you want with me?

1837 '...what the devil do you want with me, as the man said wen he seed the ghost?' (p. 125)
The Posthumous Papers of the Pickwick Club. 1837. The Oxford Illustrated Dickens, Vol. I. Oxford: Oxford University Press, 1948.
DOW 32.

To be **devil-may-care**

1841 '...I'll be a bachelor, a devil-may-care bachelor....' (p. 371)
The Old Curiosity Shop. 1841. The Oxford Illustrated Dickens, Vol. VIII. Oxford: Oxford University Press, 1951.
1846 He sang it with an assumption of a devil-may-care voice.... (p. 186)
Christmas Books. 1843-49. The Oxford Illustrated Dickens, Vol. XVI. Oxford: Oxford University Press, 1954.
APP 101; MP 163.

To be the **devil's own** something

1848 ...any proposal...would throw the whole question into what is expressively called "the Devil's own state...." (p. 385)
The Letters of Charles Dickens: Volume Five: 1847-1849. Eds. Graham Storey and K. J. Fielding. Oxford: The Clarendon Press, 1981.
1857 'There are the devil's own secrets in some families!' (p. 360)
Little Dorrit. 1857. The Oxford Illustrated Dickens, Vol. XIV. Oxford: Oxford University Press, 1953.
PARTRIDGE 217.

To beat the **Devil's tattoo**

1853 ...beating the Devil's Tattoo with his boot on the patternless carpet. (p. 550)
Bleak House. 1853. The Oxford Illustrated Dickens, Vol. III. Oxford: Oxford University Press, 1948.
PARTRIDGE 217.

Die and be damned.

1841 I think "die and be d—d" is a foolish curse. "Live and be damned" is my motto to all such vagabonds. (pp. 824-825)
The Letters of Charles Dickens: Volume Seven: 1853-1855. Eds. Graham Storey, Kathleen Tillotson, and Angus Easson. Oxford: The Clarendon Press, 1993.

Never say **die**.

1833-36 '...keep your eyes open, and niver say die!' (p. 112)
Sketches by Boz. 1833-40. The Oxford Illustrated Dickens, Vol. XII. Oxford: Oxford University Press, 1957.
1837 "Never say die, you know." (p. 448)
Sketches by Boz. 1833-40. The Oxford Illustrated Dickens, Vol. XII. Oxford: Oxford University Press, 1957.
1837 '...accidents will happen—best regulated families—never say die—...put that in his pipe....' (p. 9)
The Posthumous Papers of the Pickwick Club. 1837. The Oxford Illustrated Dickens, Vol. I. Oxford: Oxford University Press, 1948.
1838 ...she...gave utterance to various exclamations of 'Never say die!' (p. 190)
The Adventures of Oliver Twist. 1838. The Oxford Illustrated Dickens, Vol. V. Oxford: Oxford University Press, 1948.
1841 ...he cried, 'Never say die!' a great many times.... (p. 135)
1841 'Keep up your spirits, Never say die....' (p. 136)
1841 The corks, and the never say die, afforded the gentleman...much delight.... (p. 359)
1841 'Never say die....' (p. 434)
Barnaby Rudge: A Tale of the Riots of 'Eighty. 1841. The Oxford Illustrated Dickens, Vol. XV. Oxford: Oxford University Press, 1954.
1841 There's more philosophy in "never *say* die", than most people suppose. (p. 364)
The Letters of Charles Dickens: Volume Two: 1840-1841. Eds. Madeline House and Graham Storey. Oxford: The Clarendon Press, 1969.
1846 But never say die! (p. 631)
The Letters of Charles Dickens: Volume Four: 1844-1846. Ed. Kathleen Tillotson. Oxford: The Clarendon Press, 1977.
1850 'Never say die, sir!' (p. 398)
The Personal History of David Copperfield. 1850. The Oxford Illustrated Dickens, Vol. II. Oxford: Oxford University Press, 1948.
1862 The more I think of Never Say Die, the less I like. (p. 322)
The Letters of Charles Dickens, ed. Walter Dexter. Vol. III: 1858-1870. The Nonesuch Dickens. London: The Nonesuch Press, 1938.
1865 'Never say die, sir!' (p. 478)
Our Mutual Friend. 1865. The Oxford Illustrated Dickens, Vol. X. Oxford: Oxford University Press, 1952.

ODEP 563; EAP 109; MP 167; DAP 149.

One can **die** only once.

1860 "...they knew Mr. Merdle to have said to the Physician, 'man can die but once.'" (p. 354)
The Uncommercial Traveller and Reprinted Pieces Etc. 1850-1860. The Oxford Illustrated Dickens, Vol. XXI. Oxford: Oxford University Press, 1958.
APP 102; ODEP 503; EAP 109; MP 168; DAP 148.

The **die** is cast.

1837 His die's now cast. (p. 697)
The Letters of Charles Dickens: Volume One: 1820-1839. Eds. Madeline House and Graham Storey. Oxford: The Clarendon Press, 1965.
1850 'The die is cast—all is over.' (p. 263)
The Personal History of David Copperfield. 1850. The Oxford Illustrated Dickens, Vol. II. Oxford: Oxford University Press, 1948.
APP 102; ODEP 186; EAP 108; MP 167; DAP 148.

We must all **die** sometime.

1841 '...we must all die some time, or another, eh?' (p. 235)
Barnaby Rudge: A Tale of the Riots of 'Eighty. 1841. The Oxford Illustrated Dickens, Vol. XV. Oxford: Oxford University Press, 1954.
1843 "He is as dead Sir as a door-nail. But we must all die...sooner or later...." (p. 550)
The Letters of Charles Dickens: Volume Three: 1842-1843. Eds. Madeline House, Graham Storey, and Kathleen Tillotson. Oxford: The Clarendon Press, 1974.
1852-54 We must all die! (p. 140)
Master Humphrey's Clock and A Child's History of England. 1840-41, 1852-54. The Oxford Illustrated Dickens, Vol. XX. Oxford: Oxford University Press, 1958.
APP 102; ODEP 10; EAP 109; MP 167; DAP 148.

To go at it **ding-dong**

1851 But I hope...to...go at it Ding-Dong. (p. 518)
The Letters of Charles Dickens: Volume Six: 1850-1852. Eds. Madeline House, Graham Storey, and Kathleen Tillotson. Oxford: The Clarendon Press, 1988.
URDANG, *IDIOMS* 342.

Discretion is the better part of valour.

1867 OBENREIZER: As Shakespeare says, 'Discretion is the better part of valour!' (*No Thoroughfare*, IV, ii, pp. 212-213)
Complete Plays and Selected Poems of Charles Dickens. London: Vision Press, 1970.
APP 103; ODEP 189; EAP 110; CODP 54; MP 169; DAP 152.

Desperate **diseases** need desperate remedies.

1852-54 "Because," said Guy Fawkes, "desperate diseases need desperate remedies." (p. 443)
Master Humphrey's Clock and A Child's History of England. 1840-41, 1852-54. The Oxford Illustrated Dickens, Vol. XX. Oxford: Oxford University Press, 1958.
APP 103; ODEP 178; EAP 110; CODP 51; MP 169; DAP 152.

Do as you would be done by.

1844 'Here's the rule for bargains. "Do other men, for they would do you."' (p. 181)
The Life and Adventures of Martin Chuzzlewit. 1844. The Oxford Illustrated Dickens, Vol. IX. Oxford: Oxford University Press, 1951.
1846 'The grater says...Do as you-would-be—done by.' (p. 256)
1846 'Do as you would be done by! Forget and Forgive!' (p. 311)
Christmas Books. 1843-49. The Oxford Illustrated Dickens, Vol. XVI. Oxford: Oxford University Press, 1954.
1854 ...the absurd answer, 'To do unto others as I would that they should do unto me.' (p. 55)
Hard Times for These Times. 1854. The Oxford Illustrated Dickens, Vol. XVII. Oxford: Oxford University Press, 1955.
APP 104; ODEP 191; EAP 113; CODP 56; MP 171; DAP 154.

Beware of the **dog**.

1853 'Beware of the Bull-dog....' (p. 248)
Bleak House. 1853. The Oxford Illustrated Dickens, Vol. III. Oxford: Oxford University Press, 1948.
1870 ...the traffic...came sneaking in...by a back stable-way, for many years labelled at the corner: 'Beware of the Dog.' (p. 55)
The Mystery of Edwin Drood. 1870. The Oxford Illustrated Dickens, Vol. XVIII. Oxford: Oxford University Press, 1956.
STEVENSON 601:3.

A **dog** is man's best friend.

1850-56 Or does that animal that is the friend of man always degenerate in his low society? (p. 468)
The Uncommercial Traveller and Reprinted Pieces Etc. 1850-1860. The Oxford Illustrated Dickens, Vol. XXI. Oxford: Oxford University Press, 1958.
MP 174; DAP 157.

Help a lame **dog** over the stile.

1855 ...the national pig is not nearly over the stile yet.... (p. 464)
Address on Administrative Reform, London, 27 June 1855. *The Works of Charles Dickens: The Speeches*. Ed. Richard H. Shepherd. New National Edition, Vol. II. New York: Hearst's International Library Company, n. d.
ODEP 368; EAP 117; MP 178; DAP 159.

To follow like a **dog**

1851 ...his fiacre will follow him like a dog.... (p. 247)
"Common-Sense on Wheels." [with W. H. Wills and E. C. Grenville Murray]. *Charles Dickens' Uncollected Writings from* Household Words *1850-1859*, 2 vols. Ed. Harry Stone. Bloomington: Indiana University Press, 1968.
EAP 117; MP 178.

To treat someone like a **dog**

1838 '...those that treat you like a dog—like a dog!' (p. 341)
The Adventures of Oliver Twist. 1838. The Oxford Illustrated Dickens, Vol. V. Oxford: Oxford University Press, 1948.
APP 108; MP 179.

To wear a **dog-collar**

1852 ...to make it know to all men by wearing a clear-starched dog-collar round his throat. (p. 426)
"Boys to Mend." [with Henry Morley]. *Charles Dickens' Uncollected Writings from* Household Words *1850-1859*, 2 vols. Ed. Harry Stone. Bloomington: Indiana University Press, 1968.
PARTRIDGE 230.

The **dog-days** of summer

1843 ...he iced his coffee in the dog-days.... (p. 8)
Christmas Books. 1843-49. The Oxford Illustrated Dickens, Vol. XVI. Oxford: Oxford University Press, 1954.
1859 ...he declines pale horse...in the dog days. (p. 112)
The Letters of Charles Dickens, ed. Walter Dexter. Vol. III: 1858-1870. The Nonesuch Dickens. London: The Nonesuch Press, 1938.
URDANG, *IDIOMS* 356; STEVENSON 611:5.

To lead a **dog's** life

1844 ...she led her parent what is usually called, for the want of a better figure of speech, the life of a dog. (p. 470)
The Life and Adventures of Martin Chuzzlewit. 1844. The Oxford Illustrated Dickens, Vol. IX. Oxford: Oxford University Press, 1951.

APP 107; ODEP 197; EAP 118; MP 176.

Let sleeping **dogs** lie.

1850 'Let sleeping dogs lie—who wants to rouse 'em?' (p. 578)
The Personal History of David Copperfield. 1850. The Oxford Illustrated Dickens, Vol. II. Oxford: Oxford University Press, 1948.
1857 '...if it's advisable (as the proverb says it is) to let sleeping dogs lies, it's just as advisable, perhaps, to let missing dogs lie.' (p. 681)
1857 'You remember what I said to you about sleeping dogs and missing ones.' (p. 751)
Little Dorrit. 1857. The Oxford Illustrated Dickens, Vol. XIV. Oxford: Oxford University Press, 1953.
ODEP 456; CODP 205; MP 176; DAP 160.

Mad **dogs** and Englishmen go out in the noonday sun.

1851 ...the Italians have a saying to this day, that no creatures voluntarily move about in the hot summer sunlight, except mad dogs and Englishmen. (p. 247)
"Common-Sense on Wheels." [with W. H. Wills and E. C. Grenville Murray]. *Charles Dickens' Uncollected Writings from* Household Words *1850-1859*, 2 vols. Ed. Harry Stone. Bloomington: Indiana University Press, 1968.
EAP 117; MP 177; DAP 160.

To go to the **dogs**

1850 '...a grander kind of going to the dogs, I suppose.' (p. 322)
The Personal History of David Copperfield. 1850. The Oxford Illustrated Dickens, Vol. II. Oxford: Oxford University Press, 1948.
1853 Pal himself has gone to the dogs. (p. 180)
The Letters of Charles Dickens: Volume Seven: 1853-1855. Eds. Graham Storey, Kathleen Tillotson, and Angus Easson. Oxford: The Clarendon Press, 1993.
APP 107; ODEP 208; EAP 117; MP 178.

Constant **dropping** wears away a stone.

1841 'As to Nell, constant dropping will wear away a stone....; (p. 56)
The Old Curiosity Shop. 1841. The Oxford Illustrated Dickens, Vol. VIII. Oxford: Oxford University Press, 1951.
1861 '...notwithstanding the proverb, that constant dropping will wear away a stone, you may set your mind at rest....' (p. 253)
Great Expectations. 1861. The Oxford Illustrated Dickens, Vol. XIII. Oxford: Oxford University Press, 1953.
APP 111; ODEP 141; EAP 121; CODP 42; MP 186; DAP 168.

As **dry** as a bone

1870 '...I am as dry as a bone.' (p. 9)
The Mystery of Edwin Drood. 1870. The Oxford Illustrated Dickens, Vol. XVIII. Oxford: Oxford University Press, 1956.
APP 36; MP 62.

As **dry** as a chip

1853 '...your mother...was as dry as a chip....' (p. 293)
Bleak House. 1853. The Oxford Illustrated Dickens, Vol. III. Oxford: Oxford University Press, 1948.
APP 68; EAP 71; MP 113.

As **dry** as a lime-basket

1838 '...he might be busted if he warn't as dry as a lime-basket.' (p. 133)
The Adventures of Oliver Twist. 1838. The Oxford Illustrated Dickens, Vol. V. Oxford: Oxford University Press, 1948.
PARTRIDGE 484.

As **dry** as the weather

1836 JOHN: ...it's as dry as the weather.... (*The Village Coquettes*, I, i, p. 46)
Complete Plays and Selected Poems of Charles Dickens. London: Vision Press, 1970.

Like a dying **duck** in a thunderstorm

1844 ...with something of that expression which the poetry of ages has attributed to a domestic bird, when breathing its last amid the ravages of an electric storm. (p. 158)
The Life and Adventures of Martin Chuzzlewit. 1844. The Oxford Illustrated Dickens, Vol. IX. Oxford: Oxford University Press, 1951.
ODEP 210.

To make **ducks and drakes** of something

1850 'He soon made ducks and drakes of what I gave him....' (p. 689)
The Personal History of David Copperfield. 1850. The Oxford Illustrated Dickens, Vol. II. Oxford: Oxford University Press, 1948.
APP 112; ODEP 207; MP 188.

To dine with **Duke Humphrey**

1844 ...Diggory Chuzzlewit was in the habit of perpetually dining with Duke Humphrey. (p. 4)

The Life and Adventures of Martin Chuzzlewit. 1844. The Oxford Illustrated Dickens, Vol. IX. Oxford: Oxford University Press, 1951.

APP 113; ODEP 188; EAP 122.

As **dull** as a codfish

1838 I am as dull as a Codfish. (p. 353)

The Letters of Charles Dickens: Volume One: 1820-1839. Eds. Madeline House and Graham Storey. Oxford: The Clarendon Press, 1965.

WILSTACH 106.

As **dull** as ditchwater

1857 'He is as sweet as honey, and I am as dull as ditch-water.' (p. 802)

Little Dorrit. 1857. The Oxford Illustrated Dickens, Vol. XIV. Oxford: Oxford University Press, 1953.

ODEP 208; EAP 111; MP 171.

As **dull** as swipes [Cf. As dull as ditchwater.]

1838 '...it's been dull as swipes.' (p. 292)

The Adventures of Oliver Twist. 1838. The Oxford Illustrated Dickens, Vol. V. Oxford: Oxford University Press, 1948.

ODEP 208 .

As **dumb** as a drum

1837 'Dumb as a drum vith a hole in it, sir' replied Sam. (p. 342)

The Posthumous Papers of the Pickwick Club. 1837. The Oxford Illustrated Dickens, Vol. I. Oxford: Oxford University Press, 1948.

As **dumb** as a stone

1853 ...to be...stone blind and dumb! (p. 220)

Bleak House. 1853. The Oxford Illustrated Dickens, Vol. III. Oxford: Oxford University Press, 1948.

APP 356; WILKINSON 218.

To shake the **dust** from one's feet

1844 ...she shook the dust from her feet.... (p. 62)

The Life and Adventures of Martin Chuzzlewit. 1844. The Oxford Illustrated Dickens, Vol. IX. Oxford: Oxford University Press, 1951.

APP 113; ODEP 719; EAP 123; MP 189.

To throw **dust** in someone's eyes

1853 ...it flings as much dust in the eyes of Allegory as the law.... (p. 305)

Bleak House. 1853. The Oxford Illustrated Dickens, Vol. III. Oxford: Oxford University Press, 1948.

APP 114; ODEP 209; EAP 123; MP 190.

To look like a **Dutch cheese**

1853 ...looking something between the knob on top of a pair of tongs—a Chinese—and a scraped Dutch cheese. (p. 87)

The Letters of Charles Dickens: Volume Seven: 1853-1855. Eds. Graham Storey, Kathleen Tillotson, and Angus Easson. Oxford: The Clarendon Press, 1993.

PARTRIDGE 250.

A **Dutch clock**

1842 He had...manufactured a...Dutch clock from some disregarded odds and ends.... (p. 101)

American Notes and Pictures from Italy. 1842, 1846. The Oxford Illustrated Dickens, Vol. XIX. Oxford: Oxford University Press, 1957.

PARTRIDGE 250.

A **Dutch house**

1837 Mr. Tibbs bobbed up and down to the three ladies like a figure in a Dutch house.... (p. 281)

Sketches by Boz. 1833-40. The Oxford Illustrated Dickens, Vol. XII. Oxford: Oxford University Press, 1957.

1840 There is an old-fashioned weather-glass representing a house with two doorways, in one of which is the figure of a gentleman, in the other a figure of a lady. (p. 577)

Sketches by Boz. 1833-40. The Oxford Illustrated Dickens, Vol. XII. Oxford: Oxford University Press, 1957.

...or I'm a **Dutchman**

1837 'I'm one Dutchman, and you're another....' (p. 370)

The Posthumous Papers of the Pickwick Club. 1837. The Oxford Illustrated Dickens, Vol. I. Oxford: Oxford University Press, 1948.

1845 ...I will give the Turin people something...or I'm a Dutchman! (p. 409)

1845 ...I'm a Dutchman if I do it.... (p, 415)

1846 If Fireworks can't do that...I'm a Dutchman. (p. 659)

The Letters of Charles Dickens: Volume Four: 1844-1846. Ed. Kathleen Tillotson. Oxford: The Clarendon Press, 1977.

1855 And if Stanfield don't astonish 'em, I'm a Dutchman. (p. 631)

The Letters of Charles Dickens: Volume Seven: 1853-1855. Eds. Graham Storey, Kathleen Tillotson, and Angus Easson. Oxford: The Clarendon Press, 1993.

APP 114; ODEP 209; MP 191.

Dutchmen like broad cases and much clothing.

1846 There is a popular belief that Dutchmen love broad cases and much clothing for their own lower selves.... (pp. 160-161)

Christmas Books. 1843-49. The Oxford Illustrated Dickens, Vol. XVI. Oxford: Oxford University Press, 1954.

Duty is duty.

1853 'Duty is duty, and friendship is friendship.' (p. 677)

Bleak House. 1853. The Oxford Illustrated Dickens, Vol. III. Oxford: Oxford University Press, 1948.

MP 191.

E

To go in one **ear** and out the other

1844 'It come in at one ear, and went out at the other.' (p. 343)

The Life and Adventures of Martin Chuzzlewit. 1844. The Oxford Illustrated Dickens, Vol. IX. Oxford: Oxford University Press, 1951.

ODEP 402; EAP 126; MP 192.

To grin from **ear** to ear

1842 ...all the rest...grin from ear to ear incessantly. (p. 91)

1842 The black driver recognises him by...grinning from ear to ear. (p. 133)

American Notes and Pictures from Italy. 1842, 1846. The Oxford Illustrated Dickens, Vol. XIX. Oxford: Oxford University Press, 1957.

1844 I grinned from ear to ear. (p. 185)

The Letters of Charles Dickens: Volume Four: 1844-1846. Ed. Kathleen Tillotson. Oxford: The Clarendon Press, 1977.

URDANG, *IDIOMS* 394.

To turn a deaf **ear** to someone (-thing)

1833-36 ...the driver...turns a deaf ear to your earnest entreaties.... (p. 163)
Sketches by Boz. 1833-40. The Oxford Illustrated Dickens, Vol. XII. Oxford: Oxford University Press, 1957.

1841 Grip turned a deaf ear to the request.... (p. 357)
Barnaby Rudge: A Tale of the Riots of 'Eighty. 1841. The Oxford Illustrated Dickens, Vol. XV. Oxford: Oxford University Press, 1954.

1857 Affery...turned a deaf ear to all adjuration.... (p. 690)
Little Dorrit. 1857. The Oxford Illustrated Dickens, Vol. XIV. Oxford: Oxford University Press, 1953.
URDANG, *IDIOMS* 395.

The **ears** burn when one is talked about.

1845 My left ear has been burning.... (p. 337)
The Letters of Charles Dickens: Volume Four: 1844-1846. Ed. Kathleen Tillotson. Oxford: The Clarendon Press, 1977.

1853 '...according to the old superstition, it should be Rosa's ears that burn....' (p. 158)
Bleak House. 1853. The Oxford Illustrated Dickens, Vol. III. Oxford: Oxford University Press, 1948.
WILKINSON 301.

To set someone by the **ears**

1837 '...people o' the same purfession, as sets people by the ears, free gratis for nothin'....' (p. 362)
The Posthumous Papers of the Pickwick Club. 1837. The Oxford Illustrated Dickens, Vol. I. Oxford: Oxford University Press, 1948.

On **earth** peace, and good will toward men.

1847 ...such designs are practically worthy of...a practical remembrance of the words, 'On earth peace, and good will toward men.' (p. 419)
Address at the opening of the Glasgow Athenaeum, 28 Dec. 1847. *The Works of Charles Dickens: The Speeches.* Ed. Richard H. Shepherd. New National Edition, Vol. II. New York: Hearst's International Library Company, n. d.
STEVENSON 973:14.

Eat, drink, and be merry, for tomorrow we die.

1857 ...the motto of these tables is not 'Let us eat and drink, for to-morrow we die'; but 'Let us eat and drink, for to-morrow we live.' (p. 470)

Address to the Warehousemen and Clerks' Schools, London, 5 Nov. 1857. *The Works of Charles Dickens: The Speeches.* Ed. Richard H. Shepherd. New National Edition, Vol. II. New York: Hearst's International Library Company, n. d.
APP 116; EAP 127; MP 195; DAP 175.

As **eccentric** as a comet

1833-36 But these trades are as eccentric as comets.... (p. 182)
Sketches by Boz. 1833-40. The Oxford Illustrated Dickens, Vol. XII. Oxford: Oxford University Press, 1957.
WILSTACH 109 (CITING DICKENS).

To be out at the **elbow**

1841 ...Mr. Chester followed...by propounding...truisms, worn a little out at the elbow.... (p. 206)
Barnaby Rudge: A Tale of the Riots of 'Eighty. 1841. The Oxford Illustrated Dickens, Vol. XV. Oxford: Oxford University Press, 1954.
ODEP 601, EAP 129.

As **empty** as a desert

1848 ...the lines of iron road...were as empty and as silent as a desert. (p. 776)
Dealings with the Firm of Dombey and Son. 1848. The Oxford Illustrated Dickens, Vol. VII. Oxford: Oxford University Press, 1950.

All things have an **end**.

1853 All things have an end.... (p. 88)
Bleak House. 1853. The Oxford Illustrated Dickens, Vol. III. Oxford: Oxford University Press, 1948.
APP 120; ODEP 231; EAP 130; CODP 3; MP 617; DAP 179.

All will come right in the **end**.

1844 'But it'll all come right in the end, sir; it'll all come right!' (p. 555)
The Life and Adventures of Martin Chuzzlewit. 1844. The Oxford Illustrated Dickens, Vol. IX. Oxford: Oxford University Press, 1951.
DAP 179.

To be one's own worst **enemy**

1838 'Some people are nobody's enemies but their own, yer know.' (p. 327)

The Adventures of Oliver Twist. 1838. The Oxford Illustrated Dickens, Vol. V. Oxford: Oxford University Press, 1948.
URDANG, *IDIOMS* 409.

In plain **English**

1838 TOM: ...in plain English...it's all my eye and—yourself, Miss Martin. (*The Lamplighter*, I, ii, p. 127)
Complete Plays and Selected Poems of Charles Dickens. London: Vision Press, 1970.
1838 These words, in plain English, conveyed an injunction.... (p. 105)
The Adventures of Oliver Twist. 1838. The Oxford Illustrated Dickens, Vol. V. Oxford: Oxford University Press, 1948.
EAP 132; MP 203.

An **Englishman's house** is his castle.

1837 'Some people maintains than an Englishman's house is his castle.' (p. 332)
The Posthumous Papers of the Pickwick Club. 1837. The Oxford Illustrated Dickens, Vol. I. Oxford: Oxford University Press, 1948.
1848 ...an Englishwoman's house was her castle.... (p. 118)
Dealings with the Firm of Dombey and Son. 1848. The Oxford Illustrated Dickens, Vol. VII. Oxford: Oxford University Press, 1950.
1854 They made him out to be...John Bull, Habeas Corpus, the Bill of Rights, An Englishman's house is his castle...all put together. (p. 43)
Hard Times for These Times. 1854. The Oxford Illustrated Dickens, Vol. XVII. Oxford: Oxford University Press, 1955.
1861 '...a Englishman's 'ouse is his Castle....' (p. 442)
Great Expectations. 1861. The Oxford Illustrated Dickens, Vol. XIII. Oxford: Oxford University Press, 1953.
APP 193; ODEP 389; EAP 226; CODP 66; MP 328; DAP 304.

Quite **enough** to get, sir.

1837 'Oh, quite enough to get, sir, as the soldier said ven they ordered him three hundred and fifty lashes,' replied Sam. (p. 483)
The Posthumous Papers of the Pickwick Club. 1837. The Oxford Illustrated Dickens, Vol. I. Oxford: Oxford University Press, 1948.
DOW 39.

Always suspect **everybody**.

1841 '"Always suspect everybody." That's the maxim to go through life with!' (p. 499)

The Old Curiosity Shop. 1841. The Oxford Illustrated Dickens, Vol. VIII. Oxford: Oxford University Press, 1951.
STEVENSON 2253:2 (CITING DICKENS).

Everybody is as likely to be wrong as right.

1849 Everybody is, often, as likely to be wrong as right. (p. 317)
Christmas Books. 1843-49. The Oxford Illustrated Dickens, Vol. XVI. Oxford: Oxford University Press, 1954.

Everybody's business is nobody's business.

1855 ...what is everybody's business is nobody's business.... (p. 459)
Address on Administrative Reform, London, 27 June 1855. *The Works of Charles Dickens: The Speeches*. Ed. Richard H. Shepherd. New National Edition, Vol. II. New York: Hearst's International Library Company, n. d.
APP 49; ODEP 231; EAP 51; MP 205; DAP 76.

Evil be to him who thinks evil.

1852-54 The King is said to have picked up a lady's garter at a ball, and to have said, *Honi soit qui mal y pense*—in English. "Evil be to him who evil think of it." (pp. 292-293)
Master Humphrey's Clock and A Child's History of England. 1840-41, 1852-54. The Oxford Illustrated Dickens, Vol. XX. Oxford: Oxford University Press, 1958.
ODEP 397; EAP 135; MP 315; DAP 186.

Never do **evil** that good may come of it.

1842 The maxim that out of evil cometh good is strongly illustrated by these establishments at home.... (p. 28)
American Notes and Pictures from Italy. 1842, 1846. The Oxford Illustrated Dickens, Vol. XIX. Oxford: Oxford University Press, 1957.
ODEP 562; EAP 137; MP 206; DAP 186.

Of two **evils** choose the less.

1850 ...of two evils, they prefer the less. (p. 201)
"Mr. Bendigo Buster on Our National Defences Against Education." [with Henry Morley]. *Charles Dickens' Uncollected Writings from* Household Words *1850-1859*, 2 vols. Ed. Harry Stone. Bloomington: Indiana University Press, 1968.
APP 122; ODEP 233; EAP 136; CODP 70; MP 206; DAP 186.

You won't reduce me to **extremities**.

1837 '...allow me to express a hope as you won't reduce me to extremities; in saying wich, I merely quote wot the nobleman said to the fractious pennywinkle, ven he wouldn't come out of his shell by means of a pin, and he conseqvently began to be afeerd that he should be obliged to crack him in the parlour-door.' (p. 541)
The Posthumous Papers of the Pickwick Club. 1837. The Oxford Illustrated Dickens, Vol. I. Oxford: Oxford University Press, 1948.

To be all one's **eye** and Betty Martin

1838 TOM: ...in plain English...it's all my eye and—yourself, Miss Martin. (*The Lamplighter*, I, ii, p. 127)
Complete Plays and Selected Poems of Charles Dickens. London: Vision Press, 1970.
APP 26; ODEP 10; EAP 30; MP 208.

To keep an **eye** on someone (something)

1836 MARTIN: I'll keep a sharp eye upon these doings.... (*The Village Coquettes*, I, i, p. 47)
1837 LOVETOWN: ...I must keep a sharp eye upon them.... (*Is She His Wife?*, I, p. 99)
Complete Plays and Selected Poems of Charles Dickens. London: Vision Press, 1970.
1839 Still keeping his eye on Nicholas, Mr. Crummles shook his head.... (p. 628)
The Life and Adventures of Nicholas Nickleby. 1839. The Oxford Illustrated Dickens, Vol. VI. Oxford: Oxford University Press, 1950.
1843 I shall not fail to keep a sharp eye on Horne. (p. 578)
The Letters of Charles Dickens: Volume Three: 1842-1843. Eds. Madeline House, Graham Storey, and Kathleen Tillotson. Oxford: The Clarendon Press, 1974.
1844 'Always got her eye upon her country, sir!' (p. 541)
The Life and Adventures of Martin Chuzzlewit. 1844. The Oxford Illustrated Dickens, Vol. IX. Oxford: Oxford University Press, 1951.
1845 'Keep your eye on the practical man!' (p. 98)
Christmas Books. 1843-49. The Oxford Illustrated Dickens, Vol. XVI. Oxford: Oxford University Press, 1954.
1846 ...keep your eye on me.... (p. 654)
The Letters of Charles Dickens: Volume Four: 1844-1846. Ed. Kathleen Tillotson. Oxford: The Clarendon Press, 1977.
1850 ...Miss Murdstone, still keeping her eye on the pickles.... (p. 136)
The Personal History of David Copperfield. 1850. The Oxford Illustrated Dickens, Vol. II. Oxford: Oxford University Press, 1948.
1853 ...he might keep a loving eye on the river.... (p. 458)
"Received, a Blank Child." [with W. H. Wills]. *Charles Dickens' Uncollected Writings from* Household Words *1850-1859*, 2 vols. Ed. Harry Stone. Bloomington: Indiana University Press, 1968.

1855 Are you keeping your eye on the Marylebone Theatre? (p. 506)
The Letters of Charles Dickens: Volume Seven: 1853-1855. Eds. Graham Storey, Kathleen Tillotson, and Angus Easson. Oxford: The Clarendon Press, 1993.
1865 ...he...kept his eye upon her silently. (p. 558)
Our Mutual Friend. 1865. The Oxford Illustrated Dickens, Vol. X. Oxford: Oxford University Press, 1952.
URDANG, *IDIOMS* 747.

To be up to the **eyebrows** in something

1849 I am steeped to the very eyebrows in glue and paste. (p. 473)
The Letters of Charles Dickens: Volume Five: 1847-1849. Eds. Graham Storey and K. J. Fielding. Oxford: The Clarendon Press, 1981.
URDANG, *IDIOMS* 421.

To be up to the **eyes** in something

1848 I am up to the eyes...in correspondence. (p. 314)
The Letters of Charles Dickens: Volume Five: 1847-1849. Eds. Graham Storey and K. J. Fielding. Oxford: The Clarendon Press, 1981.
URDANG, *IDIOMS* 422.

To keep one's **eyes** open

1833-36 '...keep your eyes open, and niver say die!' (p. 112)
Sketches by Boz. 1833-40. The Oxford Illustrated Dickens, Vol. XII. Oxford: Oxford University Press, 1957.
APP 124; EAP 140.

F

To be **face** to face

1850 ...having to sit there, face to face, for some hours.... (p. 9.)
1850 As I recall our being opposed thus, face to face.... (p. 46)
1850 '...he sat afore me, face to face....' (p. 454)
The Personal History of David Copperfield. 1850. The Oxford Illustrated Dickens, Vol. II. Oxford: Oxford University Press, 1948.
URDANG, *IDIOMS* 427.

To fly in the **face** of Providence

1857 '...don't fly in the face of providence by attempting to deny it!' (p. 369)

Little Dorrit. 1857. The Oxford Illustrated Dickens, Vol. XIV. Oxford: Oxford University Press, 1953.
APP 126; ODEP 270; EAP 142; MP 211.

To put a good **face** upon something

1839 ...he...put the best face upon the matter.... (p. 261)
1839 ...it was as well to put a good face upon the matter.... (p. 399)
The Life and Adventures of Nicholas Nickleby. 1839. The Oxford Illustrated Dickens, Vol. VI. Oxford: Oxford University Press, 1950.
ODEP 319; EAP 142.

To do something until one is black in the **face**

1833-36 The curate coughed till he was black in the face.... (p. 9)
Sketches by Boz. 1833-40. The Oxford Illustrated Dickens, Vol. XII. Oxford: Oxford University Press, 1957.
1837 "Suddenly he became black in the face...." (p. 469)
Sketches by Boz. 1833-40. The Oxford Illustrated Dickens, Vol. XII. Oxford: Oxford University Press, 1957.
1844 ...till he was black in the face. (p. 487)
The Life and Adventures of Martin Chuzzlewit. 1844. The Oxford Illustrated Dickens, Vol. IX. Oxford: Oxford University Press, 1951.
1854 '...with...nobility of this country applauding him till they were black in the face....' (p. 169)
Hard Times for These Times. 1854. The Oxford Illustrated Dickens, Vol. XVII. Oxford: Oxford University Press, 1955.
APP 126; ODEP 792; MP 212.

Fact and fiction

1847 ...through all the facts and fictions of this library, these ladies will always be active.... (p. 419)
Address at the opening of the Glasgow Athenaeum, 28 Dec. 1847. *The Works of Charles Dickens: The Speeches.* Ed. Richard H. Shepherd. New National Edition, Vol. II. New York: Hearst's International Library Company, n. d.
1854 "I...am so divided this night between fact and fiction...." (p. 77)
Christmas Stories. 1871. The Oxford Illustrated Dickens, Vol. XI. Oxford: Oxford University Press, 1956.
APP 127; ODEP 844; CODP 75; DAP 194.

Fact or fancy

1853 ...we must close it up with such matter of fact or fancy.... (p. 36)
The Letters of Charles Dickens: Volume Seven: 1853-1855. Eds. Graham Storey, Kathleen Tillotson, and Angus Easson. Oxford: The Clarendon Press, 1993.

Facts and figures

1845 'A man...may heap up facts on figures...mountains high and dry....' (p. 98)

1845 Facts and Figures, Facts and Figures! (p. 100)

1845 'Facts and Figures, Facts and Figures!' (p. 103)

Christmas Books. 1843-49. The Oxford Illustrated Dickens, Vol. XVI. Oxford: Oxford University Press, 1954.

1846 ...I could...ascertain, by facts and figures.... (p. 527)

The Letters of Charles Dickens: Volume Four: 1844-1846. Ed. Kathleen Tillotson. Oxford: The Clarendon Press, 1977.

1854 'I wish I could collect all the Facts...and all the Figures....' (p. 52)

Hard Times for These Times. 1854. The Oxford Illustrated Dickens, Vol. XVII. Oxford: Oxford University Press, 1955.

1870 You know upon an old authority, that you may believe anything except facts and figures.... (p. 586)

Address to the Newsvendors' Benevolent and Provident Institution, London, 5 Apr. 1870. *The Works of Charles Dickens: The Speeches.* Ed. Richard H. Shepherd. New National Edition, Vol. II. New York: Hearst's International Library Company, n. d.

STEVENSON 742:4.

Facts are stubborn things.

1854 Stubborn things Facts are stubborn things (p. 251)

Dickens' Working Notes for His Novels. Ed. Harry Stone. Chicago, Ill.: University of Chicago Press, 1987.

ODEP 238; EAP 143; CODP 238; MP 212; DAP 194.

Now, gen'l'm'n, **fall on.**

1837 'Now, gen'l'm'n, "fall on," as the English said to the French when they fixed bagginets.' (p. 255)

The Posthumous Papers of the Pickwick Club. 1837. The Oxford Illustrated Dickens, Vol. I. Oxford: Oxford University Press, 1948.

DOW 42.

To run in the **family**

1837 'It runs in the family, I b'lieve, sir,' replied Mr. Weller. (p. 209)

The Posthumous Papers of the Pickwick Club. 1837. The Oxford Illustrated Dickens, Vol. I. Oxford: Oxford University Press, 1948.

URDANG, *IDIOMS* 432.

Far and near

1854 Thus Christmas begirt me, far and near.... (p. 94)

Christmas Stories. 1871. The Oxford Illustrated Dickens, Vol. XI. Oxford: Oxford University Press, 1956.
URDANG, *IDIOMS* 433.

Far and wide

1848 Here was the little society...scattered far and wide. (pp. 456-457)
Dealings with the Firm of Dombey and Son. 1848. The Oxford Illustrated Dickens, Vol. VII. Oxford: Oxford University Press, 1950.
1852-54 This touching action...is famous far and wide.... (p. 426)
Master Humphrey's Clock and A Child's History of England. 1840-41, 1852-54. The Oxford Illustrated Dickens, Vol. XX. Oxford: Oxford University Press, 1958.
URDANG, *IDIOMS* 433.

So **far**, so good.

1850 'So far so good.' (p. 512)
The Personal History of David Copperfield. 1850. The Oxford Illustrated Dickens, Vol. II. Oxford: Oxford University Press, 1948.
APP 127; ODEP 749; EAP 144; MP 214.

Fast and loose

1853 'Fast and loose in one thing, Fast and loose in everything.' (pp. 775-776)
Bleak House. 1853. The Oxford Illustrated Dickens, Vol. III. Oxford: Oxford University Press, 1948.
1854 'You didn't take your wife for fast and for loose....' (p. 75)
Hard Times for These Times. 1854. The Oxford Illustrated Dickens, Vol. XVII. Oxford: Oxford University Press, 1955.
APP 127; ODEP 630; EAP 145; MP 215.

Every man has his **faults**.

1848 'We all have our faults,' said Mrs. Chick.... (p. 48)
Dealings with the Firm of Dombey and Son. 1848. The Oxford Illustrated Dickens, Vol. VII. Oxford: Oxford University Press, 1950.
ODEP 229; DAP 201.

To be a **feather** in one's cap

1869 ...a tenacity that makes the beating of them a new feather in the proudest cap. (p. 565)
Toast to the crews of the International University Boat Race, Sydenham, 30 Aug. 1869. *The Works of Charles Dickens: The Speeches*. Ed. Richard H. Shepherd. New National Edition, Vol. II. New York: Hearst's International Library Company, n. d.

APP 129; ODEP 251; EAP 147; MP 217.

To be in high feather

1844 Todgers's was in high feather.... (p. 826)
The Life and Adventures of Martin Chuzzlewit. 1844. The Oxford Illustrated Dickens, Vol. IX. Oxford: Oxford University Press, 1951.

1849 I won't say how long I intend to give you to grow into full business feather.... (p. 583)
The Letters of Charles Dickens: Volume Five: 1847-1849. Eds. Graham Storey and K. J. Fielding. Oxford: The Clarendon Press, 1981.

1861 'He's in wonderful feather.' (p. 245)
Great Expectations. 1861. The Oxford Illustrated Dickens, Vol. XIII. Oxford: Oxford University Press, 1953.

APP 129; MP 218.

To be knocked down with a feather

1841 '...you might knock me down with a feather.' (p. 316)
Barnaby Rudge: A Tale of the Riots of 'Eighty. 1841. The Oxford Illustrated Dickens, Vol. XV. Oxford: Oxford University Press, 1954.

1844 'Bring a feather, somebody, and knock me down with it!' (p. 831)
The Life and Adventures of Martin Chuzzlewit. 1844. The Oxford Illustrated Dickens, Vol. IX. Oxford: Oxford University Press, 1951.

1851 GABBLEWIG: You might knock me down with a feather. (*Mr. Nightingale's Diary*, I, i, p. 145)
Complete Plays and Selected Poems of Charles Dickens. London: Vision Press, 1970.

APP 130; EAP 148; MP 218.

By a feather's weight

1845 ...the second is not affected by a hair's-breadth or a feather's weight. (p. 428)
The Letters of Charles Dickens: Volume Four: 1844-1846. Ed. Kathleen Tillotson. Oxford: The Clarendon Press, 1977.

To be off one's feed

1839 '...a sort of rash...rather puts 'em off their feed.' (p. 740)
The Life and Adventures of Nicholas Nickleby. 1839. The Oxford Illustrated Dickens, Vol. VI. Oxford: Oxford University Press, 1950.

APP 130; MP 218.

The feeling does you honour.

1837 'The feeling does you a great deal of honour,' replied Mr. Pickwick.... (p. 215)
The Posthumous Papers of the Pickwick Club. 1837. The Oxford Illustrated Dickens, Vol. I. Oxford: Oxford University Press, 1948.

Few and far between

1870 'I merely refer to my visits, which are few and far between.' (p. 85)
The Mystery of Edwin Drood. 1870. The Oxford Illustrated Dickens, Vol. XVIII. Oxford: Oxford University Press, 1956.
URDANG, *IDIOMS* 444.

To play first (second) **fiddle**

1844 To say that Tom had no idea of playing first fiddle in any social orchestra, but was always quite satisfied to be set down for the hundred and fiftieth violin in the band, or thereabouts, is to express his modesty in very inadequate terms. (p. 193)
The Life and Adventures of Martin Chuzzlewit. 1844. The Oxford Illustrated Dickens, Vol. IX. Oxford: Oxford University Press, 1951.

1850 Even Paxton must be second-fiddle.... (p. 166)
The Letters of Charles Dickens: Volume Six: 1850-1852. Eds. Madeline House, Graham Storey, and Kathleen Tillotson. Oxford: The Clarendon Press, 1988.
APP 131; ODEP 630; MP 220.

To laugh like a **fiend**

1841 ...he merely achieved that performance which is designated in melodramas 'laughing like a fiend....' (p. 414)
The Old Curiosity Shop. 1841. The Oxford Illustrated Dickens, Vol. VIII. Oxford: Oxford University Press, 1951.

As **fierce** as a bull

1833-36 ...says the master, as fierce as a bull in fits. (p. 28)
Sketches by Boz. 1833-40. The Oxford Illustrated Dickens, Vol. XII. Oxford: Oxford University Press, 1957.
EAP 48.

As **fierce** as a lion

1839 '...he was as fierce as a lion and as bold as brass....' (p. 69)

The Life and Adventures of Nicholas Nickleby. 1839. The Oxford Illustrated Dickens, Vol. VI. Oxford: Oxford University Press, 1950.
APP 224; MP 378.

A **fig** for something

1841 'A fig for Time, sir.' (p. 198)
1841 'A fig for 'em all....' (p. 305)
Barnaby Rudge: A Tale of the Riots of 'Eighty. 1841. The Oxford Illustrated Dickens, Vol. XV. Oxford: Oxford University Press, 1954.
APP 131; ODEP 255; EAP 149; MP 221.

(Not) to care a **fig**

1858 ...he never cared a fig for them.... (pp. 603-604)
"A House to Let." [with Wilkie Collins]. *Charles Dickens' Uncollected Writings from Household Words 1850-1859*, 2 vols. Ed. Harry Stone. Bloomington: Indiana University Press, 1968.
APP 132; EAP 150; MP 221.

To cut a **figure**

1836 STRANGE GENTLEMAN: A pretty figure I should cut before the old people.... (*The Strange Gentleman*, I, 1, p. 12)
Complete Plays and Selected Poems of Charles Dickens. London: Vision Press, 1970.
1848 'And a pretty figure he cuts with it for his pains,' returned the Uncle. (p. 35)
Dealings with the Firm of Dombey and Son. 1848. The Oxford Illustrated Dickens, Vol. VII. Oxford: Oxford University Press, 1950.
1852-54 Then she...cut...a mighty ridiculous figure.... (p. 434)
Master Humphrey's Clock and A Child's History of England. 1840-41, 1852-54. The Oxford Illustrated Dickens, Vol. XX. Oxford: Oxford University Press, 1958.
APP 132.

To be a fine (handsome) **figure** of a woman (man)

1861 '...your sister is a fine figure of a woman.' (p. 43)
1861 '...your sister is...a—fine—figure—of—a—woman!' (p. 43)
1861 '...you know'd her when she were a fine figure of a —....' (p. 265)
Great Expectations. 1861. The Oxford Illustrated Dickens, Vol. XIII. Oxford: Oxford University Press, 1953.
1863 He was a handsome figure of a man.... (p. 370)
Christmas Stories. 1871. The Oxford Illustrated Dickens, Vol. XI. Oxford: Oxford University Press, 1956.

URDANG, *IDIOMS* 450.

Placing one's **finger** beside the nose signifies a confidence.

1860 ...says Bullfinch, with his forefinger at his nose. (p. 332)
The Uncommercial Traveller and Reprinted Pieces Etc. 1850-1860. The Oxford Illustrated Dickens, Vol. XXI. Oxford: Oxford University Press, 1958.

To burn one's **finger**

1866 ...Mitchell, having of yore burnt his fingers a good deal.... (p. 458)
The Letters of Charles Dickens, ed. Walter Dexter. Vol. III: 1858-1870. The Nonesuch Dickens. London: The Nonesuch Press, 1938.
ODEP 259; EAP 151; MP 223.

To have one's **finger** in the pie

1852 Miss Coutts is...far from objecting to having Tennant's finger in the Sanitary pie in this stage of its baking.... (p. 816)
The Letters of Charles Dickens: Volume Six: 1850-1852. Eds. Madeline House, Graham Storey, and Kathleen Tillotson. Oxford: The Clarendon Press, 1988.
APP 133; ODEP 258; EAP 151; MP 224.

To wind someone around one's little **finger**

1844 '...I can wind him round my little finger.' (p. 479)
The Life and Adventures of Martin Chuzzlewit. 1844. The Oxford Illustrated Dickens, Vol. IX. Oxford: Oxford University Press, 1951.
1864 ...I could draw the Major out like a thread and wind him round my finger.... (p. 416)
Christmas Stories. 1871. The Oxford Illustrated Dickens, Vol. XI. Oxford: Oxford University Press, 1956.
APP 133; ODEP 847; EAP 152; MP 224.

To slip through one's **fingers**

1836 ...they should be *very sorry to let it slip through their hands.* (p. 163)
The Letters of Charles Dickens: Volume One: 1820-1839. Eds. Madeline House and Graham Storey. Oxford: The Clarendon Press, 1965.
1861 Mr. Jaggers was...angry at me for having 'let it slip through my fingers....' (p. 425)
Great Expectations. 1861. The Oxford Illustrated Dickens, Vol. XIII. Oxford: Oxford University Press, 1953.

APP 133; EAP 152.

Fire is a good servant but a bad master.

1841 'Fire, as the saying goes, is a good servant, but a bad master.' (p. 407)

Barnaby Rudge: A Tale of the Riots of 'Eighty. 1841. The Oxford Illustrated Dickens, Vol. XV. Oxford: Oxford University Press, 1954.

APP 134; ODEP 259; EAP 153; MP 225; DAP 209.

First and foremost

1838 'First and foremost, Faguey,' said Toby. (p. 182)

The Adventures of Oliver Twist. 1838. The Oxford Illustrated Dickens, Vol. V. Oxford: Oxford University Press, 1948.

URDANG, *IDIOMS* 455.

First come, first served.

1863 ...there is but one note to be observed, and that is, First come first served. (p. 333)

The Letters of Charles Dickens, ed. Walter Dexter. Vol. III: 1858-1870. The Nonesuch Dickens. London: The Nonesuch Press, 1938.

APP 77; ODEP 262; EAP 80; CODP 81; MP 128; DAP 211.

All is (not) **fish** that comes to the net.

1853 'And all's fish that comes to my net.' (p. 52)

Bleak House. 1853. The Oxford Illustrated Dickens, Vol. III. Oxford: Oxford University Press, 1948.

APP 135; ODEP 264; EAP 154; DAP 211.

Fish and flattery

1837 ...Mr. Tupman and the spinster aunt established a joint-stock company of fish and flattery. (p. 70)

The Posthumous Papers of the Pickwick Club. 1837. The Oxford Illustrated Dickens, Vol. I. Oxford: Oxford University Press, 1948.

To gasp like a **fish**

1846 'Why he's gasping like a gold and silver fish!' (p. 164)

Christmas Books. 1843-49. The Oxford Illustrated Dickens, Vol. XVI. Oxford: Oxford University Press, 1954.

WILSTACH 168.

Fits and starts

1844 ...he had...deemed him energetic only by fits and starts.... (p. 523)
The Life and Adventures of Martin Chuzzlewit. 1844. The Oxford Illustrated Dickens, Vol. IX. Oxford: Oxford University Press, 1951.

1846 ...it...shining on the leaves by fits and starts, made them look as if.... (p. 282)
Christmas Books. 1843-49. The Oxford Illustrated Dickens, Vol. XVI. Oxford: Oxford University Press, 1954.

1853 '...real success...ever was or could be...wrested from Fortune by fits and starts....' (p. 180)
Bleak House. 1853. The Oxford Illustrated Dickens, Vol. III. Oxford: Oxford University Press, 1948.

1866 "...it has been there, now and again, by fits and starts." (p. 532)
Christmas Stories. 1871. The Oxford Illustrated Dickens, Vol. XI. Oxford: Oxford University Press, 1956.

URDANG, *IDIOMS* 458.

To be a flash in the pan

1853 'A flash in the pan, or a shot?' (p. 472)
Bleak House. 1853. The Oxford Illustrated Dickens, Vol. III. Oxford: Oxford University Press, 1948.

EAP 156; MP 230.

As flat as a warming pan

1854 '...I was as flat as a warming pan....' (p. 135)
Hard Times for These Times. 1854. The Oxford Illustrated Dickens, Vol. XVII. Oxford: Oxford University Press, 1955.

All flesh is grass.

1853 And he is making hay of the grass which is flesh.... (p. 548)
Bleak House. 1853. The Oxford Illustrated Dickens, Vol. III. Oxford: Oxford University Press, 1948.

APP 138; EAP 157; MP 232; DAP 215.

Flesh and blood

1838 ...mere flesh and blood, no more—but such flesh, and so much blood! (p. 363)
The Adventures of Oliver Twist. 1838. The Oxford Illustrated Dickens, Vol. V. Oxford: Oxford University Press, 1948.

1839 '...there is not hardihood enough in flesh and blood to face it out.' (p. 250)

1839 'Yes, here he is, flesh and blood, flesh and blood.' (p. 588)

1839 'That master's cruel treatment of his own flesh and blood....' (p. 774)

The Life and Adventures of Nicholas Nickleby. 1839. The Oxford Illustrated Dickens, Vol. VI. Oxford: Oxford University Press, 1950.

1842 ...I couldn't accept them: being of mere flesh and blood.... (p. 146)

The Letters of Charles Dickens: Volume Three: 1842-1843. Eds. Madeline House, Graham Storey, and Kathleen Tillotson. Oxford: The Clarendon Press, 1974.

1844 ...he substituted 'flesh and blood'. (p. 14)

1844 ...as far as Mark's flesh and blood were concerned.... (p. 113)

1844 'And your own flesh and blood might come to want too...?' (p. 299)

1844 ...steel and iron are of infinitely greater account...than flesh and blood. (p. 341)

1844 ...it was in the nature of flesh and blood.... (p. 623)

The Life and Adventures of Martin Chuzzlewit. 1844. The Oxford Illustrated Dickens, Vol. IX. Oxford: Oxford University Press, 1951.

1848 'He warn't my flesh and blood,' said the Captain.... (p. 463)

Dealings with the Firm of Dombey and Son. 1848. The Oxford Illustrated Dickens, Vol. VII. Oxford: Oxford University Press, 1950.

1850 'My flesh and blood...when it rises against me, is not my flesh and blood.' (p. 82)

The Personal History of David Copperfield. 1850. The Oxford Illustrated Dickens, Vol. II. Oxford: Oxford University Press, 1948.

1853 No, it's...fair flesh and blood.... (p. 469)

1853 ...to make D better satisfied with his flesh and blood.... (p. 522)

1853 'Real flesh and blood....Real flesh and blood, Miss Dedlock' (p. 572)

1853 'He is no more like flesh and blood, than a rusty old carbine is.' (p. 643)

Bleak House. 1853. The Oxford Illustrated Dickens, Vol. III. Oxford: Oxford University Press, 1948.

1855 ...all horses in existence were of flesh and blood. (p. 536)

"By Rail to Parnassus." [with Henry Morley]. *Charles Dickens' Uncollected Writings from Household Words 1850-1859*, 2 vols. Ed. Harry Stone. Bloomington: Indiana University Press, 1968.

1864 ...to think of the brains of my poor dear Lirriper's own flesh and blood flying about the new oilcloth.... (p. 408)

Christmas Stories. 1871. The Oxford Illustrated Dickens, Vol. XI. Oxford: Oxford University Press, 1956.

1865 'Flesh and blood can't bear it.' (p. 581)

Our Mutual Friend. 1865. The Oxford Illustrated Dickens, Vol. X. Oxford: Oxford University Press, 1952.

URDANG, *IDIOMS* 462.

Flesh is weak.

1844 '...there's a wooden leg...was quite as weak as flesh, if not weaker.' (p. 625)
The Life and Adventures of Martin Chuzzlewit. 1844. The Oxford Illustrated Dickens, Vol. IX. Oxford: Oxford University Press, 1951.

As **flimsy** as a banknote

1850 ...her works are the reverse of heavy or erudite—being "flimsy" to a proverb.... (p. 128)
"The Old Lady in Threadneedle Street." [with W. H. Wills].
1850 Flimsy as a Bank note is to a proverb.... (p. 159)
"Two Chapters on Bank Note Forgeries: Chapter II." [with W. H. Wills]. *Charles Dickens' Uncollected Writings from* Household Words *1850-1859*, 2 vols. Ed. Harry Stone. Bloomington: Indiana University Press, 1968.
PARTRIDGE 287.

To be able to eat off the **floor** because of its cleanness

1848 'You might eat your dinner off the floor.' (pp. 13-14)
Dealings with the Firm of Dombey and Son. 1848. The Oxford Illustrated Dickens, Vol. VII. Oxford: Oxford University Press, 1950.
APP 139; MP 232.

A **fly** in the jug

1841 'Positively a fly in the jug.' (p. 115)
Barnaby Rudge: A Tale of the Riots of 'Eighty. 1841. The Oxford Illustrated Dickens, Vol. XV. Oxford: Oxford University Press, 1954.
MP 234.

Not to hurt a **fly**

1865 'Wouldn't have hurt a fly!' (p. 663)
Our Mutual Friend. 1865. The Oxford Illustrated Dickens, Vol. X. Oxford: Oxford University Press, 1952.
MP 234.

To be **fond** of someone (-thing)

1837 ...I am—to use a scotch expression—very fond of him. (pp. 277-278)

The Letters of Charles Dickens: Volume One: 1820-1839. Eds. Madeline House and Graham Storey. Oxford: The Clarendon Press, 1965.
SPEARS 101.

By the **foot** of Pharaoh

1845 By the foot of Pharaoh, it was a great scene! (p. 351)
The Letters of Charles Dickens: Volume Four: 1844-1846. Ed. Kathleen Tillotson. Oxford: The Clarendon Press, 1977.

To put one's **foot** in it

1837 ...Tom...always managed to put his foot in it.... (p. 359)
Sketches by Boz. 1833-40. The Oxford Illustrated Dickens, Vol. XII. Oxford: Oxford University Press, 1957.
APP 143; EAP 163; MP 239.

To be behind the **footlights**

1837 '...to be behind them [the footlights] is to be...left to sink or swim...as fortune wills it.' (p. 34)
The Posthumous Papers of the Pickwick Club. 1837. The Oxford Illustrated Dickens, Vol. I. Oxford: Oxford University Press, 1948.
URDANG, *IDIOMS* 473.

To follow in someone's **footsteps**

1841 '...my friend is following fast in the footsteps of his mother.' (p. 306)
Barnaby Rudge: A Tale of the Riots of 'Eighty. 1841. The Oxford Illustrated Dickens, Vol. XV. Oxford: Oxford University Press, 1954.
WILKINSON 208.

To act through **force** of habit

1833-36 "The force of habit" is a trite phrase in everybody's mouth.... (p. 201)
Sketches by Boz. 1833-40. The Oxford Illustrated Dickens, Vol. XII. Oxford: Oxford University Press, 1957.

Forewarned is forearmed.

1850 ...forewarned is forearmed. (p. 202)
"Mr. Bendigo Buster on Our National Defences Against Education." [with Henry Morley].*Charles Dickens' Uncollected Writings from* Household Words *1850-1859*, 2 vols. Ed. Harry Stone. Bloomington: Indiana University Press, 1968.

APP 144; ODEP 280; EAP 164; CODP 86; MP 239; DAP 228.

Forget and forgive.

1846 'It says...For-get and For-give.' (p. 255)
1846 'Do as you would be done by! Forget and Forgive!' (p. 311)
Christmas Books. 1843-49. The Oxford Illustrated Dickens, Vol. XVI. Oxford: Oxford University Press, 1954.
1849 ...you would have forgotten and forgiven all. (p. 476)
The Letters of Charles Dickens: Volume Five: 1847-1849. Eds. Graham Storey and K. J. Fielding. Oxford: The Clarendon Press, 1981.
APP 144; ODEP 281; EAP 164; MP 239; DAP 228.

As **free** as a bird

1841 '...we'll...be as free and happy as the birds.' (p. 94)
The Old Curiosity Shop. 1841. The Oxford Illustrated Dickens, Vol. VIII. Oxford: Oxford University Press, 1951.
APP 27; ODEP 286; MP 46.

As **free** as the air

1853 'I am as free as the air.' (p. 829)
Bleak House. 1853. The Oxford Illustrated Dickens, Vol. III. Oxford: Oxford University Press, 1948.
APP 4; ODEP 286; EAP 6; MP 7.

Free and easy

1841 ...none of your free-and-easy companions.... (p. 75)
Barnaby Rudge: A Tale of the Riots of 'Eighty. 1841. The Oxford Illustrated Dickens, Vol. XV. Oxford: Oxford University Press, 1954.
1842 He is a free-and-easy...kind of pig.... (p. 86)
American Notes and Pictures from Italy. 1842, 1846. The Oxford Illustrated Dickens, Vol. XIX. Oxford: Oxford University Press, 1957.
1844 '...it was something in the...free-and-easy way again.' (p. 217)
The Life and Adventures of Martin Chuzzlewit. 1844. The Oxford Illustrated Dickens, Vol. IX. Oxford: Oxford University Press, 1951.
1846 ...I was...mighty free and easy.... (p. 634)
The Letters of Charles Dickens: Volume Four: 1844-1846. Ed. Kathleen Tillotson. Oxford: The Clarendon Press, 1977.
1851 Title: A Free (and Easy) School (p. 351)
"A Free (and Easy) School." [with Henry Morley]. *Charles Dickens' Uncollected Writings from Household Words 1850-1859*, 2 vols. Ed. Harry Stone. Bloomington: Indiana University Press, 1968.
ODEP 286.

Free, gratis, and for nothing

1837 '...people o' the same purfession, as sets people by the ears, free gratis for nothin'....' (p. 362)

The Posthumous Papers of the Pickwick Club. 1837. The Oxford Illustrated Dickens, Vol. I. Oxford: Oxford University Press, 1948.

To attend a free-and-easy

1850-56 "'I was dining over at Lambeth the other day, at a free-and-easy....'" (p. 506)

The Uncommercial Traveller and Reprinted Pieces Etc. 1850-1860. The Oxford Illustrated Dickens, Vol. XXI. Oxford: Oxford University Press, 1958.
PARTRIDGE 300.

Frenchmen are slender.

1850 ...all [Frenchmen] are of very slender proportions in figure; ...their staple diet is frogs; and...they very much prefer to dance than to fight.... (p. 150)

"Foreigners' Portraits of Englishmen." [with W. H. Wills and E. C. Grenville Murray]. *Charles Dickens' Uncollected Writings from* Household Words *1850-1859*, 2 vols. Ed. Harry Stone. Bloomington: Indiana University Press, 1968.

Frenchmen are frog-eaters.

1850 ...all [Frenchmen] are of very slender proportions in figure; ...their staple diet is frogs; and...they very much prefer to dance than to fight.... (p. 150)

"Foreigners' Portraits of Englishmen." [with W. H. Wills and E. C. Grenville Murray]. *Charles Dickens' Uncollected Writings from* Household Words *1850-1859*, 2 vols. Ed. Harry Stone. Bloomington: Indiana University Press, 1968.
1850-56 ...the French are a frog-eating people.... (p. 589)
1850-56 ...but the French are a frog-eating people.... (p. 591)

The Uncommercial Traveller and Reprinted Pieces Etc. 1850-1860. The Oxford Illustrated Dickens, Vol. XXI. Oxford: Oxford University Press, 1958.
URDANG, *IDIOMS* 494.

Frenchmen would rather dance than fight.

1850 ...all [Frenchmen] are of very slender proportions in figure; ...their staple diet is frogs; and...they very much prefer to dance than to fight.... (p. 150)

"Foreigners' Portraits of Englishmen." [with W. H. Wills and E. C. Grenville Murray]. *Charles Dickens' Uncollected Writings from* Household Words *1850-1859*, 2 vols. Ed. Harry Stone. Bloomington: Indiana University Press, 1968.

As **fresh** as a daisy

1846 ...she presently came bouncing back,—the saying is, as fresh as a daisy.... (pp. 202-203)
Christmas Books. 1843-49. The Oxford Illustrated Dickens, Vol. XVI. Oxford: Oxford University Press, 1954.
1850 'The daisy of the field at sunrise, is not fresher than you are.' (p. 288)
The Personal History of David Copperfield. 1850. The Oxford Illustrated Dickens, Vol. II. Oxford: Oxford University Press, 1948.
1864 So I come back as fresh as a daisy.... (p. 403)
The Letters of Charles Dickens, ed. Walter Dexter. Vol. III: 1858-1870. The Nonesuch Dickens. London: The Nonesuch Press, 1938.
ODEP 287; MP 147.

As **fresh** as a lark

1853 '...I have been as fresh as a lark!' (p. 104)
Bleak House. 1853. The Oxford Illustrated Dickens, Vol. III. Oxford: Oxford University Press, 1948.
APP 214; MP 360.

As **fresh** as a rose

1853 ...she looks as fresh as a rose.... (p. 385)
Bleak House. 1853. The Oxford Illustrated Dickens, Vol. III. Oxford: Oxford University Press, 1948.
APP 312; ODEP 287; EAP 371; MP 538.

As **fresh** as butter

1865 'Driver says he's as fresh as butter.' (p. 251)
Our Mutual Friend. 1865. The Oxford Illustrated Dickens, Vol. X. Oxford: Oxford University Press, 1952.
WILSTACH 161 (CITING DICKENS).

A **friend** in need is a friend indeed.

1850 '...you are friends in need, and friends indeed.' (p. 705)
The Personal History of David Copperfield. 1850. The Oxford Illustrated Dickens, Vol. II. Oxford: Oxford University Press, 1948.
APP 146; ODEP 289; EAP 168; CODP 87; MP 242; DAP 233.

Friendship is friendship.

1853 'Duty is duty, and friendship is friendship.' (p. 677)

Bleak House. 1853. The Oxford Illustrated Dickens, Vol. III. Oxford: Oxford University Press, 1948.

G

The **game** is not worth the candle.

1867 ...I do not clearly see the game to be worth so large a candle. (pp. 531-532)
The Letters of Charles Dickens, ed. Walter Dexter. Vol. III: 1858-1870. The Nonesuch Dickens. London: The Nonesuch Press, 1938.
APP 150; ODEP 295; EAP 172; MP 248; DAP 82.

Gammon and spinach

1838 'Toor rul lol loo, gammon and spinach....' (p. 83)
The Adventures of Oliver Twist. 1838. The Oxford Illustrated Dickens, Vol. V. Oxford: Oxford University Press, 1948.
1850 'What a world of gammon and spinnage it is, though, ain't it!' (p. 329)
The Personal History of David Copperfield. 1850. The Oxford Illustrated Dickens, Vol. II. Oxford: Oxford University Press, 1948.
PARTRIDGE 314 (CITING DICKENS).

To be all **gammon**

1836 STRANGE GENTLEMAN: ...that's all gammon and nonsense.... (*The Strange Gentleman*, I, i, p. 8)
Complete Plays and Selected Poems of Charles Dickens. London: Vision Press, 1970.
1838 Your agreement is—in Wellerian phraseology—gammon. (p. 359)
The Letters of Charles Dickens: Volume One: 1820-1839. Eds. Madeline House and Graham Storey. Oxford: The Clarendon Press, 1965.
PARTRIDGE 314.

All is **gas and gaiters**.

1839 '...all is gas and gaiters!' (p. 648)
The Life and Adventures of Nicholas Nickleby. 1839. The Oxford Illustrated Dickens, Vol. VI. Oxford: Oxford University Press, 1950.
MP 8.

To throw down the **gauntlet**

1842 ...the Great Writers...have...flung their gauntlets down.... (p. 219)

The Letters of Charles Dickens: Volume Three: 1842-1843. Eds. Madeline House, Graham Storey, and Kathleen Tillotson. Oxford: The Clarendon Press, 1974.

1846 My hat shall ever be ready to be thrown up, and my glove ever ready to be thrown down.... (p. 661)

The Letters of Charles Dickens: Volume Four: 1844-1846. Ed. Kathleen Tillotson. Oxford: The Clarendon Press, 1977.

APP 151; ODEP 689; EAP 173; MP 250.

As **gay** as a butterfly

1850 'I want our pet to...be as gay as a butterfly.' (p. 638)

The Personal History of David Copperfield. 1850. The Oxford Illustrated Dickens, Vol. II. Oxford: Oxford University Press, 1948.

MP 85.

As **gay** as a lark

1848 'We'll be as gay as larks....' (p. 259)

Dealings with the Firm of Dombey and Son. 1848. The Oxford Illustrated Dickens, Vol. VII. Oxford: Oxford University Press, 1950.

APP 214; ODEP 527; EAP 252; MP 360.

Every man thinks his **geese** are swans.

1846 'Every man thinks his own geese swans,' observed the Toy-merchant....' (p. 189)

Christmas Books. 1843-49. The Oxford Illustrated Dickens, Vol. XVI. Oxford: Oxford University Press, 1954.

APP 156; ODEP 298; EAP 182; MP 263; DAP 262.

*Les **gens** de qualité savent tous, sans avoir jamais rien appris.*

1850 What says the comedian? 'Les gens de qualité savent tous, sans avoir jamais rien appris.' (People of quality know everything without ever learning anything.) (p. 202)

"Mr. Bendigo Buster on Our National Defences Against Education." [with Henry Morley]. *Charles Dickens' Uncollected Writings from* Household Words *1850-1859*, 2 vols. Ed. Harry Stone. Bloomington: Indiana University Press, 1968.

(Not) to have the **ghost** of a chance

1837 ...you have not the shade of a chance. (p. 298)

The Letters of Charles Dickens: Volume One: 1820-1839. Eds. Madeline House and Graham Storey. Oxford: The Clarendon Press, 1965.

1837 'Chances be d----d,' replied Price; 'he hasn't half the ghost of one.' (p. 564)
The Posthumous Papers of the Pickwick Club. 1837. The Oxford Illustrated Dickens, Vol. I. Oxford: Oxford University Press, 1948.
URDANG, *IDIOMS* 521.

As **giddy** as a drunken man

1843 'I am as light as a feather, I am as happy as an angel, I am as merry as a schoolboy. I am as giddy as a drunken man.' (p. 71)
Christmas Books. 1843-49. The Oxford Illustrated Dickens, Vol. XVI. Oxford: Oxford University Press, 1954.

To have the **gift** of the gab

1837 'Worn't one o' these chaps...with...the gift o' the gab wery gallopin'?' (p. 271)
The Posthumous Papers of the Pickwick Club. 1837. The Oxford Illustrated Dickens, Vol. I. Oxford: Oxford University Press, 1948.
ODEP 301; EAP 175; MP 252.

Give and take

1837 TAPKINS: Here, give and take is all fair, you know. (*Is She His Wife?*, I, p. 111)
Complete Plays and Selected Poems of Charles Dickens. London: Vision Press, 1970.
1848 '...it's a give and take affair.' (p. 363)
Dealings with the Firm of Dombey and Son. 1848. The Oxford Illustrated Dickens, Vol. VII. Oxford: Oxford University Press, 1950.
APP 152; ODEP 303; EAP 176; MP 253.

God (Heaven) only knows.

1835 ...when it will be done God only knows. (p. 86)
The Letters of Charles Dickens: Volume One: 1820-1839. Eds. Madeline House and Graham Storey. Oxford: The Clarendon Press, 1965.
1843 ...how many boats would cross...the Atlantic...Heaven only knows. (p. 596)
The Letters of Charles Dickens: Volume Three: 1842-1843. Eds. Madeline House, Graham Storey, and Kathleen Tillotson. Oxford: The Clarendon Press, 1974.
URDANG, *IDIOMS* 540.

All that glitters is not **gold**.

1841 "That which glitters is not always gold...." (p. 625)
The Uncommercial Traveller and Reprinted Pieces Etc. 1850-1860. The Oxford Illustrated
Dickens, Vol. XXI. Oxford: Oxford University Press, 1958.
APP 154; ODEP 316; EAP 181; CODP 92; MP 9; DAP 256.

The **Golden Age**

1850-56 ...of course it was in a Golden Age.... (p. 544)
1860 A happy Golden Age, and a serene tranquillity. (p. 168)
The Uncommercial Traveller and Reprinted Pieces Etc. 1850-1860. The Oxford Illustrated
Dickens, Vol. XXI. Oxford: Oxford University Press, 1958.
1857 To come out of the shop...was...the Golden Age revived. (p. 574)
Little Dorrit. 1857. The Oxford Illustrated Dickens, Vol. XIV. Oxford: Oxford University
Press, 1953.
URDANG, *IDIOMS* 543; STEVENSON 47:3-11.

A **Golden Rule**

1840-41 ...he gave them golden rules for discovering witches.... (p. 58)
Master Humphrey's Clock and A Child's History of England. 1840-41, 1852-54. The
Oxford Illustrated Dickens, Vol. XX. Oxford: Oxford University Press, 1958.
1846 '...she'd find it to be the golden rule of half her clients.' (p. 256)
Christmas Books. 1843-49. The Oxford Illustrated Dickens, Vol. XVI. Oxford: Oxford
University Press, 1954.
1857 '...there is his golden rule.' (p. 802)
Little Dorrit. 1857. The Oxford Illustrated Dickens, Vol. XIV. Oxford: Oxford University
Press, 1953.
URDANG, *IDIOMS* 543; BARTLETT 34:NOTE 1.

As **good** as a play

1838 '...it's as good as a play—as good as a play!' (p. 37)
The Adventures of Oliver Twist. 1838. The Oxford Illustrated Dickens, Vol. V. Oxford:
Oxford University Press, 1948.
1841 '...they was as clear as a bell, and as good as a play.' (p. 502)
Barnaby Rudge: A Tale of the Riots of 'Eighty. 1841. The Oxford Illustrated Dickens, Vol.
XV. Oxford: Oxford University Press, 1954.
APP 289; ODEP 317; MP 500.

As **good** as gold

1841 There was the baby...who had sat as good as gold.... (p. 295)
The Old Curiosity Shop. 1841. The Oxford Illustrated Dickens, Vol. VIII. Oxford: Oxford
University Press, 1951.
1850 He was...as good as gold.... (p. 33)

The Personal History of David Copperfield. 1850. The Oxford Illustrated Dickens, Vol. II. Oxford: Oxford University Press, 1948.
APP 155; ODEP 317; MP 262.

As **good** as new

1841 '...their clothes looked as good as new....' (p. 291)
The Old Curiosity Shop. 1841. The Oxford Illustrated Dickens, Vol. VIII. Oxford: Oxford University Press, 1951.
WILSTACH 183.

As **good** as one's word

1842 He was as good as his word.... (p. 72)
American Notes and Pictures from Italy. 1842, 1846. The Oxford Illustrated Dickens, Vol. XIX. Oxford: Oxford University Press, 1957.
1843 Scrooge was better than his word. (p. 76)
Christmas Books. 1843-49. The Oxford Illustrated Dickens, Vol. XVI. Oxford: Oxford University Press, 1954.
1850 He was as good as his word.... (p. 85)
1850 She was as good as her word. (p. 650)
The Personal History of David Copperfield. 1850. The Oxford Illustrated Dickens, Vol. II. Oxford: Oxford University Press, 1948.
APP 412; ODEP 317; EAP 497; MP 700.

As **good** as the bank

1837 'His money was always as good as the bank....' (p. 360)
The Posthumous Papers of the Pickwick Club. 1837. The Oxford Illustrated Dickens, Vol. I. Oxford: Oxford University Press, 1948.

Good, bad, or indifferent

1837 It is strange with how little notice, good, bad, or indifferent, a man may live and die in London. (p. 215)
Sketches by Boz. 1833-40. The Oxford Illustrated Dickens, Vol. XII. Oxford: Oxford University Press, 1957.

He is **good-for-nothing**.

1841 a soft-hearted, good-for-nothing, vagabond kind of fellow.... (p. 465)
Barnaby Rudge: A Tale of the Riots of 'Eighty. 1841. The Oxford Illustrated Dickens, Vol. XV. Oxford: Oxford University Press, 1954.
1868 Any such story is good for nothing.... (p. 676)

The Letters of Charles Dickens, ed. Walter Dexter. Vol. III: 1858-1870. The Nonesuch Dickens. London: The Nonesuch Press, 1938.
ODEP 319; URDANG, *IDIOMS* 546.

Goody-poody

1860 ...he must be goody-poody, and do as he is toldy-poldy, and not be a manny-panny or a voter-poter, but fold his handy-pandys, and be a childy-pildy. (p. 259)
The Uncommercial Traveller and Reprinted Pieces Etc. 1850-1860. The Oxford Illustrated Dickens, Vol. XXI. Oxford: Oxford University Press, 1958.

To be **goosed** [=hissed at the theatre]

1854 'He was goosed last night, he was goosed the night before last, he was goosed to-day. He has lately got in the way of being always goosed....' ¶'Why has he been—so very much—Goosed?' asked Mr. Gradgrind....'...his daughter knew of his being goosed....' (p. 32)
Hard Times for These Times. 1854. The Oxford Illustrated Dickens, Vol. XVII. Oxford: Oxford University Press, 1955.
PARTRIDGE 343.

Gordian knot

1848 Will you cut this Gordian Knot? (p. 334)
The Letters of Charles Dickens: Volume Five: 1847-1849. Eds. Graham Storey and K. J. Fielding. Oxford: The Clarendon Press, 1981.
1868 I shall be delighted to have the Gordian Knot.... (p. 652)
The Letters of Charles Dickens, ed. Walter Dexter. Vol. III: 1858-1870. The Nonesuch Dickens. London: The Nonesuch Press, 1938.
APP 211; ODEP 328; EAP 183; MP 266; BARTLETT 184:22.

To be **got along**

1868 ...if I could be "got along," he was the man to get me along: and if I couldn't be got along, I might conclude that it could possibly be fixed. (p. 636)
The Letters of Charles Dickens, ed. Walter Dexter. Vol. III: 1858-1870. The Nonesuch Dickens. London: The Nonesuch Press, 1938.

To contain a **grain** of truth

1851 ...I must concede half a grain or so of truth to that superstition.... (p. 426)

Toast at a banquet in honor of William Charles Macready, London, 1 Mar. 1851. *The Works of Charles Dickens: The Speeches*. Ed. Richard H. Shepherd. New National Edition, Vol. II. New York: Hearst's International Library Company, n. d.

To go against the **grain**

1840 I wrote...against the grain.... (p. 126)
The Letters of Charles Dickens: Volume Two: 1840-1841. Eds. Madeline House and Graham Storey. Oxford: The Clarendon Press, 1969.
1846 It went against the grain with me.... (p. 581)
The Letters of Charles Dickens: Volume Four: 1844-1846. Ed. Kathleen Tillotson. Oxford: The Clarendon Press, 1977.
APP 158; ODEP 6; EAP 184; MP 266.

To take with a **grain** of salt

1865 Title: Chapter II: To Be Taken with a Grain of Salt (p. 455)
Christmas Stories. 1871. The Oxford Illustrated Dickens, Vol. XI. Oxford: Oxford University Press, 1956.
ODEP 330; EAP 184; MP 267.

(Not) to let the **grass** grow under one's feet

1852 ...no grass grew under the horses' iron shoes betwen Poland Street and the Forest. (p. 633)
The Uncommercial Traveller and Reprinted Pieces Etc. 1850-1860. The Oxford Illustrated Dickens, Vol. XXI. Oxford: Oxford University Press, 1958.
APP 159; ODEP 331; EAP 186; MP 269; DAP 265.

While the **grass** grows, the steed starves.

1870 'Else I might have proved the proverb, that while the grass grows, the steed starves!' (p. 198)
The Mystery of Edwin Drood. 1870. The Oxford Illustrated Dickens, Vol. XVIII. Oxford: Oxford University Press, 1956.
ODEP 331; EAP 186; CODP 100; MP 269; DAP 265.

Some are born great; some achieve **greatness**....

1851 But My Uncle is a concentration of all the different sorts of greatness...—he was born great; he has had greatness thrust upon him; he has achieved greatness. (p. 368)
"My Uncle." [with W. H. Wills]. *Charles Dickens' Uncollected Writings from* Household Words *1850-1859*, 2 vols. Ed. Harry Stone. Bloomington: Indiana University Press, 1968.
DAP 267; STEVENSON 1031: 9.

It's all **Greek** to me.

1841 '...I am a stranger, and this is Greek to me?' (p. 7)
Barnaby Rudge: A Tale of the Riots of 'Eighty. 1841. The Oxford Illustrated Dickens, Vol.
XV. Oxford: Oxford University Press, 1954.
APP 161; ODEP 336; EAP 187; MP 271.

The **green-eyed monster**, jealousy

1862 "It [jealousy] is the green-eyed monster...." (p. 353)
Christmas Stories. 1871. The Oxford Illustrated Dickens, Vol. XI. Oxford: Oxford
University Press, 1956.
WILKINSON 410.

The **Green Room** of a theatre

1843 I...peep in at the Green Room.... (p. 510)
The Letters of Charles Dickens: Volume Three: 1842-1843. Eds. Madeline House, Graham
Storey, and Kathleen Tillotson. Oxford: The Clarendon Press, 1974.
1851 ...to paint a picture for the Guild, representing the Green Room at
your house. (p. 347)
The Letters of Charles Dickens: Volume Six: 1850-1852. Eds. Madeline House, Graham
Storey, and Kathleen Tillotson. Oxford: The Clarendon Press, 1988.
URDANG, *IDIOMS* 560.

To go to **Gretna Green**

1836 MARY: My...swain...implores me to...accompany him on an
expedition to Gretna Green. (*The Strange Gentleman*, I, i, p. 15)
1838 GALILEO: ...we could go to Gretna Green.... (*The Lamplighter*, I,
ii, p. 123)
Complete Plays and Selected Poems of Charles Dickens. London: Vision Press, 1970.
1837 "...you can go the Gretna Green together...." (p. 411)
1837 ...they had better go to Gretna Green.... (p. 420)
Sketches by Boz. 1833-40. The Oxford Illustrated Dickens, Vol. XII. Oxford: Oxford
University Press, 1957.
1855 ...I was on the shortest road to Gretna Green. What had *I* to do
with Gretna Green? (p. 103)
1855 What does the Infant do...but cut away...on an expedition to go to
Gretna Green and be married? (p. 119)
1855 "...do you suppose I should be going to Gretna Green without
her?" (p. 128)
Christmas Stories. 1871. The Oxford Illustrated Dickens, Vol. XI. Oxford: Oxford
University Press, 1956.
URDANG, *IDIOMS* 560.

As **grey** as iron; iron-grey

1854 ...his iron-grey hair lay long and thin. (p. 63)
Hard Times for These Times. 1854. The Oxford Illustrated Dickens, Vol. XVII. Oxford: Oxford University Press, 1955.

1859 ...he was a...man, with iron-grey hair.... (p. 684)
The Uncommercial Traveller and Reprinted Pieces Etc. 1850-1860. The Oxford Illustrated Dickens, Vol. XXI. Oxford: Oxford University Press, 1958.

URDANG, *IDIOMS* 719.

All is **grist** that comes to one's mill.

1853 ...its owner...is perhaps prompted to...send up to H. W. a little bag—or a large sack—of grist. So the mill goes. (p. 475)
"H. W." [with Henry Morley]. *Charles Dickens' Uncollected Writings from* Household Words *1850-1859*, 2 vols. Ed. Harry Stone. Bloomington: Indiana University Press, 1968.

APP 162; ODEP 339; EAP 188; CODP 102; MP 9; DAP 269.

To worship the **ground** someone walks upon

1841 '...he seems to despise the very ground he walks on!' (p. 211)
Barnaby Rudge: A Tale of the Riots of 'Eighty. 1841. The Oxford Illustrated Dickens, Vol. XV. Oxford: Oxford University Press, 1954.

1850 ...'I love the ground my Agnes walks on!' (p. 381)
The Personal History of David Copperfield. 1850. The Oxford Illustrated Dickens, Vol. II. Oxford: Oxford University Press, 1948.

ODEP 493; MP 273.

What will Mrs. **Grundy** say?

1854 ...as if Mr. Bounderby had been Mrs. Grundy. (p. 13)
1854 Not being Mrs. Grundy, who *was* Mr. Bounderby? (p. 14)
Hard Times for These Times. 1854. The Oxford Illustrated Dickens, Vol. XVII. Oxford: Oxford University Press, 1955.

APP 163; ODEP 536; MP 273.

To blow great **guns**

1841 'It blows great guns, indeed.' (p. 250)
Barnaby Rudge: A Tale of the Riots of 'Eighty. 1841. The Oxford Illustrated Dickens, Vol. XV. Oxford: Oxford University Press, 1954.

1844 ...it blows great guns with a raging storm. (p. 210)
The Letters of Charles Dickens: Volume Four: 1844-1846. Ed. Kathleen Tillotson. Oxford: The Clarendon Press, 1977.

1855 It is blowing great guns.... (p. 773)

The Letters of Charles Dickens: Volume Seven: 1853-1855. Eds. Graham Storey, Kathleen Tillotson, and Angus Easson. Oxford: The Clarendon Press, 1993.
ODEP 70; MP 275.

To stand (stick) to one's **guns**

1851 We must stand to our Guns.... (p. 448)
The Letters of Charles Dickens: Volume Six: 1850-1852. Eds. Madeline House, Graham Storey, and Kathleen Tillotson. Oxford: The Clarendon Press, 1988.
APP 164; ODEP 770; MP 276; DAP 271.

H

A **hair** of the dog that bit you

1841 'Another hair of the dog that bit you, captain!' (p. 399)
Barnaby Rudge: A Tale of the Riots of 'Eighty. 1841. The Oxford Illustrated Dickens, Vol. XV. Oxford: Oxford University Press, 1954.
APP 166; ODEP 343; EAP 191; MP 278; DAP 273.

(Not) to harm a **hair** of someone's head

1838 '...do you think I would harm a hair of his head?' (p. 217)
The Adventures of Oliver Twist. 1838. The Oxford Illustrated Dickens, Vol. V. Oxford: Oxford University Press, 1948.
1839 '...don't hurt a hair of his head, I beg. On no account hurt a hair of his head.' (p. 646)
1839 It would not...have been quite so easy to hurt a hair of the gentleman's head.... (p. 646)
The Life and Adventures of Nicholas Nickleby. 1839. The Oxford Illustrated Dickens, Vol. VI. Oxford: Oxford University Press, 1950.
1841 '...think of the mischief you'll bring...upon some innocent heads that you wouldn't wish to hurt a hair of.' (p. 160)
Barnaby Rudge: A Tale of the Riots of 'Eighty. 1841. The Oxford Illustrated Dickens, Vol. XV. Oxford: Oxford University Press, 1954.
1842 ...not a hair on the head of one of those men has been hurt.... (p. 197)
The Letters of Charles Dickens: Volume Three: 1842-1843. Eds. Madeline House, Graham Storey, and Kathleen Tillotson. Oxford: The Clarendon Press, 1974.
1852-54 ...the Parliament "should not hurt one hair of his head." (p. 460)
Master Humphrey's Clock and A Child's History of England. 1840-41, 1852-54. The Oxford Illustrated Dickens, Vol. XX. Oxford: Oxford University Press, 1958.
1866 No Port captain shall hurt a hair of your head. (p. 457)

The Letters of Charles Dickens, ed. Walter Dexter. Vol. III: 1858-1870. The Nonesuch Dickens. London: The Nonesuch Press, 1938.
APP 167; EAP 191; MP 278.

To drag someone by the **hair**

1845 Frederick I will drag to Miss Kelly's by the hair of his head. (p. 428)
The Letters of Charles Dickens: Volume Four: 1844-1846. Ed. Kathleen Tillotson. Oxford: The Clarendon Press, 1977.
1869 I was dragged out of London by the hair of my head.... (p. 750)
The Letters of Charles Dickens, ed. Walter Dexter. Vol. III: 1858-1870. The Nonesuch Dickens. London: The Nonesuch Press, 1938.

To let down one's back **hair**

1852 ...she let her back hair down.... (p. 416)
"First Fruits." [with George Augustus Sala]. *Charles Dickens' Uncollected Writings from Household Words 1850-1859*, 2 vols. Ed. Harry Stone. Bloomington: Indiana University Press, 1968.
MP 279.

To make one's **hair** stand on end

1840 ...the bare mention of which would make the hair of all human creatures stand on end with wonder. (p. 817)
The Letters of Charles Dickens: Volume Seven: 1853-1855. Eds. Graham Storey, Kathleen Tillotson, and Angus Easson. Oxford: The Clarendon Press, 1993.
1840-41 Joe Toddyhigh...felt his hair stand on end.... (p. 18)
Master Humphrey's Clock and A Child's History of England. 1840-41, 1852-54. The Oxford Illustrated Dickens, Vol. XX. Oxford: Oxford University Press, 1958.
1844 'So did his hair...which...stood bolt upright....' (p. 13)
The Life and Adventures of Martin Chuzzlewit. 1844. The Oxford Illustrated Dickens, Vol. IX. Oxford: Oxford University Press, 1951.
1845 ...such vile obscenity as positively made one's hair stand on end. (p. 299)
The Letters of Charles Dickens: Volume Four: 1844-1846. Ed. Kathleen Tillotson. Oxford: The Clarendon Press, 1977.
1846 ...every curl...had made a man's hair stand on end. (p. 260)
1849 ...Mr. William's light hair stood on end.... (p. 323)
Christmas Books. 1843-49. The Oxford Illustrated Dickens, Vol. XVI. Oxford: Oxford University Press, 1954.
1847 Expect a letter...as shall make your hair stand on end! (p. 11)
1848 ...I imagine your hair standing on end... (p. 330)
1849 ...my hair is even now standing on end. (p. 646)

The Letters of Charles Dickens: Volume Five: 1847-1849. Eds. Graham Storey and K. J. Fielding. Oxford: The Clarendon Press, 1981.

1851 NIGHTINGALE: ...your hair would stand on end. (*Mr. Nightingale's Diary*, I, i, p. 151)
Complete Plays and Selected Poems of Charles Dickens. London: Vision Press, 1970.

1852 My hair stands on end at the bare notion of those suits at law you tell me of. (p. 591)
The Letters of Charles Dickens: Volume Six: 1850-1852. Eds. Madeline House, Graham Storey, and Kathleen Tillotson. Oxford: The Clarendon Press, 1988.

1866 You make my hair stand on end.... (p. 490)
The Letters of Charles Dickens, ed. Walter Dexter. Vol. III: 1858-1870. The Nonesuch Dickens. London: The Nonesuch Press, 1938.

URDANG, *IDIOMS* 573.

By a **hair's** breadth

1845 ...the second is not affected by a hair's-breadth or a feather's weight. (p. 428)
The Letters of Charles Dickens: Volume Four: 1844-1846. Ed. Kathleen Tillotson. Oxford: The Clarendon Press, 1977.

1848 The old woman had her clutch within a hair's breadth of his shock of hair.... (p. 730)
Dealings with the Firm of Dombey and Son. 1848. The Oxford Illustrated Dickens, Vol. VII. Oxford: Oxford University Press, 1950.

1850 ...the room...was dusted and arranged to a hair's breadth already. (p. 201)
The Personal History of David Copperfield. 1850. The Oxford Illustrated Dickens, Vol. II. Oxford: Oxford University Press, 1948.

1850-56 She...could never bend herself a hair's breadth.... (pp. 544-545)
The Uncommercial Traveller and Reprinted Pieces Etc. 1850-1860. The Oxford Illustrated Dickens, Vol. XXI. Oxford: Oxford University Press, 1958.

1850 ...not the hundredth part of a hair's breadth...should fail to range.... (p. 159)
"Two Chapters on Bank Note Forgeries: Chapter II." [with W. H. Wills]. *Charles Dickens' Uncollected Writings from* Household Words *1850-1859*, 2 vols. Ed. Harry Stone. Bloomington: Indiana University Press, 1968.

1857 ...it were sometimes by only a hair's-breadth.... (p. 357)
Little Dorrit. 1857. The Oxford Illustrated Dickens, Vol. XIV. Oxford: Oxford University Press, 1953.

1869 ...the rapid railway travelling was stretched a hair's breadth too far.... (p. 723)
The Letters of Charles Dickens, ed. Walter Dexter. Vol. III: 1858-1870. The Nonesuch Dickens. London: The Nonesuch Press, 1938.

1869 ...you may...call a butterfly a buffalo, without advancing's a hair's breadth towards making it one.... (p. 568)

Address to the Birmingham and Midland Institute, Birmingham, 27 Sept. 1869. *The Works of Charles Dickens: The Speeches*. Ed. Richard H. Shepherd. New National Edition, Vol. II. New York: Hearst's International Library Company, n. d.
ODEP 151; EAP 192.

Hale and hearty

1837 From its hale and hearty green. (p. 225)
Complete Plays and Selected Poems of Charles Dickens. London: Vision Press, 1970.
URDANG, *IDIOMS* 574.

Half a loaf is better than no bread at all.

1844 ...half a loaf is better than no bread.... (p. 218)
The Letters of Charles Dickens: Volume Four: 1844-1846. Ed. Kathleen Tillotson. Oxford: The Clarendon Press, 1977.
1848 'Half a loaf's better than no bread....' (p. 131)
Dealings with the Firm of Dombey and Son. 1848. The Oxford Illustrated Dickens, Vol. VII. Oxford: Oxford University Press, 1950.
APP 167; ODEP 344; EAP 192; CODP 104; MP 280; DAP 274.

The better half of a man is his wife.

1851 Your better half...saw a Sunset there. (p. 464)
The Letters of Charles Dickens: Volume Six: 1850-1852. Eds. Madeline House, Graham Storey, and Kathleen Tillotson. Oxford: The Clarendon Press, 1988.
1870 ...the sisterhood of literature also, although that 'better half of human nature,' to which Mr. Gladstone rendered his graceful tribute, is unworthily represented here.... (p. 588)
Response to a toast at the Royal Academy Dinner, London, 2 May 1870. *The Works of Charles Dickens: The Speeches*. Ed. Richard H. Shepherd. New National Edition, Vol. II. New York: Hearst's International Library Company, n. d.
ODEP 53; EAP 30.

To make a hallaballoo

1850 They made a mighty hallaballoo.... (p. 119)
The Letters of Charles Dickens: Volume Six: 1850-1852. Eds. Madeline House, Graham Storey, and Kathleen Tillotson. Oxford: The Clarendon Press, 1988.
PARTRIDGE 413.

Do nothing by halves.

1857 "A man who can do nothing by halves appears to me to be a fearful man." (p. 723)

Christmas Stories. 1871. The Oxford Illustrated Dickens, Vol. XI. Oxford: Oxford University Press, 1956.

1863 Don't do it by halves.... (p. 333)

The Letters of Charles Dickens, ed. Walter Dexter. Vol. III: 1858-1870. The Nonesuch Dickens. London: The Nonesuch Press, 1938.

1864 ...the Major does nothing by halves.... (p. 407)

Christmas Stories. 1871. The Oxford Illustrated Dickens, Vol. XI. Oxford: Oxford University Press, 1956.

ODEP 562; MP 280; DAP 273.

Like *Hamlet* with the part of Hamlet left out

1850 It was a common figure of speech, whenever anything important was left out of any great scheme, to say it was the tragedy of *Hamlet* with the part of Hamlet left out.... (p. 421)

Address on the Public Health of the Metropolis, London, 6 Feb. 1850. *The Works of Charles Dickens: The Speeches.* Ed. Richard H. Shepherd. New National Edition, Vol. II. New York: Hearst's International Library Company, n. d.

ODEP 345; EAP 193; MP 281.

Hammer and tongs

1844 On he went...hammer and tongs.... (p. 56)

The Letters of Charles Dickens: Volume Four: 1844-1846. Ed. Kathleen Tillotson. Oxford: The Clarendon Press, 1977.

APP 168; ODEP 346; EAP 193; MP 281.

Hand and foot

1852 ...I have been obliged to...bind the company, hand and foot.... (p. 732)

The Letters of Charles Dickens: Volume Six: 1850-1852. Eds. Madeline House, Graham Storey, and Kathleen Tillotson. Oxford: The Clarendon Press, 1988.

ODEP 346; MP 285.

To be brought up by **hand**

1861 ...Joe Gargery and I had been brought up by hand. (p. 6)

1861 'Who brought you up by hand?' (p. 7)

1861 '...it were the talk how she was bringing you up by hand.' (p. 43)

1861 '...be grateful, boy, to them which brought you up by hand.' (p. 22)

1861 'No bringing up by hand then.' (p. 24)

1861 'Let your behaviour here be a credit unto them which brought you up by hand!' (p. 51)

Great Expectations. 1861. The Oxford Illustrated Dickens, Vol. XIII. Oxford: Oxford University Press, 1953.

To be **hand-in-glove** with someone

1850-56 ...hand-in-glove with the penny-a-liners of that time, they became.... (p. 485)

The Uncommercial Traveller and Reprinted Pieces Etc. 1850-1860. The Oxford Illustrated Dickens, Vol. XXI. Oxford: Oxford University Press, 1958.

APP 169; ODEP 346; EAP 195; MP 283.

To get the upper **hand**

1838 'I've got the upper hand over you, Fagin....' (p. 104)

The Adventures of Oliver Twist. 1838. The Oxford Illustrated Dickens, Vol. V. Oxford: Oxford University Press, 1948.

APP 169; ODEP 856; EAP 195; MP 284.

To live from **hand** to mouth

1833-36 A poor man...just manages to live on from hand to mouth.... (p. 1)

Sketches by Boz. 1833-40. The Oxford Illustrated Dickens, Vol. XII. Oxford: Oxford University Press, 1957.

1857 ...he would have dragged on from hand to mouth.... (p. 75)

Little Dorrit. 1857. The Oxford Illustrated Dickens, Vol. XIV. Oxford: Oxford University Press, 1953.

APP 170; ODEP 474; EAP 193; MP 285.

To pass from **hand** to hand

1850 Thousands of sovereigns were jerked hither and thither from hand to hand...piles of bank notes...hustled to and fro.... (p. 126)

"The Old Lady in Threadneedle Street." [with W. H. Wills]. *Charles Dickens' Uncollected Writings from* Household Words *1850-1859,* 2 vols. Ed. Harry Stone. Bloomington: Indiana University Press, 1968.

1857 "...this will be a hand-to-hand affair, and so much the better." (p. 187)

Christmas Stories. 1871. The Oxford Illustrated Dickens, Vol. XI. Oxford: Oxford University Press, 1956.

URDANG, *IDIOMS* 580.

To have one's **hands** tied

1841 While the Clock is going, my hands are tied. (p. 272)
The Letters of Charles Dickens: Volume Two: 1840-1841. Eds. Madeline House and Graham Storey. Oxford: The Clarendon Press, 1969.
1847 May the man who has tied my hands, never know.... (p. 89)
The Letters of Charles Dickens: Volume Five: 1847-1849. Eds. Graham Storey and K. J. Fielding. Oxford: The Clarendon Press, 1981.
MP 286.

To wash one's **hands** of someone (-thing)

1839 ...Forster then washed his hands of any further interference between us.... (p. 530)
The Letters of Charles Dickens: Volume One: 1820-1839. Eds. Madeline House and Graham Storey. Oxford: The Clarendon Press, 1965.
1853 He had entirely washed his hands of the difficulty.... (p. 74)
Bleak House. 1853. The Oxford Illustrated Dickens, Vol. III. Oxford: Oxford University Press, 1948.
1861 ...I could never bear to see him wash his hands of her.... (p. 229)
Great Expectations. 1861. The Oxford Illustrated Dickens, Vol. XIII. Oxford: Oxford University Press, 1953.
APP 170; ODEP 868; EAP 197; MP 285.

Handsome is that handsome does.

1850 ...a husband...was very handsome, except in the sense of the homely adage, 'handsome is, that handsome does....' (pp. 2-3)
The Personal History of David Copperfield. 1850. The Oxford Illustrated Dickens, Vol. II. Oxford: Oxford University Press, 1948.
APP 171; ODEP 348; EAP 197; CODP 106; MP 286; DAP 278.

As **happy** as a bird

1841 '...we'll...be as free and happy as the birds.' (p. 94)
The Old Curiosity Shop. 1841. The Oxford Illustrated Dickens, Vol. VIII. Oxford: Oxford University Press, 1951.
APP 28; MP 47.

As **happy** as a cock

1837 Tom looked as happy as a cock on a drizzly morning. (p. 359)
Sketches by Boz. 1833-40. The Oxford Illustrated Dickens, Vol. XII. Oxford: Oxford University Press, 1957.

As **happy** as a king

1861 '...he'll be as happy as a king.' (p. 283)

Great Expectations. 1861. The Oxford Illustrated Dickens, Vol. XIII. Oxford: Oxford University Press, 1953.
ODEP 527; MP 349.

As **happy** as a marigold

1837 They...looked as happy and comfortable as a couple of marigolds run to seed. (p. 323)
Sketches by Boz. 1833-40. The Oxford Illustrated Dickens, Vol. XII. Oxford: Oxford University Press, 1957.

As **happy** as a tomtit

1837 ...said Mr. Minns, as happy as a tomtit on birdlime. (p. 319)
Sketches by Boz. 1833-40. The Oxford Illustrated Dickens, Vol. XII. Oxford: Oxford University Press, 1957.

As **happy** as an angel

1843 'I am as light as a feather, I am as happy as an angel, I am as merry as a schoolboy. I am as giddy as a drunken man.' (p. 71)
Christmas Books. 1843-49. The Oxford Illustrated Dickens, Vol. XVI. Oxford: Oxford University Press, 1954.

As **hard** as a flint

1843 Hard and sharp as a flint...and solitary as an oyster. (p. 8)
Christmas Books. 1843-49. The Oxford Illustrated Dickens, Vol. XVI. Oxford: Oxford University Press, 1954.
APP 139; ODEP 352; EAP 158; MP 232.

As **hard** as a nut

1850 They have got a word like a Brazil nut.... (p. 193)
"Mr. Bendigo Buster on Our National Defences Against Education." [with Henry Morley].
Charles Dickens' Uncollected Writings from Household Words *1850-1859*, 2 vols. Ed. Harry Stone. Bloomington: Indiana University Press, 1968.

As **hard** as granite

1846 The water...freezes into solid masses...as hard as granite. (p. 675)
The Letters of Charles Dickens: Volume Four: 1844-1846. Ed. Kathleen Tillotson. Oxford: The Clarendon Press, 1977.
APP 158; MP 268.

As **hard** as iron

1839 ...I *ought* to be hard as iron to my own inclinations.... (p. 540)
The Letters of Charles Dickens: Volume One: 1820-1839. Eds. Madeline House and Graham Storey. Oxford: The Clarendon Press, 1965.
APP 200; EAP 235; MP 338.

Hard and fast

1839 '...so here I am hard and fast.' (p. 780)
The Life and Adventures of Nicholas Nickleby. 1839. The Oxford Illustrated Dickens, Vol. VI. Oxford: Oxford University Press, 1950.
1841 '...the knot's tied hard and fast....' (p. 164)
The Old Curiosity Shop. 1841. The Oxford Illustrated Dickens, Vol. VIII. Oxford: Oxford University Press, 1951.
1853 'What should I have done as soon as I was hard and fast here?' (p. 706)
Bleak House. 1853. The Oxford Illustrated Dickens, Vol. III. Oxford: Oxford University Press, 1948.
WILKINSON 87.

In (out of) harm's way

1841 'To be out of harm's way he prudently thinks is something too....' (p. 249)
The Old Curiosity Shop. 1841. The Oxford Illustrated Dickens, Vol. VIII. Oxford: Oxford University Press, 1951.
1845 ...it may keep him out of other harm's way. (p. 346)
The Letters of Charles Dickens: Volume Four: 1844-1846. Ed. Kathleen Tillotson. Oxford: The Clarendon Press, 1977.
URDANG, *IDIOMS* 588; BARTLETT 348:9.

Harum-scarum

1853 'Before I begin my harum-scarum day....' (p. 112)
1853 '...I'm a harum-scarum sort of a good-for-nought, that more kicks than halfpence come natural to....' (p. 480)
1853 '...I...went away and 'listed, harum-scarum....' (p. 749)
Bleak House. 1853. The Oxford Illustrated Dickens, Vol. III. Oxford: Oxford University Press, 1948.
PARTRIDGE 377.

To eat one's hat

1837 '...I'd eat my hat and swallow the buckle whole,' said the clarical gentleman. (p. 592)

The Posthumous Papers of the Pickwick Club. 1837. The Oxford Illustrated Dickens, Vol. I. Oxford: Oxford University Press, 1948.

To play **havoc** with something

1850 It is playing havoc with the villainous literature. (p. 83)
The Letters of Charles Dickens: Volume Six: 1850-1852. Eds. Madeline House, Graham Storey, and Kathleen Tillotson. Oxford: The Clarendon Press, 1988.
URDANG, *IDIOMS* 602.

Make **hay** while the sun shines.

1844 'Get in your hay while the sun shines.' (p. 400)
The Life and Adventures of Martin Chuzzlewit. 1844. The Oxford Illustrated Dickens, Vol. IX. Oxford: Oxford University Press, 1951.
1853 And he is making hay of the grass which is flesh.... (p. 548)
Bleak House. 1853. The Oxford Illustrated Dickens, Vol. III. Oxford: Oxford University Press, 1948.
APP 175; ODEP 501; EAP 202; CODP 143; MP 293; DAP 286.

Head and shoulders

1842 He...drew nothing in, as the saying is, by the head and shoulders.... (p. 58)
American Notes and Pictures from Italy. 1842, 1846. The Oxford Illustrated Dickens, Vol. XIX. Oxford: Oxford University Press, 1957.
ODEP 360.

(Not) to make **head or tail** of something

1836 OVERTON: ...which I could make neither head nor tail of. (*The Strange Gentleman*, I, ii, p. 22)
Complete Plays and Selected Poems of Charles Dickens. London: Vision Press, 1970.
ODEP 360; EAP 205; MP 294.

Off with his **head**!

1833-36 ...that's only one pound ten, including the "off with his head!" (p. 119)
Sketches by Boz. 1833-40. The Oxford Illustrated Dickens, Vol. XII. Oxford: Oxford University Press, 1957.
STEVENSON 1096:3.

The hardest **head** may co-exist with the softest heart.

1858 The hardest head may co-exist with the softest heart. (p. 501)

Address to the Institutional Association of Lancashire and Cheshire, Manchester, 3 Dec. 1858. *The Works of Charles Dickens: The Speeches*. Ed. Richard H. Shepherd. New National Edition, Vol. II. New York: Hearst's International Library Company, n. d.

To beat one's **head** against a stone wall

1843 I am beating my head against the door.... (p. 496)
The Letters of Charles Dickens: Volume Three: 1842-1843. Eds. Madeline House, Graham Storey, and Kathleen Tillotson. Oxford: The Clarendon Press, 1974.
1853 "—bosh! what's my head running against!" (p. 306)
1853 "...I don't see how an innocent man is to make up his mind to this kind of thing without knocking his head against the walls." (p. 619)
1853 "...a married woman, possessing your attraction ... goes and runs he delicate-formed head against a wall." (p. 709)
Bleak House. 1853. The Oxford Illustrated Dickens, Vol. III. Oxford: Oxford University Press, 1948.
1854 ...and knock his ed agen the wall.... (p. 458)
The Letters of Charles Dickens: Volume Seven: 1853-1855. Eds. grahem Storey, Kathleen Tillotson, and Angus Easson. Oxford: The Clarendon Press, 1993.
ODEP 688; MP 294.

To be over **head** and ears

1837 "I am as regularly over head and ears as the Royal George...." (p. 448)
Sketches by Boz. 1833-40. The Oxford Illustrated Dickens, Vol. XII. Oxford: Oxford University Press, 1957.
1846 ...it is a plunge straight over head and ears.... (p. 573)
The Letters of Charles Dickens: Volume Four: 1844-1846. Ed. Kathleen Tillotson. Oxford: The Clarendon Press, 1977.
1850 I was not merely over head and ears in love with her.... (p. 474)
The Personal History of David Copperfield. 1850. The Oxford Illustrated Dickens, Vol. II. Oxford: Oxford University Press, 1948.
1852 I have taken the liberty of...knocking it over heads and heels. (p. 796)
The Letters of Charles Dickens: Volume Six: 1850-1852. Eds. Madeline House, Graham Storey, and Kathleen Tillotson. Oxford: The Clarendon Press, 1988.
APP 176; EAP 203; MP 294.

To go **head** over heels

1861 ...he made it go head over heels before me.... (p. 2)
Great Expectations. 1861. The Oxford Illustrated Dickens, Vol. XIII. Oxford: Oxford University Press, 1953.
APP 177; EAP 203; MP 295.

To lose one's **head**

1848 ...our footman..."losing his head" as they call it.... (p. 389)
The Letters of Charles Dickens: Volume Five: 1847-1849. Eds. Graham Storey and K. J. Fielding. Oxford: The Clarendon Press, 1981.
WILKINSON 299.

To turn someone's **head**

1837 ...you will turn my head. (p. 281)
The Letters of Charles Dickens: Volume One: 1820-1839. Eds. Madeline House and Graham Storey. Oxford: The Clarendon Press, 1965.
URDANG, *IDIOMS* 607.

To work one's **head** off

1852 I write shortly, having been working my head off. (p. 809)
The Letters of Charles Dickens: Volume Six: 1850-1852. Eds. Madeline House, Graham Storey, and Kathleen Tillotson. Oxford: The Clarendon Press, 1988.
CRAIG 229.

Do not expect to find old **heads** on young shoulders.

1844 An ancient proverb warns us that we should not expect to find old heads upon young shoulders.... (p. 176)
The Life and Adventures of Martin Chuzzlewit. 1844. The Oxford Illustrated Dickens, Vol. IX. Oxford: Oxford University Press, 1951.
1850 '...you don't expect...old heads on young shoulders.' (p. 650)
The Personal History of David Copperfield. 1850. The Oxford Illustrated Dickens, Vol. II. Oxford: Oxford University Press, 1948.
APP 176; ODEP 589; EAP 204; CODP 167; MP 296; DAP 288.

Two **heads** are better than just one.

1837 '...four heads is better than two, Sammy,' said Mr. Weller.... (p. 771)
The Posthumous Papers of the Pickwick Club. 1837. The Oxford Illustrated Dickens, Vol. I. Oxford: Oxford University Press, 1948.
APP 177; ODEP 851; EAP 206; CODP 233; MP 297; DAP 288.

To be struck of a **heap**

1838 '..."I was so struck all of a heap...."'" (p. 228)
The Adventures of Oliver Twist. 1838. The Oxford Illustrated Dickens, Vol. V. Oxford: Oxford University Press, 1948.
1844 'It strikes one all of a heap.' (p. 514)

The Life and Adventures of Martin Chuzzlewit. 1844. The Oxford Illustrated Dickens, Vol. IX. Oxford: Oxford University Press, 1951.

1850 'I'm struck of a heap....' (p. 453)'

The Personal History of David Copperfield. 1850. The Oxford Illustrated Dickens, Vol. II. Oxford: Oxford University Press, 1948.

1870 '...can you suppose that anyone...could fail to be struck all of a heap...?' (p. 149)

The Mystery of Edwin Drood. 1870. The Oxford Illustrated Dickens, Vol. XVIII. Oxford: Oxford University Press, 1956.

APP 178; ODEP 781; EAP 206; MP 297.

To **hear** is to obey.

1841 What can I do but say with the good Mussulmen—"to hear is to obey?" (p. 416)

The Letters of Charles Dickens: Volume Two: 1840-1841. Eds. Madeline House and Graham Storey. Oxford: The Clarendon Press, 1969.

1854 To which Mrs. Sparsit returned...'To hear is to obey.' (p. 201)

Hard Times for These Times. 1854. The Oxford Illustrated Dickens, Vol. XVII. Oxford: Oxford University Press, 1955.

DAP 290.

Faint **heart** never won fair lady.

1839 '"Faint heart never won fair lady."' (p. 702)

The Life and Adventures of Nicholas Nickleby. 1839. The Oxford Illustrated Dickens, Vol. VI. Oxford: Oxford University Press, 1950.

APP 178; ODEP 238; EAP 207; CODP 75; MP 298; DAP 292.

Heart and soul

1836 BENSON: ...I have a heart and soul within me.... (*The Village Coquettes*, I, iii, p. 66)

1837 TAPKINS: Bless my heart and soul...! (*Is She His Wife?*, I, p. 99)

Complete Plays and Selected Poems of Charles Dickens. London: Vision Press, 1970.

1839 '...I pity her with all my heart and soul....' (p. 619)

The Life and Adventures of Nicholas Nickleby. 1839. The Oxford Illustrated Dickens, Vol. VI. Oxford: Oxford University Press, 1950.

1842 Loving you with all my heart and soul...I would not condemn you.... (pp. 156-157)

1842 Bless your heart and soul, my dear fellow.... (p. 169)

1842 ...I will ever be, heart and soul, your faithful friend! (p. 176)

1843 ...Talfourd...will echo with all his heart and soul.... (p. 511)

1843 Now don't you in your own heart and soul...quarrel with me...? (p. 547)
The Letters of Charles Dickens: Volume Three: 1842-1843. Eds. Madeline House, Graham Storey, and Kathleen Tillotson. Oxford: The Clarendon Press, 1974.

1844 I congratulate you, with all my heart and soul.... (p. 89)
The Letters of Charles Dickens: Volume Four: 1844-1846. Ed. Kathleen Tillotson. Oxford: The Clarendon Press, 1977.

1846 ...I congratulate you on it, with all my heart and soul. (p. 643)
The Letters of Charles Dickens: Volume Four: 1844-1846. Ed. Kathleen Tillotson. Oxford: The Clarendon Press, 1977.

1848 I...congratulate you with all my heart and soul. (p. 279)
The Letters of Charles Dickens: Volume Five: 1847-1849. Eds. Graham Storey and K. J. Fielding. Oxford: The Clarendon Press, 1981.

1850 ...I have been believing such things with all my heart and soul.... (p. 179)
The Letters of Charles Dickens: Volume Six: 1850-1852. Eds. Madeline House, Graham Storey, and Kathleen Tillotson. Oxford: The Clarendon Press, 1988.

1853 '...dead suitors, broken, heart and soul, upon the wheel of Chancery....' (p. 492)
Bleak House. 1853. The Oxford Illustrated Dickens, Vol. III. Oxford: Oxford University Press, 1948.

1857 Every man lying-to at his work, with a will that had all his heart and soul in it. (p. 199)
Christmas Stories. 1871. The Oxford Illustrated Dickens, Vol. XI. Oxford: Oxford University Press, 1956.

URDANG, *IDIOMS* 613.

Heart of oak

1841 'Give it a name, heart of oak....' (p. 62)
Barnaby Rudge: A Tale of the Riots of 'Eighty. 1841. The Oxford Illustrated Dickens, Vol. XV. Oxford: Oxford University Press, 1954.

1870 ...Providence made a distinct mistake in originating so small a nation of hearts of oak.... (page 128)
The Mystery of Edwin Drood. 1870. The Oxford Illustrated Dickens, Vol. XVIII. Oxford: Oxford University Press, 1956.

ODEP 364; EAP 207.

In one's **heart** of hearts

1842 ...in your heart of hearts, you think and feel with me. (p. 346)
The Letters of Charles Dickens: Volume Three: 1842-1843. Eds. Madeline House, Graham Storey, and Kathleen Tillotson. Oxford: The Clarendon Press, 1974.

1860 ...I love Calais with my heart of hearts! (p. 184)

The Uncommercial Traveller and Reprinted Pieces Etc. 1850-1860. The Oxford Illustrated
Dickens, Vol. XXI. Oxford: Oxford University Press, 1958.
1867 That done, from my heart of hearts.... (p. 502)
The Letters of Charles Dickens, ed. Walter Dexter. Vol. III: 1858-1870. The Nonesuch
Dickens. London: The Nonesuch Press, 1938.
URDANG, *IDIOMS* 612; STEVENSON 1113:7, 1749:15.

It is a poor **heart** that never rejoices.

1844 'It is a poor heart that never rejoices....' (p. 83)
The Life and Adventures of Martin Chuzzlewit. 1844. The Oxford Illustrated Dickens, Vol.
IX. Oxford: Oxford University Press, 1951.
1850 Its [*sic*] a poor heart which *never* rejoices! (p. 88)
The Letters of Charles Dickens: Volume Six: 1850-1852. Eds. Madeline House, Graham
Storey, and Kathleen Tillotson. Oxford: The Clarendon Press, 1988.
ODEP 638; CODP 180; MP 298; DAP 292.

To break one's **heart**

1843 It is enough to break one's heart.... (p. 562)
The Letters of Charles Dickens: Volume Three: 1842-1843. Eds. Madeline House, Graham
Storey, and Kathleen Tillotson. Oxford: The Clarendon Press, 1974.
1844 ...I verily think I should have broken my heart. (p. 60)
The Letters of Charles Dickens: Volume Four: 1844-1846. Ed. Kathleen Tillotson. Oxford:
The Clarendon Press, 1977.
1846 'It breaks my heart.' (p. 259)
1849 '...you'll die of a broken heart....' (p. 346)
1849 'I must have nearly broke your heart....' (p. 384)
Christmas Books. 1843-49. The Oxford Illustrated Dickens, Vol. XVI. Oxford: Oxford
University Press, 1954.
1850 ...she means to break her heart.... (p. 203)
1850 I am at present breaking my man's heart.... (p. 241)
The Letters of Charles Dickens: Volume Six: 1850-1852. Eds. Madeline House, Graham
Storey, and Kathleen Tillotson. Oxford: The Clarendon Press, 1988.
1851 ...although Olivia...had...tried...to break my heart, there was
"balm in Gilead." [Jeremiah 8:22] (pp. 217-218)
"My Mahogany Friend." [with Mary Boyle]. *Charles Dickens' Uncollected Writings from
Household Words 1850-1859*, 2 vols. Ed. Harry Stone. Bloomington: Indiana University
Press, 1968.
1859 ...it will break his heart. (p. 119)
1860 ...Elliotson...would break his heart.... (p. 152)
The Letters of Charles Dickens, ed. Walter Dexter. Vol. III: 1858-1870. The Nonesuch
Dickens. London: The Nonesuch Press, 1938.
URDANG, *IDIOMS* 612.

To do one's **heart** good

1838 It has done my heart good.... (p. 387)
The Letters of Charles Dickens: Volume One: 1820-1839. Eds. Madeline House and Graham Storey. Oxford: The Clarendon Press, 1965.
URDANG, *IDIOMS* 613.

To have a bleeding **heart**

1855 Bleeding Heart Yard (p. 275)
1855 Bleeding Heart Yard (p. 277)
Dickens' Working Notes for His Novels. Ed. Harry Stone. Chicago, Ill.: University of Chicago Press, 1987.
URDANG, *IDIOMS* 612.

He's a...windictive creetur, with a hard **heart**.

1837 'He's a ma-licious, bad-disposed, vorldly-minded, spiteful, windictive creetur, with a hard heart as there ain't no soft'nin'. As the wirtuous clergyman remarked of the old gen'l'm'n with the dropsy, ven he said, that upon the whole he thought he'd rayther leave his property to his vife than build a chapel vith it.' (p. 615)
The Posthumous Papers of the Pickwick Club. 1837. The Oxford Illustrated Dickens, Vol. I. Oxford: Oxford University Press, 1948.

To have a heavy **heart**

1842 We...would have gone on our way with heavy hearts. (p. 175)
The Letters of Charles Dickens: Volume Three: 1842-1843. Eds. Madeline House, Graham Storey, and Kathleen Tillotson. Oxford: The Clarendon Press, 1974.
URDANG, *IDIOMS* 612.

To have one's **heart** in one's mouth

1853 'My heart's in my mouth.' (p. 110)
Bleak House. 1853. The Oxford Illustrated Dickens, Vol. III. Oxford: Oxford University Press, 1948.
APP 178; ODEP 364; EAP 207; MP 299.

To have one's **heart** in the right place

1850 '...my heart is no longer in the right place....' (p. 702)
The Personal History of David Copperfield. 1850. The Oxford Illustrated Dickens, Vol. II. Oxford: Oxford University Press, 1948.
1854 His heart was in the right place.... (p. 78)

Christmas Stories. 1871. The Oxford Illustrated Dickens, Vol. XI. Oxford: Oxford University Press, 1956.

1857 'My son has a art, and my son's art is in the right place.' (p. 721)

Little Dorrit. 1857. The Oxford Illustrated Dickens, Vol. XIV. Oxford: Oxford University Press, 1953.

WILKINSON 304.

To move a **heart** of stone

1852 ...he...groans in a way that might move a heart of stone.... (p. 619)

The Uncommercial Traveller and Reprinted Pieces Etc. 1850-1860. The Oxford Illustrated Dickens, Vol. XXI. Oxford: Oxford University Press, 1958.

APP 179; EAP 207; MP 299.

To take something to **heart**

1848 ...you have taken my letter so much to heart.... (p. 357)
1849 ...you took the complaints...so much to heart. (p. 536)

The Letters of Charles Dickens: Volume Five: 1847-1849. Eds. Graham Storey and K. J. Fielding. Oxford: The Clarendon Press, 1981.

URDANG, *IDIOMS* 612.

To be one's **heart's desire**

1853 ...as if it were her heart's desire.... (p. 653)

Bleak House. 1853. The Oxford Illustrated Dickens, Vol. III. Oxford: Oxford University Press, 1948.

URDANG, *IDIOMS* 334.

Heaven helps those who help themselves.

1847 ...the axiom, 'Heaven helps those who help themselves,' is truer in no case than it is in this.... (p. 417)

Address at the opening of the Glasgow Athenaeum, 28 Dec. 1847.

1854 ...I will say in the words of the French proverb, 'Heaven helps those who help themselves.' (p. 454)

Address to the Commercial Travellers, London, 30 Dec. 1854. *The Works of Charles Dickens: The Speeches.* Ed. Richard H. Shepherd. New National Edition, Vol. II. New York: Hearst's International Library Company, n. d.

ODEP 310; EAP 178; CODP 93; MP 259; DAP 294.

Heaven suits the back to the burden.

1839 'Heaven suits the back to the burden.' (p. 218)

The Life and Adventures of Nicholas Nickleby. 1839. The Oxford Illustrated Dickens, Vol. VI. Oxford: Oxford University Press, 1950.
ODEP 312; CODP 94; MP 259; DAP 255.

To be tied by the **heels**

1845 ...I am tied by the heels—both heels.... (p. 335)
The Letters of Charles Dickens: Volume Four: 1844-1846. Ed. Kathleen Tillotson. Oxford: The Clarendon Press, 1977.
URDANG, *IDIOMS* 616.

To cool one's **heels**

1839 'He shall cool his heels in jail....' (p. 676)
The Life and Adventures of Nicholas Nickleby. 1839. The Oxford Illustrated Dickens, Vol. VI. Oxford: Oxford University Press, 1950.
ODEP 143; EAP 209; MP 300.

To kick one's **heels**

1842 ...two or three half-drunken loafers...will be seen kicking their heels in rocking-chairs.... (p. 188)
American Notes and Pictures from Italy. 1842, 1846. The Oxford Illustrated Dickens, Vol. XIX. Oxford: Oxford University Press, 1957.
ODEP 422; EAP 209; MP 301.

To lay someone by the **heels**

1870 ...I am literally laid by the heels.... (p. 776)
555)
The Letters of Charles Dickens, ed. Walter Dexter. Vol. III: 1858-1870. The Nonesuch Dickens. London: The Nonesuch Press, 1938.
EAP 209; MP 301.

It's over and can't be **helped**.

1837 'It's over, and can't be helped, and that's one consolation, as they always say in Turkey, ven they cuts a wrong man's head off.' (p. 315)
The Posthumous Papers of the Pickwick Club. 1837. The Oxford Illustrated Dickens, Vol. I. Oxford: Oxford University Press, 1948.
DOW 26.

Helter-skelter

1841 'Who won the Helter-Skelter Plate, child?' (p. 196)
1841 'The Helter-Skelter Plate at the races, child....' (p. 196)

1841 'Can't you say who won the Helter-Skelter Plate...?' (p. 196)
The Old Curiosity Shop. 1841. The Oxford Illustrated Dickens, Vol. VIII. Oxford: Oxford University Press, 1951.
PARTRIDGE 387.

Here and there

1842 Here and there, were drops of its blood.... (p. 120)
American Notes and Pictures from Italy. 1842, 1846. The Oxford Illustrated Dickens, Vol. XIX. Oxford: Oxford University Press, 1957.
1864 ...I have laid a trifle of timber here and there.... (p. 521)
Address in support of the Shakespeare Schools, London, 11 May 1864. *The Works of Charles Dickens: The Speeches*. Ed. Richard H. Shepherd. New National Edition, Vol. II. New York: Hearst's International Library Company, n. d.
1868 The charred trunks of the trees...stand here and there.... (p. 640)
The Letters of Charles Dickens, ed. Walter Dexter. Vol. III: 1858-1870. The Nonesuch Dickens. London: The Nonesuch Press, 1938.
URDANG, *IDIOMS* 621.

Here, there, and everywhere

1857 '...I have been here and there and everywhere!' (p. 354)
Little Dorrit. 1857. The Oxford Illustrated Dickens, Vol. XIV. Oxford: Oxford University Press, 1953.
URDANG, *IDIOMS* 621.

To be neither **here** nor there

1850-56 "That's neither here nor there." (p. 504)
The Uncommercial Traveller and Reprinted Pieces Etc. 1850-1860. The Oxford Illustrated Dickens, Vol. XXI. Oxford: Oxford University Press, 1958.
1857 'But she's neither here nor there....' (p. 280)
Little Dorrit. 1857. The Oxford Illustrated Dickens, Vol. XIV. Oxford: Oxford University Press, 1953.
APP 182; ODEP 561; EAP 211; MP 305.

To be **hey-go-mad**

1854 'Yo was hey-go-mad about her....' (p. 157)
Hard Times for These Times. 1854. The Oxford Illustrated Dickens, Vol. XVII. Oxford: Oxford University Press, 1955.

Hide-and-seek

1843 ...it was a young house, playing at hide-and-seek with other houses.... (p. 14)

Christmas Books. 1843-49. The Oxford Illustrated Dickens, Vol. XVI. Oxford: Oxford University Press, 1954.

1857 ...they...played at hide-and-seek.... (p. 69)

Little Dorrit. 1857. The Oxford Illustrated Dickens, Vol. XIV. Oxford: Oxford University Press, 1953.

URDANG, *IDIOMS* 623.

Higgledy-piggledy

1850 ...'his name's...higgledy-piggledy.' (p. 330)

The Personal History of David Copperfield. 1850. The Oxford Illustrated Dickens, Vol. II. Oxford: Oxford University Press, 1948.

1860 ...the stock was higgledy-piggledy.... (p. 249)

The Uncommercial Traveller and Reprinted Pieces Etc. 1850-1860. The Oxford Illustrated Dickens, Vol. XXI. Oxford: Oxford University Press, 1958.

PARTRIDGE 389.

As **high** as the sky; sky-high

1842 ...the Steamer Alcohol blowing up sky-high. (p. 193)

The Letters of Charles Dickens: Volume Three: 1842-1843. Eds. Madeline House, Graham Storey, and Kathleen Tillotson. Oxford: The Clarendon Press, 1974.

1848 'She aspires sky-high.' (p. 274)

Dealings with the Firm of Dombey and Son. 1848. The Oxford Illustrated Dickens, Vol. VII. Oxford: Oxford University Press, 1950.

APP 338; EAP 398; MP 573.

High and dry

1838 ...I no sooner get myself up, high and dry.... (p. 421)

The Letters of Charles Dickens: Volume One: 1820-1839. Eds. Madeline House and Graham Storey. Oxford: The Clarendon Press, 1965.

1841 I am going to...get down on Hampstead Heath or some high and dry road to walk. (p. 200)

The Letters of Charles Dickens: Volume Two: 1840-1841. Eds. Madeline House and Graham Storey. Oxford: The Clarendon Press, 1969.

1844 '...leaves me high and dry, without a leg to stand upon.' (p. 737)

The Life and Adventures of Martin Chuzzlewit. 1844. The Oxford Illustrated Dickens, Vol. IX. Oxford: Oxford University Press, 1951.

1845 'A man...may heap up facts on figures...mountains high and dry....' (p. 98)

Christmas Books. 1843-49. The Oxford Illustrated Dickens, Vol. XVI. Oxford: Oxford University Press, 1954.

1847 ...leaving a good-sized audience high and dry behind the actor.... (p. 95)

The Letters of Charles Dickens: Volume Five: 1847-1849. Eds. Graham Storey and K. J. Fielding. Oxford: The Clarendon Press, 1981.

1850 There was a black barge...high and dry on the ground.... (p. 29)
The Personal History of David Copperfield. 1850. The Oxford Illustrated Dickens, Vol. II. Oxford: Oxford University Press, 1948.

1852 ...the sluggish tide shall...land it high and dry upon the beach. (p. 412)
"First Fruits." [with George Augustus Sala]. *Charles Dickens' Uncollected Writings from Household Words 1850-1859*, 2 vols. Ed. Harry Stone. Bloomington: Indiana University Press, 1968.

ODEP 372; MP 307.

High and low

1846 ...I looked high and low for your card.... (p. 678)
The Letters of Charles Dickens: Volume Four: 1844-1846. Ed. Kathleen Tillotson. Oxford: The Clarendon Press, 1977.

1847 ...I am looking about, high and low.... (p. 187)
The Letters of Charles Dickens: Volume Five: 1847-1849. Eds. Graham Storey and K. J. Fielding. Oxford: The Clarendon Press, 1981.

URDANG, *IDIOMS* 623.

Highways and byways

1860 ...we were...poor workers in a hundred highways and byways. (p. 32)
The Uncommercial Traveller and Reprinted Pieces Etc. 1850-1860. The Oxford Illustrated Dickens, Vol. XXI. Oxford: Oxford University Press, 1958.

URDANG, *IDIOMS* 626.

The squeaky **hinge** gets the oil.

1844 ...each one a tiny drop of oil upon my hinges: and the only oil they ever get. (p. 170)
The Letters of Charles Dickens: Volume Four: 1844-1846. Ed. Kathleen Tillotson. Oxford: The Clarendon Press, 1977.

CODP 211; MP 678; DAP 650.

Hither and thither

1850 Thousands of sovereigns were jerked hither and thither from hand to hand...piles of bank notes...hustled to and fro.... (p. 126)
"The Old Lady in Threadneedle Street." [with W. H. Wills]. *Charles Dickens' Uncollected Writings from Household Words 1850-1859*, 2 vols. Ed. Harry Stone. Bloomington: Indiana University Press, 1968.

URDANG, *IDIOMS* 635.

Hob-nob

1864 ...you and I would take a special hob-nob together.... (p. 392)
The Letters of Charles Dickens, ed. Walter Dexter. Vol. III: 1858-1870. The Nonesuch Dickens. London: The Nonesuch Press, 1938.
ODEP 342; EAP 212.

Hocus-pocus

1842 ...rather than hint at the possibility of their guests being versed in the vagabond arts of sleight-of-hand and hocus-pocus. (p. 169)
American Notes and Pictures from Italy. 1842, 1846. The Oxford Illustrated Dickens, Vol. XIX. Oxford: Oxford University Press, 1957.
1857 'All the rest is hocus-pocus.' (p. 403)
Little Dorrit. 1857. The Oxford Illustrated Dickens, Vol. XIV. Oxford: Oxford University Press, 1953.
EAP 213; URDANG, *IDIOMS* 636.

Hodge Styles

1851 If I set Hodge Styles a moral lesson.... (p. 278)
"Cain in the Fields." [with R. H. Horne]. *Charles Dickens' Uncollected Writings from Household Words 1850-1859*, 2 vols. Ed. Harry Stone. Bloomington: Indiana University Press, 1968.

To go the whole hog

1842 ...a kind of opposition...may be called...whole-hog opposition. (p. 281)
The Letters of Charles Dickens: Volume Three: 1842-1843. Eds. Madeline House, Graham Storey, and Kathleen Tillotson. Oxford: The Clarendon Press, 1974.
1853 ...every moderately sane man...does not carry his pigs to a Whole Hog market. (p. 480)
"In and Out of Jail." [with Henry Morley and W. H. Wills]. *Charles Dickens' Uncollected Writings from Household Words 1850-1859*, 2 vols. Ed. Harry Stone. Bloomington: Indiana University Press, 1968.
APP 184; ODEP 307; EAP 215; MP 311.

Hoity-toity

1848 'Hoity-toity!' exclaimed Mrs. Pipchin.... (p. 140)
1848 'Hoity, toity!' (p. 720)
1848 'Hoity toity!' says Mrs. Pipchin.... (p. 834)

Dealings with the Firm of Dombey and Son. 1848. The Oxford Illustrated Dickens, Vol. VII. Oxford: Oxford University Press, 1950.

1864 "Hoity toity, Major," I says.... (p. 417)

Christmas Stories. 1871. The Oxford Illustrated Dickens, Vol. XI. Oxford: Oxford University Press, 1956.

1868 "Hoity toity me!" (p. 701)

The Uncommercial Traveller and Reprinted Pieces Etc. 1850-1860. The Oxford Illustrated Dickens, Vol. XXI. Oxford: Oxford University Press, 1958.

PARTRIDGE 391.

Hole-and-corner

1864 ...the actors are wise...in seeking not a little hole-and-corner place of education.... (p. 521)

Address in support of the Shakespeare Schools, London, 11 May 1864. *The Works of Charles Dickens: The Speeches.* Ed. Richard H. Shepherd. New National Edition, Vol. II. New York: Hearst's International Library Company, n. d.

1870 '...we are to make a moonlight hole-and-corner exploration....' (p. 130)

The Mystery of Edwin Drood. 1870. The Oxford Illustrated Dickens, Vol. XVIII. Oxford: Oxford University Press, 1956.

MP 312.

To make a **hole** in the water [=to drown oneself]

1853 'I don't know why I don't go and make a hole in the water.' (p. 631)

Bleak House. 1853. The Oxford Illustrated Dickens, Vol. III. Oxford: Oxford University Press, 1948.

ODEP 378; MP 312.

Home is home, though it be never so homely.

1857 'Just as Home is Home though it's never so Homely, why you see,' said Mr. Meagles, adding a new version to the proverb, 'Rome is Rome, though it's never so Romely.' (p. 527)

Little Dorrit. 1857. The Oxford Illustrated Dickens, Vol. XIV. Oxford: Oxford University Press, 1953.

APP 186; ODEP 379; EAP 216; DAP 304.

Home, sweet home

1842 ...with what feeling I play *Home Sweet Home* every night.... (p. 166)

The Letters of Charles Dickens: Volume Three: 1842-1843. Eds. Madeline House, Graham Storey, and Kathleen Tillotson. Oxford: The Clarendon Press, 1974.

1865 '...you'd been called upon for Home, Sweet Home....' (p. 499)
Our Mutual Friend. 1865. The Oxford Illustrated Dickens, Vol. X. Oxford: Oxford University Press, 1952.
STEVENSON 1153:8.

To go to one's long **home**

1844 '...Gamp was summoned to his long home....' (p. 313)
The Life and Adventures of Martin Chuzzlewit. 1844. The Oxford Illustrated Dickens, Vol. IX. Oxford: Oxford University Press, 1951.
APP 186; ODEP 479; EAP 216; MP 314.

As **honest** as the sun

1857 '...he is as honest as the sun....' (p. 199)
Little Dorrit. 1857. The Oxford Illustrated Dickens, Vol. XIV. Oxford: Oxford University Press, 1953.
WILKINSON 210.

Honesty is the best policy.

1839 '"Honesty is the best policy," is it?' (p. 368)
The Life and Adventures of Nicholas Nickleby. 1839. The Oxford Illustrated Dickens, Vol. VI. Oxford: Oxford University Press, 1950.
APP 186; ODEP 380; EAP 217; CODP 113; MP 314; DAP 305.

To turn **honey** into gall

1864 ...having had my honey turned into Gall.... (p. 399)
The Letters of Charles Dickens, ed. Walter Dexter. Vol. III: 1858-1870. The Nonesuch Dickens. London: The Nonesuch Press, 1938.
ODEP 381; EAP 218.

Honi soit qui mal y pense.

1852-54 The King is said to have picked up a lady's garter at a ball, and to have said, *Honi soit qui mal y pense*—in English. "Evil be to him who evil think of it." (pp. 292-293)
Master Humphrey's Clock and A Child's History of England. 1840-41, 1852-54. The Oxford Illustrated Dickens, Vol. XX. Oxford: Oxford University Press, 1958.
ODEP 397; EAP 135; MP 315; DAP 186.

By **hook** or by crook

1841 ...passengers...are got across by hook or by crook.... (p. 326)
The Letters of Charles Dickens: Volume Two: 1840-1841. Eds. Madeline House and Graham Storey. Oxford: The Clarendon Press, 1969.
1845 ...you must produce yourself here somehow, by hook or by crook.... (p. 1845)
The Letters of Charles Dickens: Volume Four: 1844-1846. Ed. Kathleen Tillotson. Oxford: The Clarendon Press, 1977.
APP 187; ODEP 382; EAP 218; MP 315.

Hope deferred maketh the heart sick.

1852 The promise; the hope deferred.... (p. 415)
"First Fruits." [with George Augustus Sala]. *Charles Dickens' Uncollected Writings from Household Words 1850-1859*, 2 vols. Ed. Harry Stone. Bloomington: Indiana University Press, 1968.
APP 188; ODEP 384; EAP 219; CODP 114; MP 317; DAP 308.

There is always **hope**.

1839 'There is always hope,' said Nicholas.... (p. 97)
The Life and Adventures of Nicholas Nickleby. 1839. The Oxford Illustrated Dickens, Vol. VI. Oxford: Oxford University Press, 1950.

Do not look a gift **horse** in the mouth.

1850 'I don't want to look a gift-horse in the mouth....' (p. 231)
The Personal History of David Copperfield. 1850. The Oxford Illustrated Dickens, Vol. II. Oxford: Oxford University Press, 1948.
APP 191; ODEP 301; CODP 91; MP 324; DAP 311.

To be a good **horse** to look at but a bad one to go

1842 It's a good horse to look at, but—to follow out the common saying—an uncommon bad 'un to go.... (pp. 115-116)
The Letters of Charles Dickens: Volume Three: 1842-1843. Eds. Madeline House, Graham Storey, and Kathleen Tillotson. Oxford: The Clarendon Press, 1974.

To work like a **horse**

1842 I have already begun working like a dray-horse.... (p. 269)
The Letters of Charles Dickens: Volume Three: 1842-1843. Eds. Madeline House, Graham Storey, and Kathleen Tillotson. Oxford: The Clarendon Press, 1974.
APP 192; ODEP 917; EAP 224; MP 325.

Wild **horses** could not....

1845 Man shall not force, nor horses drag, this poor gentleman-like carcass.... (p. 334)
The Letters of Charles Dickens: Volume Four: 1844-1846. Ed. Kathleen Tillotson. Oxford: The Clarendon Press, 1977.
1857 'A team of horses couldn't draw her back now....' (p. 320)
Little Dorrit. 1857. The Oxford Illustrated Dickens, Vol. XIV. Oxford: Oxford University Press, 1953.
APP 192; ODEP 889; EAP 223; MP 326.

A **horseshoe** nailed above the door brings luck.

1840-41 ...the towns-people went to work nailing up horseshoes over every door.... (p. 58)
Master Humphrey's Clock and A Child's History of England. 1840-41, 1852-54. The Oxford Illustrated Dickens, Vol. XX. Oxford: Oxford University Press, 1958.
URDANG, *IDIOMS* 652.

To blow both **hot and cold**

1859 Though he bloweth both hot and cold. (p. 245)
Complete Plays and Selected Poems of Charles Dickens. London: Vision Press, 1970.
APP 193; ODEP 70; EAP 37; MP 58.

To be a **house** of cards

1850 I felt as if I had been living in a palace of cards, which had tumbled down.... (p. 561)
The Personal History of David Copperfield. 1850. The Oxford Illustrated Dickens, Vol. II. Oxford: Oxford University Press, 1948.
MP 329.

To be like a **house** afire

1857 '...he is making out his case like a house a-fire.' (p. 822)
Little Dorrit. 1857. The Oxford Illustrated Dickens, Vol. XIV. Oxford: Oxford University Press, 1953.
APP 194; ODEP 390; MP 330.

To bring down the **house**

1843 ...I expect he will bring the house down. (p. 510)
The Letters of Charles Dickens: Volume Three: 1842-1843. Eds. Madeline House, Graham Storey, and Kathleen Tillotson. Oxford: The Clarendon Press, 1974.
URDANG, *IDIOMS* 656.

To play to a shy **house** in the theatre

1841 ...a full house is distinctly better than what is called, in theatrical slang, a "shy" one. (p. 878)
The Letters of Charles Dickens: Volume Seven: 1853-1855. Eds. Graham Storey, Kathleen Tillotson, and Angus Easson. Oxford: The Clarendon Press, 1993.

When **house** and lands are gone and spent, | Then learning is most excellent.

1843 The old doggerel rhyme...says that 'When house and lands are gone and spent, | Then learning is most excellent'; but I should be strongly disposed...to say that 'Though house and lands he never got, | Learning can give what they can*not*.' (p. 391)
Address at the Manchester Athenaeum, 5 Oct. 1843. *The Works of Charles Dickens: The Speeches*. Ed. Richard H. Shepherd. New National Edition, Vol. II. New York: Hearst's International Library Company, n. d.
ODEP 389.

To be a **household word**

1851 ...the place which was a Nuisance, is become quite a household word. (p. 349)
"Shakspeare and Newgate." [with R. H. Horne].
1852 That it is *"le premier pas qui coûte"*—that the first step is the great point—is...a household word.... (p. 410)
"First Fruits." [with George Augustus Sala]. *Charles Dickens' Uncollected Writings from Household Words 1850-1859*, 2 vols. Ed. Harry Stone. Bloomington: Indiana University Press, 1968.
URDANG, *IDIOMS* 658.

The **Hub** of the Universe is Boston.

1867 ...Boston, the Hub of the Universe as they call it.... (p. 587)
The Letters of Charles Dickens, ed. Walter Dexter. Vol. III: 1858-1870. The Nonesuch Dickens. London: The Nonesuch Press, 1938.
STEVENSON 225:6.

Hubbub

1839 ...his quick ear caught the sound of a...hubbub of voices.... (p. 576)
The Life and Adventures of Nicholas Nickleby. 1839. The Oxford Illustrated Dickens, Vol. VI. Oxford: Oxford University Press, 1950.
PARTRIDGE 412.

To raise the **hue and cry**

1838 ...the Dodger...joined in the hue-and-cry which was raised.... (p. 82)

1838 ...he was deeply absorbed in the interesting pages of the Hue-and-Cry. (p. 106)

1838 'They set up a hue-and-cry....' (p. 227)

The Adventures of Oliver Twist. 1838. The Oxford Illustrated Dickens, Vol. V. Oxford: Oxford University Press, 1948.

1841 'There was one...raised the hue-and-cry....' (p. 128)

1841 'There's a great cry there, Mr. Willet, but very little wool.' (p. 234)

Barnaby Rudge: A Tale of the Riots of 'Eighty. 1841. The Oxford Illustrated Dickens, Vol. XV. Oxford: Oxford University Press, 1954.

1854 ...the Lawyer...wanted a description of the murderer to send to the Police Hue and Cry.... (p. 529)

"The Seven Poor Travellers." *Charles Dickens' Uncollected Writings from* Household Words *1850-1859*, 2 vols. Ed. Harry Stone. Bloomington: Indiana University Press, 1968.
WILKINSON 261.

To be in a **huff**

1864 ...some other dignitaries resigned in a huff.... (p. 390)

The Letters of Charles Dickens, ed. Walter Dexter. Vol. III: 1858-1870. The Nonesuch Dickens. London: The Nonesuch Press, 1938.
URDANG, *IDIOMS* 660.

Human nature is weak.

1862 "Human nature is weak." (p. 340)

Christmas Stories. 1871. The Oxford Illustrated Dickens, Vol. XI. Oxford: Oxford University Press, 1956.

To eat **humble pie**

1850 'I ate umble pie with an appetite.' (p. 575)

The Personal History of David Copperfield. 1850. The Oxford Illustrated Dickens, Vol. II. Oxford: Oxford University Press, 1948.
APP 195; ODEP 391; EAP 228; MP 331.

Humdrum

1850 ...we'd group in miniature your humdrum baby-trainers.... (pp. 192-193)

"Mr. Bendigo Buster on Our National Defences Against Education." [with Henry Morley]. *Charles Dickens' Uncollected Writings from* Household Words *1850-1859*, 2 vols. Ed. Harry Stone. Bloomington: Indiana University Press, 1968.
PARTRIDGE 414.

Hurly-burly

1839 '...when it cooms—ecod, such a hoorly-boorly!' (p. 545)
The Life and Adventures of Nicholas Nickleby. 1839. The Oxford Illustrated Dickens, Vol. VI. Oxford: Oxford University Press, 1950.
PARTRIDGE 416.

To play a **hurry** as an actor enters

1833-36 ...the wrongful heir comes in to two bars of quick music (technically called "a hurry...." (p. 116)
Sketches by Boz. 1833-40. The Oxford Illustrated Dickens, Vol. XII. Oxford: Oxford University Press, 1957.
PARTRIDGE 416 (CITING DICKENS).

I

To dot the **i**'s and cross the **t**'s

1836 STRANGE GENTLEMAN: ...there's a ferocious recklessness in the cross to this 'T,' and a baleful malignity in the dot of that 'I....' (*The Strange Gentleman*, I, i, p. 11)
Complete Plays and Selected Poems of Charles Dickens. London: Vision Press, 1970.
1839 '...he dots all his small i's and crosses every t as he writes it.' (p. 472)
The Life and Adventures of Nicholas Nickleby. 1839. The Oxford Illustrated Dickens, Vol. VI. Oxford: Oxford University Press, 1950.
1842 The letter is...from...the cross of every t, and the dot of every i, a most wicked and nefarious Forgery. (p. 327)
The Letters of Charles Dickens: Volume Three: 1842-1843. Eds. Madeline House, Graham Storey, and Kathleen Tillotson. Oxford: The Clarendon Press, 1974.
APP 197; ODEP 200; EAP 230; MP 333.

To break the **ice**

1837 "I'll break the ice, my love," said Mr. Budden.... (p. 313)
Sketches by Boz. 1833-40. The Oxford Illustrated Dickens, Vol. XII. Oxford: Oxford University Press, 1957.
1841 'We have broken the ice, though.' (p. 335)

Barnaby Rudge: A Tale of the Riots of 'Eighty. 1841. The Oxford Illustrated Dickens, Vol. XV. Oxford: Oxford University Press, 1954.
APP 197; ODEP 83; EAP 230; MP 334.

Idleness is the root of all evil.

1850 '...idleness is the root of all evil.' (p. 136)
The Personal History of David Copperfield. 1850. The Oxford Illustrated Dickens, Vol. II. Oxford: Oxford University Press, 1948.
APP 198; ODEP 396; EAP 231; CODP 118; MP 334; DAP 324.

Ignorance is bliss.

1837 Poor thing! there are times when ignorance is bliss indeed. (p. 85)
The Posthumous Papers of the Pickwick Club. 1837. The Oxford Illustrated Dickens, Vol. I. Oxford: Oxford University Press, 1948.
APP 198; ODEP 396; CODP 118; MP 335; DAP 325.

First **impressions** are most lasting.

1844 '...first impressions...often go a long way, and last a long time.' (p. 75)
The Life and Adventures of Martin Chuzzlewit. 1844. The Oxford Illustrated Dickens, Vol. IX. Oxford: Oxford University Press, 1951.

Give an **inch**, take an ell.

1841 A homely proverb recognizes the existence of a troublesome class of persons who, having an inch conceded them, will take an ell. (p. 228)
1841 Old John having long encroached a good standard inch...and having snipped off a Flemish ell...grew...despotic.... (p. 228)
Barnaby Rudge: A Tale of the Riots of 'Eighty. 1841. The Oxford Illustrated Dickens, Vol. XV. Oxford: Oxford University Press, 1954.
1865 'Give him an inch, and he'll take an ell.' (p. 581)
Our Mutual Friend. 1865. The Oxford Illustrated Dickens, Vol. X. Oxford: Oxford University Press, 1952.
1867 ...if you were to give me a happy inch, I should take an ell.... (p. 555)
The Letters of Charles Dickens, ed. Walter Dexter. Vol. III: 1858-1870. The Nonesuch Dickens. London: The Nonesuch Press, 1938.
APP 198; ODEP 303; EAP 232; MP 336; DAP 328.

Annual **income** twenty pounds, annual expenditure nineteen six, result happiness....

1850 Annual income twenty pounds, annual expenditure nineteen six, result happiness. Annual income twenty pounds, annual expenditure twenty pounds ought and six, result misery. (p. 175)
The Personal History of David Copperfield. 1850. The Oxford Illustrated Dickens, Vol. II. Oxford: Oxford University Press, 1948.
STEVENSON 2196-2197:14.

Werry sorry to 'casion any personal **inconvenience**.

1837 'Werry sorry to 'casion any personal inconwenience, ma'am, as the house-breaker said to the old lady when he put her on the fire....' (p. 360)
The Posthumous Papers of the Pickwick Club. 1837. The Oxford Illustrated Dickens, Vol. I. Oxford: Oxford University Press, 1948.
DOW 66.

To walk **Indian file**

1851 The sections march off Indian file.... (p. 259)
"The Metropolitan Protectives." [with W. H. Wills]. *Charles Dickens' Uncollected Writings from* Household Words *1850-1859*, 2 vols. Ed. Harry Stone. Bloomington: Indiana University Press, 1968.
URDANG, *IDIOMS* 705.

Ins and outs

1865 '...I know more of the ins and outs of him than any living person does.' (p. 64)
Our Mutual Friend. 1865. The Oxford Illustrated Dickens, Vol. X. Oxford: Oxford University Press, 1952.
EAP 234; MP 338.

This I call adding **insult** to injury.

1837 '...vich I call addin' insult to injury, as the parrot said ven they not only took him from his native land, but made him talk the English langvidg arterwards.' (p. 493)
The Posthumous Papers of the Pickwick Club. 1837. The Oxford Illustrated Dickens, Vol. I. Oxford: Oxford University Press, 1948.
APP 200; ODEP 405; EAP 234; MP 338; DAP 332; DOW 67.

The wery best **intentions**, sir.

1837 '...the wery best intentions, as the gen'l'm'n said ven he run away from his wife 'cos she seemed unhappy with him,' replied Mr. Weller. (p. 364)

The Posthumous Papers of the Pickwick Club. 1837. The Oxford Illustrated Dickens, Vol. I. Oxford: Oxford University Press, 1948.

DOW 68.

To all **intents and purposes**

1849 ...she was, to all intents and purposes, *well*, next day. (p. 487)

The Letters of Charles Dickens: Volume Five: 1847-1849. Eds. Graham Storey and K. J. Fielding. Oxford: The Clarendon Press, 1981.

URDANG, *IDIOMS* 711.

Sorry to...cause an **interruption** to such wery pleasant proceedings.

1837 'Sorry to do anythin' as may cause an interruption to such wery pleasant proceedin's, as the king said wen he dissolved parliament,' interposed Mr. Weller.... (p. 674)

The Posthumous Papers of the Pickwick Club. 1837. The Oxford Illustrated Dickens, Vol. I. Oxford: Oxford University Press, 1948.

DOW 68.

As **invisible** as the air

1841 To any body else Man Woman or Child I shall be as invisible as the Air.... (p. 838)

The Letters of Charles Dickens: Volume Seven: 1853-1855. Eds. Graham Storey, Kathleen Tillotson, and Angus Easson. Oxford: The Clarendon Press, 1993.

WILSTACH 218.

Strike while the **iron** is hot.

1841 'Strike while the iron's hot; that's what I say.' (p. 336)

Barnaby Rudge: A Tale of the Riots of 'Eighty. 1841. The Oxford Illustrated Dickens, Vol. XV. Oxford: Oxford University Press, 1954.

1848 The iron was now hot, and Richards striking on it.... (p. 28)

Dealings with the Firm of Dombey and Son. 1848. The Oxford Illustrated Dickens, Vol. VII. Oxford: Oxford University Press, 1950.

1850 It was one of the irons I began to heat immediately, and one of the irons I kept hot, and hammered at, with the perseverance I may honestly admire. (p. 545)

The Personal History of David Copperfield. 1850. The Oxford Illustrated Dickens, Vol. II. Oxford: Oxford University Press, 1948.

1862 ...I am...ready...to strike in and hammer the hot iron out. (p. 310)

1863 ...if I don't strike while the iron (meaning myself) is hot, I shall drift off again.... (p. 364)

The Letters of Charles Dickens, ed. Walter Dexter. Vol. III: 1858-1870. The Nonesuch Dickens. London: The Nonesuch Press, 1938.

APP 201; ODEP 781; EAP 235; CODP 215; MP 338; DAP 334.

To have other **irons** in the fire

1836 ...the numerous Irons that I have been putting in the fire...are only just beginning to get warm.... (p. 143)

The Letters of Charles Dickens: Volume One: 1820-1839. Eds. Madeline House and Graham Storey. Oxford: The Clarendon Press, 1965.

1849 ...he will be none the worse for having two irons in the fire. (p. 685)

The Letters of Charles Dickens: Volume Five: 1847-1849. Eds. Graham Storey and K. J. Fielding. Oxford: The Clarendon Press, 1981.

1850 You have other irons in the fire. (p. 202)

"Mr. Bendigo Buster on Our National Defences Against Education." [with Henry Morley]. *Charles Dickens' Uncollected Writings from Household Words 1850-1859*, 2 vols. Ed. Harry Stone. Bloomington: Indiana University Press, 1968.

1861 All the iron is in the fire, and I have "only" to beat it out.... (p. 217)

The Letters of Charles Dickens, ed. Walter Dexter. Vol. III: 1858-1870. The Nonesuch Dickens. London: The Nonesuch Press, 1938.

APP 201; ODEP 509; EAP 235; MP 339.

J

Jack-in-office

1833-36 "You're a Jack-in-office, sir." (p. 154)
1833-36 "A Jack-in office, sir...." (p. 154)

Sketches by Boz. 1833-40. The Oxford Illustrated Dickens, Vol. XII. Oxford: Oxford University Press, 1957.

1857 '...that is a type of Jack-in-office insolence....' (p. 18)

Little Dorrit. 1857. The Oxford Illustrated Dickens, Vol. XIV. Oxford: Oxford University Press, 1953.

ODEP 408; EAP 238; MP 340.

Jack-in-the-box

1833-36 Pedestrians linger...unable to resist the allurements of the stout proprietress of the "Jack-in-the-box, three shies a penny. (p. 112)

Sketches by Boz. 1833-40. The Oxford Illustrated Dickens, Vol. XII. Oxford: Oxford University Press, 1957.

ODEP 408.

Jack-in-the-green

1837 ...falling about with every jerk of the machine...like a "Jack-in-the-green," on May-day.... (p. 472)

Sketches by Boz. 1833-40. The Oxford Illustrated Dickens, Vol. XII. Oxford: Oxford University Press, 1957.

PARTRIDGE 420.

Jack Ketch

1833-36 ...we half expected to see a brass plate, with the inscription "Mr. Ketch...." (p. 196)

Sketches by Boz. 1833-40. The Oxford Illustrated Dickens, Vol. XII. Oxford: Oxford University Press, 1957.

1838 '...you would have to escape Jack Ketch.' (p. 189)

The Adventures of Oliver Twist. 1838. The Oxford Illustrated Dickens, Vol. V. Oxford: Oxford University Press, 1948.

PARTRIDGE 430.

Jack of all trades is master of none.

1833-36 ...he is a bit of a Jack of all trades.... (p. 11)

Sketches by Boz. 1833-40. The Oxford Illustrated Dickens, Vol. XII. Oxford: Oxford University Press, 1957.

1861 'I am my own...Jack of all Trades,' said Wemmick.... (p. 196)

Great Expectations. 1861. The Oxford Illustrated Dickens, Vol. XIII. Oxford: Oxford University Press, 1953.

APP 202; ODEP 408; EAP 237; MP 340; DAP 337.

Before one can say **Jack Robinson**

1839 '...Tim was at him, sir, before you could say "Jack Robinson."' (p. 596)

The Life and Adventures of Nicholas Nickleby. 1839. The Oxford Illustrated Dickens, Vol. VI. Oxford: Oxford University Press, 1950.

1842 ...great writers...are as familiar to our lips as household words. (p. 378)

Remarks at a dinner given by the young men of Boston, Massachusetts, 1 Feb. 1842. *The Works of Charles Dickens: The Speeches*. Ed. Richard H. Shepherd. New National Edition, Vol. II. New York: Hearst's International Library Company, n. d.

1843 'Let's have the shutters up...before a man can say Jack Robinson!' (p. 31)

Christmas Books. 1843-49. The Oxford Illustrated Dickens, Vol. XVI. Oxford: Oxford University Press, 1954.

1852 The portly constable will whisk you into a back office before you can say Jack Robinson.... (p. 397)

"Post-Office Money-Orders." [with W. H. Wills]. *Charles Dickens' Uncollected Writings from* Household Words *1850-1859*, 2 vols. Ed. Harry Stone. Bloomington: Indiana University Press, 1968.

APP 202; ODEP 40; EAP 238; MP 341.

Jim Crow

1842 ...he finishes...with the chuckle of a million counterfeit Jim Crows.... (p. 91)

American Notes and Pictures from Italy. 1842, 1846. The Oxford Illustrated Dickens, Vol. XIX. Oxford: Oxford University Press, 1957.

PARTRIDGE 1224.

John Bull

1850-56 ...Dogginson—regarded in our Vestry as "a regular John Bull...." (p. 575)

The Uncommercial Traveller and Reprinted Pieces Etc. 1850-1860. The Oxford Illustrated Dickens, Vol. XXI. Oxford: Oxford University Press, 1958.

ODEP 412.

John Doe and Richard Roe

1841 'Those charming creations of the poet, John Doe and Richard Roe...will open a new world....' (p. 250)

The Old Curiosity Shop. 1841. The Oxford Illustrated Dickens, Vol. VIII. Oxford: Oxford University Press, 1951.

ODEP 413.

To be a **Johnny Cake**

1842 "Down Easters and Johnny Cakes can follow if they please. I an't a Johnny Cake...I an't a Johnny Cake...." (p. 151)

American Notes and Pictures from Italy. 1842, 1846. The Oxford Illustrated Dickens, Vol. XIX. Oxford: Oxford University Press, 1957.

URDANG, IDIOMS 738.

A **joke** is a joke.

1833-36 A joke's a joke.... (p. 43)
Sketches by Boz. 1833-40. The Oxford Illustrated Dickens, Vol. XII. Oxford: Oxford University Press, 1957.
1854 'A joke's a joke.' (p. 135)
Hard Times for These Times. 1854. The Oxford Illustrated Dickens, Vol. XVII. Oxford: Oxford University Press, 1955.
APP 205; MP 345.

(Not) to matter a **jot**

1840-41 Will...cared not a jot for hard knocks.... (p. 66)
Master Humphrey's Clock and A Child's History of England. 1840-41, 1852-54. The Oxford Illustrated Dickens, Vol. XX. Oxford: Oxford University Press, 1958.
1844 Whether he were in the humour to profit by it, mattered not a jot. (p. 375)
The Life and Adventures of Martin Chuzzlewit. 1844. The Oxford Illustrated Dickens, Vol. IX. Oxford: Oxford University Press, 1951.
EAP 241; MP 345.

Judas kiss
1865 A Judas order of kiss.... (p. 471)
Our Mutual Friend. 1865. The Oxford Illustrated Dickens, Vol. X. Oxford: Oxford University Press, 1952.
ODEP 414; EAP 342; MP 345.

Be **just** before you are generous.

1844 'There is a most remarkably long-headed, flowing-bearded, and patriarchal proverb, which observes that it is the duty of a man to be just before he is generous.' (p. 221)
The Life and Adventures of Martin Chuzzlewit. 1844. The Oxford Illustrated Dickens, Vol. IX. Oxford: Oxford University Press, 1951.
ODEP 416; EAP 242; CODP 123; MP 346; DAP 342; BARTLETT 352:31.

K

To be a pretty **kettle** of fish

1845 Here's a pretty kettle of Fish! (p. 415)
The Letters of Charles Dickens: Volume Four: 1844-1846. Ed. Kathleen Tillotson. Oxford: The Clarendon Press, 1977.
1850 ...'there'll be a pretty kettle of fish!' (p. 275)

The Personal History of David Copperfield. 1850. The Oxford Illustrated Dickens, Vol. II. Oxford: Oxford University Press, 1948.
APP 207; ODEP 421; EAP 243; MP 347.

To have the **kicks** but not the halfpence

1857 "...it's hard...that you should have all the halfpence, and I all the kicks...." (p. 167)
Christmas Stories. 1871. The Oxford Illustrated Dickens, Vol. XI. Oxford: Oxford University Press, 1956.
APP 208; ODEP 541; EAP 243; MP 348.

Kill or cure

1833-36 If an elephant run mad, we are all ready for him—kill or cure.... (p. 182)
Sketches by Boz. 1833-40. The Oxford Illustrated Dickens, Vol. XII. Oxford: Oxford University Press, 1957.
APP 87; ODEP 422; EAP 244; MP 349.

King Charles the First's head

1850 'Do you recollect the date...when King Charles the First had his head cut off?' (p. 202)
The Personal History of David Copperfield. 1850. The Oxford Illustrated Dickens, Vol. II. Oxford: Oxford University Press, 1948.
ODEP 425.

To touch for the **King's Evil**

1852-54 This was called "touching for the King's Evil...." (p. 170)
Master Humphrey's Clock and A Child's History of England. 1840-41, 1852-54. The Oxford Illustrated Dickens, Vol. XX. Oxford: Oxford University Press, 1958.
URDANG, *IDIOMS* 754.

Don't **kiss** and tell.

18441 A caution from Mr. Tapley; a hasty exchange of farewlls, and of something else which the proverb says must not be told of afterwards. (p. 673)
The Life and Adventures of Martin Chuzzlewit. 1844. The Oxford Illustrated Dickens, Vol. IX. Oxford: Oxford University Press, 1951.
ODEP 429; EAP 246, MP 351; DAP 349.

Kith and kin

1841 'I reject you, and all of your kith and kin.' (p. 111)

Barnaby Rudge: A Tale of the Riots of 'Eighty. 1841. The Oxford Illustrated Dickens, Vol. XV. Oxford: Oxford University Press, 1954.

1843 'There are some...who are...strange to us and all our kith and kin....' (p. 43)

Christmas Books. 1843-49. The Oxford Illustrated Dickens, Vol. XVI. Oxford: Oxford University Press, 1954.

1844 '...he's kith and kin to me....' (p. 75)

The Life and Adventures of Martin Chuzzlewit. 1844. The Oxford Illustrated Dickens, Vol. IX. Oxford: Oxford University Press, 1951.

1853 ...some...occasioned inconvenience...by claiming kith and kin with them. (p. 461)

"Received, a Blank Child." [with W. H. Wills]. *Charles Dickens' Uncollected Writings from* Household Words *1850-1859,* 2 vols. Ed. Harry Stone. Bloomington: Indiana University Press, 1968.

MP 352.

Cab-horse **knees**

1845 ...they begin to feel like used-up cab horses—going perceptibly at the knees. (p. 376)

1845 ...they feel themselves *going at the knees.* (p. 384)

The Letters of Charles Dickens: Volume Four: 1844-1846. Ed. Kathleen Tillotson. Oxford: The Clarendon Press, 1977.

WILKINSON 101.

Know thyself.

1839 The only scriptural admonition...was 'know thyself.' (p. 567)

The Life and Adventures of Nicholas Nickleby. 1839. The Oxford Illustrated Dickens, Vol. VI. Oxford: Oxford University Press, 1950.

ODEP 435; EAP 247; CODP 126; MP 355; DAP 352.

Knowledge is power.

1847 ...'knowledge is power, and...it won't do to have too much power abroad.' (p. 411)

Address at the opening of the Glasgow Athenaeum, 28 Dec. 1847. *The Works of Charles Dickens: The Speeches.* Ed. Richard H. Shepherd. New National Edition, Vol. II. New York: Hearst's International Library Company, n. d.

ODEP 436; EAP 247; CODP 126; MP 356; DAP 354.

To put the **kye-bosh** (kybosh) on someone (-thing)

1833-36 ..."Hooroar...put the kye-bosh on her, Mary!" (p. 70)

Sketches by Boz. 1833-40. The Oxford Illustrated Dickens, Vol. XII. Oxford: Oxford University Press, 1957.
URDANG, *IDIOMS* 762; PARTRIDGE 1235.

L

To be a **labour** of love
1852 ...I could not make a new engagement...with the least regard to my labours of love. (p. 728)
The Letters of Charles Dickens: Volume Six: 1850-1852. Eds. Madeline House, Graham Storey, and Kathleen Tillotson. Oxford: The Clarendon Press, 1988.
APP 212; EAP 248; MP 357.

The **labourer** is worthy of his hire.

1844 'The labourer is worthy of his hire.' (p. 438)
The Life and Adventures of Martin Chuzzlewit. 1844. The Oxford Illustrated Dickens, Vol. IX. Oxford: Oxford University Press, 1951.
APP 212; ODEP 439; EAP 249; CODP 128; MP 357; DAP 358.

To climb the **ladder** of success

1850 Some happy talent...may form the two sides of the ladder on which some men mount.... (p. 606)
The Personal History of David Copperfield. 1850. The Oxford Illustrated Dickens, Vol. II. Oxford: Oxford University Press, 1948.
CRAIG 122.

It snows when the old **lady** in the sky picks her geese.

1855 "...the old lady up in the sky was picking her geese pretty hard to-day." (p. 100)
Christmas Stories. 1871. The Oxford Illustrated Dickens, Vol. XI. Oxford: Oxford University Press, 1956.
ODEP 887.

The **lady** doth protest too much, methinks.

1864 ...the Lady Britannia, like the Lady Desdemona, 'doth protest too much.' (p. 513)
Toast at a banquet in aid of the University Hospital, London, 12 Apr. 1864. *The Works of Charles Dickens: The Speeches*. Ed. Richard H. Shepherd. New National Edition, Vol. II. New York: Hearst's International Library Company, n. d.

STEVENSON 551:8.

The Old **Lady** of Threadneedle Street

1850 Title: The Old Lady in Threadneedle Street (p. 123)
1850 Even the Old Lady who lived on a hill...or that other Old Lady who lived in a shoe...are unknown to fame, compared with the Old Lady of Threadneedle Street. (p. 123)
1850 The kind Old Lady of Threadneedle Street has...managed to attach her dependents to her by the strongest of ties—that of love. (pp. 134-135)
"The Old Lady in Threadneedle Street." [with W. H. Wills]. *Charles Dickens' Uncollected Writings from* Household Words *1850-1859,* 2 vols. Ed. Harry Stone. Bloomington: Indiana University Press, 1968.
WILKINSON 384.

Long is the **lane** that has no turning.

1854 ...they looked as long as the lane that hath no turning. (p. 527)
"The Seven Poor Travellers." *Charles Dickens' Uncollected Writings from* Household Words *1850-1859,* 2 vols. Ed. Harry Stone. Bloomington: Indiana University Press, 1968.
APP 214; ODEP 480; EAP 251; CODP 137; MP 360; DAP 359.

To be in the **lap** of luxury

1849 '...and you rolling in the lap of luxury....' (p. 341)
Christmas Books. 1843-49. The Oxford Illustrated Dickens, Vol. XVI. Oxford: Oxford University Press, 1954.
1854 '...you were born in the lap of luxury....you know you were born in the lap of luxury.' (p. 46)
Hard Times for These Times. 1854. The Oxford Illustrated Dickens, Vol. XVII. Oxford: Oxford University Press, 1955.
1857 ...Mrs. Sparkler had...been lying at full length in the lap of luxury.... (p. 619)
Little Dorrit. 1857. The Oxford Illustrated Dickens, Vol. XIV. Oxford: Oxford University Press, 1953.
1858 ...you wouldn't...deprive yourself, to support that Indian in the lap of luxury. (p. 214)
Christmas Stories. 1871. The Oxford Illustrated Dickens, Vol. XI. Oxford: Oxford University Press, 1956.
1868 ...the Mare shall roll in the lap of luxury (which is very much dried up by the bye).... (p. 656)
The Letters of Charles Dickens, ed. Walter Dexter. Vol. III: 1858-1870. The Nonesuch Dickens. London: The Nonesuch Press, 1938.

WILKINSON 276.

As **large** as life

1850-56 "What did I see...but a green parrot on a stand, as large as life!" (p. 502)
The Uncommercial Traveller and Reprinted Pieces Etc. 1850-1860. The Oxford Illustrated Dickens, Vol. XXI. Oxford: Oxford University Press, 1958.
1865 There you have me again, as large as life. (p. 436)
Christmas Stories. 1871. The Oxford Illustrated Dickens, Vol. XI. Oxford: Oxford University Press, 1956.
APP 219; ODEP 442; MP 370.

To be **last**, but not least

1843 ...though last not least...its opportunities of blameless, rational enjoyment.... (p. 389)
Address at the Manchester Athenaeum, 5 Oct. 1843. *The Works of Charles Dickens: The Speeches.* Ed. Richard H. Shepherd. New National Edition, Vol. II. New York: Hearst's International Library Company, n. d.
1847 Best love from both of us...last, and not least, to you. (p. 217)
The Letters of Charles Dickens: Volume Five: 1847-1849. Eds. Graham Storey and K. J. Fielding. Oxford: The Clarendon Press, 1981.
ODEP 442; EAP 252; MP 361; DAP 360.

Let them **laugh** that win.

1850-56 Let them laugh that win. (p. 461)
The Uncommercial Traveller and Reprinted Pieces Etc. 1850-1860. The Oxford Illustrated Dickens, Vol. XXI. Oxford: Oxford University Press, 1958.
APP 215; ODEP 445; EAP 253; CODP 129; MP 363; DAP 362.

One must either **laugh** or cry.

1846 'One must either laugh or cry at such stupendous inconsistencies; and I prefer to laugh.' (p. 252)
Christmas Books. 1843-49. The Oxford Illustrated Dickens, Vol. XVI. Oxford: Oxford University Press, 1954.
STEVENSON 1357:7.

(Not) to be a **laughing matter**

1844 '...I don't consider it by any means a laughing matter....' (p. 205)
The Life and Adventures of Martin Chuzzlewit. 1844. The Oxford Illustrated Dickens, Vol. IX. Oxford: Oxford University Press, 1951.
1861 It was no laughing matter with Estella.... (p. 253)

Great Expectations. 1861. The Oxford Illustrated Dickens, Vol. XIII. Oxford: Oxford University Press, 1953.
ODEP 445; URDANG, *IDIOMS* 848.

To be a **laughing-stock**

1841 '...they are the laughing-stock of young and old....' (p. 24)
Barnaby Rudge: A Tale of the Riots of 'Eighty. 1841. The Oxford Illustrated Dickens, Vol. XV. Oxford: Oxford University Press, 1954.
URDANG, *IDIOMS* 772; STEVENSON 1354:13.

The **law** is a ass.

1838 'If the law supposes that...the law is a ass—a idiot.' (p. 399)
The Adventures of Oliver Twist. 1838. The Oxford Illustrated Dickens, Vol. V. Oxford: Oxford University Press, 1948.
ODEP 446; MP 363.

Lawyers, sharks, and leeches are not easily satisfied.

1850 'But lawyers, sharks, and leeches, are not easily satisfied, you know! (p. 746)
The Personal History of David Copperfield. 1850. The Oxford Illustrated Dickens, Vol. II. Oxford: Oxford University Press, 1948.

To shake like a **leaf**

1841 ...trembling like a leaf and supporting herself against the wall.... (p. 512)
The Old Curiosity Shop. 1841. The Oxford Illustrated Dickens, Vol. VIII. Oxford: Oxford University Press, 1951.
1848 ...her palsied head shook like a leaf.... (p. 433)
Dealings with the Firm of Dombey and Son. 1848. The Oxford Illustrated Dickens, Vol. VII. Oxford: Oxford University Press, 1950.
APP 216; ODEP 21; EAP 256; MP 365.

To take a **leaf** from someone's book

1852-54 ...some lords and gentlemen...would have taken a leaf out of Oliver Cromwell's book. (p. 488)
Master Humphrey's Clock and A Child's History of England. 1840-41, 1852-54. The Oxford Illustrated Dickens, Vol. XX. Oxford: Oxford University Press, 1958.
APP 216; ODEP 798; EAP 256; MP 365.

To turn over a new **leaf**

1853 'Now turn over a new leaf....' (p. 590)
Bleak House. 1853. The Oxford Illustrated Dickens, Vol. III. Oxford: Oxford University Press, 1948.
APP 217; ODEP 846; EAP 256; MP 366.

A little **learning** is a dangerous thing.

1843 ...the axiom that a little Learning is a dangerous thing. (p. 593)
The Letters of Charles Dickens: Volume Three: 1842-1843. Eds. Madeline House, Graham Storey, and Kathleen Tillotson. Oxford: The Clarendon Press, 1974.
1843 ...how often have we heard from them...that 'a little learning is a dangerous thing'? (p. 390)
1843 I should be glad to hear such people's estimate of the comparative danger of 'a little learning' and a vast amount of ignorance.... (p. 390)
Address at the Manchester Athenaeum, 5 Oct. 1843.
1858 ...a parrot...was once always saying...that knowledge was a dangerous thing. (pp. 500-501)
Address to the Institutional Association of Lancashire and Cheshire, Manchester, 3 Dec. 1858. *The Works of Charles Dickens: The Speeches.* Ed. Richard H. Shepherd. New National Edition, Vol. II. New York: Hearst's International Library Company, n. d.
APP 217; CODP 131; MP 366; DAP 367.

Least said, soonest mended.

1833 "Least said soonest mended." (p. 26)
The Letters of Charles Dickens: Volume One: 1820-1839. Eds. Madeline House and Graham Storey. Oxford: The Clarendon Press, 1965.
1837 ...the least said soonest mended.... (p. 677)
The Posthumous Papers of the Pickwick Club. 1837. The Oxford Illustrated Dickens, Vol. I. Oxford: Oxford University Press, 1948.
1850 'Least said, soonest mended!' (p. 513)
1850 '...least said, soonest mended.' (p. 748)
The Personal History of David Copperfield. 1850. The Oxford Illustrated Dickens, Vol. II. Oxford: Oxford University Press, 1948.
APP 217; ODEP 472; EAP 257; CODP 131; MP 366; DAP 367.

To stick like a **leech**

1839 ...I should stick like a leech to Nicholas to-night. (p. 508)
The Letters of Charles Dickens: Volume One: 1820-1839. Eds. Madeline House and Graham Storey. Oxford: The Clarendon Press, 1965.
APP 217; EAP 257; MP 367.

To speak over the **left shoulder**

1837 ...'over the left'...its expression is one of light and playful sarcasm. (p. 592)

The Posthumous Papers of the Pickwick Club. 1837. The Oxford Illustrated Dickens, Vol. I. Oxford: Oxford University Press, 1948.

ODEP 603.

Not to have a **leg** to stand upon

1844 '...leaves me high and dry, without a leg to stand upon.' (p. 737)

The Life and Adventures of Martin Chuzzlewit. 1844. The Oxford Illustrated Dickens, Vol. IX. Oxford: Oxford University Press, 1951.

1851 He...would not have had a leg to stand upon.... (p. 254)

The Letters of Charles Dickens: Volume Six: 1850-1852. Eds. Madeline House, Graham Storey, and Kathleen Tillotson. Oxford: The Clarendon Press, 1988.

APP 218; MP 367.

The **legitimate drama**

1838 Let the Legitimate Drama put this, and Joan of Arc as a first piece into her pipe.... (pp. 355-356)

The Letters of Charles Dickens: Volume One: 1820-1839. Eds. Madeline House and Graham Storey. Oxford: The Clarendon Press, 1965.

PARTRIDGE 477.

To land on one's **legs** like a cat

1857 'He has fallen on his legs, has Dan.' (p. 822)

Little Dorrit. 1857. The Oxford Illustrated Dickens, Vol. XIV. Oxford: Oxford University Press, 1953.

ODEP 107.

To have so many **lengths** of an acting part

1839 '...I've got a part of twelve lengths here....' (p. 292)

The Life and Adventures of Nicholas Nickleby. 1839. The Oxford Illustrated Dickens, Vol. VI. Oxford: Oxford University Press, 1950.

PARTRIDGE 477.

The **less** said, the better.

1844 'The less you say...the better.' (p. 18)

The Life and Adventures of Martin Chuzzlewit. 1844. The Oxford Illustrated Dickens, Vol. IX. Oxford: Oxford University Press, 1951.

1850 'The less said, the better.' (p. 324)

The Personal History of David Copperfield. 1850. The Oxford Illustrated Dickens, Vol. II. Oxford: Oxford University Press, 1948.

APP 218; EAP 259; MP 269; DAP 369.

To observe the **letter**, not the spirit, of the law

1850 He may even be...a stickler by the letter, not by the spirit.... (p. 166)
"The Doom of English Wills." [with W. H. Wills]. *Charles Dickens' Uncollected Writings from* Household Words *1850-1859*, 2 vols. Ed. Harry Stone. Bloomington: Indiana University Press, 1968.
STEVENSON 1365:7.

For the **life** of me

1850 For the life of me I can't think of anybody else.... (p. 47)
The Letters of Charles Dickens: Volume Six: 1850-1852. Eds. Madeline House, Graham Storey, and Kathleen Tillotson. Oxford: The Clarendon Press, 1988.
PARTRIDGE 481.

Life and death

1837 ...it is a matter of life or death to us.... (p. 249)
The Letters of Charles Dickens: Volume One: 1820-1839. Eds. Madeline House and Graham Storey. Oxford: The Clarendon Press, 1965.
1841 ...urging on his stout little horse as if for life or death. (p. 27)
Barnaby Rudge: A Tale of the Riots of 'Eighty. 1841. The Oxford Illustrated Dickens, Vol. XV. Oxford: Oxford University Press, 1954.
1842 He never hears of...the life or death of any single creature. (pp. 100-101)
American Notes and Pictures from Italy. 1842, 1846. The Oxford Illustrated Dickens, Vol. XIX. Oxford: Oxford University Press, 1957.
1846 ...professional assistants, hastily called in...as on a point of life or death, ran against each other.... (p. 230)
Christmas Books. 1843-49. The Oxford Illustrated Dickens, Vol. XVI. Oxford: Oxford University Press, 1954.
1848 He had risen...in the course of life and death, from Son to Dombey.... (p. 2)
Dealings with the Firm of Dombey and Son. 1848. The Oxford Illustrated Dickens, Vol. VII. Oxford: Oxford University Press, 1950.
1858 ...it has a power over life and death, the body and the soul.... (p. 502)
Address to the Institutional Association of Lancashire and Cheshire, Manchester, 3 Dec. 1858. *The Works of Charles Dickens: The Speeches*. Ed. Richard H. Shepherd. New National Edition, Vol. II. New York: Hearst's International Library Company, n. d.
1869 ...that Shining Source...holds in His mighty hands the unapproachable mysteries of life and death. (p. 575)

Address to the Birmingham and Midland Institute, Birmingham, 27 Sept. 1869. *The Works of Charles Dickens: The Speeches.* Ed. Richard H. Shepherd. New National Edition, Vol. II. New York: Hearst's International Library Company, n. d.
URDANG, *IDIOMS* 791.

Life and limb

1850-56 ...he submits his life and limbs.... (p. 469)
The Uncommercial Traveller and Reprinted Pieces Etc. 1850-1860. The Oxford Illustrated Dickens, Vol. XXI. Oxford: Oxford University Press, 1958.
1852 ...limb and life were in peril.... (p. 384)
"A Curious Dance Round a Curious Tree." [with W. H. Wills]. *Charles Dickens' Uncollected Writings from Household Words 1850-1859,* 2 vols. Ed. Harry Stone. Bloomington: Indiana University Press, 1968.
1860 ...he was...robbed with...a gracious consideration for life and limb.... (p. 304)
The Uncommercial Traveller and Reprinted Pieces Etc. 1850-1860. The Oxford Illustrated Dickens, Vol. XXI. Oxford: Oxford University Press, 1958.
URDANG, *IDIOMS* 791; STEVENSON 1405:13.

Life is a fight and must be fought out.

1860 Life is a fight and must be fought out. (p. 172)
The Letters of Charles Dickens, ed. Walter Dexter. Vol. III: 1858-1870. The Nonesuch Dickens. London: The Nonesuch Press, 1938.
STEVENSON 1399:7.

Life is not a bed of roses.

1838 'A porochial [*sic*] life is not a bed of roses, Mrs. Mann.' (p. 119)
The Adventures of Oliver Twist. 1838. The Oxford Illustrated Dickens, Vol. V. Oxford: Oxford University Press, 1948.
1846 The beds of such men are not of roses.... (p. 407)
Toast on the anniversary of the General Theatrical Fund, London, 6 Apr. 1846. *The Works of Charles Dickens: The Speeches.* Ed. Richard H. Shepherd. New National Edition, Vol. II. New York: Hearst's International Library Company, n. d.
1852-54 ...thorns were springing up under his bed of roses.... (p. 341)
Master Humphrey's Clock and A Child's History of England. 1840-41, 1852-54. The Oxford Illustrated Dickens, Vol. XX. Oxford: Oxford University Press, 1958.
EAP 24; MP 371; DAP 374.

Life is short, and why should speeches be long?

1865 ...it was said by that remarkable man, 'Life is short, and why should speeches be long?' (p. 532)

Toast in appreciation of Lord Lytton of the Guild of Literature, Knebworth, 29 July 1865.
The Works of Charles Dickens: The Speeches. Ed. Richard H. Shepherd. New National
Edition, Vol. II. New York: Hearst's International Library Company, n. d.
APP 220; EAP 259; MP 371; DAP 374.

If you walley my precious **life**, don't upset me.

1837 'If you walley my precious life don't upset me, as the gen'l'm'n
said to the driver when they was a carryin' him to Tyburn.' (p. 254)
The Posthumous Papers of the Pickwick Club. 1837. The Oxford Illustrated Dickens, Vol.
I. Oxford: Oxford University Press, 1948.
DOW 73.

Upon my **life** and soul

1864 "No, upon my life and soul, I can't!" (p. 347)
Dickens' Working Notes for His Novels. Ed. Harry Stone. Chicago, Ill.: University of
Chicago Press, 1987. xxiv +
URDANG, *IDIOMS* 791.

Where **life's** flowers freshest blow, | The sharpest thorns and keenest
briars grow.

1842 ...where life's flowers freshest blow, | The sharpest thorns and
keenest briars grow.... (p. 235)
Complete Plays and Selected Poems of Charles Dickens. London: Vision Press, 1970.

As **light** as a feather

1843 'I am as light as a feather, I am as happy as an angel, I am as
merry as a schoolboy. I am as giddy as a drunken man.' (p. 71)
Christmas Books. 1843-49. The Oxford Illustrated Dickens, Vol. XVI. Oxford: Oxford
University Press, 1954.
APP 129; ODEP 462; EAP 147; MP 217.

Let there be **light**.

1842 ...'God said, Let there be light, and there was none.' (p. 380)
Remarks at Hartford, Connecticut, 7 Feb. 1842. *The Works of Charles Dickens: The
Speeches*. Ed. Richard H. Shepherd. New National Edition, Vol. II. New York: Hearst's
International Library Company, n. d.
STEVENSON 1422:2.

Like it or lump it.

1848 'If she don't like it...she must be taught to lump it.' (p. 140)

Dealings with the Firm of Dombey and Son. 1848. The Oxford Illustrated Dickens, Vol. VII. Oxford: Oxford University Press, 1950.

1865 'If you don't like it, it's open to you to lump it.' (p. 653)

Our Mutual Friend. 1865. The Oxford Illustrated Dickens, Vol. X. Oxford: Oxford University Press, 1952.

APP 223; ODEP 464; EAP 262; MP 375.

Like will to like.

1844 ...the old axiom is reversed, and like clings to unlike more than to like. (p. 100)

The Life and Adventures of Martin Chuzzlewit. 1844. The Oxford Illustrated Dickens, Vol. IX. Oxford: Oxford University Press, 1951.

APP 222; ODEP 464; EAP 262; MP 375; DAP 377.

To tear someone (-thing) **limb** from limb

1839 The phenomenon was really in a fair way of being torn limb from limb.... (p. 314)

The Life and Adventures of Nicholas Nickleby. 1839. The Oxford Illustrated Dickens, Vol. VI. Oxford: Oxford University Press, 1950.

1840-41 'Let them tear me from limb to limb....' (p. 47)

Master Humphrey's Clock and A Child's History of England. 1840-41, 1852-54. The Oxford Illustrated Dickens, Vol. XX. Oxford: Oxford University Press, 1958.

1846 It makes me so damned savage that I could rend him limb from limb. (p. 463)

The Letters of Charles Dickens: Volume Four: 1844-1846. Ed. Kathleen Tillotson. Oxford: The Clarendon Press, 1977.

1857 '...they're a-coming around the corner, to tear him limb from limb.' (p. 162)

Little Dorrit. 1857. The Oxford Illustrated Dickens, Vol. XIV. Oxford: Oxford University Press, 1953.

1860 ...he was persuaded to...rend the murderer limb from limb.... (p. 98)

1860 ...by travelling to and fro...as though they...would be rent limb from limb.... (p. 263)

The Uncommercial Traveller and Reprinted Pieces Etc. 1850-1860. The Oxford Illustrated Dickens, Vol. XXI. Oxford: Oxford University Press, 1958.

STEVENSON 1432:9.

The **line** of business

1839 'I never saw a young fellow so regularly cut out for that line, since I've been in the profession.' (p. 281)

1839 '...I can come it pretty well—nobody better, perhaps, in my own line....' (p. 291)
The Life and Adventures of Nicholas Nickleby. 1839. The Oxford Illustrated Dickens, Vol. VI. Oxford: Oxford University Press, 1950.
1860 Chapter I: HIS GENERAL LINE OF BUSINESS (p. 1)
The Uncommercial Traveller and Reprinted Pieces Etc. 1850-1860. The Oxford Illustrated Dickens, Vol. XXI. Oxford: Oxford University Press, 1958.
URDANG, *IDIOMS* 798.

To draw the line

1850 '...we draw a line.' (p. 565)
The Personal History of David Copperfield. 1850. The Oxford Illustrated Dickens, Vol. II. Oxford: Oxford University Press, 1948.
1854 'Here's my father drawing what he calls a line....' (p. 176)
Hard Times for These Times. 1854. The Oxford Illustrated Dickens, Vol. XVII. Oxford: Oxford University Press, 1955.
1865 For the general rule is...to draw the line at dressing up. (p. 447)
Christmas Stories. 1871. The Oxford Illustrated Dickens, Vol. XI. Oxford: Oxford University Press, 1956.
ODEP 21.

To fight like a lion

1841 'He fought like a lion to-night....' (p. 462)
Barnaby Rudge: A Tale of the Riots of 'Eighty. 1841. The Oxford Illustrated Dickens, Vol. XV. Oxford: Oxford University Press, 1954.
APP 224; EAP 263; MP 378.

To take the lion's share

1841 ...taking the lion's share of the mulled wine.... (p. 270)
Barnaby Rudge: A Tale of the Riots of 'Eighty. 1841. The Oxford Illustrated Dickens, Vol. XV. Oxford: Oxford University Press, 1954.
ODEP 467; MP 378.

Live and learn.

1844 'But live and learn, Mr. Bevan!' (p. 545)
The Life and Adventures of Martin Chuzzlewit. 1844. The Oxford Illustrated Dickens, Vol. IX. Oxford: Oxford University Press, 1951.
1850 'Live and learn.' (p. 294)
The Personal History of David Copperfield. 1850. The Oxford Illustrated Dickens, Vol. II. Oxford: Oxford University Press, 1948.

1867 "...perhaps you know our English proverb, 'Live and Learn.'" (p. 569)

Christmas Stories. 1871. The Oxford Illustrated Dickens, Vol. XI. Oxford: Oxford University Press, 1956.

APP 225; ODEP 473; EAP 265; CODP 136; MP 380; DAP 381.

Let us **live** while we are living.

1839 *Dum vivimus*—live while we may— (p. 542)

The Letters of Charles Dickens: Volume One: 1820-1839. Eds. Madeline House and Graham Storey. Oxford: The Clarendon Press, 1965.

STEVENSON 1413:1.

To **live** happy ever afterwards

1850-56 ...he lived happy ever afterwards.... (p. 549)

1868 "Be good, then,...and live happy ever afterwards." (p. 706)

The Uncommercial Traveller and Reprinted Pieces Etc. 1850-1860. The Oxford Illustrated Dickens, Vol. XXI. Oxford: Oxford University Press, 1958.

1867 ...and they lived happy ever afterwards. (p. 547)

Address to the Railway Benevolent Society, London, 5 June 1867. *The Works of Charles Dickens: The Speeches*. Ed. Richard H. Shepherd. New National Edition, Vol. II. New York: Hearst's International Library Company, n. d.

URDANG, *IDIOMS* 585.

To be a **load** off of one's mind

1853 'This is a load off my mind....' (p. 703)

Bleak House. 1853. The Oxford Illustrated Dickens, Vol. III. Oxford: Oxford University Press, 1948.

WILKINSON 193.

Lock and key

1855 ...you have them under lock and key again. (p. 494)

The Letters of Charles Dickens: Volume Seven: 1853-1855. Eds. Graham Storey, Kathleen Tillotson, and Angus Easson. Oxford: The Clarendon Press, 1993.

URDANG, *IDIOMS* 807; STEVENSON 1446:10.

To be at **loggerheads**

1854 ...that British subject immediately falling foul of every other British subject in the place...all at loggerheads. (p. 501)

"On Her Majesty's Service." [with E. C. Grenville Murray]. *Charles Dickens' Uncollected Writings from* Household Words *1850-1859*, 2 vols. Ed. Harry Stone. Bloomington: Indiana University Press, 1968.

APP 227; EAP 266; MP 382.

Long and short [Cf. Short and long.]

1844 'The long and the short of it,' said Jonas. 'The long and the short of it is, what's the security?' (p. 443)
The Life and Adventures of Martin Chuzzlewit. 1844. The Oxford Illustrated Dickens, Vol. IX. Oxford: Oxford University Press, 1951.
APP 227; ODEP 478; EAP 392; MP 382.

Too **long** and too much

1843 You stand by your order too long and too much. (p. 462)
The Letters of Charles Dickens: Volume Three: 1842-1843. Eds. Madeline House, Graham Storey, and Kathleen Tillotson. Oxford: The Clarendon Press, 1974.

Look before you leap.

1853 'We will look before we leap....' (p. 233)
Bleak House. 1853. The Oxford Illustrated Dickens, Vol. III. Oxford: Oxford University Press, 1948.
APP 228; ODEP 482; EAP 267; CODP 138; MP 383; DAP 384.

The **Lord** tempers the wind to the newly-shorn lamb.

1859 "Lord temper the wind to you, my lamb," said the good Mesrour...." (p. 251)
Christmas Stories. 1871. The Oxford Illustrated Dickens, Vol. XI. Oxford: Oxford University Press, 1956.
APP 154; ODEP 312; EAP 179; CODP 95; MP 260; DAP 385.

Like **Lot's wife**

1855 I returned from Shepherd's Bush, like Lot's wife after she became the pillar of Salt. (p. 528)
The Letters of Charles Dickens: Volume Seven: 1853-1855. Eds. Graham Storey, Kathleen Tillotson, and Angus Easson. Oxford: The Clarendon Press, 1993.
STEVENSON 2028:7.

Love at first sight

1857 "Love at first sight!...But the course of it doesn't run smooth." (p. 702)
Christmas Stories. 1871. The Oxford Illustrated Dickens, Vol. XI. Oxford: Oxford University Press, 1956.
APP 229; ODEP 493; EAP 269; MP 385.

Love is blind.

1838 Poets tell us that love is blind. (p. 422)
The Letters of Charles Dickens: Volume One: 1820-1839. Eds. Madeline House and Graham Storey. Oxford: The Clarendon Press, 1965.
1842 ...a lover's love is blind, and...a mother's love is blind.... (p. 376)
Remarks at a dinner given by the young men of Boston, Massachusetts, 1 Feb. 1842. *The Works of Charles Dickens: The Speeches*. Ed. Richard H. Shepherd. New National Edition, Vol. II. New York: Hearst's International Library Company, n. d.
APP 230; ODEP 490; EAP 269; CODP 140; MP 386; DAP 388.

Love makes the world go round.

1865 '...what a bright old song it is, that oh, 'tis love, 'tis love, 'tis love that makes the world go round!' (p. 671)
Our Mutual Friend. 1865. The Oxford Illustrated Dickens, Vol. X. Oxford: Oxford University Press, 1952.
ODEP 492; CODP 140; MP 386; DAP 389.

No **love** lost between one and another

1839 'There's no love lost between us, I assure you,' said Miss Price.... (p. 112)
The Life and Adventures of Nicholas Nickleby. 1839. The Oxford Illustrated Dickens, Vol. VI. Oxford: Oxford University Press, 1950.
ODEP 492; EAP 270; MP 387.

Better **luck** next time.

1839 "Better luck next time" I hope. (p. 557)
The Letters of Charles Dickens: Volume One: 1820-1839. Eds. Madeline House and Graham Storey. Oxford: The Clarendon Press, 1965.
1861 We will all hope for "better luck next time...." (p. 239)
The Letters of Charles Dickens, ed. Walter Dexter. Vol. III: 1858-1870. The Nonesuch Dickens. London: The Nonesuch Press, 1938.
APP 231; ODEP 54; EAP 271; MP 388.

Never change **luck** when it is good.

1867 JOEY: Never change luck when it is good, sir! never change luck. (*No Thoroughfare*, I, i, p. 183)
Complete Plays and Selected Poems of Charles Dickens. London: Vision Press, 1970.

M

As **mad** as a March hare

1837 Like a March Hare he's Mad. (p. 697)
The Letters of Charles Dickens: Volume One: 1820-1839. Eds. Madeline House and Graham Storey. Oxford: The Clarendon Press, 1965.
1844 'He's as mad as a March hare!' (p. 717)
The Life and Adventures of Martin Chuzzlewit. 1844. The Oxford Illustrated Dickens, Vol. IX. Oxford: Oxford University Press, 1951.
APP 171; ODEP 497; EAP 198; MP 287.

As **mad** as Bedlam

1850 'Mad as Bedlam, boy!' said Mr. Dick.... (p. 202)
The Personal History of David Copperfield. 1850. The Oxford Illustrated Dickens, Vol. II. Oxford: Oxford University Press, 1948.
MP 38.

To get to the middle like a **maggot** in a nut

1854 '...here, got into the middle of it, like a maggot into a nut, is Josiah Bounderby.' (p. 169)
Hard Times for These Times. 1854. The Oxford Illustrated Dickens, Vol. XVII. Oxford: Oxford University Press, 1955.

*Parvis componere **magna**.*

1838 *Parvis componere magna.* (p. 382)
The Letters of Charles Dickens: Volume One: 1820-1839. Eds. Madeline House and Graham Storey. Oxford: The Clarendon Press, 1965.
STEVENSON 1037:6.

Mag's diversions

1849 ..."And in short it led to the very Mag's Diversions. *Old Saying.*" Or..."And in short they all played Mag's Diversions. *Old Saying*"? (p. 500)
The Letters of Charles Dickens: Volume Five: 1847-1849. Eds. Graham Storey and K. J. Fielding. Oxford: The Clarendon Press, 1981.

Look to the **main chance**.

1844 The education of Mr. Jonas had been conducted...on the strictest principles of the main chance. (p. 119)

The Life and Adventures of Martin Chuzzlewit. 1844. The Oxford Illustrated Dickens, Vol. IX. Oxford: Oxford University Press, 1951.
APP 124; ODEP 411; EAP 140; MP 207.

Make or break.

1841 '...chance will neither make or or break her.' (p. 25)
Barnaby Rudge: A Tale of the Riots of 'Eighty. 1841. The Oxford Illustrated Dickens, Vol. XV. Oxford: Oxford University Press, 1954.
APP 233; ODEP 385, 501; EAP 274; MP 393.

Good **malt** makes good beer.

1854 Good malt makes good beer.... (p. 29)
Hard Times for These Times. 1854. The Oxford Illustrated Dickens, Vol. XVII. Oxford: Oxford University Press, 1955.

A **man** cannot serve two masters.

1855 ...I cannot serve two masters. (p. 459)
Address on Administrative Reform, London, 27 June 1855. *The Works of Charles Dickens: The Speeches.* Ed. Richard H. Shepherd. New National Edition, Vol. II. New York: Hearst's International Library Company, n. d.
APP 239; ODEP 569; EAP 279; CODP 162; MP 399; DAP 402.

A wilful **man** must have his way.

1849 But "a wilful man must have his way"—and of course a wilful woman must. (p. 666)
The Letters of Charles Dickens: Volume Five: 1847-1849. Eds. Graham Storey and K. J. Fielding. Oxford: The Clarendon Press, 1981.
ODEP 890.

Every **man** for himself, and God for us all.

1844 'Every man for himself, and no creature for me!' (p. 42)
The Life and Adventures of Martin Chuzzlewit. 1844. The Oxford Illustrated Dickens, Vol. IX. Oxford: Oxford University Press, 1951.
APP 234; ODEP 229; EAP 134; CODP 67; MP 394; DAP 398.

Every **man** is his own friend.

1838 'Every man's his own friend....' (p. 327)
The Adventures of Oliver Twist. 1838. The Oxford Illustrated Dickens, Vol. V. Oxford: Oxford University Press, 1948.
DAP 399.

Every **man** to his own trade.

1857 Every man lying-to at his work, with a will that had all his heart and soul in it. (p. 199)
Christmas Stories. 1871. The Oxford Illustrated Dickens, Vol. XI. Oxford: Oxford University Press, 1956.
1867 "How they stick to their trade!" (p. 631)
Christmas Stories. 1871. The Oxford Illustrated Dickens, Vol. XI. Oxford: Oxford University Press, 1956.
APP 235; ODEP 230; EAP 135; CODP 69; MP 396; DAP 399.

Man proposes; God disposes.

1870 '...Man proposes, Heaven disposes.' (p. 35)
The Mystery of Edwin Drood. 1870. The Oxford Illustrated Dickens, Vol. XVIII. Oxford: Oxford University Press, 1956.
APP 235; ODEP 506; EAP 278; CODP 144; MP 398; DAP 401.

Man, woman, or child

1844 ...one...needs no favor from any man, woman, or child.... (p. 74)
The Letters of Charles Dickens: Volume Four: 1844-1846. Ed. Kathleen Tillotson. Oxford: The Clarendon Press, 1977.

No **man** is to be esteemed guilty until he is proven so to be.

1840 The maxim that "No man is to be esteemed guilty until he is proven so to be," is one which has ever been acted on in our courts.... (p. 491)
The Letters of Charles Dickens: Volume Two: 1840-1841. Eds. Madeline House and Graham Storey. Oxford: The Clarendon Press, 1969.
STEVENSON 1249:6.

The **man** in the moon

1841 '...he knows no more than the man in the moon.' (p. 139)
The Old Curiosity Shop. 1841. The Oxford Illustrated Dickens, Vol. VIII. Oxford: Oxford University Press, 1951.
1850 ...I should have thought the Man in the Moon a more likely one. (p. 63)
The Letters of Charles Dickens: Volume Six: 1850-1852. Eds. Madeline House, Graham Storey, and Kathleen Tillotson. Oxford: The Clarendon Press, 1988.
ODEP 504; EAP 277; MP 396.

To be a **man** of the world

1839 '...I should have no other course, as a man of the world....' (p. 249)

1839 '...you are too much a man of the world....' (p. 619)
The Life and Adventures of Nicholas Nickleby. 1839. The Oxford Illustrated Dickens, Vol. VI. Oxford: Oxford University Press, 1950.

1844 'Men of the world, my dear sir,' Jobling whispered to Jonas.... (p. 453)
The Life and Adventures of Martin Chuzzlewit. 1844. The Oxford Illustrated Dickens, Vol. IX. Oxford: Oxford University Press, 1951.

1853 'You're a man of the world, and I'm a man of the world.' (p. 349)

1853 '...we are men and women of the world here....' (p. 735)
Bleak House. 1853. The Oxford Illustrated Dickens, Vol. III. Oxford: Oxford University Press, 1948.

1857 '...how can you, as a man of the world....' (p. 520)
Little Dorrit. 1857. The Oxford Illustrated Dickens, Vol. XIV. Oxford: Oxford University Press, 1953.

URDANG, *IDIOMS* 839; STEVENSON 2628:9.

To make a **man** of someone

1838 'The kind and blessed gentlemen...are a going to...make a man of you....' (p. 18)
The Adventures of Oliver Twist. 1838. The Oxford Illustrated Dickens, Vol. V. Oxford: Oxford University Press, 1948.

Why is a **man** in jail like a man out of it?

1844 '...like that celebrated conundrum, "Why's a man in jail like a man out of jail?" there's no answer to it.' (p. 48)
The Life and Adventures of Martin Chuzzlewit. 1844. The Oxford Illustrated Dickens, Vol. IX. Oxford: Oxford University Press, 1951.

Il faut **manger.**

1846 *Mais il faut manger.* (p. 608)
The Letters of Charles Dickens: Volume Four: 1844-1846. Ed. Kathleen Tillotson. Oxford: The Clarendon Press, 1977.

1853 'Ill fo manger. That's the French saying....' (p. 277)
Bleak House. 1853. The Oxford Illustrated Dickens, Vol. III. Oxford: Oxford University Press, 1948.

STEVENSON 664:12.

The **march** of time

1850 ...they have not kept up with the march of time.... (p. 199)

"Mr. Bendigo Buster on Our National Defences Against Education." [with Henry Morley].*Charles Dickens' Uncollected Writings from* Household Words *1850-1859,* 2 vols. Ed. Harry Stone. Bloomington: Indiana University Press, 1968.
URDANG, *IDIOMS* 842.

To steal a **march** on someone

1838 I do not however see the least possibility of any other Theatre being able to steal a march upon you. (p. 389)
The Letters of Charles Dickens: Volume One: 1820-1839. Eds. Madeline House and Graham Storey. Oxford: The Clarendon Press, 1965.
APP 238; ODEP 772; EAP 282; MP 404.

Marriages are made in heaven.

1836 STRANGE GENTLEMAN: Marriages are made above—I'm quite certain ours is booked.... (*The Strange Gentleman,* II, i, p. 38)
Complete Plays and Selected Poems of Charles Dickens. London: Vision Press, 1970.
1850 In spite of the old saw, far fewer marriages are made in Heaven, than with an eye to Threadneedle Street. (p. 123)
"The Old Lady in Threadneedle Street." [with W. H. Wills]. *Charles Dickens' Uncollected Writings from* Household Words *1850-1859,* 2 vols. Ed. Harry Stone. Bloomington: Indiana University Press, 1968.
APP 239; ODEP 514; EAP 284; CODP 147; MP 405; DAP 407.

Matrimony is a serious undertaking.

1837 Matrimony is proverbially a serious undertaking. (p. 431)
Sketches by Boz. 1833-40. The Oxford Illustrated Dickens, Vol. XII. Oxford: Oxford University Press, 1957.

Away with **melancholy**.

1837 'Avay with melincholly, as the little boy said ven his school-missis died.' (p. 623)
The Posthumous Papers of the Pickwick Club. 1837. The Oxford Illustrated Dickens, Vol. I. Oxford: Oxford University Press, 1948.
DOW 84.

All **men** are created equal.

1842 ...publicly exhibited...is the Unanimous Declaration of the Thirteen United States of America, which solemnly declares that All Men are created Equal; and are endowed by their Creator with the Inalienable Rights of Life, Liberty, and the Pursuit of Happiness! (p. 119)

American Notes and Pictures from Italy. 1842, 1846. The Oxford Illustrated Dickens, Vol. XIX. Oxford: Oxford University Press, 1957.
DAP 398; BARTLETT 783:20.

Down among the dead **men**

1848 ...with it vaults of gold and silver 'down among the dead men....' (p. 32)
Dealings with the Firm of Dombey and Son. 1848. The Oxford Illustrated Dickens, Vol. VII. Oxford: Oxford University Press, 1950.
URDANG, *IDIOMS* 855; STEVENSON 634:3.

Men must live.

1839 'Men must live....' (p. 619)
1839 'Men must live, sir' said the literary gentleman.... (p. 634)
The Life and Adventures of Nicholas Nickleby. 1839. The Oxford Illustrated Dickens, Vol. VI. Oxford: Oxford University Press, 1950.

As **merry** as a cricket

1845 So I...am as merry again as my own Cricket.... (p. 429)
The Letters of Charles Dickens: Volume Four: 1844-1846. Ed. Kathleen Tillotson. Oxford: The Clarendon Press, 1977.
APP 84; ODEP 527; EAP 87; MP 138.

As **merry** as a grig

1853 The learned gentleman...is as merry as a grig at a French watering-place. (p. 259)
Bleak House. 1853. The Oxford Illustrated Dickens, Vol. III. Oxford: Oxford University Press, 1948.
APP 162; ODEP 527; EAP 188; MP 272.

As **merry** as a schoolboy

1843 'I am as light as a feather, I am as happy as an angel, I am as merry as a schoolboy. I am as giddy as a drunken man.' (p. 71)
Christmas Books. 1843-49. The Oxford Illustrated Dickens, Vol. XVI. Oxford: Oxford University Press, 1954.

To have the **Midas touch**

1857 Mr. Merdle was...a Midas without the ears, who turned all he touched to gold. (p. 246)

Little Dorrit. 1857. The Oxford Illustrated Dickens, Vol. XIV. Oxford: Oxford University Press, 1953.
MP 409.

To burn the **midnight oil**

1860 ...he will get up an abstruse subject...utterly regardless of the price of midnight oil.... (p. 343)
The Uncommercial Traveller and Reprinted Pieces Etc. 1850-1860. The Oxford Illustrated Dickens, Vol. XXI. Oxford: Oxford University Press, 1958.
ODEP 92; EAP 321; MP 460.

Do not cry over spilt **milk**.

1865 '...but, however, that's spilt milk.' (p. 558)
Our Mutual Friend. 1865. The Oxford Illustrated Dickens, Vol. X. Oxford: Oxford University Press, 1952.
APP 243; ODEP 159; EAP 289; CODP 46; MP 411; DAP 410.

Milk and honey

1839 '...he was all milk and honey....' (p. 194)
The Life and Adventures of Nicholas Nickleby. 1839. The Oxford Illustrated Dickens, Vol. VI. Oxford: Oxford University Press, 1950.
ODEP 531.

Milk and water

1840-41 ...he became quite a tame and milk-and-water character. (p. 74)
Master Humphrey's Clock and A Child's History of England. 1840-41, 1852-54. The Oxford Illustrated Dickens, Vol. XX. Oxford: Oxford University Press, 1958.
APP 244; EAP 289; MP 410.

The **milk** of human kindness

1844 ...any amount of butter might have been made out of him, by churning the milk of human kindness, as it spouted upwards from his heart. (p. 38)
The Life and Adventures of Martin Chuzzlewit. 1844. The Oxford Illustrated Dickens, Vol. IX. Oxford: Oxford University Press, 1951.
1848 ...all her...milk of human kindness, had been pumped out dry.... (p. 99)
Dealings with the Firm of Dombey and Son. 1848. The Oxford Illustrated Dickens, Vol. VII. Oxford: Oxford University Press, 1950.
EAP 289.

To have a **millstone** around one's neck

1846-49 "...it were better for him that he had a millstone tied about his neck...." (p. 59)
The Life of Our Lord: Written for His Children... New York: Simon and Schuster, 1934.
1851 Stone...is a Millstone...round my neck. (p. 330)
The Letters of Charles Dickens: Volume Six: 1850-1852. Eds. Madeline House, Graham Storey, and Kathleen Tillotson. Oxford: The Clarendon Press, 1988.
APP 244; EAP 290; MP 412; BARTLETT 39:4.

To see with one's **mind's eye**

1837 ...he was in our mind's eye all night. (p. 263)
Sketches by Boz. 1833-40. The Oxford Illustrated Dickens, Vol. XII. Oxford: Oxford University Press, 1957.

1838 Oliver *did* see it in his mind's eye.... (p. 80)
The Adventures of Oliver Twist. 1838. The Oxford Illustrated Dickens, Vol. V. Oxford: Oxford University Press, 1948.
1839 ...laying open a new and magic world before the mental eye.... (p. 311)
The Life and Adventures of Nicholas Nickleby. 1839. The Oxford Illustrated Dickens, Vol. VI. Oxford: Oxford University Press, 1950.
1839 ...laying open a new and magic world before the mental eye.... (p. 311)
The Letters of Charles Dickens: Volume One: 1820-1839. Eds. Madeline House and Graham Storey. Oxford: The Clarendon Press, 1965.
1841 ...which in his mind's eye represented the sconce or head of Joseph Willet. (p. 241)
Barnaby Rudge: A Tale of the Riots of 'Eighty. 1841. The Oxford Illustrated Dickens, Vol. XV. Oxford: Oxford University Press, 1954.
1841 I have in my mind's eye...the expression of a face.... (p. 249)
1841 ...having in their mind's eye, the example of Scott.... (p. 421)
The Letters of Charles Dickens: Volume Two: 1840-1841. Eds. Madeline House and Graham Storey. Oxford: The Clarendon Press, 1969.
1844 In my mind's eye, Horatio. (p. 200)
1846 ...I shall often and often look that way with my mind's eye.... (p. 667)
The Letters of Charles Dickens: Volume Four: 1844-1846. Ed. Kathleen Tillotson. Oxford: The Clarendon Press, 1977.
1848 ...it may be that his mind's eye followed him.... (p. 80)
1848 He saw himself, in his mind's eye, put meekly in a hackney-coach.... (p. 453)
Dealings with the Firm of Dombey and Son. 1848. The Oxford Illustrated Dickens, Vol. VII. Oxford: Oxford University Press, 1950.

1850 I see you (in my mind's eye) unable to eat.... (p. 188)
The Letters of Charles Dickens: Volume Six: 1850-1852. Eds. Madeline House, Graham Storey, and Kathleen Tillotson. Oxford: The Clarendon Press, 1988.

1850-56 ...my mind's eye can discern some traces.... (p. 370)

1850-56 ...our mind's eye now recalls a worthy Frenchman.... (p. 400)
The Uncommercial Traveller and Reprinted Pieces Etc. 1850-1860. The Oxford Illustrated Dickens, Vol. XXI. Oxford: Oxford University Press, 1958.

1857 In her mind's eye...she saw the fair bosom.... (pp. 613-614)
Little Dorrit. 1857. The Oxford Illustrated Dickens, Vol. XIV. Oxford: Oxford University Press, 1953.

1859 ...I saw the beast...(with my mind's eye)...delivering his cut-and-dried speech.... (p. 118)

1860 In my mind's eye I behold Mrs. Bouncer.... (p. 180)

1868 I can see nothing with my mind's eye.... (p. 662)
The Letters of Charles Dickens, ed. Walter Dexter. Vol. III: 1858-1870. The Nonesuch Dickens. London: The Nonesuch Press, 1938.

1860 The chance use of the word...brought that numerous fraternity so vividly before my mind's eye.... (p. 104)

1860 For my mind's eye saw him.... (p. 339)
The Uncommercial Traveller and Reprinted Pieces Etc. 1850-1860. The Oxford Illustrated Dickens, Vol. XXI. Oxford: Oxford University Press, 1958.

WILKINSON 300; STEVENSON 1579:5.

To hold...the **mirror** up to Nature

1850 It is not long since the mirror held up to Nature...revealed to us.... (p. 144)
"Foreigners' Portraits of Englishmen." [with W. H. Wills and E. C. Grenville Murray]. *Charles Dickens' Uncollected Writings from* Household Words *1850-1859*, 2 vols. Ed. Harry Stone. Bloomington: Indiana University Press, 1968.
STEVENSON 1586:2.

Misfortunes never come singly.

1841 Misfortunes, saith the adage, never come singly. (p. 242)
Barnaby Rudge: A Tale of the Riots of 'Eighty. 1841. The Oxford Illustrated Dickens, Vol. XV. Oxford: Oxford University Press, 1954.
APP 246; ODEP 535; EAP 292; CODP 151; MP 414; DAP 413.

To **modley-coddley** someone

1870 'Don't moddley-coddley....I like anything better than being moddley-coddleyed.' (p. 9)

1870 'He...moddley-coddleys in the merest trifles.' (p. 149)

The Mystery of Edwin Drood. 1870. The Oxford Illustrated Dickens, Vol. XVIII. Oxford: Oxford University Press, 1956.
STEVENSON 1606:12 (CITING DICKENS).

It takes **money** to make money.

1865 '...money makes money, as well as makes everything else.' (p. 464)
Our Mutual Friend. 1865. The Oxford Illustrated Dickens, Vol. X. Oxford: Oxford University Press, 1952.
ODEP 538; CODP 154; MP 417; DAP 416.

Money is money.

1848 'Money is money....' (p. 494)
Dealings with the Firm of Dombey and Son. 1848. The Oxford Illustrated Dickens, Vol. VII. Oxford: Oxford University Press, 1950.

Money is the root of all evil.

1844 'Money...is the root of all evil.' (p. 19)
The Life and Adventures of Martin Chuzzlewit. 1844. The Oxford Illustrated Dickens, Vol. IX. Oxford: Oxford University Press, 1951.

Money makes the man.

1850 '...it isn't money makes the man....' (p. 517)
The Personal History of David Copperfield. 1850. The Oxford Illustrated Dickens, Vol. II. Oxford: Oxford University Press, 1948.
ODEP 539; MP 417.

To coin **money**

1857 ...nobody knew...what Mr. Merdle's business was, except that it was to coin money.... (p. 394)
Little Dorrit. 1857. The Oxford Illustrated Dickens, Vol. XIV. Oxford: Oxford University Press, 1953.

To let **money** burn a hole in one's pocket

1852 ...seeing the danger of allowing the savings of its servants to burn holes in their pockets.... (pp. 392-393)
"Post-Office Money-Orders." [with W. H. Wills]. *Charles Dickens' Uncollected Writings from Household Words 1850-1859*, 2 vols. Ed. Harry Stone. Bloomington: Indiana University Press, 1968.
APP 247; ODEP 538; MP 416.

To come the double **monkey**

1833-36 ...Bill Thompson can "come the double monkey...." (p. 55)
Sketches by Boz. 1833-40. The Oxford Illustrated Dickens, Vol. XII. Oxford: Oxford University Press, 1957.

To follow the **monkey**

1863 ...he adds "He followed the Monkey." (p. 390)
Christmas Stories. 1871. The Oxford Illustrated Dickens, Vol. XI. Oxford: Oxford University Press, 1956.

To rouse someone with a **monkey's tail**

1859 I wouldn't...shiver my ould timbers and rouse me up with a monkey's tail (man-of-war metaphor), not to chuck a biscuit into Davy Jones's weather eye.... (p. 123)
The Letters of Charles Dickens, ed. Walter Dexter. Vol. III: 1858-1870. The Nonesuch Dickens. London: The Nonesuch Press, 1938.
PARTRIDGE 529.

To be a **monster** in human form

1849 Engaged in links of adamant to a "monster in human form"—a remarkable expression...in a newspaper.... (p. 479)
The Letters of Charles Dickens: Volume Five: 1847-1849. Eds. Graham Storey and K. J. Fielding. Oxford: The Clarendon Press, 1981.

To cry for the **moon**

1853 ...he didn't cry for the moon. (p. 70)
Bleak House. 1853. The Oxford Illustrated Dickens, Vol. III. Oxford: Oxford University Press, 1948.
ODEP 158; MP 423.

To be all **moonshine**

1852 He says..."its [*sic*] all moonshine...." (p. 595)
The Letters of Charles Dickens: Volume Six: 1850-1852. Eds. Madeline House, Graham Storey, and Kathleen Tillotson. Oxford: The Clarendon Press, 1988.
APP 424; ODEP 549; MP 424.

From **morning** till night

1854 Slander and backbiting...were going on from morning till night. (p. 501)

"On Her Majesty's Service." [with E. C. Grenville Murray]. *Charles Dickens' Uncollected Writings from* Household Words *1850-1859*, 2 vols. Ed. Harry Stone. Bloomington: Indiana University Press, 1968.
URDANG, *IDIOMS* 876.

Morning, noon, and night

1836 ...I have been superintending its preparation, morning, noon, and night. (pp. 177-178)
The Letters of Charles Dickens: Volume One: 1820-1839. Eds. Madeline House and Graham Storey. Oxford: The Clarendon Press, 1965.
1837 ...I am worried about it, morning, noon, and night. (p. 783)
The Letters of Charles Dickens: Volume Seven: 1853-1855. Eds. Graham Storey, Kathleen Tillotson, and Angus Easson. Oxford: The Clarendon Press, 1993.
1839 '...I have thought of nothing...morning, noon, and night.' (p. 486)
1839 '...he the very man who has been wearying us morning, noon, and night....' (p. 813)
The Life and Adventures of Nicholas Nickleby. 1839. The Oxford Illustrated Dickens, Vol. VI. Oxford: Oxford University Press, 1950.
1842 He...has an intolerable headache, morning, noon, and night. (p. 100)
The Letters of Charles Dickens: Volume Three: 1842-1843. Eds. Madeline House, Graham Storey, and Kathleen Tillotson. Oxford: The Clarendon Press, 1974.
1853 ...Mr. Bucket takes into the conversation in right of his importance, 'morning, noon, and night.' (p. 718)
Bleak House. 1853. The Oxford Illustrated Dickens, Vol. III. Oxford: Oxford University Press, 1948.
1857 Morning, noon, and night, morning, noon, and night, each recurring with its accompanying monotony.... (p. 339)
1857 'I have...worried myself morning, noon, and night....' (p. 393)
Little Dorrit. 1857. The Oxford Illustrated Dickens, Vol. XIV. Oxford: Oxford University Press, 1953.
BARTLETT 357:8.

To beam like the morning

1853 ...I beam like the morning. (p. 220)
The Letters of Charles Dickens: Volume Seven: 1853-1855. Eds. Graham Storey, Kathleen Tillotson, and Angus Easson. Oxford: The Clarendon Press, 1993.
WILSTACH 14.

Mother Carey's chickens

1842 ...we could watch...those small creatures ever on the wing, the Mother Carey's chickens.... (p. 221)

American Notes and Pictures from Italy. 1842, 1846. The Oxford Illustrated Dickens, Vol. XIX. Oxford: Oxford University Press, 1957.
APP 251; ODEP 546; EAP 297.

Do not make a **mountain** out of a molehill.

1857 '...we do...make mountains of molehills....' (p. 321)
Little Dorrit. 1857. The Oxford Illustrated Dickens, Vol. XIV. Oxford: Oxford University Press, 1953.
APP 252; ODEP 547; EAP 300; MP 428; DAP 419.

The country **mouse** and the city mouse

1857 ...like the country mouse in the second year of famine, come to see the town mouse.... (p. 363)
Little Dorrit. 1857. The Oxford Illustrated Dickens, Vol. XIV. Oxford: Oxford University Press, 1953.

One can have too **much** of a good thing.

1840 There cannot be a better practical illustration of the wise saw and ancient instance, that there may be too much of a good thing.... (p. 563)
Sketches by Boz. 1833-40. The Oxford Illustrated Dickens, Vol. XII. Oxford: Oxford University Press, 1957.
1858 ...it is too much of a good thing. (p. 603)
"A House to Let." [with Wilkie Collins]. *Charles Dickens' Uncollected Writings from Household Words 1850-1859*, 2 vols. Ed. Harry Stone. Bloomington: Indiana University Press, 1968.
APP 253; ODEP 831; EAP 302; CODP 228; MP 620; DAP 260.

So **much** the better

1836 FLAM: So much the better for my purpose.... (*The Village Coquettes*, II, i, p. 71)
Complete Plays and Selected Poems of Charles Dickens. London: Vision Press, 1970.
1836 So much the better.... (p. 160)
The Letters of Charles Dickens: Volume One: 1820-1839. Eds. Madeline House and Graham Storey. Oxford: The Clarendon Press, 1965.
1841 'So much the better,' growled Dennis.... (p. 454)
Barnaby Rudge: A Tale of the Riots of 'Eighty. 1841. The Oxford Illustrated Dickens, Vol. XV. Oxford: Oxford University Press, 1954.
1857 "...this will be a hand-to-hand affair, and so much the better." (p. 187)
Christmas Stories. 1871. The Oxford Illustrated Dickens, Vol. XI. Oxford: Oxford University Press, 1956.

URDANG, *IDIOMS* 882.

...vether it's worth while goin' through so **much** to learn so little....

1837 '...vether it's worth while goin' through so much, to learn so little, as the charity-boy said ven he got to the end of the alphabet, is a matter o' taste.' (p. 373)
The Posthumous Papers of the Pickwick Club. 1837. The Oxford Illustrated Dickens, Vol. I. Oxford: Oxford University Press, 1948.
DOW 72.

Mug of a bell

1846 About the 'mug of a bell....' (p. 499)
The Letters of Charles Dickens: Volume Four: 1844-1846. Ed. Kathleen Tillotson. Oxford: The Clarendon Press, 1977.

Mum is the word.

1838 Mum is the word 'till [*sic*] we see how it goes. (p. 794)
The Letters of Charles Dickens: Volume Seven: 1853-1855. Eds. Graham Storey, Kathleen Tillotson, and Angus Easson. Oxford: The Clarendon Press, 1993.
APP 254; ODEP 551; EAP 303; MP 433; BARTLETT 151:13.

Murder will out.

1837 'Now the murder's out....' (p. 614)
The Posthumous Papers of the Pickwick Club. 1837. The Oxford Illustrated Dickens, Vol. I. Oxford: Oxford University Press, 1948.
1850 Now the murder's out! (p. 30)
The Letters of Charles Dickens: Volume Six: 1850-1852. Eds. Madeline House, Graham Storey, and Kathleen Tillotson. Oxford: The Clarendon Press, 1988.
APP 254; ODEP 551; EAP 303; CODP 157; MP 434; DAP 421.

As **mute** as a poker

1844 '...he wasn't as mute as a poker.' (p. 451)
The Life and Adventures of Martin Chuzzlewit. 1844. The Oxford Illustrated Dickens, Vol. IX. Oxford: Oxford University Press, 1951.
WILSTACH 269.

N

To hit the **nail** on the head

1838 ...they have hit the right nail on the very centre of its head. (p. 525)
Sketches by Boz. 1833-40. The Oxford Illustrated Dickens, Vol. XII. Oxford: Oxford University Press, 1957.
APP 256; ODEP 374; EAP 305; MP 438.

My **name** is Jack Robinson.

1865 'If you don't see those three at the altar in Bond Street, in a jiffy, my name's Jack Robinson!' (p. 734)
Our Mutual Friend. 1865. The Oxford Illustrated Dickens, Vol. X. Oxford: Oxford University Press, 1952.

To take someone's **name** in vain

1864 ...we propose by and by to take his name, but by no means to take it in vain. (p. 517)
Address in support of the Shakespeare Schools, London, 11 May 1864. *The Works of Charles Dickens: The Speeches.* Ed. Richard H. Shepherd. New National Edition, Vol. II. New York: Hearst's International Library Company, n. d.
STEVENSON 2256:5.

...whose **name** is Legion.

1850 ...the occupants of this hall (whose name was Legion) appeared.... (p. 73) "Valentine's Day at the Post-Office." [with W. H. Wills].
1851 ...their name having since become Legion. (p. 370) "My Uncle." [with W. H. Wills].
1853 His name is Legion. (p. 468)
"H. W." [with Henry Morley]. *Charles Dickens' Uncollected Writings from* Household Words *1850-1859,* 2 vols. Ed. Harry Stone. Bloomington: Indiana University Press, 1968.
1857 ...*its* name was Legion. (p. 106)
Little Dorrit. 1857. The Oxford Illustrated Dickens, Vol. XIV. Oxford: Oxford University Press, 1953.
STEVENSON 1654:14.

I only assisted **natur'**, ma'm.

1837 'I only assisted natur', ma'm; as the doctor said to the boy's mother, arter he'd bled him to death.' (p. 664)
The Posthumous Papers of the Pickwick Club. 1837. The Oxford Illustrated Dickens, Vol. I. Oxford: Oxford University Press, 1948.
DOW 88.

Nearest and dearest

1842 ...you have given those who are nearest and dearest to me a new reason.... (p. 383)

Remarks at Hartford, Connecticut, 7 Feb. 1842. *The Works of Charles Dickens: The Speeches*. Ed. Richard H. Shepherd. New National Edition, Vol. II. New York: Hearst's International Library Company, n. d.

STEVENSON 1469:5.

Necessity is the mother of invention.

1842 Necessity and two-pronged forks are the mothers of invention. (p. 183)

The Letters of Charles Dickens: Volume Three: 1842-1843. Eds. Madeline House, Graham Storey, and Kathleen Tillotson. Oxford: The Clarendon Press, 1974.

APP 258; ODEP 558; EAP 307; CODP 159; MP 441; DAP 425.

Neck and crop

1837 'When I wos first pitched neck and crop into the world....' (p. 209)

The Posthumous Papers of the Pickwick Club. 1837. The Oxford Illustrated Dickens, Vol. I. Oxford: Oxford University Press, 1948.

1848 'In my desire to save young what's-his-name from being kicked out of this place, neck and crop....' (p. 467)

Dealings with the Firm of Dombey and Son. 1848. The Oxford Illustrated Dickens, Vol. VII. Oxford: Oxford University Press, 1950.

1853 '...as being able to tumble me out of this place neck and crop.' (p. 643)

Bleak House. 1853. The Oxford Illustrated Dickens, Vol. III. Oxford: Oxford University Press, 1948.

1854 'To be tumbled out of doors neck and crop....' (p. 240)

Hard Times for These Times. 1854. The Oxford Illustrated Dickens, Vol. XVII. Oxford: Oxford University Press, 1955.

1865 'I'd ha' liked to plump down aboard of him, neck and crop....' (p. 632)

Our Mutual Friend. 1865. The Oxford Illustrated Dickens, Vol. X. Oxford: Oxford University Press, 1952.

ODEP 558; MP 441.

Neck and heels

1846 ...I am plunging neck and heels into a new Book. (p. 608)

The Letters of Charles Dickens: Volume Four: 1844-1846. Ed. Kathleen Tillotson. Oxford: The Clarendon Press, 1977.

URDANG, *IDIOMS* 896.

Neck or nothing

1842 On it...dashes on haphazard, pell-mell, neck-or-nothing, down the middle of the road. (p. 64)
American Notes and Pictures from Italy. 1842, 1846. The Oxford Illustrated Dickens, Vol. XIX. Oxford: Oxford University Press, 1957.
APP 259; ODEP 558; EAP 308; MP 441.

To look for a **needle** in a haystack

1850 ...threading the needle with the golden eye all through the labyrinth of the National Debt, and hiding it in such dry hay-stacks as are rotting here! (p. 134)
"The Old Lady in Threadneedle Street." [with W. H. Wills]. *Charles Dickens' Uncollected Writings from* Household Words *1850-1859*, 2 vols. Ed. Harry Stone. Bloomington: Indiana University Press, 1968.
1870 'I came here looking for a needle in a haystack....' (p. 162)
The Mystery of Edwin Drood. 1870. The Oxford Illustrated Dickens, Vol. XVIII. Oxford: Oxford University Press, 1956.
APP 259; ODEP 559; EAP 309; MP 443.

Thou shalt love thy **neighbour** as thyself.

1846-49 *"Thou shalt love thy neighbour as thyself."* (p. 68)
The Life of Our Lord: Written for His Children... New York: Simon and Schuster, 1934.
DAP 427; STEVENSON 1676:6.

Ill **news** travels fast.

1839 'Ill news travels fast....' (p. 424)
The Life and Adventures of Nicholas Nickleby. 1839. The Oxford Illustrated Dickens, Vol. VI. Oxford: Oxford University Press, 1950.
APP 261; ODEP 400; EAP 311; CODP 8; MP 445; DAP 429.

Nick-nack

1857 What it most developed was, an unexpected taste for little ornaments and nick-nacks.... (p. 669)
Christmas Stories. 1871. The Oxford Illustrated Dickens, Vol. XI. Oxford: Oxford University Press, 1956.
URDANG, *IDIOMS* 902.

To be in the **nick** of time

1837 ...the latter for...turning up in the very nick of time.... (p. 266)

Sketches by Boz. 1833-40. The Oxford Illustrated Dickens, Vol. XII. Oxford: Oxford University Press, 1957.

1837 ...this sixteenth Pickwick | Which is just in the nick.... (p. 287)

The Letters of Charles Dickens: Volume One: 1820-1839. Eds. Madeline House and Graham Storey. Oxford: The Clarendon Press, 1965.

1846 ...the change comes in the very nick of time.... (p. 638)

The Letters of Charles Dickens: Volume Four: 1844-1846. Ed. Kathleen Tillotson. Oxford: The Clarendon Press, 1977.

1848 ...the expatriated Native...had accidentally arrived in the very nick of time.... (p. 415)

Dealings with the Firm of Dombey and Son. 1848. The Oxford Illustrated Dickens, Vol. VII. Oxford: Oxford University Press, 1950.

ODEP 565; EAP 312; MP 446.

Night and day

1841 I am still haunted by visions of America, night and day. (p. 380)

The Letters of Charles Dickens: Volume Two: 1840-1841. Eds. Madeline House and Graham Storey. Oxford: The Clarendon Press, 1969.

URDANG, *IDIOMS* 903; STEVENSON 1687:4.

To make a **night** of it

1837 ...they would "make a night of it"—an expressive term.... (p. 267)

Sketches by Boz. 1833-40. The Oxford Illustrated Dickens, Vol. XII. Oxford: Oxford University Press, 1957.

1844 ...material was at hand for making quite a heavy night of it. (p. 91)

The Life and Adventures of Martin Chuzzlewit. 1844. The Oxford Illustrated Dickens, Vol. IX. Oxford: Oxford University Press, 1951.

ODEP 566.

Nine out of ten

1866 ...in nine cases out of ten the author is at a disadvantage.... (p. 490)

The Letters of Charles Dickens, ed. Walter Dexter. Vol. III: 1858-1870. The Nonesuch Dickens. London: The Nonesuch Press, 1938.

The **Noble Savage**

1850-56 Title: The Noble Savage (p. 467)

1850-56 Mine are no new views of the noble savage. (p. 468)

1850-56 It is not the miserable nature of the noble savage.... (p. 468)

1850-56 ...conscious of an affectionate yearning towards that noble savage.... (p. 468)

1850-56 These noble savages are represented in a most agreeable manner.... (p. 469)

1850-56 ...see what the noble savage does in Zulu Kaffirland. (p. 469)

1850-56 The noble savage sets a king to reign over him.... (p. 469)

1850-56 All the noble savage's wars...are wars of extermination.... (p. 469)

1850-56 Some of the noble savages...greatly affected him.... (p. 471)

1850-56 ...war is afoot among the noble savages.... (p. 471)

1850-56 ...if we retained in us anything of the noble savage, we could not get rid of it.... (p. 472)

1850-56 ...if we have anything to learn from the Noble Savage, it is what to avoid. (p. 472)

The Uncommercial Traveller and Reprinted Pieces Etc. 1850-1860. The Oxford Illustrated Dickens, Vol. XXI. Oxford: Oxford University Press, 1958.

URDANG, *IDIOMS* 908; STEVENSON 2035:7.

Nook and corner

1846 '...there are...noble acts of heroism...done every day in nooks and corners....' (p. 252)

Christmas Books. 1843-49. The Oxford Illustrated Dickens, Vol. XVI. Oxford: Oxford University Press, 1954.

1849 ...I want...to be in...all nooks and corners.... (p. 1849)

The Letters of Charles Dickens: Volume Five: 1847-1849. Eds. Graham Storey and K. J. Fielding. Oxford: The Clarendon Press, 1981.

1852 ...may I...leave its counterpart in as fair a form in many a nook and corner of the world.... (p. 389)

"A Curious Dance Round a Curious Tree." [with W. H. Wills]. *Charles Dickens' Uncollected Writings from* Household Words *1850-1859*, 2 vols. Ed. Harry Stone. Bloomington: Indiana University Press, 1968.

1855 I can...bring you acquainted with every nook and corner.... (p. 557)

The Letters of Charles Dickens: Volume Seven: 1853-1855. Eds. Graham Storey, Kathleen Tillotson, and Angus Easson. Oxford: The Clarendon Press, 1993.

1860 ...I...roam about its deserted nooks and corners. (p. 233)

The Uncommercial Traveller and Reprinted Pieces Etc. 1850-1860. The Oxford Illustrated Dickens, Vol. XXI. Oxford: Oxford University Press, 1958.

URDANG, *IDIOMS* 909.

Do not cut off your **nose** to spite your face.

1846 But to interfere with other people's writings...is to slice at your own Nose with a sharp Razor. (p. 621)

The Letters of Charles Dickens: Volume Four: 1844-1846. Ed. Kathleen Tillotson. Oxford: The Clarendon Press, 1977.

1855 ...the medical authority will not...cut your nose off, to be revenged on your face. (p. 585)

The Letters of Charles Dickens: Volume Seven: 1853-1855. Eds. Graham Storey, Kathleen Tillotson, and Angus Easson. Oxford: The Clarendon Press, 1993.

APP 263; ODEP 163; EAP 314; CODP 47; MP 450; DAP 432.

To keep one's **nose** to the grindstone

1865 'And his nose shall be put to the grindstone for it.' (p. 581)
1865 'To put his nose to the grindstone?' (p. 582)

Our Mutual Friend. 1865. The Oxford Illustrated Dickens, Vol. X. Oxford: Oxford University Press, 1952.

APP 264; ODEP 578; EAP 314; MP 451; DAP 432.

To pay through the **nose**

1850 'Pays as he speaks...through the nose,' replied Miss Mowcher. (p. 330)

The Personal History of David Copperfield. 1850. The Oxford Illustrated Dickens, Vol. II. Oxford: Oxford University Press, 1948.

ODEP 615; MP 451.

You'd change your **note**.

1837 'If you know'd who was near, sir, I rayther think you'd change your note. As the hawk remarked to himself with a cheerful laugh, ven he heerd the robin redbreast a singin' round the corner.' (p. 662)

The Posthumous Papers of the Pickwick Club. 1837. The Oxford Illustrated Dickens, Vol. I. Oxford: Oxford University Press, 1948.

EAP 315; DOW 90.

Nothing comes of nothing.

1860 "...nothing can come of nothing...." (p. 266)

Christmas Stories. 1871. The Oxford Illustrated Dickens, Vol. XI. Oxford: Oxford University Press, 1956.

ODEP 579; MP 453; DAP 433.

Nothing venture, nothing have.

1841 '...nothing venture, nothing have....' (p. 223)

The Old Curiosity Shop. 1841. The Oxford Illustrated Dickens, Vol. VIII. Oxford: Oxford University Press, 1951.

APP 265; ODEP 581; EAP 316; CODP 165; MP 454; DAP 433.

There is **nothing** little to the great in spirit.

1870 There is nothing little to the really great in spirit. (p. 193)
The Mystery of Edwin Drood. 1870. The Oxford Illustrated Dickens, Vol. XVIII. Oxford: Oxford University Press, 1956.
STEVENSON 1443:7.

Now and again

1866 "...it has been there, now and again, by fits and starts." (p. 532)
Christmas Stories. 1871. The Oxford Illustrated Dickens, Vol. XI. Oxford: Oxford University Press, 1956.
URDANG, *IDIOMS* 919.

Now and then

1844 'It does, now and then.' (p. 264)
The Life and Adventures of Martin Chuzzlewit. 1844. The Oxford Illustrated Dickens, Vol. IX. Oxford: Oxford University Press, 1951.
URDANG, *IDIOMS* 919.

Nullus eo

1836 ...the sale was nullus eo. (p. 181)
The Letters of Charles Dickens: Volume One: 1820-1839. Eds. Madeline House and Graham Storey. Oxford: The Clarendon Press, 1965.

Look after **Number one.**

1839 '...the only number...is number one....' (p. 782)
The Life and Adventures of Nicholas Nickleby. 1839. The Oxford Illustrated Dickens, Vol. VI. Oxford: Oxford University Press, 1950.
APP 270; ODEP 583; EAP 317; MP 456.

It is **nuts** to him.

1843 It...was what the knowing ones call 'nuts' to Scrooge. (p. 8)
Christmas Books. 1843-49. The Oxford Illustrated Dickens, Vol. XVI. Oxford: Oxford University Press, 1954.
APP 266; ODEP 583; EAP 317.

To put in a **nutshell**

1838 'It all lies in a nutshell, my dear....' (p. 132)

The Adventures of Oliver Twist. 1838. The Oxford Illustrated Dickens, Vol. V. Oxford: Oxford University Press, 1948.

1841 'It lies in a nutshell.' (p. 226)

Barnaby Rudge: A Tale of the Riots of 'Eighty. 1841. The Oxford Illustrated Dickens, Vol. XV. Oxford: Oxford University Press, 1954.

1850 It lay in a nut-shell. (p. 388)

The Personal History of David Copperfield. 1850. The Oxford Illustrated Dickens, Vol. II. Oxford: Oxford University Press, 1948.

1865 'In a nut-shell, there's the state of the case.' (p. 125)

Our Mutual Friend. 1865. The Oxford Illustrated Dickens, Vol. X. Oxford: Oxford University Press, 1952.

APP 267; EAP 318; MP 456.

O

Great **oaks** from little acorns grow.

1853 Many a child grows into a giant and acorns into oaks. (p. 74)

The Letters of Charles Dickens: Volume Seven: 1853-1855. Eds. Graham Storey, Kathleen Tillotson, and Angus Easson. Oxford: The Clarendon Press, 1993.

APP 268; ODEP 584; CODP 101; MP 458; DAP 435.

To know what **o'clock** it is

1844 "...he hoped he knowed wot o'clock it wos in gineral." (p. 153)

The Life and Adventures of Martin Chuzzlewit. 1844. The Oxford Illustrated Dickens, Vol. IX. Oxford: Oxford University Press, 1951.

WILKINSON 375.

Odds and ends

1844 ...he had been...scraping all sorts of valuable odds and ends into his pouch. (p. 328)

The Life and Adventures of Martin Chuzzlewit. 1844. The Oxford Illustrated Dickens, Vol. IX. Oxford: Oxford University Press, 1951.

1854 ...other people...wanted other odds and ends.... (p. 206)

Hard Times for These Times. 1854. The Oxford Illustrated Dickens, Vol. XVII. Oxford: Oxford University Press, 1955.

1857 'I have been doing odds and ends....' (p. 131)

1857 '...we lawyers are always...picking up odds and ends....' (p. 564)

Little Dorrit. 1857. The Oxford Illustrated Dickens, Vol. XIV. Oxford: Oxford University Press, 1953.

1860 ...his native "Medicine" is a comical mixture of old odds and ends.... (p. 280)

The Uncommercial Traveller and Reprinted Pieces Etc. 1850-1860. The Oxford Illustrated Dickens, Vol. XXI. Oxford: Oxford University Press, 1958.
URDANG, *IDIOMS* 926.

What's the **odds** so long as you're happy?

1845 ...there is a vulgar saying in England "Wot's the odds so long as you're happy!" (p. 389)
The Letters of Charles Dickens: Volume Four: 1844-1846. Ed. Kathleen Tillotson. Oxford: The Clarendon Press, 1977.
PARTRIDGE 579.

To pour **oil** on troubled waters

She would throw oil on the waters. (p. 561)
The Life and Adventures of Martin Chuzzlewit. 1844. The Oxford Illustrated Dickens, Vol. IX. Oxford: Oxford University Press, 1951.
APP 269; ODEP 587; EAP 321; MP 460.

As **old** as Methuselah

1845 'A man may live to be as old as Methuselah....' (p. 98)
Christmas Books. 1843-49. The Oxford Illustrated Dickens, Vol. XVI. Oxford: Oxford University Press, 1954.
APP 242; ODEP 588; EAP 287; MP 408.

As **old** as the hills

1861 Old Barley might be as old as the hills, and might swear like a whole field of troopers.... (p. 359)
Great Expectations. 1861. The Oxford Illustrated Dickens, Vol. XIII. Oxford: Oxford University Press, 1953.
APP 183; ODEP 588; EAP 212; MP 307.

Old Nick

1841 '...he's as good...as Old Nick himself.' (p. 407)
Barnaby Rudge: A Tale of the Riots of 'Eighty. 1841. The Oxford Illustrated Dickens, Vol. XV. Oxford: Oxford University Press, 1954.
ODEP 591.

Old Parr

1850 ...the greater part must have been uttered before Old Parr.... (p. 189)

The Letters of Charles Dickens: Volume Six: 1850-1852. Eds. Madeline House, Graham Storey, and Kathleen Tillotson. Oxford: The Clarendon Press, 1988.
BREWER 805.

Ab uno disce omnes.

1838 *Ex uno disce omnes.* (p. 483)
The Letters of Charles Dickens: Volume One: 1820-1839. Eds. Madeline House and Graham Storey. Oxford: The Clarendon Press, 1965.
STEVENSON 1133:1.

All will be the same one hundred years hence.

1839 ...it would be all the same one hundred years hence.... (p. 101)
The Life and Adventures of Nicholas Nickleby. 1839. The Oxford Illustrated Dickens, Vol. VI. Oxford: Oxford University Press, 1950.
ODEP 10.

Like one of the family

1837 ...you are "one of the family". (p. 232)
The Letters of Charles Dickens: Volume One: 1820-1839. Eds. Madeline House and Graham Storey. Oxford: The Clarendon Press, 1965.

One keeps a secret better than two.

1861 'One keeps a secret better than two.' (p. 402)
Great Expectations. 1861. The Oxford Illustrated Dickens, Vol. XIII. Oxford: Oxford University Press, 1953.
STEVENSON 2053:3.

To behave like an ostrich

1844 'I should want to draw it...like a Ostrich for putting its head in the mud, and thinking nobody sees it—' (p. 547)
The Life and Adventures of Martin Chuzzlewit. 1844. The Oxford Illustrated Dickens, Vol. IX. Oxford: Oxford University Press, 1951.
ODEP 600; EAP 323; MP 465.

Out with it.

1837 '...out vith it, as the father said to the child, wen he swallowed a farden.' (p. 154)
The Posthumous Papers of the Pickwick Club. 1837. The Oxford Illustrated Dickens, Vol. I. Oxford: Oxford University Press, 1948.
DOW 93.

To swallow an **oyster** takes many men.

1854 ...it may be said...of the fat oyster in the American story, that it takes a good many men to swallow it whole. (p. 73)
Christmas Stories. 1871. The Oxford Illustrated Dickens, Vol. XI. Oxford: Oxford University Press, 1956.
ODEP 72; DAP 445.

P

To mind one's **p's and q's**

1838 ...they must mind their P's and Q's.... (p. 522)
Sketches by Boz. 1833-40. The Oxford Illustrated Dickens, Vol. XII. Oxford: Oxford University Press, 1957.
APP 274; ODEP 606; EAP 325; MP 470.

To have one's garments **paid**

1844 ...the seams of my blue jacket are "paid" [smeared with pitch to make it waterproof]—permit me to...make use of this nautical expression. (p. 183)
The Letters of Charles Dickens: Volume Four: 1844-1846. Ed. Kathleen Tillotson. Oxford: The Clarendon Press, 1977.

Not to touch with a **pair of tongs**

1854 '...you wouldn't have touched me with a pair of tongs.' (p. 15)
Hard Times for These Times. 1854. The Oxford Illustrated Dickens, Vol. XVII. Oxford: Oxford University Press, 1955.
APP 274; ODEP 833; EAP 325; MP 471.

As **pale** as a candle

1865 'You are as pale as a candle.' (p. 489)
Our Mutual Friend. 1865. The Oxford Illustrated Dickens, Vol. X. Oxford: Oxford University Press, 1952.
WILSTACH 282 (CITING DICKENS).

As **pale** as a maggot

1851 ...the boys...were as pale as maggots.... (p. 379)
"Chips: A Free (and Easy) School." *Charles Dickens' Uncollected Writings from Household Words 1850-1859*, 2 vols. Ed. Harry Stone. Bloomington: Indiana University Press, 1968.

As **pale** as a muffin

1844 'He's as pale as a muffin,' said one lady.... (p. 312)
The Life and Adventures of Martin Chuzzlewit. 1844. The Oxford Illustrated Dickens, Vol. IX. Oxford: Oxford University Press, 1951.
WILSTACH 282 (CITING DICKENS).

To be beyond the **pale**

1838 'You put yourself beyond its pale,' said the gentleman. (p. 353)
The Adventures of Oliver Twist. 1838. The Oxford Illustrated Dickens, Vol. V. Oxford: Oxford University Press, 1948.
WILKINSON 105.

In the **palmy days**

1837 ...I hope that you will meet with every happiness...in these palmy days.... (p. 232)
The Letters of Charles Dickens: Volume One: 1820-1839. Eds. Madeline House and Graham Storey. Oxford: The Clarendon Press, 1965.
1839 '...the theatre was in its high and palmy days....' (p. 311)
The Life and Adventures of Nicholas Nickleby. 1839. The Oxford Illustrated Dickens, Vol. VI. Oxford: Oxford University Press, 1950.
1844 I should prefer an intimate association with it now...in its high and palmy days. (p. 399)
Address to the Liverpool Mechanics' Institution, 26 Feb. 1844. *The Works of Charles Dickens: The Speeches.* Ed. Richard H. Shepherd. New National Edition, Vol. II. New York: Hearst's International Library Company, n. d.
1860 Those wonderful houses...in the palmy days of theatres were prosperous.... (p. 29)
The Uncommercial Traveller and Reprinted Pieces Etc. 1850-1860. The Oxford Illustrated Dickens, Vol. XXI. Oxford: Oxford University Press, 1958.
WILKINSON 399.

Pandora's box

1845 ...Hope stepped out of Pandora's box.... (p. 252)
The Letters of Charles Dickens: Volume Four: 1844-1846. Ed. Kathleen Tillotson. Oxford: The Clarendon Press, 1977.
ODEP 608; EAP 326; MP 473.

A **part** is better than the whole.

1843 I call it...A Part is Better than the Whole. (p. 509)
The Letters of Charles Dickens: Volume Three: 1842-1843. Eds. Madeline House, Graham Storey, and Kathleen Tillotson. Oxford: The Clarendon Press, 1974.

DAP 652; STEVENSON 1056:2.

Part and parcel

1833-36 Hackney-coaches are part and parcel of the law of the land....
(p. 81)
Sketches by Boz. 1833-40. The Oxford Illustrated Dickens, Vol. XII. Oxford: Oxford
University Press, 1957.
1840-41 ...coming to be part and parcel—nay nearly the whole sum and
substance of my daily thought.... (p. 43)
Master Humphrey's Clock and A Child's History of England. 1840-41, 1852-54. The
Oxford Illustrated Dickens, Vol. XX. Oxford: Oxford University Press, 1958.
1842 ...what pen...has made Rip Van Winkle...as much part and parcel
of the Catskill Mountains as any tree or crag...? (p. 387)
Remarks at a dinner, New York, 18 Feb. 1842. *The Works of Charles Dickens: The
Speeches*. Ed. Richard H. Shepherd. New National Edition, Vol. II. New York: Hearst's
International Library Company, n. d.
URDANG, *IDIOMS* 1090.

To play a part

1854 No parts to play (p. 253)
Dickens' Working Notes for His Novels. Ed. Harry Stone. Chicago, Ill.: University of
Chicago Press, 1987. xxiv +
WILKINSON 472.

C'est le premier pas qui coûte.

1852 That it is *"le premier pas qui coûte"*—that the first step is the great
point—is...a household word.... (p. 410)
"First Fruits." [with George Augustus Sala]. *Charles Dickens' Uncollected Writings from
Household Words 1850-1859*, 2 vols. Ed. Harry Stone. Bloomington: Indiana University
Press, 1968.
ODEP 773; EAP 414; CODP 82; MP 593; DAP 562.

Patience, and shuffle the cards.

1868 And as Sancho says—"Patience, and shuffle the cards." (p. 662)
1869 Let us shuffle the cards, as Sancho says, and begin again. (p. 743)
The Letters of Charles Dickens, ed. Walter Dexter. Vol. III: 1858-1870. The Nonesuch
Dickens. London: The Nonesuch Press, 1938.
ODEP 612; EAP 328; MP 475.

Peace and quiet

1854 ...this girl could never hope for peace and quiet. (p. 315)
The Letters of Charles Dickens: Volume Seven: 1853-1855. Eds. Graham Storey, Kathleen Tillotson, and Angus Easson. Oxford: The Clarendon Press, 1993.

1864 ...here am I...going out of town...to keep Shakespeare's birthday in peace and quiet. (p. 385)
The Letters of Charles Dickens, ed. Walter Dexter. Vol. III: 1858-1870. The Nonesuch Dickens. London: The Nonesuch Press, 1938.

1870 '...and having an idea of doing it in this lovely place in peace and quiet....' (p. 210)
The Mystery of Edwin Drood. 1870. The Oxford Illustrated Dickens, Vol. XVIII. Oxford: Oxford University Press, 1956.

URDANG, *IDIOMS* 1097.

Do not cast **pearls** before swine.

1848 '...I do a thankless thing, and cast pearls before swine!' (p. 329)
Dealings with the Firm of Dombey and Son. 1848. The Oxford Illustrated Dickens, Vol. VII. Oxford: Oxford University Press, 1950.

APP 278; ODEP 617; EAP 330; CODP 176; MP 478; DAP 456.

To be in a **peck** of trouble

1854 He had known, to use his words, a peck of trouble. (p. 63)
Hard Times for These Times. 1854. The Oxford Illustrated Dickens, Vol. XVII. Oxford: Oxford University Press, 1955.

APP 279; ODEP 618; EAP 331; MP 479.

To haggle like a **pedlar**

1844 ..."I won't...haggle like a pedlar...." (p. 68)
The Letters of Charles Dickens: Volume Four: 1844-1846. Ed. Kathleen Tillotson. Oxford: The Clarendon Press, 1977.

Pell-mell

1833-36 ...the people scampered away, pell-mell.... (p. 127)
1833-36 ...away rush the members pell-mell. (p. 162)
Sketches by Boz. 1833-40. The Oxford Illustrated Dickens, Vol. XII. Oxford: Oxford University Press, 1957.

1837 Horses...had brought him there, pell-mell. (p. 596)
The Posthumous Papers of the Pickwick Club. 1837. The Oxford Illustrated Dickens, Vol. I. Oxford: Oxford University Press, 1948.

1838 ...to see a charity-boy tearing through the streets pell-mell.... (p. 43)

The Adventures of Oliver Twist. 1838. The Oxford Illustrated Dickens, Vol. V. Oxford: Oxford University Press, 1948.

1841 ...the throng of people...came pouring out pell-mell.... (p. 331)

Barnaby Rudge: A Tale of the Riots of 'Eighty. 1841. The Oxford Illustrated Dickens, Vol. XV. Oxford: Oxford University Press, 1954.

1842 On it...dashes on haphazard, pell-mell, neck-or-nothing, down the middle of the road. (p. 64)

American Notes and Pictures from Italy. 1842, 1846. The Oxford Illustrated Dickens, Vol. XIX. Oxford: Oxford University Press, 1957.

1844 ...then going to work again, pell-mell.... (p. 452)

The Life and Adventures of Martin Chuzzlewit. 1844. The Oxford Illustrated Dickens, Vol. IX. Oxford: Oxford University Press, 1951.

1850 ...the little elephant...rattled it off, pell-mell.... (p. 736)

The Personal History of David Copperfield. 1850. The Oxford Illustrated Dickens, Vol. II. Oxford: Oxford University Press, 1948.

URDANG, *IDIOMS* 1099.

To set **pen** to paper

1835 ...I have not yet set pen to paper.... (p. 73)

1836 I have been...wholly unable to set pen to paper.... (p. 188)

The Letters of Charles Dickens: Volume One: 1820-1839. Eds. Madeline House and Graham Storey. Oxford: The Clarendon Press, 1965.

URDANG, *IDIOMS* 1100.

To take up one's **pen**

1847 I "take up my pen," as the young ladies write.... (p. 216)

The Letters of Charles Dickens: Volume Five: 1847-1849. Eds. Graham Storey and K. J. Fielding. Oxford: The Clarendon Press, 1981.

A **penny** saved is a penny got.

1853 '...let me tell you: a penny saved, is a penny got!' (p. 114)

Bleak House. 1853. The Oxford Illustrated Dickens, Vol. III. Oxford: Oxford University Press, 1948.

APP 279; ODEP 619; EAP 332; CODP 176; MP 482; DAP 458.

In for a **penny**, in for a pound.

1839 '...if you're in for a penny, you're in for a pound.' (p. 748)

The Life and Adventures of Nicholas Nickleby. 1839. The Oxford Illustrated Dickens, Vol. VI. Oxford: Oxford University Press, 1950.

APP 280; ODEP 402; EAP 332; CODP 120; MP 481; DAP 458.

(Not) to have a **penny** to bless oneself with

1844 '...he landed there without a penny to bless himself with....' (p. 217)
The Life and Adventures of Martin Chuzzlewit. 1844. The Oxford Illustrated Dickens, Vol. IX. Oxford: Oxford University Press, 1951.
ODEP 156; MP 482.

People of quality know everything without ever learning anything.

1850 What says the comedian? ....People of quality know everything without ever learning anything. (p. 202)
"Mr. Bendigo Buster on Our National Defences Against Education." [with Henry Morley].
Charles Dickens' Uncollected Writings from Household Words *1850-1859*, 2 vols. Ed. Harry Stone. Bloomington: Indiana University Press, 1968.

Peter Piper picked a peck of pickled peppers....

1860 ...if patriotic Peckham picked a peck of pickled poetry, this *was* the peck of pickled poetry which patriotic Peckham picked. (p. 360)
The Uncommercial Traveller and Reprinted Pieces Etc. 1850-1860. The Oxford Illustrated Dickens, Vol. XXI. Oxford: Oxford University Press, 1958.
1865 '"If Peter Piper picked a peck of pickled pepper, where's the peck," &c?' (p. 536)
Our Mutual Friend. 1865. The Oxford Illustrated Dickens, Vol. X. Oxford: Oxford University Press, 1952.
STEVENSON 1777:8.

Pick and choose

1839 ...Kate must now pick and choose.... (p. 339)
The Life and Adventures of Nicholas Nickleby. 1839. The Oxford Illustrated Dickens, Vol. VI. Oxford: Oxford University Press, 1950.
URDANG, *IDIOMS* 1110.

To carry someone **pick-a-back**

1837 '...I find it necessary to carry you away, pick-a-back....' (p. 541)
The Posthumous Papers of the Pickwick Club. 1837. The Oxford Illustrated Dickens, Vol. I. Oxford: Oxford University Press, 1948.
WILKINSON 277.

To be in a **pickle**

1842 But my best rod is in pickle. (p. 230)
1842 I am steeping a little rod in strong Pickle.... (p. 238)

1842 I have thought of a rod...and have put it in Pickle. (p. 240)
The Letters of Charles Dickens: Volume Three: 1842-1843. Eds. Madeline House, Graham Storey, and Kathleen Tillotson. Oxford: The Clarendon Press, 1974.
APP 282; ODEP 623; EAP 334; MP 486.

To give someone a **piece** of one's mind

1836 MARTIN: ...I might tell Miss Lucy Benson a bit of my mind....
(*The Village Coquettes*, I, i, p. 47)
Complete Plays and Selected Poems of Charles Dickens. London: Vision Press, 1970.
1838 Kate boasts...of having told you "a piece of her mind". (p. 445)
The Letters of Charles Dickens: Volume One: 1820-1839. Eds. Madeline House and Graham Storey. Oxford: The Clarendon Press, 1965.
1842 ...I...told him a piece of my mind. (p. 196)
1843 ...Mr. Hall shall have a piece of my mind. (p. 517)
The Letters of Charles Dickens: Volume Three: 1842-1843. Eds. Madeline House, Graham Storey, and Kathleen Tillotson. Oxford: The Clarendon Press, 1974.
1843 'I'd give him a piece of my mind....' (p. 48)
Christmas Books. 1843-49. The Oxford Illustrated Dickens, Vol. XVI. Oxford: Oxford University Press, 1954.
APP 283; EAP 335.

To be enough to disgust a **pig**

1861 "Ain't it enough to disgust a pig, if he could give his mind to it?" (p. 312)
Christmas Stories. 1871. The Oxford Illustrated Dickens, Vol. XI. Oxford: Oxford University Press, 1956.

To stare like a stuck **pig**

1861 '...what's the matter...you staring great stuck pig.' (p. 9)
Great Expectations. 1861. The Oxford Illustrated Dickens, Vol. XIII. Oxford: Oxford University Press, 1953.
APP 244; ODEP 771; EAP 336; MP 490.

To take one's **pigs** to a fine market

1853 ...every moderately sane man...does not carry his pigs to a Whole Hog market. (p. 480)
"In and Out of Jail." [with Henry Morley and W. H. Wills]. *Charles Dickens' Uncollected Writings from* Household Words *1850-1859*, 2 vols. Ed. Harry Stone. Bloomington: Indiana University Press, 1968.
1857 '...you have brought your pigs to a very indifferent market, Arthur.' (p. 751)

Little Dorrit. 1857. The Oxford Illustrated Dickens, Vol. XIV. Oxford: Oxford University Press, 1953.
APP 284; ODEP 204; MP 489.

(Not) to care a **pin**

1844 ...he didn't care a pin for Fortune.... (p. 215)
The Life and Adventures of Martin Chuzzlewit. 1844. The Oxford Illustrated Dickens, Vol. IX. Oxford: Oxford University Press, 1951.
APP 286; ODEP 102; EAP 337; MP 493.

To be quiet enough to hear a **pin** drop

1839 You might have heard a pin fall.... (p. 15)
The Life and Adventures of Nicholas Nickleby. 1839. The Oxford Illustrated Dickens, Vol. VI. Oxford: Oxford University Press, 1950.
1855 ...a pin-drop's silence strikes o'er all the place. (p. 533)
"By Rail to Parnassus." [with Henry Morley]. *Charles Dickens' Uncollected Writings from Household Words 1850-1859,* 2 vols. Ed. Harry Stone. Bloomington: Indiana University Press, 1968.
1850-56 To say that a pin might have been heard to fall, would be feeble to express the all-absorbing interest and silence. (p. 579)
The Uncommercial Traveller and Reprinted Pieces Etc. 1850-1860. The Oxford Illustrated Dickens, Vol. XXI. Oxford: Oxford University Press, 1958.
APP 286; ODEP 363; EAP 338; MP 492.

To get (be on) **pins and needles**

1844 ...by all the pins and needles that run up and down in angry veins, Tom was in a most unusual tingle all at once! (p. 570)
The Life and Adventures of Martin Chuzzlewit. 1844. The Oxford Illustrated Dickens, Vol. IX. Oxford: Oxford University Press, 1951.
1848 '...it turns all the blood in a person's body into pins and needles....' (p. 605)
Dealings with the Firm of Dombey and Son. 1848. The Oxford Illustrated Dickens, Vol. VII. Oxford: Oxford University Press, 1950.
ODEP 626; EAP 338; MP 493.

Put that in your **pipe** and smoke it.

1837 '...accidents will happen—best regulated families—never say die—...put that in his pipe....' (p. 9)
1837 '...fill your pipe with that 'ere reflection....' (pp. 215-216)
The Posthumous Papers of the Pickwick Club. 1837. The Oxford Illustrated Dickens, Vol. I. Oxford: Oxford University Press, 1948.

1838 Let the Legitimate Drama put this, and Joan of Arc as a first piece into her pipe.... (pp. 355-356)
1839 So please to put that in your pipe.... (p. 541)
The Letters of Charles Dickens: Volume One: 1820-1839. Eds. Madeline House and Graham Storey. Oxford: The Clarendon Press, 1965.
APP 256; ODEP 657; MP 494.

To smoke the **pipe of peace**

1850-56 ...he laughs and smokes his pipe of peace. (p. 409)
The Uncommercial Traveller and Reprinted Pieces Etc. 1850-1860. The Oxford Illustrated Dickens, Vol. XXI. Oxford: Oxford University Press, 1958.
ODEP 627; EAP 339; MP 495.

To pay the **piper**

1844 ...another man's mission was to pay the piper.... (p. 509)
The Life and Adventures of Martin Chuzzlewit. 1844. The Oxford Illustrated Dickens, Vol. IX. Oxford: Oxford University Press, 1951.
1850-56 "....I will pay the piper." (p. 546)
The Uncommercial Traveller and Reprinted Pieces Etc. 1850-1860. The Oxford Illustrated Dickens, Vol. XXI. Oxford: Oxford University Press, 1958.
1855 ...we venture to claim that right in virtue of his orchestra, consisting of a very powerful piper, whom we always pay. (p. 458)
Address on Administrative Reform, London, 27 June 1855. *The Works of Charles Dickens: The Speeches.* Ed. Richard H. Shepherd. New National Edition, Vol. II. New York: Hearst's International Library Company, n. d.
APP 287; ODEP 615; EAP 339; MP 495.

He who handles **pitch** will be defiled.

1857 'He provides the pitch, and I handle it, and its sticks to me.' (p. 802)
Little Dorrit. 1857. The Oxford Illustrated Dickens, Vol. XIV. Oxford: Oxford University Press, 1953.
APP 287; ODEP 834; EAP 340; CODP 228; MP 497; DAP 466.

To rain **pitchforks**

1843 If the day be anything short of cats, dogs, and pitchforks, in its dampness.... (p. 444)
The Letters of Charles Dickens: Volume Three: 1842-1843. Eds. Madeline House, Graham Storey, and Kathleen Tillotson. Oxford: The Clarendon Press, 1974.
1854 Unless it should rain cats, dogs, pitchforks and Cochin China poultry, the Train...is my means of going down. (p. 267)

The Letters of Charles Dickens: Volume Seven: 1853-1855. Eds. Graham Storey, Kathleen Tillotson, and Angus Easson. Oxford: The Clarendon Press, 1993.
APP 288; EAP 340; MP 498.

As **plain** as print

1841 ...there it was before him, as plain as print. (p. 519)
The Old Curiosity Shop. 1841. The Oxford Illustrated Dickens, Vol. VIII. Oxford: Oxford University Press, 1951.
1853 '...I see sold up in your face, George, as plain as print....' (p. 475)
Bleak House. 1853. The Oxford Illustrated Dickens, Vol. III. Oxford: Oxford University Press, 1948.
APP 296; EAP 348; MP 512.

As **plain** as Salisbury

1837 '...it's as plain as Salisbury.' (p. 588)
The Posthumous Papers of the Pickwick Club. 1837. The Oxford Illustrated Dickens, Vol. I. Oxford: Oxford University Press, 1948.
WILKINSON 206.

As **plain** as the sun

1844 All of which...spoke as plain English as the shining sun. (p. 511)
The Life and Adventures of Martin Chuzzlewit. 1844. The Oxford Illustrated Dickens, Vol. IX. Oxford: Oxford University Press, 1951.
APP 360; EAP 423; MP 605.

If you do not **play**, you cannot win.

1833-36 '...them as don't play can't vin....' (p. 112)
Sketches by Boz. 1833-40. The Oxford Illustrated Dickens, Vol. XII. Oxford: Oxford University Press, 1957.
1847 ...the people...on the race-courses, call, "a firm heart and a bold resolution, them as don't play can't win...." (p. 59)
The Letters of Charles Dickens: Volume Five: 1847-1849. Eds. Graham Storey and K. J. Fielding. Oxford: The Clarendon Press, 1981.

As **pleased** as a pug dog

1865 I was as pleased and as proud as a Pug Dog with his muzzle black-leaded for an evening party, and his tail extra curled by machinery. (p. 486)
Christmas Stories. 1871. The Oxford Illustrated Dickens, Vol. XI. Oxford: Oxford University Press, 1956.

A **pleasure** is a pleasure all the world over.

1861 'A pleasure's a pleasure all the world over.' (p. 98)
Great Expectations. 1861. The Oxford Illustrated Dickens, Vol. XIII. Oxford: Oxford University Press, 1953.

To give **pleasure** to the Devil

1861 "...a deteriorated spectacle calculated to give the Devil (and perhaps the monkeys) pleasure...." (p. 299)
Christmas Stories. 1871. The Oxford Illustrated Dickens, Vol. XI. Oxford: Oxford University Press, 1956.

As **plentiful** as blackberries

1845 Even, and edds...were as plentiful as blackberries.... (p. 358)
The Letters of Charles Dickens: Volume Four: 1844-1846. Ed. Kathleen Tillotson. Oxford: The Clarendon Press, 1977.
APP 31; ODEP 634; EAP 35; MP 55.

To make the **plunge**

1869 I made the plunge.... (p. 724)
The Letters of Charles Dickens, ed. Walter Dexter. Vol. III: 1858-1870. The Nonesuch Dickens. London: The Nonesuch Press, 1938.
WILKINSON 75.

Not to put too fine a **point** on it

1853 '...not to put too fine a point upon it—' a favourite apology for plain-speaking with Mr. Snagsby.... (p. 142)
1853 '....not to put too fine a point upon it—that you're rather greasy here, sir?' (p. 445)
1853 '...not to put too fine a point upon it—that they were quite fresh....' (p. 445)
1853 'A little—not to put too fine a point upon it—drop of shrub?' (p. 460)
1853 '...it is relating—not to put too fine a point upon it—to the foreigner, sir.' (p. 584)
1853 'Why, not to put too fine a point upon it, this is Bedlam, sir!' (p. 646)
Bleak House. 1853. The Oxford Illustrated Dickens, Vol. III. Oxford: Oxford University Press, 1948.
APP 290; MP 502.

As **poor** as a churchmouse

1857 '...you therefore know the reasons for my being as poor as Thingummy.' ¶'A church mouse?' Mrs. Merdle suggested with a smile. ¶'I was thinking of the other proverbial church person—Job.' (p. 392)
1857 'I suppose they'as as poor as mice...?' (p. 520)
Little Dorrit. 1857. The Oxford Illustrated Dickens, Vol. XIV. Oxford: Oxford University Press, 1953.
APP 70; ODEP 638; EAP 73; MP 116.

As **poor** as Job

1857 '...you therefore know the reasons for my being as poor as Thingummy.' ¶'A church mouse?' Mrs. Merdle suggested with a smile. ¶'I was thinking of the other proverbial church person—Job.' (p. 392)
1857 'I suppose they'as as poor as mice...?' (p. 520)
Little Dorrit. 1857. The Oxford Illustrated Dickens, Vol. XIV. Oxford: Oxford University Press, 1953.
APP 204; ODEP 638; EAP 240; MP 344.

Between you and me and the **post**

1839 '...between you and me and the post, sir, it will be a very nice portrait....' (p. 117)
The Life and Adventures of Nicholas Nickleby. 1839. The Oxford Illustrated Dickens, Vol. VI. Oxford: Oxford University Press, 1950.
ODEP 57; MP 250.

From **post** to pillar

1844 '...skimming from post to pillar, like the butterfly....' (p. 306)
The Life and Adventures of Martin Chuzzlewit. 1844. The Oxford Illustrated Dickens, Vol. IX. Oxford: Oxford University Press, 1951.
1847 I had been...driven from pillar to post.... (p. 44)
The Letters of Charles Dickens: Volume Five: 1847-1849. Eds. Graham Storey and K. J. Fielding. Oxford: The Clarendon Press, 1981.
1853 '...the man was so...tortured, by being knocked about from post to pillar, and from pillar to post....' (pp. 342-343)
Bleak House. 1853. The Oxford Illustrated Dickens, Vol. III. Oxford: Oxford University Press, 1948.
1865 ...how the worn-out people...get driven from post to pillar, and pillar to post.... (p. 199)
Our Mutual Friend. 1865. The Oxford Illustrated Dickens, Vol. X. Oxford: Oxford University Press, 1952.
APP 285; ODEP 625; EAP 344; MP 491.

To keep the **pot** boiling

1837 'Keep the pot a bilin', sir!' said Sam. (p. 413)
The Posthumous Papers of the Pickwick Club. 1837. The Oxford Illustrated Dickens, Vol.
I. Oxford: Oxford University Press, 1948.
ODEP 418; EAP 345.

To take **pot-luck**

1870 '...*you* are very kind to...take pot-luck.' (p. 115)
The Mystery of Edwin Drood. 1870. The Oxford Illustrated Dickens, Vol. XVIII. Oxford:
Oxford University Press, 1956.
APP 294; EAP 345; MP 508.

Pounds, shillings, and pence

1839 'I don't believe he ever had an appetite...except for pounds,
shillings, and pence....' (p. 609)
The Life and Adventures of Nicholas Nickleby. 1839. The Oxford Illustrated Dickens, Vol.
VI. Oxford: Oxford University Press, 1950.
1870 '"Pounds, shillings, and pence," is my next note....Life is pounds,
shillings, and pence....Death is *not* pounds, shillings, and
pence....Pounds, shillings, and pence.' (pp. 86-87)
The Mystery of Edwin Drood. 1870. The Oxford Illustrated Dickens, Vol. XVIII. Oxford:
Oxford University Press, 1956.

Practice makes perfect.

1839 'Practice makes perfect, you know.' (p. 616)
The Life and Adventures of Nicholas Nickleby. 1839. The Oxford Illustrated Dickens, Vol.
VI. Oxford: Oxford University Press, 1950.
APP 295; ODEP 856; EAP 346; CODP 182; MP 509; DAP 479.

One should **practise** what he preaches.

1840-41 'I will not preach to you what I have not practised, indeed.' (p.
36)
Master Humphrey's Clock and A Child's History of England. 1840-41, 1852-54. The
Oxford Illustrated Dickens, Vol. XX. Oxford: Oxford University Press, 1958.
1857 Thomas Idle...practised what he would have preached if he had not
been too idle to preach.... (p. 664)
Christmas Stories. 1871. The Oxford Illustrated Dickens, Vol. XI. Oxford: Oxford
University Press, 1956.
APP 295; ODEP 643; EAP 346; CODP 182; MP 510; DAP 479.

To be a blue-nosed **Presbyterian**

1845 ...the New President...is what they call in America "a blue-nosed Presbyterian". (p. 360)

The Letters of Charles Dickens: Volume Four: 1844-1846. Ed. Kathleen Tillotson. Oxford: The Clarendon Press, 1977.

STEVENSON 205:6.

Prevention is better than cure.

1851 ...some of the wealthy...have been induced to assist in carrying out that excellent motto, 'Prevention is better than cure.' (p. 239)

"Chips: Small Beginnings." [with W. H. Wills]. *Charles Dickens' Uncollected Writings from Household Words 1850-1859*, 2 vols. Ed. Harry Stone. Bloomington: Indiana University Press, 1968.

APP 272; ODEP 646; EAP 347; CODP 183; MP 465; DAP 483.

Pride and joy

1840-41 '...cuttin' and curlin' was his pride and glory.' (p. 90)

Master Humphrey's Clock and A Child's History of England. 1840-41, 1852-54. The Oxford Illustrated Dickens, Vol. XX. Oxford: Oxford University Press, 1958.

1851 GABBLEWIG: ...no more will I leave this 'ouse until I find a parent's 'ope—a mother's pride—and nobody's...joy. (*Mr. Nightingale's Diary*, I, i, p. 165)

Complete Plays and Selected Poems of Charles Dickens. London: Vision Press, 1970.

1864 "He has been my pride and joy ever since." (p. 426)

Christmas Stories. 1871. The Oxford Illustrated Dickens, Vol. XI. Oxford: Oxford University Press, 1956.

URDANG, *IDIOMS* 1147.

Pride goeth before a fall.

1848 'Pride shall have a fall, and it always was and will be so!' (p. 829)

Dealings with the Firm of Dombey and Son. 1848. The Oxford Illustrated Dickens, Vol. VII. Oxford: Oxford University Press, 1950.

APP 296; ODEP 647; EAP 348; CODP 183; MP 511; DAP 483.

Hooroar for the **principle**.

1837 'Hooroar for the principle, as the money-lender said ven he vouldn't renew the bill,' observed Mr. Weller.... (p. 489)

The Posthumous Papers of the Pickwick Club. 1837. The Oxford Illustrated Dickens, Vol. I. Oxford: Oxford University Press, 1948.

1842 So "Hoo-roar for the principle, as the money-lender said, ven he vouldn't renoo the bill." (p. 92)
The Letters of Charles Dickens: Volume Three: 1842-1843. Eds. Madeline House, Graham Storey, and Kathleen Tillotson. Oxford: The Clarendon Press, 1974.
DOW 100.

Pro and con

1844 We must formally...vote pro and con.... (p. 25)
The Letters of Charles Dickens: Volume Four: 1844-1846. Ed. Kathleen Tillotson. Oxford: The Clarendon Press, 1977.
1854 Except the crowds...reading the placards pro and con.... (p. 260)
The Letters of Charles Dickens: Volume Seven: 1853-1855. Eds. Graham Storey, Kathleen Tillotson, and Angus Easson. Oxford: The Clarendon Press, 1993.
URDANG, *IDIOMS* 1149.

Procrastination is the thief of time.

1850 'Procrastination is the thief of time.' (p. 174)
The Personal History of David Copperfield. 1850. The Oxford Illustrated Dickens, Vol. II. Oxford: Oxford University Press, 1948.
APP 296; ODEP 648; EAP 349; CODP 184; MP 512; DAP 485.

He'd rather leave his **property** to his wife....

1837 'As the wirtuous clergyman remarked of the old gen'l'm'n with the dropsy, ven he said, that upon the whole he thought he'd rather leave his property to his wife than build a chapel vith it.' (p. 615)
The Posthumous Papers of the Pickwick Club. 1837. The Oxford Illustrated Dickens, Vol. I. Oxford: Oxford University Press, 1948.

That's what I call a self-evident **proposition**.

1837 'That's what I call a self-evident proposition, as the dog's-meat man said, when the housemaid told him he warn't a gentleman.' (p. 299)
The Posthumous Papers of the Pickwick Club. 1837. The Oxford Illustrated Dickens, Vol. I. Oxford: Oxford University Press, 1948.
DOW 101.

Pros and cons

1835 ...I never act upon them without...deliberation of the *pro's* [*sic*] and *cons*.... (p. 56)
The Letters of Charles Dickens: Volume One: 1820-1839. Eds. Madeline House and Graham Storey. Oxford: The Clarendon Press, 1965.

1841 ...as if she were...discussing the pros and cons of some very weighty matter. (p. 205)

The Old Curiosity Shop. 1841. The Oxford Illustrated Dickens, Vol. VIII. Oxford: Oxford University Press, 1951.

URDANG, *IDIOMS* 1155.

Prunes and prism

1857 'Papa, potatoes, poultry, prunes, and prism, are all very good words for the lips: especially prunes and prism.' (p. 476)

Little Dorrit. 1857. The Oxford Illustrated Dickens, Vol. XIV. Oxford: Oxford University Press, 1953.

As **punctual** as the almanac

1850-56 "There's another queer old customer...comes over, as punctual as the almanack...." (p. 531)

The Uncommercial Traveller and Reprinted Pieces Etc. 1850-1860. The Oxford Illustrated Dickens, Vol. XXI. Oxford: Oxford University Press, 1958.

As **punctual** as the sun

1853 'You are as punctual as the sun,' said Mr. Jarndyce. (p. 341)

Bleak House. 1853. The Oxford Illustrated Dickens, Vol. III. Oxford: Oxford University Press, 1948.

You cannot make a silk **purse** out of a sow's ear.

1851 ...your conducting them would change them, from a sow's ear to a silk purse. (p. 494)

The Letters of Charles Dickens: Volume Six: 1850-1852. Eds. Madeline House, Graham Storey, and Kathleen Tillotson. Oxford: The Clarendon Press, 1988.

APP 298; ODEP 733; EAP 352; CODP 204; MP 515; DAP 491.

Q

To live in **Queer Street**

1837 '...you would have found yourself in Queer Street before this.' (p. 776)

The Posthumous Papers of the Pickwick Club. 1837. The Oxford Illustrated Dickens, Vol. I. Oxford: Oxford University Press, 1948.

1865 'Queer Street is full of lodgers just at present!' (p. 423)

1865 Chapter I: Lodgers in Queer Street (p. 420)

Our Mutual Friend. 1865. The Oxford Illustrated Dickens, Vol. X. Oxford: Oxford University Press, 1952.
ODEP 659; MP 519.

Ask no **questions**, and you'll be told no lies.

1861 'Ask no questions, and you'll be told no lies.' (p. 11)
Great Expectations. 1861. The Oxford Illustrated Dickens, Vol. XIII. Oxford: Oxford University Press, 1953.
APP 300; ODEP 20; EAP 353; CODP 7; MP 519; DAP 494.

As **quick** as powder

1853 'The old girl...is as quick. As powder.' (p. 670)
Bleak House. 1853. The Oxford Illustrated Dickens, Vol. III. Oxford: Oxford University Press, 1948.
WILKINSON 41.

As **quiet** as a church at midnight

1851 ...a room...where all is as quiet as a...church at midnight.... (p. 228)
"Spitalfields." [with W. H. Wills]. *Charles Dickens' Uncollected Writings from Household Words 1850-1859*, 2 vols. Ed. Harry Stone. Bloomington: Indiana University Press, 1968.
MP 115.

As **quiet** as a churchyard

1846 'It's as quiet as a churchyard,' said Clemency.... (p. 276)
Christmas Books. 1843-49. The Oxford Illustrated Dickens, Vol. XVI. Oxford: Oxford University Press, 1954.
MP 116.

As **quiet** as a lamb

1850 He...would be as quiet and tractable as any Lamb. (p. 186)
The Letters of Charles Dickens: Volume Six: 1850-1852. Eds. Madeline House, Graham Storey, and Kathleen Tillotson. Oxford: The Clarendon Press, 1988.
APP 213; ODEP 298; EAP 250; MP 358.

As **quiet** as a monastery

1850 'As quiet as a monastery, and almost as roomy.' (p. 222)
The Personal History of David Copperfield. 1850. The Oxford Illustrated Dickens, Vol. II. Oxford: Oxford University Press, 1948.
WILSTACH 309.

As **quiet** as a mouse

1853 ...they...were as quiet as mice.... (p. 40)
1853 ...I was as quiet as a mouse. They were as quiet as mice, too.... (p. 112)
Bleak House. 1853. The Oxford Illustrated Dickens, Vol. III. Oxford: Oxford University Press, 1948.
APP 252; EAP 301; MP 429.

As **quiet** as a playhouse at daybreak

1851 ...a room...where all is as quiet as a playhouse at daybreak.... (p. 228)
"Spitalfields." [with W. H. Wills].*Charles Dickens' Uncollected Writings from* Household Words *1850-1859*, 2 vols. Ed. Harry Stone. Bloomington: Indiana University Press, 1968.

As **quiet** as a sepulchre

1844 ...the house was as quiet as a sepulchre.... (p. 413)
The Life and Adventures of Martin Chuzzlewit. 1844. The Oxford Illustrated Dickens, Vol. IX. Oxford: Oxford University Press, 1951.
WILSTACH 309 (CITING DICKENS).

As **quiet** as quiet can be

1844 Quiet as quiet can be. (p. 174)
The Letters of Charles Dickens: Volume Four: 1844-1846. Ed. Kathleen Tillotson. Oxford: The Clarendon Press, 1977.

As **quiet** as the North Pole

1850 'Distant and quiet as the North Pole.' (p. 325)
The Personal History of David Copperfield. 1850. The Oxford Illustrated Dickens, Vol. II. Oxford: Oxford University Press, 1948.

R

To go to **rack and ruin**

1839 '...so we must go to rack and ruin....' (p. 253)
The Life and Adventures of Nicholas Nickleby. 1839. The Oxford Illustrated Dickens, Vol. VI. Oxford: Oxford University Press, 1950.
1853 '...I have so many things here...going to rack and ruin....' (p. 52)
1853 ...the housekeeping was going to rack and ruin.... (p. 515)

Bleak House. 1853. The Oxford Illustrated Dickens, Vol. III. Oxford: Oxford University Press, 1948.
MP 706.

Like a red **rag** to a bull

1855 ...in the Spanish case, the bull rushes at the scarlet, in the Ninevite case, the scarlet rushes at the bull.... (p. 462)
Address on Administrative Reform, London, 27 June 1855. *The Works of Charles Dickens: The Speeches.* Ed. Richard H. Shepherd. New National Edition, Vol. II. New York: Hearst's International Library Company, n. d.
ODEP 668; MP 522.

To move at **railroad speed**

1847 You run away at Railroad speed (and more than Railroad speed)....
(p. 11)
The Letters of Charles Dickens: Volume Five: 1847-1849. Eds. Graham Storey and K. J. Fielding. Oxford: The Clarendon Press, 1981.

It never **rains** but it pours.

1842 ...the Proverb says it never rains but it pours.... (p. 231)
The Letters of Charles Dickens: Volume Three: 1842-1843. Eds. Madeline House, Graham Storey, and Kathleen Tillotson. Oxford: The Clarendon Press, 1974.
APP 303; ODEP 663; EAP 356; CODP 188; MP 523; DAP 498.

Rank and file

1853? The story of Nobody is the story of the rank and file of the earth.
(p. 66)
Christmas Stories. 1871. The Oxford Illustrated Dickens, Vol. XI. Oxford: Oxford University Press, 1956.
WILKINSON 52.

To close up **ranks**

1863 ...we must close up the ranks.... (p. 370)
The Letters of Charles Dickens, ed. Walter Dexter. Vol. III: 1858-1870. The Nonesuch Dickens. London: The Nonesuch Press, 1938.
WILKINSON 46.

Rats will leave a sinking ship.

1844 'When vessels are about to founder, the rats are said to leave 'em.'
(p. 257)

The Life and Adventures of Martin Chuzzlewit. 1844. The Oxford Illustrated Dickens, Vol. IX. Oxford: Oxford University Press, 1951.
ODEP 664; EAP 357; MP 526; DAP 499; BARTLETT 104:NOTE 9.

Do not laugh without **reason** lest you cry with it.

1844 'Let us take heed how we laugh without reason, lest we cry with it.' (p. 16)
The Life and Adventures of Martin Chuzzlewit. 1844. The Oxford Illustrated Dickens, Vol. IX. Oxford: Oxford University Press, 1951.

A **receipt** is a receipt.

1863 "A receipt's a receipt." (p. 386)
Christmas Stories. 1871. The Oxford Illustrated Dickens, Vol. XI. Oxford: Oxford University Press, 1956.

Red tape

1851 I call it "Red Tape". (p. 273)
The Letters of Charles Dickens: Volume Six: 1850-1852. Eds. Madeline House, Graham Storey, and Kathleen Tillotson. Oxford: The Clarendon Press, 1988.
1855 All the red tape in this country grew redder.... (p. 463)
Address on Administrative Reform, London, 27 June 1855. *The Works of Charles Dickens: The Speeches.* Ed. Richard H. Shepherd. New National Edition, Vol. II. New York: Hearst's International Library Company, n. d.
WILKINSON 65.

To be caught **red-handed**

1861 '...I had been taken red-handed....' (p. 98)
Great Expectations. 1861. The Oxford Illustrated Dickens, Vol. XIII. Oxford: Oxford University Press, 1953.
APP 305; MP 528.

To be a **red-letter day**

1841 ...what red-letter day or saint's day the almanack said it was.... (p. 190)
The Old Curiosity Shop. 1841. The Oxford Illustrated Dickens, Vol. VIII. Oxford: Oxford University Press, 1951.
1845 So wind and frost and snow...were Toby Veck's red-letter days. (p. 83)
Christmas Books. 1843-49. The Oxford Illustrated Dickens, Vol. XVI. Oxford: Oxford University Press, 1954.
URDANG, *IDIOMS* 1193.

To lean upon a broken **reed**

1855 ...she has leaned thus long upon a broken reed.... (p. 549)
"The Holly-Tree Inn." *Charles Dickens' Uncollected Writings from* Household Words *1850-1859*, 2 vols. Ed. Harry Stone. Bloomington: Indiana University Press, 1968.
ODEP 88; EAP 359; MP 529.

To be off the **reel**

1866 It seems to me to be so constituted as to require to be read "off the reel." (p. 462)
The Letters of Charles Dickens, ed. Walter Dexter. Vol. III: 1858-1870. The Nonesuch Dickens. London: The Nonesuch Press, 1938.
MP 529.

As **regular** as clockwork

1837 Regular as clockwork—breakfast at nine.... (p. 245)
Sketches by Boz. 1833-40. The Oxford Illustrated Dickens, Vol. XII. Oxford: Oxford University Press, 1957.
1850-56 "He comes back...as reg'lar as the clock strikes three in the morning...." (p. 531)
The Uncommercial Traveller and Reprinted Pieces Etc. 1850-1860. The Oxford Illustrated Dickens, Vol. XXI. Oxford: Oxford University Press, 1958.
1857 "As sober as a judge, and as regular as clock-work in his habits." (p. 690)
Christmas Stories. 1871. The Oxford Illustrated Dickens, Vol. XI. Oxford: Oxford University Press, 1956.
APP 72; MP 119.

Three **removes** are as bad as a fire.

1839 There is an old proverb that three removes are as bad as a fire. (p. 602)
The Letters of Charles Dickens: Volume One: 1820-1839. Eds. Madeline House and Graham Storey. Oxford: The Clarendon Press, 1965.
APP 306; ODEP 817; EAP 361; CODP 224; DAP 505.

As **rich** as a Jew

1853 'We would make him as rich as a Jew....' (p. 686)
Bleak House. 1853. The Oxford Illustrated Dickens, Vol. III. Oxford: Oxford University Press, 1948.
STEVENSON 1985:6.

This is rayther too **rich**.

1837 '...this is rayther too rich, as the young lady said, wen she remonstrated with the pastry-cook, arter he'd sold her a pork-pie as had got nothin' but fat inside.' (p. 541)
The Posthumous Papers of the Pickwick Club. 1837. The Oxford Illustrated Dickens, Vol. I. Oxford: Oxford University Press, 1948.
DOW 107.

As **rickety** as a hackney coach

1859 'I am as rickety as a hackney-coach, I'm as sleepy as laudanum....' (p. 53)
A Tale of Two Cities. 1859. The Oxford Illustrated Dickens, Vol. IV. Oxford: Oxford University Press, 1948.

Good **riddance** to bad rubbish.

1848 'A good riddance of bad rubbish!' said that wrathful old lady. (p. 617)
Dealings with the Firm of Dombey and Son. 1848. The Oxford Illustrated Dickens, Vol. VII. Oxford: Oxford University Press, 1950.
ODEP 323; EAP 363; MP 531; DAP 510.

Riddle-me, riddle-me ree.

1864 "Riddle-me, riddle-me ree, perhaps you can't tell me what this may be?" (p. 347)
Dickens' Working Notes for His Novels. Ed. Harry Stone. Chicago, Ill.: University of Chicago Press, 1987. xxiv +
1865 'The old nursery form runs, "Riddle-me-riddle-me-ree, p'raps you can tell me what this may be?"' (p. 286)
1865 'Riddle-me, riddle-me-ree, perhaps you can't tell me what this may be?' (p. 295)
Our Mutual Friend. 1865. The Oxford Illustrated Dickens, Vol. X. Oxford: Oxford University Press, 1952.
URDANG, *IDIOMS* 1203.

To **ride** roughshod over someone (-thing)

1843 ...a cold...has ridden rough-shod—to use the favorite newspaper expression—over my features. (p. 584)
The Letters of Charles Dickens: Volume Three: 1842-1843. Eds. Madeline House, Graham Storey, and Kathleen Tillotson. Oxford: The Clarendon Press, 1974.
1850 'Ride on! Rough-shod if need be...!' (p. 426)

The Personal History of David Copperfield. 1850. The Oxford Illustrated Dickens, Vol. II. Oxford: Oxford University Press, 1948.

1850-56 ...it will be clamorous to know whether it is to be..."ridden over rough-shod." (p. 575)

The Uncommercial Traveller and Reprinted Pieces Etc. 1850-1860. The Oxford Illustrated Dickens, Vol. XXI. Oxford: Oxford University Press, 1958.

WILKINSON 122.

Riff-raff

1854 '...I am a bit of dirty riff-raff, and a genuine scrap of tag, rag, and bobtail.' (p. 126)

Hard Times for These Times. 1854. The Oxford Illustrated Dickens, Vol. XVII. Oxford: Oxford University Press, 1955.

WILKINSON 376.

As **right** as a trivet

1844 'He's righter than a trivet!' (p. 457)

The Life and Adventures of Martin Chuzzlewit. 1844. The Oxford Illustrated Dickens, Vol. IX. Oxford: Oxford University Press, 1951.

APP 382; ODEP 677; MP 644.

To be the **right** something in the wrong place

1864 She and Colenso seem to me to be the right man and woman in the wrong places. (p. 406)

The Letters of Charles Dickens, ed. Walter Dexter. Vol. III: 1858-1870. The Nonesuch Dickens. London: The Nonesuch Press, 1938.

URDANG, *IDIOMS* 1206.

To read the **Riot Act**

1841 That the Riot Act being read.... (p. 510)

Barnaby Rudge: A Tale of the Riots of 'Eighty. 1841. The Oxford Illustrated Dickens, Vol. XV. Oxford: Oxford University Press, 1954.

APP 307; MP 531.

The **road** to ruin is in good repair.

1842 All these are roads to ruin. (p. 229)

American Notes and Pictures from Italy. 1842, 1846. The Oxford Illustrated Dickens, Vol. XIX. Oxford: Oxford University Press, 1957.

URDANG, *IDIOMS* 1212; STEVENSON 2012:9.

A **Roland** for an Oliver

1842 We shall play...A Roland for an Oliver [by Thomas M. Morton]...and Deaf as a Post [by John Poole]. (p. 235)
1842 The Theatricals...are, *A Roland for an Oliver*...and...*Deaf as a Post*. (pp. 236-237)
1842 We perform a Roland for an Oliver...and Deaf as a Post. (p. 244)
The Letters of Charles Dickens: Volume Three: 1842-1843. Eds. Madeline House, Graham Storey, and Kathleen Tillotson. Oxford: The Clarendon Press, 1974.
APP 309; ODEP 682; EAP 368; MP 535.

Rome was not built in a day.

1850 '...Rome was not built in a day, nor in a year.' (p. 638)
The Personal History of David Copperfield. 1850. The Oxford Illustrated Dickens, Vol. II. Oxford: Oxford University Press, 1948.
1854 'Rome wasn't built in a day, ma'am.' (p. 202)
Hard Times for These Times. 1854. The Oxford Illustrated Dickens, Vol. XVII. Oxford: Oxford University Press, 1955.
APP 310; ODEP 683; EAP 368; CODP 193; MP 535; DAP 515.

When in **Rome**, do as the Romans do.

1859 'When you go to Rome, do as Rome does.' (p. 152)
A Tale of Two Cities. 1859. The Oxford Illustrated Dickens, Vol. IV. Oxford: Oxford University Press, 1948.
APP 310; ODEP 683; EAP 368; CODP 193; MP 536; DAP 515.

(Not) enough **room** to swing a cat in

1850 ...there wasn't room to swing a cat there.... (p. 500)
The Personal History of David Copperfield. 1850. The Oxford Illustrated Dickens, Vol. II. Oxford: Oxford University Press, 1948.
APP 59; ODEP 683; EAP 62; MP 536.

Root and branch

1850-56 ...the Railway had cut it up root and branch. (p. 566)
The Uncommercial Traveller and Reprinted Pieces Etc. 1850-1860. The Oxford Illustrated Dickens, Vol. XXI. Oxford: Oxford University Press, 1958.
APP 311; EAP 369.

Give a man **rope** enough, and he will hang himself.

1845 ...having plenty of rope, he hanged himself.... (p. 346)

The Letters of Charles Dickens: Volume Four: 1844-1846. Ed. Kathleen Tillotson. Oxford: The Clarendon Press, 1977.
APP 311; ODEP 683; EAP 369; CODP 194; MP 537; DAP 516.

To be on the high **ropes**

1839 '...she was quite on the high ropes about something....' (p. 404)
The Life and Adventures of Nicholas Nickleby. 1839. The Oxford Illustrated Dickens, Vol. VI. Oxford: Oxford University Press, 1950.
ODEP 372; EAP 370.

Regular **rotation**.

1837 'No, no; reg'lar rotation, as Jack Ketch said, wen he tied the men up.' (p. 119)
The Posthumous Papers of the Pickwick Club. 1837. The Oxford Illustrated Dickens, Vol. I. Oxford: Oxford University Press, 1948.
DOW 108.

Rough and ready

1850 'You'll find us rough, sir, but you'll find us ready.' (p. 31)
The Personal History of David Copperfield. 1850. The Oxford Illustrated Dickens, Vol. II. Oxford: Oxford University Press, 1948.
ODEP 685; EAP 372; MP 539.

Rough and tough

1839 'How is the old rough-and-tough monster of Golden Square?' (p. 404)
The Life and Adventures of Nicholas Nickleby. 1839. The Oxford Illustrated Dickens, Vol. VI. Oxford: Oxford University Press, 1950.
1848 'Joe is rough and tough....' (p. 717)
Dealings with the Firm of Dombey and Son. 1848. The Oxford Illustrated Dickens, Vol. VII. Oxford: Oxford University Press, 1950.
PARTRIDGE 708.

As **round** as a hedgehog

1841 ...rolling himself up as round as a hedgehog.... (p. 372)
The Old Curiosity Shop. 1841. The Oxford Illustrated Dickens, Vol. VIII. Oxford: Oxford University Press, 1951.

There's the **rub**.

1840 ...there's the Rub. (p. 123)

The Letters of Charles Dickens: Volume Two: 1840-1841. Eds. Madeline House and Graham Storey. Oxford: The Clarendon Press, 1969.

1844 There was the rub! (p. 510)

The Life and Adventures of Martin Chuzzlewit. 1844. The Oxford Illustrated Dickens, Vol. IX. Oxford: Oxford University Press, 1951.

1847 ...but there's the rub. (p. 165)

The Letters of Charles Dickens: Volume Five: 1847-1849. Eds. Graham Storey and K. J. Fielding. Oxford: The Clarendon Press, 1981.

APP 313; ODEP 686; EAP 372; MP 540.

To cross the **Rubicon**

1852 We...felt that we had passed the Rubicon too. (p. 419)

"First Fruits." [with George Augustus Sala]. "First Fruits." [with George Augustus Sala]. *Charles Dickens' Uncollected Writings from* Household Words *1850-1859*, 2 vols. Ed. Harry Stone. Bloomington: Indiana University Press, 1968.

APP 313; ODEP 687; EAP 372; MP 540.

As **ruddy** as a berry

1846 ...his brown face as ruddy as a winter berry.... (p. 204)

Christmas Books. 1843-49. The Oxford Illustrated Dickens, Vol. XVI. Oxford: Oxford University Press, 1954.

MP 44.

Every **rule** has an exception.

1852 The only exception to this general rule is the child.... (p. 31)

Christmas Stories. 1871. The Oxford Illustrated Dickens, Vol. XI. Oxford: Oxford University Press, 1956.

APP 313; ODEP 687; CODP 71; DAP 518.

Rules and regulations

1838 '...the rules and regulations...would soon bring their spirit down for 'em.' (p. 24)

The Adventures of Oliver Twist. 1838. The Oxford Illustrated Dickens, Vol. V. Oxford: Oxford University Press, 1948.

1852 ...too many unbending rules and regulations.... (p. 427)

"Boys to Mend." [with Henry Morley]. *Charles Dickens' Uncollected Writings from* Household Words *1850-1859*, 2 vols. Ed. Harry Stone. Bloomington: Indiana University Press, 1968.

In the long (short) **run**

1843 I quite agree with you...in the long run. But in the short run.... (p. 432)
The Letters of Charles Dickens: Volume Three: 1842-1843. Eds. Madeline House, Graham Storey, and Kathleen Tillotson. Oxford: The Clarendon Press, 1974.
WILKINSON 452.

S

To get the sack

1837 'I should get the sack, I s'pose—eh?' (p. 263)
The Posthumous Papers of the Pickwick Club. 1837. The Oxford Illustrated Dickens, Vol. I. Oxford: Oxford University Press, 1948.
1853 'Say, got the sack!' cries Mr. Jobling.... (p. 278)
Bleak House. 1853. The Oxford Illustrated Dickens, Vol. III. Oxford: Oxford University Press, 1948.
APP 315; ODEP 26; MP 543.

Sackcloth and ashes

1850 He attended on us, as I may say, in sackcloth and ashes. (p. 290)
The Personal History of David Copperfield. 1850. The Oxford Illustrated Dickens, Vol. II. Oxford: Oxford University Press, 1948.
WILKINSON 4:19.

As safe as the Bank of England

1845 ...you were as cool as a Cucumber, and safer than the Bank.... (p. 428)
The Letters of Charles Dickens: Volume Four: 1844-1846. Ed. Kathleen Tillotson. Oxford: The Clarendon Press, 1977.
1865 ...it is as safe as the Bank.... (p. 525)
Address to the Newsvendors' Benevolent and Provident Association, London, 9 May 1865.
The Works of Charles Dickens: The Speeches. Ed. Richard H. Shepherd. New National Edition, Vol. II. New York: Hearst's International Library Company, n. d.
ODEP 691; MP 30.

Safe and sound

1842 I was delighted...to think of your sitting down...safe and sound again. (p. 407)
The Letters of Charles Dickens: Volume Three: 1842-1843. Eds. Madeline House, Graham Storey, and Kathleen Tillotson. Oxford: The Clarendon Press, 1974.
1844 ...I think of you safe and sound.... (p. 202)

The Letters of Charles Dickens: Volume Four: 1844-1846. Ed. Kathleen Tillotson. Oxford: The Clarendon Press, 1977.

1862 You got to London safe and sound.... (p. 321)

The Letters of Charles Dickens, ed. Walter Dexter. Vol. III: 1858-1870. The Nonesuch Dickens. London: The Nonesuch Press, 1938.

APP 315; ODEP 691; EAP 376; MP 543.

To be no sooner **said** than done

1846 'No sooner said than done, Bertha.' (p. 189)

Christmas Books. 1843-49. The Oxford Illustrated Dickens, Vol. XVI. Oxford: Oxford University Press, 1954.

APP 319; ODEP 574; EAP 380; MP 549.

In one's **salad days**

'...what used to be called in my young times—in the salad days of Jemmy Jackman....' (p. 396)

"Mrs. Lirriper's Lodgings." *Christmas Stories*. 1871. The Oxford Illustrated Dickens, Vol. XI. Oxford: Oxford University Press, 1956.

1860 My salad-days...being gone...no coming event cast its shadow before. (p. 309)

The Uncommercial Traveller and Reprinted Pieces Etc. 1850-1860. The Oxford Illustrated Dickens, Vol. XXI. Oxford: Oxford University Press, 1958.

URDANG, *IDIOMS* 1235; STEVENSON 1039:15.

(Not) to be worth one's **salt**

1839 '...there's not a skipper or mate that would think you worth your salt....' (p. 283)

The Life and Adventures of Nicholas Nickleby. 1839. The Oxford Illustrated Dickens, Vol. VI. Oxford: Oxford University Press, 1950.

1854 'He is not worth his salt, ma'am.' (p. 116)

Hard Times for These Times. 1854. The Oxford Illustrated Dickens, Vol. XVII. Oxford: Oxford University Press, 1955.

APP 316; ODEP 922; EAP 378; MP 545.

To put **salt** on a bird's tail

1841 ...having dropped a pinch of salt on the tails of all cardinal virtues, and caught them every one. (p. 206)

Barnaby Rudge: A Tale of the Riots of 'Eighty. 1841. The Oxford Illustrated Dickens, Vol. XV. Oxford: Oxford University Press, 1954.

1842 Can a pinch of salt be dropped upon his tail? (p. 304)

The Letters of Charles Dickens: Volume Three: 1842-1843. Eds. Madeline House, Graham Storey, and Kathleen Tillotson. Oxford: The Clarendon Press, 1974.

1846 ...I ...shall hope to put a pinch of salt on the tail of the sliding number in advance.... (p. 628)

The Letters of Charles Dickens: Volume Four: 1844-1846. Ed. Kathleen Tillotson. Oxford: The Clarendon Press, 1977.

1847 I have some of the salt of my youth left in me...and sprinkled it upon him. (p. 106)

The Letters of Charles Dickens: Volume Five: 1847-1849. Eds. Graham Storey and K. J. Fielding. Oxford: The Clarendon Press, 1981.

APP 316; ODEP 697; EAP 378; MP 545.

Ye are the **salt** of the earth.

1870 Of such is the salt of the earth. (p. 127)

The Mystery of Edwin Drood. 1870. The Oxford Illustrated Dickens, Vol. XVIII. Oxford: Oxford University Press, 1956.

EAP 378; MP 545.

To write on **sand**

1847 ...some part of your letter has been written on the sand.... (p. 73)

The Letters of Charles Dickens: Volume Five: 1847-1849. Eds. Graham Storey and K. J. Fielding. Oxford: The Clarendon Press, 1981.

EAP 379.

Satan finds some mischief still for idle hands to do.

1850 ...he added...'"Satan finds some mischief still, for idle hands to do."' (p. 227)

The Personal History of David Copperfield. 1850. The Oxford Illustrated Dickens, Vol. II. Oxford: Oxford University Press, 1948.

APP 318; ODEP 180; EAP 104; CODP 51; MP 162; DAP 523.

Full of wise **saws** and modern instances

1840 There cannot be a better practical illustration of the wise saw and ancient instance, that there may be too much of a good thing.... (p. 563)

Sketches by Boz. 1833-40. The Oxford Illustrated Dickens, Vol. XII. Oxford: Oxford University Press, 1957.

STEVENSON 1278:10.

...though I **say** it who should not

1846 ...who wants a house...though I say it who "didn't oughtn't—as the Americans observe.... (p. 540)
The Letters of Charles Dickens: Volume Four: 1844-1846. Ed. Kathleen Tillotson. Oxford: The Clarendon Press, 1977.
ODEP 814; EAP 380; MP 549.

To be on a **scale** of magnitude never before attempted

1837 Preparations, to make use of theatrical phraseology, "on a scale of magnitude never before attempted," were incessantly made.... (p. 327)
Sketches by Boz. 1833-40. The Oxford Illustrated Dickens, Vol. XII. Oxford: Oxford University Press, 1957.

To go behind the **scenes**

1837-39 All people who have been behind the scenes...know that.... (p. 672)
Sketches by Boz. 1833-40. The Oxford Illustrated Dickens, Vol. XII. Oxford: Oxford University Press, 1957.
1844 'You're behind the scenes.' (p. 441)
The Life and Adventures of Martin Chuzzlewit. 1844. The Oxford Illustrated Dickens, Vol. IX. Oxford: Oxford University Press, 1951.
WILKINSON 471; STEVENSON 2040:1.

To be of the old **school**

1833-36 Take a...London hackney-coach of the old school.... (p. 81)
Sketches by Boz. 1833-40. The Oxford Illustrated Dickens, Vol. XII. Oxford: Oxford University Press, 1957.
URDANG, *IDIOMS* 1245; WILKINSON 29.

To pay **scot and lot**

1844 'I'll pay you off scot and lot by and bye.' [get page number]
The Life and Adventures of Martin Chuzzlewit. 1844. The Oxford Illustrated Dickens, Vol. IX. Oxford: Oxford University Press, 1951.
ODEP 615.

To go **scot-free**

1841 'We may get off scot-free.' (p. 571)
Barnaby Rudge: A Tale of the Riots of 'Eighty. 1841. The Oxford Illustrated Dickens, Vol. XV. Oxford: Oxford University Press, 1954.
1841 '...she might go scot-free for aught I cared.' (p. 491)
The Old Curiosity Shop. 1841. The Oxford Illustrated Dickens, Vol. VIII. Oxford: Oxford University Press, 1951.

1853 'Your are not to...escape scot free.' (p. 484)
Bleak House. 1853. The Oxford Illustrated Dickens, Vol. III. Oxford: Oxford University Press, 1948.
ODEP 705; WILKINSON 65.

To come up to the **scratch**

1843 Up to the scratch in good season! (p. 607)
The Letters of Charles Dickens: Volume Three: 1842-1843. Eds. Madeline House, Graham Storey, and Kathleen Tillotson. Oxford: The Clarendon Press, 1974.
1854 To continue in fistic phraseology, he had a genius for coming up to the scratch.... (p. 5)
Hard Times for These Times. 1854. The Oxford Illustrated Dickens, Vol. XVII. Oxford: Oxford University Press, 1955.
1854 I am ready to come up to the scratch...and to shoulder the wheel. (p. 439)
The Letters of Charles Dickens: Volume Seven: 1853-1855. Eds. Graham Storey, Kathleen Tillotson, and Angus Easson. Oxford: The Clarendon Press, 1993.
1860 Adam...will not be up to the scratch when Collins's sponge is thrown up. (p. 151)
The Letters of Charles Dickens, ed. Walter Dexter. Vol. III: 1858-1870. The Nonesuch Dickens. London: The Nonesuch Press, 1938.
APP 320; ODEP 706; EAP 381; MP 549.

To have a **screw** loose

1837 '...as he always said himself, that "there was a screw loose somewhere."' (p. 689)
The Posthumous Papers of the Pickwick Club. 1837. The Oxford Illustrated Dickens, Vol. I. Oxford: Oxford University Press, 1948.
1844 'I see well enough there's a screw loose in your affairs.' (p. 228)
The Life and Adventures of Martin Chuzzlewit. 1844. The Oxford Illustrated Dickens, Vol. IX. Oxford: Oxford University Press, 1951.
1846 ...there was a screw loose in his arrangements. (p. 230)
Christmas Books. 1843-49. The Oxford Illustrated Dickens, Vol. XVI. Oxford: Oxford University Press, 1954.
1850 I have been endeavouring to tighten the screws of my head.... (p. 122)
The Letters of Charles Dickens: Volume Six: 1850-1852. Eds. Madeline House, Graham Storey, and Kathleen Tillotson. Oxford: The Clarendon Press, 1988.
APP 320; ODEP 706; MP 550.

To be **scum** of the earth

1850 '...my clerk...is the very scum of society....' (p. 748)

The Personal History of David Copperfield. 1850. The Oxford Illustrated Dickens, Vol. II. Oxford: Oxford University Press, 1948.

1854 '...I come of the scum of the earth.' (p. 47)

Hard Times for These Times. 1854. The Oxford Illustrated Dickens, Vol. XVII. Oxford: Oxford University Press, 1955.

1859 '...the vilest scum of the earth that ever did murder by whole-sale....' (p. 228)

A Tale of Two Cities. 1859. The Oxford Illustrated Dickens, Vol. IV. Oxford: Oxford University Press, 1948.

URDANG, *IDIOMS* 1249; BARTLETT 371:10.

To be at **sea** about something

1865 ...I am rather at sea about the No.... (p. 418)

The Letters of Charles Dickens, ed. Walter Dexter. Vol. III: 1858-1870. The Nonesuch Dickens. London: The Nonesuch Press, 1938.

APP 321; MP 550.

Let me **see.**

1865 "Let me see, said the blind man...." (p. 233)

Our Mutual Friend. 1865. The Oxford Illustrated Dickens, Vol. X. Oxford: Oxford University Press, 1952.

ODEP 456; DOW 113.

Sow the **seed.**

1854 Sow the seed. It will come up in the spot where it is sown.... (p. 312)

The Letters of Charles Dickens: Volume Seven: 1853-1855. Eds. Graham Storey, Kathleen Tillotson, and Angus Easson. Oxford: The Clarendon Press, 1993.

WILKINSON 421.

To run to **seed**

1861 ...he had not been running to seed.... (p. 110)

Great Expectations. 1861. The Oxford Illustrated Dickens, Vol. XIII. Oxford: Oxford University Press, 1953.

WILKINSON 386.

As **seedy** as a cucumber

1833-36 '...I was as seedy as a cheap cowcumber.' (p. 27)

Sketches by Boz. 1833-40. The Oxford Illustrated Dickens, Vol. XII. Oxford: Oxford University Press, 1957.

Seeing is believing.

1842 Seeing only is believing, very often isn't that, and even Being the
the thing falls a long way short of believing it. (p. 333)
The Letters of Charles Dickens: Volume Three: 1842-1843. Eds. Madeline House, Graham
Storey, and Kathleen Tillotson. Oxford: The Clarendon Press, 1974.
1852   Says he, immediately, "Seeing is believing." (p. 447)
"Discovery of a Treasure Near Cheapside." [with Henry Morley]. *Charles Dickens' Uncol-
lected Writings from* Household Words *1850-1859*, 2 vols. Ed. Harry Stone. Bloomington:
Indiana University Press, 1968.
APP 321; ODEP 710; EAP 27; CODP 199; MP 551; DAP 530.

Self-praise is no recommendation.

1865 '...the old adage that self-praise is no recommendation.' (p. 643)
Our Mutual Friend. 1865. The Oxford Illustrated Dickens, Vol. X. Oxford: Oxford
University Press, 1952.
ODEP 507; EAP 347; CODP 507; MP 552; DAP 531.

To be in the **seventh heaven**

1844 ...rare incense...curling upward to the seventh heaven of Fame. (p.
274)
The Life and Adventures of Martin Chuzzlewit. 1844. The Oxford Illustrated Dickens, Vol.
IX. Oxford: Oxford University Press, 1951.
ODEP 718; MP 300.

(Not) to have a **shadow** of a doubt

1853 ...I have not a shadow of doubt.... (p. 97)
The Letters of Charles Dickens: Volume Seven: 1853-1855. Eds. Graham Storey, Kathleen
Tillotson, and Angus Easson. Oxford: The Clarendon Press, 1993.
URDANG, *IDIOMS* 1267.

As **sharp** as a ferret

1841 'I'm as sharp...as sharp as a ferret....' (p. 172)
The Old Curiosity Shop. 1841. The Oxford Illustrated Dickens, Vol. VIII. Oxford: Oxford
University Press, 1951.
MP 220.

As **sharp** as a flint

1843 Hard and sharp as a flint...and solitary as an oyster. (p. 8)
Christmas Books. 1843-49. The Oxford Illustrated Dickens, Vol. XVI. Oxford: Oxford
University Press, 1954.

As **sharp** as a lancet

1851 SLAP: You're as sharp as a lancet. (*Mr. Nightingale's Diary*, I, i, p. 153)
Complete Plays and Selected Poems of Charles Dickens. London: Vision Press, 1970.
WILSTACH 343.

As **sharp** as a serpent's tooth

1866 She is infinitely sharper than the serpent's Tooth. (p. 476)
The Letters of Charles Dickens, ed. Walter Dexter. Vol. III: 1858-1870. The Nonesuch
Dickens. London: The Nonesuch Press, 1938.
STEVENSON 342:1.

Sharp enough to open an oyster

1864 The East wind on the top of this hill today would open an oyster.
(p. 407)
The Letters of Charles Dickens, ed. Walter Dexter. Vol. III: 1858-1870. The Nonesuch
Dickens. London: The Nonesuch Press, 1938.

To have a close **shave**

1859 ...the National Razor shaved him close. (p. 279)
A Tale of Two Cities. 1859. The Oxford Illustrated Dickens, Vol. IV. Oxford: Oxford
University Press, 1948.
WILKINSON 312; PARTRIDGE 751.

It is as well to be hanged for a **sheep** as a lamb.

1841 ...others...comforted themselves with the homely proverb, that,
being hanged at all, they might as well be hanged for a sheep as a lamb.
(p. 402)
Barnaby Rudge: A Tale of the Riots of 'Eighty. 1841. The Oxford Illustrated Dickens, Vol.
XV. Oxford: Oxford University Press, 1954.
APP 324; ODEP 350; EAP 386; CODP 106; MP 554; DAP 278, 534.

To have a wet **sheet** and a flowing sail

1864 ...you will come up with a wet sheet and a flowing sail—as we say
in these parts. (p. 401)
The Letters of Charles Dickens, ed. Walter Dexter. Vol. III: 1858-1870. The Nonesuch
Dickens. London: The Nonesuch Press, 1938.
EAP 388.

To blow something to **shivers**

1851 Your suggestion fired...a rain of damp gunpowder, which blew my head to shivers. (pp. 551-552)
The Letters of Charles Dickens: Volume Six: 1850-1852. Eds. Madeline House, Graham Storey, and Kathleen Tillotson. Oxford: The Clarendon Press, 1988.

To walk in someone else's **shoes**

1844 '...show me a man in this city who is worthy to walk in the shoes of the departed Mr. Chuzzlewit.' (p. 315)
The Life and Adventures of Martin Chuzzlewit. 1844. The Oxford Illustrated Dickens, Vol. IX. Oxford: Oxford University Press, 1951.
APP 328; EAP 391; MP 560.

Short and long [Cf. Long and short.]

1838 'The short and long of what you mean...is that....' (p. 149)
The Adventures of Oliver Twist. 1838. The Oxford Illustrated Dickens, Vol. V. Oxford: Oxford University Press, 1948.
1841 '...the short and long of it is....' (p. 265)
The Old Curiosity Shop. 1841. The Oxford Illustrated Dickens, Vol. VIII. Oxford: Oxford University Press, 1951.
APP 227; ODEP 478; EAP 392; MP 382.

Put your **shoulder** to the wheel.

1851 ...the wagoner...has resolutely put his own shoulder to the wheel.... (p. 429)
Toast at a banquet in honor of the General Theatrical Fund, London, 14 Apr. 1851. *The Works of Charles Dickens: The Speeches*. Ed. Richard H. Shepherd. New National Edition, Vol. II. New York: Hearst's International Library Company, n. d.
1853 'We have put our shoulders to the wheel....' (p. 550)
Bleak House. 1853. The Oxford Illustrated Dickens, Vol. III. Oxford: Oxford University Press, 1948.
1854 I am ready to come up to the scratch...and to shoulder the wheel. (p. 439)
The Letters of Charles Dickens: Volume Seven: 1853-1855. Eds. Graham Storey, Kathleen Tillotson, and Angus Easson. Oxford: The Clarendon Press, 1993.
1855 We must put our shoulders to the wheel...throwing ourselves into the tide, and going with the stream.... (p. 700)
The Letters of Charles Dickens: Volume Seven: 1853-1855. Eds. Graham Storey, Kathleen Tillotson, and Angus Easson. Oxford: The Clarendon Press, 1993.
APP 331; ODEP 729; EAP 393; MP 563; DAP 538.

To give the cold **shoulder** to someone

1841 'He gives me the cold shoulder on this very matter....' (p. 498)
The Old Curiosity Shop. 1841. The Oxford Illustrated Dickens, Vol. VIII. Oxford: Oxford University Press, 1951.
1844 'Let me see the man who should give the cold shoulder to anybody I chose to protect....' (p. 191)
The Life and Adventures of Martin Chuzzlewit. 1844. The Oxford Illustrated Dickens, Vol. IX. Oxford: Oxford University Press, 1951.
APP 331; ODEP 133; MP 563.

To be on the safe **side**

1860 "It's as well to be on the safe side, Sir," replied Tom. (p. 257)
Christmas Stories. 1871. The Oxford Illustrated Dickens, Vol. XI. Oxford: Oxford University Press, 1956.
ODEP 691; MP 564.

To come out on the other **side**

1843 ...as Mr. Weller says, "come out on the other side." (p. 551)
The Letters of Charles Dickens: Volume Three: 1842-1843. Eds. Madeline House, Graham Storey, and Kathleen Tillotson. Oxford: The Clarendon Press, 1974.

To laugh on the other **side** of one's mouth

1842 "...he'd make honorable members sing out, a little more on the other side of their mouths". (p. 119)
The Letters of Charles Dickens: Volume Three: 1842-1843. Eds. Madeline House, Graham Storey, and Kathleen Tillotson. Oxford: The Clarendon Press, 1974.
APP 333; ODEP 445; EAP 393; MP 565.

There are two **sides** to every question.

1852-54 But there were two sides to this question.... (p. 392)
Master Humphrey's Clock and A Child's History of England. 1840-41, 1852-54. The Oxford Illustrated Dickens, Vol. XX. Oxford: Oxford University Press, 1958.
APP 332; ODEP 852; EAP 393; CODP 234; MP 564; DAP 539.

Out of **sight**, out of mind.

1837 The unfortunate individual...found...the perfect truth of the old adage, "out of sight, out of mind...." (p. 426)
Sketches by Boz. 1833-40. The Oxford Illustrated Dickens, Vol. XII. Oxford: Oxford University Press, 1957.
APP 333; ODEP 602; EAP 394; CODP 172; MP 566; DAP 540.

Signed, sealed, and delivered

1843 ...I will sign, seal, and deliver, at that hour. (p. 486)
The Letters of Charles Dickens: Volume Three: 1842-1843. Eds. Madeline House, Graham Storey, and Kathleen Tillotson. Oxford: The Clarendon Press, 1974.
1846 '...we'll sign, seal, and deliver as soon as possible....' (p. 256)
Christmas Books. 1843-49. The Oxford Illustrated Dickens, Vol. XVI. Oxford: Oxford University Press, 1954.
1850 '...the dear creature has signed, sealed, and delivered....' (p. 656)
The Personal History of David Copperfield. 1850. The Oxford Illustrated Dickens, Vol. II. Oxford: Oxford University Press, 1948.
SPEARS 296.

Silence is golden.

1869 ...I should immediately and at once subside into a golden silence.... (p. 567)
Address to the Birmingham and Midland Institute, Birmingham, 27 Sept. 1869.
The Works of Charles Dickens: The Speeches. Ed. Richard H. Shepherd. New National Edition, Vol. II. New York: Hearst's International Library Company, n. d.
ODEP 763; CODP 203; MP 586; DAP 540.

As **silent** as a desert

1848 ...the lines of iron road...were as empty and as silent as a desert. (p. 776)
Dealings with the Firm of Dombey and Son. 1848. The Oxford Illustrated Dickens, Vol. VII. Oxford: Oxford University Press, 1950.

As **silent** as the grave

1839 The house was silent as the grave. (p. 736)
The Life and Adventures of Nicholas Nickleby. 1839. The Oxford Illustrated Dickens, Vol. VI. Oxford: Oxford University Press, 1950.
APP 160; ODEP 733; EAP 187; MP 270.

As **silent** as the tomb

1844 '...I would be as silent as the tomb.' (p. 184)
The Life and Adventures of Martin Chuzzlewit. 1844. The Oxford Illustrated Dickens, Vol. IX. Oxford: Oxford University Press, 1951.
ODEP 733; EAP 445; MP 635.

Similia similibus curantur.

1852 ...their motto must have been, *Similia similibus curantur*.... (p. 383)

"A Curious Dance Round a Curious Tree." [with W. H. Wills]. *Charles Dickens' Uncollected Writings from* Household Words *1850-1859*, 2 vols. Ed. Harry Stone. Bloomington: Indiana University Press, 1968.
STEVENSON 1557:15.

Sink or swim

1837 '...to be behind them [the footlights] is to be...left to sink or swim...as fortune wills it.' (p. 34)

The Posthumous Papers of the Pickwick Club. 1837. The Oxford Illustrated Dickens, Vol. I. Oxford: Oxford University Press, 1948.

1869 ...one of those young American gentlemen...sailed in her to sink or swim with the men who believed in him. (p. 566)

Toast to the crews of the International University Boat Race, Sydenham, 30 Aug. 1869. *The Works of Charles Dickens: The Speeches*. Ed. Richard H. Shepherd. New National Edition, Vol. II. New York: Hearst's International Library Company, n. d.
APP 335; ODEP 737; EAP 396; MP 569; DAP 543.

The sins of the fathers....

1853 '...the virtues of the mothers shall, occasionally, be visited on the children, as well as the sins of the fathers.' (p. 234)
1853 'Pray daily that the sins of others be not visited upon your head.' (p. 514)

Bleak House. 1853. The Oxford Illustrated Dickens, Vol. III. Oxford: Oxford University Press, 1948.
STEVENSON 2117:5.

To be at sixes and sevens

1836 ...everything is at sixes and sevens.... (p. 178)

The Letters of Charles Dickens: Volume One: 1820-1839. Eds. Madeline House and Graham Storey. Oxford: The Clarendon Press, 1965.

1850 ...the castors...were all at sixes and sevens.... (p. 642)

The Personal History of David Copperfield. 1850. The Oxford Illustrated Dickens, Vol. II. Oxford: Oxford University Press, 1948.

1865 'Everything is so at sixes and sevens.' (p. 584)

Our Mutual Friend. 1865. The Oxford Illustrated Dickens, Vol. X. Oxford: Oxford University Press, 1952.
APP 336; ODEP 739; EAP 397; MP 569.

There is a skeleton in every house (closet, cupboard).

1865 Perhaps the skeleton in the cupboard comes out to be talked to, on such domestic occasions? (p. 556)

1865 ...the skeleton retired into the closet, and shut itself up. (p. 557)

Our Mutual Friend. 1865. The Oxford Illustrated Dickens, Vol. X. Oxford: Oxford University Press, 1952.

1870 'There is said to be a hidden skeleton in every house....' (p. 13)

The Mystery of Edwin Drood. 1870. The Oxford Illustrated Dickens, Vol. XVIII. Oxford: Oxford University Press, 1956.

APP 336; ODEP 739; MP 571; DAP 544.

Skin and bone

1841 'It was once mere skin and bone....' (p. 178)

Barnaby Rudge: A Tale of the Riots of 'Eighty. 1841. The Oxford Illustrated Dickens, Vol. XV. Oxford: Oxford University Press, 1954.

1850 it was...nothing but skin and bone. (p. 129)

"The Old Lady in Threadneedle Street." [with W. H. Wills]. *Charles Dickens' Uncollected Writings from Household Words 1850-1859,* 2 vols. Ed. Harry Stone. Bloomington: Indiana University Press, 1968.

1853 '...I'm worritted to skins and bones.' (p. 631)

Bleak House. 1853. The Oxford Illustrated Dickens, Vol. III. Oxford: Oxford University Press, 1948.

1861 'Little more than skin and bone!' mused Mr. Pumblechook.... (p. 450)

Great Expectations. 1861. The Oxford Illustrated Dickens, Vol. XIII. Oxford: Oxford University Press, 1953.

ODEP 740.

Out of a clear blue sky

1852 ...the stars are shining brightly out of a clear blue sky. (p. 829)

The Letters of Charles Dickens: Volume Six: 1850-1852. Eds. Madeline House, Graham Storey, and Kathleen Tillotson. Oxford: The Clarendon Press, 1988.

MP 58; URDANG, *IDIOMS* 1301.

To beat something into a sky-blue fit

1849 ...Broadstairs beats all watering places into what the Americans call "sky-blue fits". (p. 568)

The Letters of Charles Dickens: Volume Five: 1847-1849. Eds. Graham Storey and K. J. Fielding. Oxford: The Clarendon Press, 1981.

As sleek as a moke

1850 "...you'll come out as bright as a star, and as sleek as this here Moke." (p. 120)

"A Popular Delusion." [with W. H. Wills]. *Charles Dickens' Uncollected Writings from Household Words 1850-1859*, 2 vols. Ed. Harry Stone. Bloomington: Indiana University Press, 1968.

There's nothin' so refreshin' as **sleep**.

1837 'There's nothin' so refreshin' as sleep, sir, as the servant-girl said afore she drank the egg-cupful o' laudanum.' (p. 211)

The Posthumous Papers of the Pickwick Club. 1837. The Oxford Illustrated Dickens, Vol. I. Oxford: Oxford University Press, 1948.

DOW 121.

As **sleepy** as laudanum

1859 'I am as rickety as a hackney-coach, I'm as sleepy as laudanum....' (p. 53)

A Tale of Two Cities. 1859. The Oxford Illustrated Dickens, Vol. IV. Oxford: Oxford University Press, 1948.

To do something with **slickness and sprydom**

1844 I left my house...as the Americans would say, "with sich everlass'n slickness and al-mitty sprydom...." (p. 89)

The Letters of Charles Dickens: Volume Four: 1844-1846. Ed. Kathleen Tillotson. Oxford: The Clarendon Press, 1977.

There's many a **slip** between cup and lip.

1864 "Many a slip" for Mr Riderhood (p. 341)

Dickens' Working Notes for His Novels. Ed. Harry Stone. Chicago, Ill.: University of Chicago Press, 1987. xxiv +

APP 339; ODEP 160; EAP 399; CODP 146; MP 575; DAP 546.

To have a **slip** of the tongue

1853 ...excusing himself for this slip of the tongue.... (p. 377)

Bleak House. 1853. The Oxford Illustrated Dickens, Vol. III. Oxford: Oxford University Press, 1948.

APP 399; ODEP 55.

Slopping around

1868 "Slopping around," so used means untidyness and disorder. It is a comically expressive phrase, and has many meanings. (p. 632)

The Letters of Charles Dickens, ed. Walter Dexter. Vol. III: 1858-1870. The Nonesuch Dickens. London: The Nonesuch Press, 1938.

As **slow** as a tortoise

1841 'You're as slow as a tortoise, and more thick-headed than a rhinoceros,' returned his obliging client.... (p. 383)
The Old Curiosity Shop. 1841. The Oxford Illustrated Dickens, Vol. VIII. Oxford: Oxford University Press, 1951.
SOMMER 630.

Slow and sure.

1839 '"Slow and steddy," I says to myself....' (p. 545)
The Life and Adventures of Nicholas Nickleby. 1839. The Oxford Illustrated Dickens, Vol. VI. Oxford: Oxford University Press, 1950.
APP 399; ODEP 743; EAP 400; CODP 205; MP 575; DAP 547.

As **smart** as sixpence

1838 '...we would have...made you as smart as sixpence!' (p. 94)
The Adventures of Oliver Twist. 1838. The Oxford Illustrated Dickens, Vol. V. Oxford: Oxford University Press, 1948.
MP 570.

To reduce something to eternal **smash**

1844 '...there ain't an ĕn-gīne...frizzled to a most e-tarnal smash....' (p. 345)
The Life and Adventures of Martin Chuzzlewit. 1844. The Oxford Illustrated Dickens, Vol. IX. Oxford: Oxford University Press, 1951.
1845 Lord and Lady Lansdowne and the 'Tarnal Smash knows who.... (p. 415)
The Letters of Charles Dickens: Volume Four: 1844-1846. Ed. Kathleen Tillotson. Oxford: The Clarendon Press, 1977.
1849 ...reducing to 'tarnal smash (as we say in our country) all the other couples.... (p. 488)
The Letters of Charles Dickens: Volume Five: 1847-1849. Eds. Graham Storey and K. J. Fielding. Oxford: The Clarendon Press, 1981.
URDANG, *IDIOMS* 1308.

As **smooth** as an egg

1844 His chin was as smooth as a new-laid egg.... (p. 460)
The Life and Adventures of Martin Chuzzlewit. 1844. The Oxford Illustrated Dickens, Vol. IX. Oxford: Oxford University Press, 1951.

APP 117; MP 197.

To have a cold **snap**

1842 ...but for an odd phrase now and then—such as *Snap of cold weather*.... (p. 36)
The Letters of Charles Dickens: Volume Three: 1842-1843. Eds. Madeline House, Graham Storey, and Kathleen Tillotson. Oxford: The Clarendon Press, 1974.
URDANG, *IDIOMS* 1310.

To be up to **snuff**

1837 'Up to snuff and a pinch or two over—eh?' (p. 154)
The Posthumous Papers of the Pickwick Club. 1837. The Oxford Illustrated Dickens, Vol. I. Oxford: Oxford University Press, 1948.
APP 343; ODEP 749; MP 581.

As **sober** as a judge

1837-39 Mr. Twigger at once solemnly pledged himself to be as sober as a judge.... (p. 615)
Sketches by Boz. 1833-40. The Oxford Illustrated Dickens, Vol. XII. Oxford: Oxford University Press, 1957.
1857 "As sober as a judge, and as regular as clock-work in his habits." (p. 690)
Christmas Stories. 1871. The Oxford Illustrated Dickens, Vol. XI. Oxford: Oxford University Press, 1956.
APP 205; ODEP 749; EAP 242; MP 345.

As **soft** as a mouse

1850 'Be as soft as a mouse, or the Cat'll hear us.' (p. 60)
The Personal History of David Copperfield. 1850. The Oxford Illustrated Dickens, Vol. II. Oxford: Oxford University Press, 1948.

As **solitary** as an oyster

1843 Hard and sharp as a flint...and solitary as an oyster. (p. 8)
Christmas Books. 1843-49. The Oxford Illustrated Dickens, Vol. XVI. Oxford: Oxford University Press, 1954.
SOMMER 26 (CITING DICKENS).

Something is rotten in the state of Denmark.

1849 ...there is something a leetle rotten in the State of Denmark? (p. 485)

The Letters of Charles Dickens: Volume Five: 1847-1849. Eds. Graham Storey and K. J. Fielding. Oxford: The Clarendon Press, 1981.

EAP 162; MP 160.

To sell something for a **song**

1859 ...then it went for a song. (p. 251)

Christmas Stories. 1871. The Oxford Illustrated Dickens, Vol. XI. Oxford: Oxford University Press, 1956.

APP 345; ODEP 712; EAP 406; MP 583.

Sooner or later

1839 'I must know it sooner or later....' (p. 174)

The Life and Adventures of Nicholas Nickleby. 1839. The Oxford Illustrated Dickens, Vol. VI. Oxford: Oxford University Press, 1950.

1841 '...sooner or later, that man will be discovered.' (p. 14)

Barnaby Rudge: A Tale of the Riots of 'Eighty. 1841. The Oxford Illustrated Dickens, Vol. XV. Oxford: Oxford University Press, 1954.

1843 ...I must write his name, sooner or later. (p. 465)

1843 "He is as dead Sir as a door-nail. But we must all die...sooner or later...." (p. 550)

The Letters of Charles Dickens: Volume Three: 1842-1843. Eds. Madeline House, Graham Storey, and Kathleen Tillotson. Oxford: The Clarendon Press, 1974.

1850 ...King Charles the First always strayed into it, sooner or later.... (p. 216)

The Personal History of David Copperfield. 1850. The Oxford Illustrated Dickens, Vol. II. Oxford: Oxford University Press, 1948.

1853 '...he would do it, of a certainty sooner or later....' (p. 53)

Bleak House. 1853. The Oxford Illustrated Dickens, Vol. III. Oxford: Oxford University Press, 1948.

1861 ...she would, sooner or later, find me out.... (p. 101)

Great Expectations. 1861. The Oxford Illustrated Dickens, Vol. XIII. Oxford: Oxford University Press, 1953.

1865 'Sooner or later, of course, he'd drop down upon me....' (p. 584)

Our Mutual Friend. 1865. The Oxford Illustrated Dickens, Vol. X. Oxford: Oxford University Press, 1952.

URDANG, *IDIOMS* 1326; STEVENSON 2167:2.

The **sooner** the better.

1836 CHARLES: ...the sooner we start forward on our journey farther North the better. (*The Strange Gentleman*, II, i, p. 29)

1836 FLAM: ...the sooner you create a scarcity of such animals in this market, the better. (*The Village Coquettes*, I, ii, p. 56)
Complete Plays and Selected Poems of Charles Dickens. London: Vision Press, 1970.

1836 ...I wrote word back that the sooner he did it, the better. (p. 120)

1836 The sooner the better, of course.... (p. 154)
The Letters of Charles Dickens: Volume One: 1820-1839. Eds. Madeline House and Graham Storey. Oxford: The Clarendon Press, 1965.

1837 'The sooner you go the better.' (p. 529)
The Posthumous Papers of the Pickwick Club. 1837. The Oxford Illustrated Dickens, Vol. I. Oxford: Oxford University Press, 1948.

1839 '...the sooner we go the better.' (p. 253)
The Life and Adventures of Nicholas Nickleby. 1839. The Oxford Illustrated Dickens, Vol. VI. Oxford: Oxford University Press, 1950.

1841 'The sooner the better,' said Dennis.... (p. 286)

1841 '...the sooner we get back to the Black Lion, the better, perhaps.' (p. 551)

1841 '...as soon as they please—the sooner the better.' (p. 572)
Barnaby Rudge: A Tale of the Riots of 'Eighty. 1841. The Oxford Illustrated Dickens, Vol. XV. Oxford: Oxford University Press, 1954.

1842 ...the sooner we begin, the better. (p. 357)

1843 The sooner after 12, the better. (p. 505)
The Letters of Charles Dickens: Volume Three: 1842-1843. Eds. Madeline House, Graham Storey, and Kathleen Tillotson. Oxford: The Clarendon Press, 1974.

1844 '...the sooner you desist...the better.' (p. 56)

1844 '...the sooner we are rid of their company the better.' (pp. 105-106)
The Life and Adventures of Martin Chuzzlewit. 1844. The Oxford Illustrated Dickens, Vol. IX. Oxford: Oxford University Press, 1951.

1848 '...the sooner you and me goes...the better for both....' (p. 249)
Dealings with the Firm of Dombey and Son. 1848. The Oxford Illustrated Dickens, Vol. VII. Oxford: Oxford University Press, 1950.

1849 'And the sooner the better, I think.' (p. 384)
Christmas Books. 1843-49. The Oxford Illustrated Dickens, Vol. XVI. Oxford: Oxford University Press, 1954.

1850 '...the sooner they bring it to an issue the better.' (p. 158)

1850 '...the sooner I am off, the better.' (p. 231)

1850 'The sooner the better.' (p. 702)
The Personal History of David Copperfield. 1850. The Oxford Illustrated Dickens, Vol. II. Oxford: Oxford University Press, 1948.

1854 '...the sooner I am dead, the better.' (p. 75)
Hard Times for These Times. 1854. The Oxford Illustrated Dickens, Vol. XVII. Oxford: Oxford University Press, 1955.

1865 '...the sooner you are gone, bag and baggage, the better....' (p. 595)

Our Mutual Friend. 1865. The Oxford Illustrated Dickens, Vol. X. Oxford: Oxford University Press, 1952.
APP 345; ODEP 753; EAP 406; MP 583; DAP 552.

As **sound** as a church

1839 ...asleep she did fall, sound as a church.... (p. 289)
The Life and Adventures of Nicholas Nickleby. 1839. The Oxford Illustrated Dickens, Vol. VI. Oxford: Oxford University Press, 1950.
WILKINSON 427.

As **sound** as an apple

1853 ...she looks as...sound as an apple. (p. 385)
Bleak House. 1853. The Oxford Illustrated Dickens, Vol. III. Oxford: Oxford University Press, 1948.
WILKINSON 343.

As ye **sow**, so shall ye reap.

1841 'He reaps what he has sown—no more.' (p. 605)
Barnaby Rudge: A Tale of the Riots of 'Eighty. 1841. The Oxford Illustrated Dickens, Vol. XV. Oxford: Oxford University Press, 1954.
1845 As my father would observe, she has sown and must reap. (p. 309)
The Letters of Charles Dickens: Volume Four: 1844-1846. Ed. Kathleen Tillotson. Oxford: The Clarendon Press, 1977.
1850 'She had sown this. Let her moan for the harvest that she reaps to-day!' (p. 801)
The Personal History of David Copperfield. 1850. The Oxford Illustrated Dickens, Vol. II. Oxford: Oxford University Press, 1948.
1850-56 "Because," I remark, "the harvest that is reaped, has sometimes been sown." (p. 477)
The Uncommercial Traveller and Reprinted Pieces Etc. 1850-1860. The Oxford Illustrated Dickens, Vol. XXI. Oxford: Oxford University Press, 1958.
1851 ...'I am reaping what I sowed long ago.' (p. 429)
Toast at a banquet in honor of the General Theatrical Fund, London, 14 Apr. 1851. *The Works of Charles Dickens: The Speeches.* Ed. Richard H. Shepherd. New National Edition, Vol. II. New York: Hearst's International Library Company, n. d.
ODEP 757; EAP 408; CODP 208; MP 585; DAP 554.

To call a **spade** a spade

1854 'I call a spade a spade....' (p. 32)
Hard Times for These Times. 1854. The Oxford Illustrated Dickens, Vol. XVII. Oxford: Oxford University Press, 1955.
APP 346; ODEP 98; EAP 408; MP 585.

To fawn like a **spaniel**

1841 He...fawned like a spaniel dog. (p. 267)
Barnaby Rudge: A Tale of the Riots of 'Eighty. 1841. The Oxford Illustrated Dickens, Vol. XV. Oxford: Oxford University Press, 1954.
ODEP 249; EAP 409.

The **Spartan boy** and the biting fox

1857 '...like the Spartan boy with the fox biting him....' (p. 284)
Little Dorrit. 1857. The Oxford Illustrated Dickens, Vol. XIV. Oxford: Oxford University Press, 1953.

To **speak** as one finds

1839 ...everybody should speak as they found. (p. 50)
The Life and Adventures of Nicholas Nickleby. 1839. The Oxford Illustrated Dickens, Vol. VI. Oxford: Oxford University Press, 1950.
ODEP 760; MP 586.

To **speak** plainly

1833 I have not hesitated to speak plainly.... (p. 27)
The Letters of Charles Dickens: Volume One: 1820-1839. Eds. Madeline House and Graham Storey. Oxford: The Clarendon Press, 1965.
STEVENSON 2193:3 AND 10.

To be one's **sphere** of action

1855 My sphere of action...I shall never overstep.... (p. 459)
Address on Administrative Reform, London, 27 June 1855. *The Works of Charles Dickens: The Speeches*. Ed. Richard H. Shepherd. New National Edition, Vol. II. New York: Hearst's International Library Company, n. d.

To keep up one's **spirits**

1846 ...one must keep one's spirits up.... (p. 676)
The Letters of Charles Dickens: Volume Four: 1844-1846. Ed. Kathleen Tillotson. Oxford: The Clarendon Press, 1977.
URDANG, *IDIOMS* 1335.

To throw up the **sponge**

1860 Adam...will not be up to the scratch when Collins's sponge is thrown up. (p. 151)

The Letters of Charles Dickens, ed. Walter Dexter. Vol. III: 1858-1870. The Nonesuch Dickens. London: The Nonesuch Press, 1938.
APP 347; ODEP 819; MP 588.

To be born with a silver **spoon** in one's mouth

1844 'I must have been born with a silver spoon in my mouth....' (p. 89)
The Life and Adventures of Martin Chuzzlewit. 1844. The Oxford Illustrated Dickens, Vol. IX. Oxford: Oxford University Press, 1951.
1850 ...a man who had been born, not to say with a silver spoon, but with a scaling-ladder.... (p. 373)
The Personal History of David Copperfield. 1850. The Oxford Illustrated Dickens, Vol. II. Oxford: Oxford University Press, 1948.
1851 Many people are born with silver spoons in their mouths, many more with wooden ladles.... (p. 342)
"One Man in a Dockyard." [with R. H. Horne]. *Charles Dickens' Uncollected Writings from Household Words 1850-1859*, 2 vols. Ed. Harry Stone. Bloomington: Indiana University Press, 1968.
APP 348; ODEP 76; EAP 410; CODP 217; MP 588; DAP 559.

Two **spoons** in a saucer mean a wedding in the house.

1846 'We shall have a wedding in the house—there was two spoons in my saucer this morning.' (p. 270)
Christmas Books. 1843-49. The Oxford Illustrated Dickens, Vol. XVI. Oxford: Oxford University Press, 1954.
URDANG, *IDIOMS* 1338.

To be on the **spot**

1836 JOHN: I could raise the money...were I on the spot.... (*The Strange Gentleman*, II, i, p. 34)
Complete Plays and Selected Poems of Charles Dickens. London: Vision Press, 1970.
1844 And I want to be "on the spot" as it were. (p. 200)
The Letters of Charles Dickens: Volume Four: 1844-1846. Ed. Kathleen Tillotson. Oxford: The Clarendon Press, 1977.
1850 'To be on the spot.' (p. 259)
The Personal History of David Copperfield. 1850. The Oxford Illustrated Dickens, Vol. II. Oxford: Oxford University Press, 1948.
1857 'It is not indispensable for him to be on the spot.' (p. 563)
Little Dorrit. 1857. The Oxford Illustrated Dickens, Vol. XIV. Oxford: Oxford University Press, 1953.
URDANG, *IDIOMS* 1338.

To nail someone to the **spot**

1836 STRANGE GENTLEMAN: I have nailed him—nailed him to the spot!
(*The Strange Gentleman*, I, i, p. 18)
Complete Plays and Selected Poems of Charles Dickens. London: Vision Press, 1970.

There are **spots** on the sun.

1844 '...there were spots on the sun!' (p. 48)
The Life and Adventures of Martin Chuzzlewit. 1844. The Oxford Illustrated Dickens, Vol.
IX. Oxford: Oxford University Press, 1951.
ODEP 767.

To be up the **spout** [=to be pawned]

1851 ...remembering that popular figure of speech, The Spout, he would
enquire of My Uncle whether those bundles had been up the Spout, and
were now coming down? (p. 373)
"My Uncle." [with W. H. Wills]. *Charles Dickens' Uncollected Writings from* Household
Words *1850-1859*, 2 vols. Ed. Harry Stone. Bloomington: Indiana University Press, 1968.
APP 348; EAP 410; MP 589.

Throw out a **sprat** to catch a whale.

1844 ...it was their custom...never to throw away sprats, but as bait for
whales. (p. 119)
The Life and Adventures of Martin Chuzzlewit. 1844. The Oxford Illustrated Dickens, Vol.
IX. Oxford: Oxford University Press, 1951.
APP 348; ODEP 768; EAP 441; MP 589; DAP 559.

It is too late to shut the **stable-door** after the steed is stolen.

1841 'The stable door is shut, but the steed's gone, master.' (p. 216)
Barnaby Rudge: A Tale of the Riots of 'Eighty. 1841. The Oxford Illustrated Dickens, Vol.
XV. Oxford: Oxford University Press, 1954.
APP 109; ODEP 730; EAP 414; CODP 211; MP 182; DAP 560.

A clear **stage** and no favour for the goblins

1837 A clear stage and no favour for the goblins, ladies and gentlemen,
if you please. (p. 395)
The Posthumous Papers of the Pickwick Club. 1837. The Oxford Illustrated Dickens, Vol.
I. Oxford: Oxford University Press, 1948.
APP 131; ODEP 239; MP 221.

To lumber on like a **stage-waggon**

1849 ...I am lumbering on like a stage-waggon. (p. 526)
The Letters of Charles Dickens: Volume Five: 1847-1849. Eds. Graham Storey and K. J. Fielding. Oxford: The Clarendon Press, 1981.

Star and garter

1839 'Stars and garters, chap!' said John.... (p. 542)
The Life and Adventures of Nicholas Nickleby. 1839. The Oxford Illustrated Dickens, Vol. VI. Oxford: Oxford University Press, 1950.
URDANG, *IDIOMS* 1348.

Like the **starling** that could not get out

1837 I...like that same starling who is so very seldom quoted, can't get out. (p. 274)
The Letters of Charles Dickens: Volume One: 1820-1839. Eds. Madeline House and Graham Storey. Oxford: The Clarendon Press, 1965.

Stars and Stripes

1846 There is better metal in them than in all the stars and stripes.... (p. 601)
The Letters of Charles Dickens: Volume Four: 1844-1846. Ed. Kathleen Tillotson. Oxford: The Clarendon Press, 1977.
1853 I *must* write...to say how very starry and stripy our little Bleaburn experience appears to me to be. (p. 67)
1853 ...he being...not at all starry, *or* stripey.... (p. 80)
The Letters of Charles Dickens: Volume Seven: 1853-1855. Eds. Graham Storey, Kathleen Tillotson, and Angus Easson. Oxford: The Clarendon Press, 1993.
STEVENSON 826:1.

To thank one's **stars**

1842 I, thank my stars, was on the box. (p. 167)
The Letters of Charles Dickens: Volume Three: 1842-1843. Eds. Madeline House, Graham Storey, and Kathleen Tillotson. Oxford: The Clarendon Press, 1974.
URDANG, *IDIOMS* 1349.

My **starts and halters**

1841 'My starts and halters, Muster Gashford....' (p. 336)
Barnaby Rudge: A Tale of the Riots of 'Eighty. 1841. The Oxford Illustrated Dickens, Vol. XV. Oxford: Oxford University Press, 1954.

To blow off **steam**

1855 ...I have been blowing off a little of the indignant steam which would otherwise blow me up.... (p. 716)
The Letters of Charles Dickens: Volume Seven: 1853-1855. Eds. Graham Storey, Kathleen Tillotson, and Angus Easson. Oxford: The Clarendon Press, 1993.
APP 351; MP 592.

It is the first **step** that matters.

1852 That it is *"le premier pas qui coûte"*—that the first step is the great point—is...a household word.... (p. 410)
"First Fruits." [with George Augustus Sala]. *Charles Dickens' Uncollected Writings from Household Words 1850-1859*, 2 vols. Ed. Harry Stone. Bloomington: Indiana University Press, 1968.
ODEP 773; EAP 414; CODP 82; MP 593; DAP 562.

To be a **stepping-stone**

1844 ...he could not endure the thought of...making him the stepping-stone to his fortune.... (p. 225)
The Life and Adventures of Martin Chuzzlewit. 1844. The Oxford Illustrated Dickens, Vol. IX. Oxford: Oxford University Press, 1951.
EAP 414.

To be a **stick-in-the-mud**

1837-39 ...one man had the boldness to designate Mr. Slug aloud by the opprobious epithet of 'Stick-in-the-mud!' (p. 632)
Sketches by Boz. 1833-40. The Oxford Illustrated Dickens, Vol. XII. Oxford: Oxford University Press, 1957.
APP 354; MP 595.

To be a **stick** of an actor

1839 '...you're a regular stick of an actor....' (p. 387)
The Life and Adventures of Nicholas Nickleby. 1839. The Oxford Illustrated Dickens, Vol. VI. Oxford: Oxford University Press, 1950.
PARTRIDGE 828.

To be in a cleft **stick**

1850-56 "You are put in a cleft stick, John." (p. 463)
The Uncommercial Traveller and Reprinted Pieces Etc. 1850-1860. The Oxford Illustrated Dickens, Vol. XXI. Oxford: Oxford University Press, 1958.
MP 595.

As **still** as death

1838 ...all was still as death. (p. 194)
The Adventures of Oliver Twist. 1838. The Oxford Illustrated Dickens, Vol. V. Oxford: Oxford University Press, 1948.
APP 95; EAP 98; MP 158.

To make a **stock** for soup

1846 This is what cooks call "the stock of the soup." (p. 590)
The Letters of Charles Dickens: Volume Four: 1844-1846. Ed. Kathleen Tillotson. Oxford: The Clarendon Press, 1977.

A rolling **stone** gathers no moss.

1841 'Roving stones gather no moss, Joe,' said Gabriel. (p. 24)
Barnaby Rudge: A Tale of the Riots of 'Eighty. 1841. The Oxford Illustrated Dickens, Vol. XV. Oxford: Oxford University Press, 1954.
1841 ...popular rumour, unlike the rolling stone of the proverb, is one which gathers a deal of moss in its wanderings up and down.... (p. 356)
The Old Curiosity Shop. 1841. The Oxford Illustrated Dickens, Vol. VIII. Oxford: Oxford University Press, 1951.
1842 ...I have completely baulked the ancient proverb that 'a rolling stone gathers no moss....' (p. 383)
Remarks at a dinner, New York, 18 Feb. 1842. *The Works of Charles Dickens: The Speeches*. Ed. Richard H. Shepherd. New National Edition, Vol. II. New York: Hearst's International Library Company, n. d.
1853 'I always knew you to be a rolling stone that gathered no moss....' (p. 476)
Bleak House. 1853. The Oxford Illustrated Dickens, Vol. III. Oxford: Oxford University Press, 1948.
APP 355; ODEP 682; EAP 416; CODP 193; MP 597; DAP 565.

...let him cast the first **stone**.

1846-49 ..."He that is without sin among you, let him throw the first stone at her." (p. 64)
The Life of Our Lord: Written for His Children... New York: Simon and Schuster, 1934.
DAP 542; WILKINSON 422; STEVENSON 2118:4; BARTLETT 40:8.

To leave no **stone** unturned

1848 'We mustn't leave a stone unturned....' (p. 122)
Dealings with the Firm of Dombey and Son. 1848. The Oxford Illustrated Dickens, Vol. VII. Oxford: Oxford University Press, 1950.
APP 356; ODEP 453; EAP 417; MP 598.

To be within a **stone's throw**

1839 Within a stone's throw was another retreat.... (p. 830)
The Life and Adventures of Nicholas Nickleby. 1839. The Oxford Illustrated Dickens, Vol. VI. Oxford: Oxford University Press, 1950.

1842 ...the hotel...is within a stone's throw of the boat wharf. (p. 182)
The Letters of Charles Dickens: Volume Three: 1842-1843. Eds. Madeline House, Graham Storey, and Kathleen Tillotson. Oxford: The Clarendon Press, 1974.

1846 Within a stone's throw...the audience at the Day Theatre sit.... (p. 307)
American Notes and Pictures from Italy. 1842, 1846. The Oxford Illustrated Dickens, Vol. XIX. Oxford: Oxford University Press, 1957.

1857 "Eleven homicidal linen-drapers' shops within a short stone's throw...!" (p. 681)
Christmas Stories. 1871. The Oxford Illustrated Dickens, Vol. XI. Oxford: Oxford University Press, 1956.

1858 ...there were no...children playing...within a stone's throw of him.... (p. 479)
Address in honor of the Hospital for Sick Children, London, 9 Feb. 1858. *The Works of Charles Dickens: The Speeches.* Ed. Richard H. Shepherd. New National Edition, Vol. II. New York: Hearst's International Library Company, n. d.

1870 '...it is not a stone's throw from Minor Canon Corner.' (p. 73)
The Mystery of Edwin Drood. 1870. The Oxford Illustrated Dickens, Vol. XVIII. Oxford: Oxford University Press, 1956.
MP 598.

To drive gently over the **stones**

1844 'Gently over the stones, Poll.' (p. 461)
The Life and Adventures of Martin Chuzzlewit. 1844. The Oxford Illustrated Dickens, Vol. IX. Oxford: Oxford University Press, 1951.
ODEP 300.

To be the same old **story**

1847 ...they...would say, "its [*sic*] the old story after all...." (p. 182)
The Letters of Charles Dickens: Volume Five: 1847-1849. Eds. Graham Storey and K. J. Fielding. Oxford: The Clarendon Press, 1981.
URDANG, *IDIOMS* 1364.

To cut a long **story** short

1859 To cut this part of the story short, I was piqued.... (p. 232)
Christmas Stories. 1871. The Oxford Illustrated Dickens, Vol. XI. Oxford: Oxford University Press, 1956.
APP 357; EAP 418; MP 600.

The last **straw** breaks the camel's back.

1848 ...the last straw breaks the laden camel's back.... (p. 18)
Dealings with the Firm of Dombey and Son. 1848. The Oxford Illustrated Dickens, Vol. VII. Oxford: Oxford University Press, 1950.
1852 ...you shall hear again from the undersigned Camel that his back is broken by the addition of the last overbalancing straw. (p. 756)
The Letters of Charles Dickens: Volume Six: 1850-1852. Eds. Madeline House, Graham Storey, and Kathleen Tillotson. Oxford: The Clarendon Press, 1988.
APP 54; ODEP 443; CODP 128; MP 600; DAP 567.

To throw up a **straw** to see which way the wind blows

1858 We have no little straws of our own to throw up to show us which way the wind blows.... (p. 494)
Address to the Institutional Association of Lancashire and Cheshire, Manchester, 3 Dec. 1858. *The Works of Charles Dickens: The Speeches*. Ed. Richard H. Shepherd. New National Edition, Vol. II. New York: Hearst's International Library Company, n. d.
APP 357; ODEP 779; EAP 419; CODP 214; MP 601; DAP 567.

To grasp at **straws**

1865 ...he had over-reached himself...by grasping at Mr. Venus's mere straws of hints.... (pp. 500-501)
Our Mutual Friend. 1865. The Oxford Illustrated Dickens, Vol. X. Oxford: Oxford University Press, 1952.
APP 233; ODEP 205; EAP 275; CODP 60; MP 394; DAP 169.

A noisy **stream** is not deep.

1841 ...a stream so very noisy is not very deep. (p. 407)
The Letters of Charles Dickens: Volume Two: 1840-1841. Eds. Madeline House and Graham Storey. Oxford: The Clarendon Press, 1969.
ODEP 719; DAP 567.

To swim against the **stream**

1855 We must put our shoulders to the wheel...throwing ourselves into the tide, and going with the stream.... (p. 700)
The Letters of Charles Dickens: Volume Seven: 1853-1855. Eds. Graham Storey, Kathleen Tillotson, and Angus Easson. Oxford: The Clarendon Press, 1993.
ODEP 782; EAP 420.

To have two **strings** to one's bow

1868 ...we shall be none the worse for having two strings to our bow. (p. 656)
The Letters of Charles Dickens, ed. Walter Dexter. Vol. III: 1858-1870. The Nonesuch Dickens. London: The Nonesuch Press, 1938.
APP 358; ODEP 852; EAP 421; MP 603; DAP 568.

As **strong** as a lion

1845 '...I am as strong as a lion....' (p. 87)
Christmas Books. 1843-49. The Oxford Illustrated Dickens, Vol. XVI. Oxford: Oxford University Press, 1954.
APP 224; EAP 262; MP 378.

To be a quick **study**

1847 ...I believe you are...not a "quick study...." (p. 121)
The Letters of Charles Dickens: Volume Five: 1847-1849. Eds. Graham Storey and K. J. Fielding. Oxford: The Clarendon Press, 1981.
CRAIG 200.

To be in a brown **study**

1844 ...thought Jonas in a brown study.... (p. 301)
The Life and Adventures of Martin Chuzzlewit. 1844. The Oxford Illustrated Dickens, Vol. IX. Oxford: Oxford University Press, 1951.
APP 358; MP 603; MP 603.

Stuff and nonsense

1850 'Stuff and nonsense, Trot!' replied my aunt. (p. 502)
The Personal History of David Copperfield. 1850. The Oxford Illustrated Dickens, Vol. II. Oxford: Oxford University Press, 1948.
1857 'Stuff and nonsense,' said Mr. Meagles. (p. 123)
1857 'Stuff and nonsense!' replied the young lady.... (p. 588)
Little Dorrit. 1857. The Oxford Illustrated Dickens, Vol. XIV. Oxford: Oxford University Press, 1953.
URDANG, *IDIOMS* 1374.

To be a **stumbling-block**

1840 A roast goose is universally allowed to be the great stumbling-block.... (p. 585)
Sketches by Boz. 1833-40. The Oxford Illustrated Dickens, Vol. XII. Oxford: Oxford University Press, 1957.
1846 She was a stumbling-block in the passage.... (p. 231)

Christmas Books. 1843-49. The Oxford Illustrated Dickens, Vol. XVI. Oxford: Oxford University Press, 1954.

1857 This drawback...was a large stumbling-block.... (p. 574)

Little Dorrit. 1857. The Oxford Illustrated Dickens, Vol. XIV. Oxford: Oxford University Press, 1953.

1860 Help them over that first stumbling-block.... (p. 39)

The Uncommercial Traveller and Reprinted Pieces Etc. 1850-1860. The Oxford Illustrated Dickens, Vol. XXI. Oxford: Oxford University Press, 1958.

ODEP 68; EAP 422; MP 604.

As **sulky** as a bear

1850 'As sulky as a bear!' said Miss Murdstone. (p. 118)

The Personal History of David Copperfield. 1850. The Oxford Illustrated Dickens, Vol. II. Oxford: Oxford University Press, 1948.

APP 20; MP 35.

Sum and substance

1840-41 ...coming to be part and parcel—nay nearly the whole sum and substance of my daily thought.... (p. 43)

Master Humphrey's Clock and A Child's History of England. 1840-41, 1852-54. The Oxford Illustrated Dickens, Vol. XX. Oxford: Oxford University Press, 1958.

URDANG, *IDIOMS* 1378.

Sun, moon, and stars

1855 ...I take to be as clearly established as the sun, moon, and stars. (p. 464)

Address on Administrative Reform, London, 27 June 1855. *The Works of Charles Dickens: The Speeches*. Ed. Richard H. Shepherd. New National Edition, Vol. II. New York: Hearst's International Library Company, n. d.

WILSTACH 56.

...upon which the **sun** ever shone

1844 'I am in love with one of the most beautiful girls the sun ever shone upon.' (p. 94)

The Life and Adventures of Martin Chuzzlewit. 1844. The Oxford Illustrated Dickens, Vol. IX. Oxford: Oxford University Press, 1951.

As **sure** as death

1852 ...the thing itself is as sure as Death, our honourable friend. (p. 432)

"Boys to Mend." [with Henry Morley]. *Charles Dickens' Uncollected Writings from Household Words 1850-1859*, 2 vols. Ed. Harry Stone. Bloomington: Indiana University Press, 1968.
APP 95; ODEP 789; MP 158.

As **sure** as eggs is eggs

1837 And the Bishop says, 'Sure as eggs is eggs, | This here's the bold Turpin!' (p. 227)
Complete Plays and Selected Poems of Charles Dickens. London: Vision Press, 1970.
1837 And the Bishop says, 'Sure as eggs is eggs | This here's the bold Turpin!' (p. 611)
The Posthumous Papers of the Pickwick Club. 1837. The Oxford Illustrated Dickens, Vol. I. Oxford: Oxford University Press, 1948.
APP 118; ODEP 789; MP 197.

A black **swan**

1843 ...a feathered phenomenon to which a black swan was a matter of course.... (p. 45)
Christmas Books. 1843-49. The Oxford Illustrated Dickens, Vol. XVI. Oxford: Oxford University Press, 1954.
APP 362; ODEP 65; EAP 425; MP 607.

To earn (something) by the **sweat** of one's brow

1862 ...extorting the fruits of the earth...with the sweat of his brow? (p. 336)
Christmas Stories. 1871. The Oxford Illustrated Dickens, Vol. XI. Oxford: Oxford University Press, 1956.
1864 To Earn the reward "by the sweat of his brow." (p. 341)
Dickens' Working Notes for His Novels. Ed. Harry Stone. Chicago, Ill.: University of Chicago Press, 1987. xxiv +
1865 'I'm going to earn from five to ten thousand pound by the sweat of my brow; and as a poor man doing justice to the sweat of my brow....' (p. 149)
1865 'Don't do nothing to keep back from an honest man the fruits of the sweat of his brow!' (p. 152)
1865 '...not for the sum as I expect to earn from you by the sweat of my brow....' (p. 153)
1865 ...perhaps considering how his answer might affect the fruits of the sweat of his brow.... (p. 156)
Our Mutual Friend. 1865. The Oxford Illustrated Dickens, Vol. X. Oxford: Oxford University Press, 1952.

EAP 426; MP 608; STEVENSON 2258:2; BARTLETT 478:9.

As **sweet** as honey

1857 'He is as sweet as honey, and I am as dull as ditch-water.' (p. 802)
Little Dorrit. 1857. The Oxford Illustrated Dickens, Vol. XIV. Oxford: Oxford University
Press, 1953.
ODEP 793; EAP 218; MP 317.

As **sweet** as honeysuckle

1841 'As sweet as honey-suckle I warrant you.' (p. 178)
Barnaby Rudge: A Tale of the Riots of 'Eighty. 1841. The Oxford Illustrated Dickens, Vol.
XV. Oxford: Oxford University Press, 1954.

As **swift** as an arrow

1862 Swift as the arrow from the bow, I had formed my resolution.... (p. 363)
Christmas Stories. 1871. The Oxford Illustrated Dickens, Vol. XI. Oxford: Oxford
University Press, 1956.
ODEP 794; EAP 12; MP 18.

To be in the full **swing**

1861 "We" are in the full swing.... (p. 204)
The Letters of Charles Dickens, ed. Walter Dexter. Vol. III: 1858-1870. The Nonesuch
Dickens. London: The Nonesuch Press, 1938.
URDANG, *IDIOMS* 1386.

The **Swiss** are mercenary.

1867 "You Englishmen say we Swiss are mercenary." (p. 631)
Christmas Stories. 1871. The Oxford Illustrated Dickens, Vol. XI. Oxford: Oxford
University Press, 1956.
ODEP 572.

T

To a **T**

1842 Your plans are mine, to a T. (p. 237)
The Letters of Charles Dickens: Volume Three: 1842-1843. Eds. Madeline House, Graham
Storey, and Kathleen Tillotson. Oxford: The Clarendon Press, 1974.

1859 ...I have got exactly the name for the story that...will fit the opening to a T. (p. 95)
The Letters of Charles Dickens, ed. Walter Dexter. Vol. III: 1858-1870. The Nonesuch Dickens. London: The Nonesuch Press, 1938.
APP 364; EAP 429; MP 610.

To turn the **tables** on someone

1839 '...suppose I were to turn the tables...?' (p. 378)
The Life and Adventures of Nicholas Nickleby. 1839. The Oxford Illustrated Dickens, Vol. VI. Oxford: Oxford University Press, 1950.
1857 '...you shall turn the tables on society....' (p. 352)
Little Dorrit. 1857. The Oxford Illustrated Dickens, Vol. XIV. Oxford: Oxford University Press, 1953.
1862 But I turned the tables on 'em.... (p. 328)
Christmas Stories. 1871. The Oxford Illustrated Dickens, Vol. XI. Oxford: Oxford University Press, 1956.
APP 364; ODEP 847; EAP 429; MP 610.

Tag, rag, and bobtail

1841 'We don't take in no tagrag and bobtail at our house, sir,' answered John. (p. 263)
Barnaby Rudge: A Tale of the Riots of 'Eighty. 1841. The Oxford Illustrated Dickens, Vol. XV. Oxford: Oxford University Press, 1954.
1848 There was hardly room to stand...among the...tag rag and bobtail.... (p. 254)
The Letters of Charles Dickens: Volume Five: 1847-1849. Eds. Graham Storey and K. J. Fielding. Oxford: The Clarendon Press, 1981.
1854 '...I am a bit of dirty riff-raff, and a genuine scrap of tag, rag, and bobtail.' (p. 126)
Hard Times for These Times. 1854. The Oxford Illustrated Dickens, Vol. XVII. Oxford: Oxford University Press, 1955.
APP 302; ODEP 797; EAP 429; MP 522.

Take it or leave it.

1841 I offer subjects they may take or leave. (p. 232)
Complete Plays and Selected Poems of Charles Dickens. London: Vision Press, 1970.
ODEP 799; MP 612; DAP 580.

To **take** it easy

1844 I "took it easy" after this (p. 188)

The Letters of Charles Dickens: Volume Four: 1844-1846. Ed. Kathleen Tillotson. Oxford: The Clarendon Press, 1977.
URDANG, *IDIOMS* 1399.

As **tall** as a spectre

1859 'All covered with dust, white as a spectre, tall as a spectre!' (p. 109)
A Tale of Two Cities. 1859. The Oxford Illustrated Dickens, Vol. IV. Oxford: Oxford University Press, 1948.

To be armed to the **teeth**

1852 ...they found arrayed on the other bank the white population of the district, armed to the teeth.... (p. 439)
"North American Slavery." [with Henry Morley]. *Charles Dickens' Uncollected Writings from* Household Words *1850-1859*, 2 vols. Ed. Harry Stone. Bloomington: Indiana University Press, 1968.
MP 638.

As **tender** as a lamb

1839 'Tender as a lamb,' replied Squeers. (p. 80)
The Life and Adventures of Nicholas Nickleby. 1839. The Oxford Illustrated Dickens, Vol. VI. Oxford: Oxford University Press, 1950.
WILSTACH 418 (CITING DICKENS).

To be on **tenterhooks**

1838 '...I'm on—on—' Mr. Bumble...could not immediately think of the word 'tenter-hooks....' (p. 197)
The Adventures of Oliver Twist. 1838. The Oxford Illustrated Dickens, Vol. V. Oxford: Oxford University Press, 1948.
ODEP 808; EAP 432; MP 615.

As **thick** as scarecrows in England

1844 'As thick as scarecrows in England, sir,' interposed Mark.... (p. 343)
The Life and Adventures of Martin Chuzzlewit. 1844. The Oxford Illustrated Dickens, Vol. IX. Oxford: Oxford University Press, 1951.
WILSTACH 421 (CITING DICKENS).

Through **thick and thin**

1841 '...for all old Luke's winning through thick and thin of late years....' (p. 220)

The Old Curiosity Shop. 1841. The Oxford Illustrated Dickens, Vol. VIII. Oxford: Oxford University Press, 1951.

1846 ...his Snitcheys were to be justified through thick and thin...? (p. 284)

Christmas Books. 1843-49. The Oxford Illustrated Dickens, Vol. XVI. Oxford: Oxford University Press, 1954.

1850-56 ...supported he may be, through thick and thin.... (p. 577)

The Uncommercial Traveller and Reprinted Pieces Etc. 1850-1860. The Oxford Illustrated Dickens, Vol. XXI. Oxford: Oxford University Press, 1958.

APP 368; ODEP 810; EAP 483; MP 616.

To be in the **thick**

1841 ...we are in the thick of the story. (p. 352)

The Letters of Charles Dickens: Volume Two: 1840-1841. Eds. Madeline House and Graham Storey. Oxford: The Clarendon Press, 1969.

1860 ...I was in the thick of my story.... (p. 159)

The Letters of Charles Dickens, ed. Walter Dexter. Vol. III: 1858-1870. The Nonesuch Dickens. London: The Nonesuch Press, 1938.

STEVENSON 2295:2.

As **thick-headed** as a rhinoceros

1841 'You're as slow as a tortoise, and more thick-headed than a rhinoceros,' returned his obliging client.... (p. 383)

The Old Curiosity Shop. 1841. The Oxford Illustrated Dickens, Vol. VIII. Oxford: Oxford University Press, 1951.

Once a **thief**, always a thief.

1860 Always a Ruffian, always a Thief. Always a Thief, always a Ruffian. (p. 303)

The Uncommercial Traveller and Reprinted Pieces Etc. 1850-1860. The Oxford Illustrated Dickens, Vol. XXI. Oxford: Oxford University Press, 1958.

ODEP 594; DAP 588.

When **thieves** fall out, honest men come to their own.

1844 '...which confirms the old saying that when rogues fall out, honest people get what they want.' (p. 761)

The Life and Adventures of Martin Chuzzlewit. 1844. The Oxford Illustrated Dickens, Vol. IX. Oxford: Oxford University Press, 1951.

ODEP 810; EAP 368; MP 616; DAP 588.

To know a **thing** or two

1844 ...who had a sort of interest in his eyes, as jolly dogs who knew a thing or two.... (p. 70)
The Life and Adventures of Martin Chuzzlewit. 1844. The Oxford Illustrated Dickens, Vol. IX. Oxford: Oxford University Press, 1951.
1850 I know a thing or two.... (p. 202)
"Mr. Bendigo Buster on Our National Defences Against Education." [with Henry Morley]. *Charles Dickens' Uncollected Writings from* Household Words *1850-1859*, 2 vols. Ed. Harry Stone. Bloomington: Indiana University Press, 1968.
APP 369; MP 620.

All **things** considered

1866 ...I...feel, all things considered, in very good tone. (p. 466)
The Letters of Charles Dickens, ed. Walter Dexter. Vol. III: 1858-1870. The Nonesuch Dickens. London: The Nonesuch Press, 1938.
URDANG, *IDIOMS* 1429.

When **things** are at their worst, they will mend.

1841 '...when things are at the worst they are sure to mend.' (p. 153)
Barnaby Rudge: A Tale of the Riots of 'Eighty. 1841. The Oxford Illustrated Dickens, Vol. XV. Oxford: Oxford University Press, 1954.
ODEP 811; EAP 435.

Thirteen at table is unlucky.

1847 ...keep Georgina away, to prevent your being Thirteen at table.... (p. 98)
The Letters of Charles Dickens: Volume Five: 1847-1849. Eds. Graham Storey and K. J. Fielding. Oxford: The Clarendon Press, 1981.
BREWER 1075.

To be a **thorn** in one's side

1846 They are a thorn in the side of European despots.... (p. 601)
1846 They are a thorn in the sides of European despots.... (p. 661)
The Letters of Charles Dickens: Volume Four: 1844-1846. Ed. Kathleen Tillotson. Oxford: The Clarendon Press, 1977.
1857 '...I am handsome enough to be a thorn in her side.' (p. 592)
Little Dorrit. 1857. The Oxford Illustrated Dickens, Vol. XIV. Oxford: Oxford University Press, 1953.
APP 370; EAP 435; MP 621.

He who sows **thorns** will never reap grapes.

1850 We could not expect 'to gather grapes from thorns or figs from thistles.' (p. 422)

Address on the Public Health of the Metropolis, London, 6 Feb. 1850. *The Works of Charles Dickens: The Speeches.* Ed. Richard H. Shepherd. New National Edition, Vol. II. New York: Hearst's International Library Company, n. d.
ODEP 331; DAP 592.

To ram something down someone's **throat**

1839 'Isn't it enough to make a man crusty to see that little sprawler...being forced down the people's throats...?' (p. 291)

The Life and Adventures of Nicholas Nickleby. 1839. The Oxford Illustrated Dickens, Vol. VI. Oxford: Oxford University Press, 1950.
URDANG, *IDIOMS* 1433; WILKINSON 355.

To stick in one's **throat**

1842 ...it stuck in my throat like Macbeth's amen. (p. 111)
1843 Your dedication to Peel stuck in my throat.... (p. 434)
1843 But his father's letter...chokes the words in my throat. (p. 576)

The Letters of Charles Dickens: Volume Three: 1842-1843. Eds. Madeline House, Graham Storey, and Kathleen Tillotson. Oxford: The Clarendon Press, 1974.

1844 Filer sticks in his throat.... (p. 242)

The Letters of Charles Dickens: Volume Four: 1844-1846. Ed. Kathleen Tillotson. Oxford: The Clarendon Press, 1977.
WILKINSON 355.

To be under someone's **thumb**

1850 ...'he would have had Mr. Wickfield...under his thumb. Un—der—his thumb,' said Uriah.... (p. 379)

The Personal History of David Copperfield. 1850. The Oxford Illustrated Dickens, Vol. II. Oxford: Oxford University Press, 1948.

1852-54 ...he now had Scotland (according to the common saying) under his thumb. (p. 264)

Master Humphrey's Clock and A Child's History of England. 1840-41, 1852-54. The Oxford Illustrated Dickens, Vol. XX. Oxford: Oxford University Press, 1958.
APP 371; ODEP 820; EAP 437; MP 623.

As **tight** as a gooseberry

1844 She...was comely, dimpled, plump, and tight as a gooseberry.... (p. 27)

The Life and Adventures of Martin Chuzzlewit. 1844. The Oxford Illustrated Dickens, Vol. IX. Oxford: Oxford University Press, 1951.
WILSTACH 426.

As **tight** as a horse-leech

1865 '...he holds as tight as a horse-leech.' (p. 267)
Our Mutual Friend. 1865. The Oxford Illustrated Dickens, Vol. X. Oxford: Oxford University Press, 1952.

To be on the **tight**

1854 'You're on the Tight-Jeff, ain't you?' (p. 31)
Hard Times for These Times. 1854. The Oxford Illustrated Dickens, Vol. XVII. Oxford: Oxford University Press, 1955.
PARTRIDGE 885.

To shiver one's **timbers**

1859 I wouldn't...shiver my ould timbers and rouse me up with a monkey's tail (man-of-war metaphor), not to chuck a biscuit into Davy Jones's weather eye.... (p. 123)
The Letters of Charles Dickens, ed. Walter Dexter. Vol. III: 1858-1870. The Nonesuch Dickens. London: The Nonesuch Press, 1938.
PARTRIDGE 886.

Fine **time** for them as is well wropped up.

1837 'Fine time for them as is well wropped up, as the Polar Bear said to himself, ven he was practising his skating,' replied Mr. Weller. (p. 406)
The Posthumous Papers of the Pickwick Club. 1837. The Oxford Illustrated Dickens, Vol. I. Oxford: Oxford University Press, 1948.
DOW 138.

There is a good **time** coming.

1855 ...better times are in store.... (p. 700)
The Letters of Charles Dickens: Volume Seven: 1853-1855. Eds. Graham Storey, Kathleen Tillotson, and Angus Easson. Oxford: The Clarendon Press, 1993.
ODEP 324.

There is no **time** like the present.

1837 "No time like the present—at once, if you please." (p. 385)

Sketches by Boz. 1833-40. The Oxford Illustrated Dickens, Vol. XII. Oxford: Oxford University Press, 1957.

1839 '...we'll take it now; there being no time like the present, and no two birds in the hand worth one in the bush....' (p. 477)

The Life and Adventures of Nicholas Nickleby. 1839. The Oxford Illustrated Dickens, Vol. VI. Oxford: Oxford University Press, 1950.

APP 373; ODEP 824; EAP 439; CODP 226; MP 626; DAP 598.

Time and tide wait for no man.

1833-36 ...the old adage, "time and tide wait for no man," applies with equal force to the fairer portion of the creation.... (p. 13)

Sketches by Boz. 1833-40. The Oxford Illustrated Dickens, Vol. XII. Oxford: Oxford University Press, 1957.

1844 Time and tide wait for no man, saith the adage. (p. 154)

The Life and Adventures of Martin Chuzzlewit. 1844. The Oxford Illustrated Dickens, Vol. IX. Oxford: Oxford University Press, 1951.

1859 ...according to rule, time and tide waited for no man.... (p. 106)

A Tale of Two Cities. 1859. The Oxford Illustrated Dickens, Vol. IV. Oxford: Oxford University Press, 1948.

1860 ...I have to work against time and tide.... (p. 170)

The Letters of Charles Dickens, ed. Walter Dexter. Vol. III: 1858-1870. The Nonesuch Dickens. London: The Nonesuch Press, 1938.

APP 373; ODEP 822; EAP 438; CODP 225; MP 628; DAP 598.

Time flies.

1841 'The time has flown.' (p. 39)

1841 'How fast time flies.' (p. 175)

The Old Curiosity Shop. 1841. The Oxford Illustrated Dickens, Vol. VIII. Oxford: Oxford University Press, 1951.

1846 'Time flies, Alfred.' (p. 257)

1846 'Time flies, Alfred,' said the Doctor. (p. 258)

Christmas Books. 1843-49. The Oxford Illustrated Dickens, Vol. XVI. Oxford: Oxford University Press, 1954.

1850 'How the time goes!' (p. 511)

The Personal History of David Copperfield. 1850. The Oxford Illustrated Dickens, Vol. II. Oxford: Oxford University Press, 1948.

1852 Time flies so fast...! (p. 686)

The Letters of Charles Dickens: Volume Six: 1850-1852. Eds. Madeline House, Graham Storey, and Kathleen Tillotson. Oxford: The Clarendon Press, 1988.

APP 374; ODEP 823; EAP 440; CODP 226; MP 628; DAP 598.

Time heals all wounds.

1852 Time skins over the wound of later years.... (p. 410)
"First Fruits." [with George Augustus Sala]. *Charles Dickens' Uncollected Writings from Household Words 1850-1859*, 2 vols. Ed. Harry Stone. Bloomington: Indiana University Press, 1968.
ODEP 823; EAP 442; CODP 226; MP 628; DAP 598.

Time is money.

1839 'Time is money, time is money.' (p. 612)
1839 'Time is money, and very good money too....' (p. 612)
The Life and Adventures of Nicholas Nickleby. 1839. The Oxford Illustrated Dickens, Vol. VI. Oxford: Oxford University Press, 1950.
APP 374; ODEP 823; EAP 441; CODP 226; MP 629; DAP 599.

To be a long **time** coming

1849 The Minute is "a long time coming...." (p. 492)
The Letters of Charles Dickens: Volume Five: 1847-1849. Eds. Graham Storey and K. J. Fielding. Oxford: The Clarendon Press, 1981.

Take **time** by the forelock.

1837 ...I had better take time by the fore lock.... (p. 290)
The Letters of Charles Dickens: Volume One: 1820-1839. Eds. Madeline House and Graham Storey. Oxford: The Clarendon Press, 1965.
1857 'Take time by the forelock.' (p. 584)
Little Dorrit. 1857. The Oxford Illustrated Dickens, Vol. XIV. Oxford: Oxford University Press, 1953.
APP 375; ODEP 822; EAP 443; MP 630; DAP 597.

The good old **times**

1851 ...you have the comparison between...the good old times and the bad news times.... (p. 329)
"The Great Exhibition and the Little One." [with R. H. Horne].
1852 the chairs...were, in the good old times, nailed. (p. 388)
1852 ...O shades of patients who went mad in the only good old times to be mad or sane in.... (p. 390)
"A Curious Dance Round a Curious Tree." [with W. H. Wills].
1852 ...a good old time...through all the good old times...to do anything whatever for Foundlings.... (p. 458)
"Boys to Mend." [with Henry Morley].
1853 ...crime has decreased greatly since the good old times.... (p. 479)
1853 ...in the fine old time of Agincourt and so on, the...loaf would have cost...half-a-crown. (p. 480)

"In and Out of Jail." [with Henry Morley and W. H. Wills]. *Charles Dickens' Uncollected Writings from* Household Words *1850-1859*, 2 vols. Ed. Harry Stone. Bloomington: Indiana University Press, 1968.
STEVENSON 75:3.

To be on the **tip** of one's tongue

1844 It was on the tip of the boy's tongue to relate what had followed.... (p. 464)
The Life and Adventures of Martin Chuzzlewit. 1844. The Oxford Illustrated Dickens, Vol. IX. Oxford: Oxford University Press, 1951.
1859 'Why, it's on the tip of your tongue.' (p. 78)
A Tale of Two Cities. 1859. The Oxford Illustrated Dickens, Vol. IV. Oxford: Oxford University Press, 1948.
URDANG, *IDIOMS* 1448.

To be on the **tiptoe** of expectation

1850 To conclude with a bran new phrase, "I am on the tip toe of expectation"! (p. 61)
The Letters of Charles Dickens: Volume Six: 1850-1852. Eds. Madeline House, Graham Storey, and Kathleen Tillotson. Oxford: The Clarendon Press, 1988.
URDANG, *IDIOMS* 1449.

Tiptop

1840-41 I can let you into...the tiptop sort of thing. (p. 31)
Master Humphrey's Clock and A Child's History of England. 1840-41, 1852-54. The Oxford Illustrated Dickens, Vol. XX. Oxford: Oxford University Press, 1958.
1846 The cock that crowed....is usually perched on the tip-top.... (p. 360)
American Notes and Pictures from Italy. 1842, 1846. The Oxford Illustrated Dickens, Vol. XIX. Oxford: Oxford University Press, 1957.
1847 So will I play up in tip-top style.... (p. 126)
The Letters of Charles Dickens: Volume Five: 1847-1849. Eds. Graham Storey and K. J. Fielding. Oxford: The Clarendon Press, 1981.
1850 Forster was in a tip top state of amiability.... (p. 161)
The Letters of Charles Dickens: Volume Six: 1850-1852. Eds. Madeline House, Graham Storey, and Kathleen Tillotson. Oxford: The Clarendon Press, 1988.
1854 'You were in the tiptop fashion....' (p. 46)
Hard Times for These Times. 1854. The Oxford Illustrated Dickens, Vol. XVII. Oxford: Oxford University Press, 1955.
URDANG, *IDIOMS* 1449.

Tit for tat.

1839 'Tit for tats, quits....' (p. 620)
The Life and Adventures of Nicholas Nickleby. 1839. The Oxford Illustrated Dickens, Vol. VI. Oxford: Oxford University Press, 1950.
APP 375; ODEP 826; EAP 443; MP 632; BARTLETT 142:12.

Proud o' the **title**.

1837 'Proud o' the title, as the Living Skellinton said, ven they show'd him.' (p. 207)
The Posthumous Papers of the Pickwick Club. 1837. The Oxford Illustrated Dickens, Vol. I. Oxford: Oxford University Press, 1948.

To and fro

1841 ...Mr. Haredale...had been pacing to and fro.... (p. 93)
1841 '...as long as our people go backwards and forwards, to and fro, up and down....' (p. 186)
1841 ...Willet...shook him to and fro.... (p. 251)
1841 ...they walked to and fro.... (p. 334)
1841 ...they flitted to and fro.... (p. 511)
Barnaby Rudge: A Tale of the Riots of 'Eighty. 1841. The Oxford Illustrated Dickens, Vol. XV. Oxford: Oxford University Press, 1954.
1842 ...sending wil stewards...to and fro upon the breezy decks.... (p. 8)
1842 To and fro, to and fro, to and fro again a hundred times! (p. 8)
American Notes and Pictures from Italy. 1842, 1846. The Oxford Illustrated Dickens, Vol. XIX. Oxford: Oxford University Press, 1957.
1850 Five or six flushed waiters hurried to and fro.... (p. 122) "A Popular Delusion." [with W. H. Wills].
1850 Thousands of sovereigns were jerked hither and thither from hand to hand...piles of bank notes...hustled to and fro.... (p. 126) "The Old Lady in Threadneedle Street." [with W. H. Wills].
Charles Dickens' Uncollected Writings from Household Words *1850-1859*, 2 vols. Ed. Harry Stone. Bloomington: Indiana University Press, 1968.
1854 ...they heard him walking to and fro.... (p. 276)
Hard Times for These Times. 1854. The Oxford Illustrated Dickens, Vol. XVII. Oxford: Oxford University Press, 1955.
1855 I met her in the corridor, walking to and fro.... (p. 548) "The Holly-Tree Inn."
Charles Dickens' Uncollected Writings from Household Words *1850-1859*, 2 vols. Ed. Harry Stone. Bloomington: Indiana University Press, 1968.
1855 ...I observe it to be becoming very well known...among our countrymen going to and fro. (p. 741)

The Letters of Charles Dickens: Volume Seven: 1853-1855. Eds. Graham Storey, Kathleen Tillotson, and Angus Easson. Oxford: The Clarendon Press, 1993.

1860 To and fro, up and down, aboard and ashore, swarming here there and everywhere, my Emigrants. (p. 222)

1860 ...by travelling to and fro...as though they...would be rent limb from limb.... (p. 263)

The Uncommercial Traveller and Reprinted Pieces Etc. 1850-1860. The Oxford Illustrated Dickens, Vol. XXI. Oxford: Oxford University Press, 1958.

1870 'Mr. Edwin has been to and fro here.... (p. 87)

The Mystery of Edwin Drood. 1870. The Oxford Illustrated Dickens, Vol. XVIII. Oxford: Oxford University Press, 1956.

URDANG, IDIOMS 1456.

Tom, Dick, or Harry

1857 ...the question was usually all about and between...Tom, Dick, or Harry Barnacle.... (p. 314)

Little Dorrit. 1857. The Oxford Illustrated Dickens, Vol. XIV. Oxford: Oxford University Press, 1953.

APP 377; ODEP 828; EAP 445; MP 634.

Tom Tiddler's ground

1839 "I am here, my soul's delight, upon Tom Tiddler's ground, picking up the demnition gold and silver." (p. 428)

The Life and Adventures of Nicholas Nickleby. 1839. The Oxford Illustrated Dickens, Vol. VI. Oxford: Oxford University Press, 1950.

1850 '...she lost in...some such Tom Tiddler nonsense,' explained my aunt.... (p. 513)

The Personal History of David Copperfield. 1850. The Oxford Illustrated Dickens, Vol. II. Oxford: Oxford University Press, 1948.

1861 Title of story: *Tom Tiddler's Ground* (p. 289)

1861 "And why Tom Tiddler's ground?" asked the Traveller. (p. 289)

1861 "...wherever I found it; ...whether on Tom Tiddler's ground, or the Pope of Rome's ground...." (p. 290)

1861 "How far may it be to this said Tom Tiddler's ground?" asked the Traveller. (p. 290)

1861 ...he came to Tom Tiddler's ground. (p. 293)

1861 Tom Tiddler's ground could even show it ruined water.... (p. 293)

1861 The Traveller looked all around him on Tom Tiddler's ground.... (p. 293)

1861 "Tom Tiddler's ground they call this." (p. 294)

1861 "...this...is Tom Tiddler's ground." (p. 294)

1861 ...the owner of Tom Tiddler's ground opened his eyes.... (p. 295)

Christmas Stories. 1871. The Oxford Illustrated Dickens, Vol. XI. Oxford: Oxford University Press, 1956.
ODEP 828; MP 635.

To make a **Tommy** of someone

1860 ...he still walks the earth...seeking to make a Tommy of me.... (p. 341)
1860 ...I felt rather confident of coming through it without being regarded as Tommy.... (p. 342)
1860 ...he discharged it upon me, Tommy.... (p. 343)
1860 ...why is Tommy to be always the foil...? (p. 343)
1860 He makes of me a Promethean Tommy, bound.... (p. 344)
The Uncommercial Traveller and Reprinted Pieces Etc. 1850-1860. The Oxford Illustrated Dickens, Vol. XXI. Oxford: Oxford University Press, 1958.
PARTRIDGE 896.

Never put off until **tomorrow** what you can do today.

1850 'My advice is, never do to-morrow what you can do to-day.' (p. 174)
The Personal History of David Copperfield. 1850. The Oxford Illustrated Dickens, Vol. II. Oxford: Oxford University Press, 1948.
APP 377; ODEP 656; EAP 446; CODP 186; MP 636; DAP 603.

To hold one's **tongue**

1837 'Hold your tongue, sir,' said the magistrate.... (p. 342.)
1837 'Hold your tongue, sir,' interposed the magistrate.... (p. 342)
1837 'Hold your tongue,' interposed Mr. Pickwick. (p. 563)
The Posthumous Papers of the Pickwick Club. 1837. The Oxford Illustrated Dickens, Vol. I. Oxford: Oxford University Press, 1948.
1838 'Hold your tongue, sir!' said Mr. Fang.... (p. 71)
1838 'Hold your tongue this instant...!' (p. 72)
1838 'Hold your tongue, sir!' said Mr. Fang. (p. 72)
1838 'Then you hold your tongue....' (p. 142)
1838 'Hold your tongue, will you?' said the jailer. (p. 334)
The Adventures of Oliver Twist. 1838. The Oxford Illustrated Dickens, Vol. V. Oxford: Oxford University Press, 1948.
1839 'Hold your tongue, sir,' said Ralph. (p. 24)
1839 'Hold your tongue!' replied Miss Squeers.... (p. 134)
1839 'Hold your tongue!' shrieked Miss Squeers.... (p. 138)
1839 'Will you hold your tongue—female?' said Mr. Mortimer Knag.... (p. 222)

The Life and Adventures of Nicholas Nickleby. 1839. The Oxford Illustrated Dickens, Vol. VI. Oxford: Oxford University Press, 1950.

1841 'Hold your tongue, sir,' said John Willet. (p. 23)

1841 ...Mrs. Varden...acknowledged Miggs's champtionship by commanding her to hold her tongue. (p. 56)

1841 'Hold your tongue, sir'....he generally wound up by bidding him to hold his tongue. (p. 99)

1841 '...you'll hold your tongue.' (p. 572)

Barnaby Rudge: A Tale of the Riots of 'Eighty. 1841. The Oxford Illustrated Dickens, Vol. XV. Oxford: Oxford University Press, 1954.

1841 'Hold your tongue,' said his friend. (p. 19)

The Old Curiosity Shop. 1841. The Oxford Illustrated Dickens, Vol. VIII. Oxford: Oxford University Press, 1951.

1844 'Hold your tongue!' she cried.... (p. 414)

1844 'Hold your tongue!' (p. 571)

The Life and Adventures of Martin Chuzzlewit. 1844. The Oxford Illustrated Dickens, Vol. IX. Oxford: Oxford University Press, 1951.

1848 '...he said to me as a caution to hold my tongue....' (p. 734)

1848 'Will you hold your tongue, Misses Brown?' he exclaimed.... (p. 736)

Dealings with the Firm of Dombey and Son. 1848. The Oxford Illustrated Dickens, Vol. VII. Oxford: Oxford University Press, 1950.

1849 ...you can't hold your tongue! (p. 624)

The Letters of Charles Dickens: Volume Five: 1847-1849. Eds. Graham Storey and K. J. Fielding. Oxford: The Clarendon Press, 1981.

1850 'You hold your tongue, mother....' (p. 748)

1850 'Will you hold your tongue, mother...?' (p. 749)

The Personal History of David Copperfield. 1850. The Oxford Illustrated Dickens, Vol. II. Oxford: Oxford University Press, 1948.

1850-56 A man...bids her hold her tongue. (p. 524)

The Uncommercial Traveller and Reprinted Pieces Etc. 1850-1860. The Oxford Illustrated Dickens, Vol. XXI. Oxford: Oxford University Press, 1958.

1854 '...howd thee tongue!' (p. 142)

Hard Times for These Times. 1854. The Oxford Illustrated Dickens, Vol. XVII. Oxford: Oxford University Press, 1955.

1861 '...it might make you hold your tongue....' (p. 203)

Great Expectations. 1861. The Oxford Illustrated Dickens, Vol. XIII. Oxford: Oxford University Press, 1953.

1865 'Hold your tongue, you water-rat!' (p. 170)

1865. 'Then he should have held his tongue. If he had held his tongue he would have....' (p. 269)

1865 'If I had held my tongue, you would....' (p. 269)

1865 'But I can manage to hold my tongue.' (p. 269)

1865 '...I have held my tongue....' (p. 271)

1865 'Hold your tongue! ...I didn't intend to tell you to hold your tongue....Don't hold your tongue.' (p. 473)
1865 '...you hold your tongue, Bella, my dear....' (p. 590)
Our Mutual Friend. 1865. The Oxford Illustrated Dickens, Vol. X. Oxford: Oxford University Press, 1952.
ODEP 377; DAP 604.

To be **tongue-tied**

1857 ...hosts of tongue-tied and blindfolded moderns were carefully feeling their way.... (p. 512)
Little Dorrit. 1857. The Oxford Illustrated Dickens, Vol. XIV. Oxford: Oxford University Press, 1953.
URDANG, *IDIOMS* 1540.

It is ill jesting with edged **tools**.

1839 '...what an edged tool you are!' (p. 615)
The Life and Adventures of Nicholas Nickleby. 1839. The Oxford Illustrated Dickens, Vol. VI. Oxford: Oxford University Press, 1950.
APP 378; ODEP 120; EAP 447; MP 638; DAP 606.

To fight **tooth and nail**

1837 'At it they went, tooth and nail.' (p. 298)
The Posthumous Papers of the Pickwick Club. 1837. The Oxford Illustrated Dickens, Vol. I. Oxford: Oxford University Press, 1948.
1838 ...I had fallen upon him tooth and nail.... (p. 387)
The Letters of Charles Dickens: Volume One: 1820-1839. Eds. Madeline House and Graham Storey. Oxford: The Clarendon Press, 1965.
1840 ...I must concentrate myself upon it tooth and nail.... (p. 178)
The Letters of Charles Dickens: Volume Two: 1840-1841. Eds. Madeline House and Graham Storey. Oxford: The Clarendon Press, 1969.
1843 I am afraid...of writing tooth and nail.... (p. 587)
The Letters of Charles Dickens: Volume Three: 1842-1843. Eds. Madeline House, Graham Storey, and Kathleen Tillotson. Oxford: The Clarendon Press, 1974.
1848 All the intelligence and liberality...are with it, tooth and nail. (p. 254)
The Letters of Charles Dickens: Volume Five: 1847-1849. Eds. Graham Storey and K. J. Fielding. Oxford: The Clarendon Press, 1981.
1850 '...I go at it tooth and nail.' (p. 609)
The Personal History of David Copperfield. 1850. The Oxford Illustrated Dickens, Vol. II. Oxford: Oxford University Press, 1948.
1852-54 ...they fell on each other tooth and nail. (p. 261)

Master Humphrey's Clock and A Child's History of England. 1840-41, 1852-54. The Oxford Illustrated Dickens, Vol. XX. Oxford: Oxford University Press, 1958. APP 378; ODEP 832; EAP 448; MP 638.

To rise to the **top** of the tree

1844 '...if I were at the top of the tree, Tom!' (p. 191)
The Life and Adventures of Martin Chuzzlewit. 1844. The Oxford Illustrated Dickens, Vol. IX. Oxford: Oxford University Press, 1951.
1850 '...he does not...place it out of his power to rise, ultimately, to the top of the tree.' (p. 532)
The Personal History of David Copperfield. 1850. The Oxford Illustrated Dickens, Vol. II. Oxford: Oxford University Press, 1948.
WILKINSON 152.

To sleep like a **top**

1846 ...I drank brandy and water, and slept like a top. (p. 685)
The Letters of Charles Dickens: Volume Four: 1844-1846. Ed. Kathleen Tillotson. Oxford: The Clarendon Press, 1977.
APP 379; ODEP 741; EAP 449; MP 640.

Topsy-turvy

1837 ...his whole social system was...turned completely topsy-turvy.... (p. 246)
Sketches by Boz. 1833-40. The Oxford Illustrated Dickens, Vol. XII. Oxford: Oxford University Press, 1957.
1844 'If your brains is not turned topjy turjey, Mr. Sweedlepipes!' (p. 812)
The Life and Adventures of Martin Chuzzlewit. 1844. The Oxford Illustrated Dickens, Vol. IX. Oxford: Oxford University Press, 1951.
1846 ...the lid...first of all turned topsy-turvy.... (p. 160)
Christmas Books. 1843-49. The Oxford Illustrated Dickens, Vol. XVI. Oxford: Oxford University Press, 1954.
1850 'Prince Alphabet turned topsy-turvy....' (p. 330)
The Personal History of David Copperfield. 1850. The Oxford Illustrated Dickens, Vol. II. Oxford: Oxford University Press, 1948.
1850-56 ...they turned things topsy-turvy.... (p. 548)
The Uncommercial Traveller and Reprinted Pieces Etc. 1850-1860. The Oxford Illustrated Dickens, Vol. XXI. Oxford: Oxford University Press, 1958.
URDANG, *IDIOMS* 1544.

Touch and go

1839 'There's...touch-and-go farce in your laugh,' said Mr. Vincent Crummles. (p. 283)
The Life and Adventures of Nicholas Nickleby. 1839. The Oxford Illustrated Dickens, Vol. VI. Oxford: Oxford University Press, 1950.
1842 ...I never saw anything so perfectly touch and go.... (p. 246)
The Letters of Charles Dickens: Volume Three: 1842-1843. Eds. Madeline House, Graham Storey, and Kathleen Tillotson. Oxford: The Clarendon Press, 1974.
APP 379; ODEP 833; EAP 449; MP 640.

To put the finishing **touches** to something

1861 ...he put the finishing touches to his job. (p. 311)
Christmas Stories. 1871. The Oxford Illustrated Dickens, Vol. XI. Oxford: Oxford University Press, 1956.
WILKINSON 445.

As **tough** as an old yew tree

1857 ...he was as tough as an old yew-tree, and as crusty as an old jackdaw. (pp. 680-681)
Little Dorrit. 1857. The Oxford Illustrated Dickens, Vol. XIV. Oxford: Oxford University Press, 1953.

To go to **town**

1864 ...here am I...going out of town...to keep Shakespeare's birthday in peace and quiet. (p. 385)
The Letters of Charles Dickens, ed. Walter Dexter. Vol. III: 1858-1870. The Nonesuch Dickens. London: The Nonesuch Press, 1938.
WILKINSON 185.

To get into the **track**

1864 ...I...am...getting back into the track to-day.... (p. 404)
The Letters of Charles Dickens, ed. Walter Dexter. Vol. III: 1858-1870. The Nonesuch Dickens. London: The Nonesuch Press, 1938.
WILKINSON 8.

As **tractable** as a lamb

1850 He...would be as quiet and tractable as any Lamb. (p. 186)
The Letters of Charles Dickens: Volume Six: 1850-1852. Eds. Madeline House, Graham Storey, and Kathleen Tillotson. Oxford: The Clarendon Press, 1988.
WILSTACH 430.

To know a **trick** worth two of that

1837 '...he knows a trick worth a good half dozen of that....' (p. 370)
The Posthumous Papers of the Pickwick Club. 1837. The Oxford Illustrated Dickens, Vol. I. Oxford: Oxford University Press, 1948.
APP 382; ODEP 839; EAP 453; MP 644.

To lie (act) like a **Trojan**

1855 ...he went on lying like a Trojan about the pony. (p. 123)
Christmas Stories. 1871. The Oxford Illustrated Dickens, Vol. XI. Oxford: Oxford University Press, 1956.
MP 644.

To swear like a **trooper**

1861 Old Barley might be as old as the hills, and might swear like a whole field of troopers.... (p. 359)
Great Expectations. 1861. The Oxford Illustrated Dickens, Vol. XIII. Oxford: Oxford University Press, 1953.
APP 382; ODEP 792; EAP 453; MP 645.

As **true** as steel

1839 '...I was as true as steel.' (p. 794)
The Life and Adventures of Nicholas Nickleby. 1839. The Oxford Illustrated Dickens, Vol. VI. Oxford: Oxford University Press, 1950.
1850 He was...as true as steel.... (p. 33)
The Personal History of David Copperfield. 1850. The Oxford Illustrated Dickens, Vol. II. Oxford: Oxford University Press, 1948.
APP 352; ODEP 840; EAP 414; MP 592.

As **true** as taxes

1850 'It was as true...as taxes is.' (p. 308)
The Personal History of David Copperfield. 1850. The Oxford Illustrated Dickens, Vol. II. Oxford: Oxford University Press, 1948.

As **true** as the Bank of England [Cf. Safe.]

1839 'It's...true as the Bank of England....' (p. 701)
The Life and Adventures of Nicholas Nickleby. 1839. The Oxford Illustrated Dickens, Vol. VI. Oxford: Oxford University Press, 1950.
ODEP 691; MP 30.

As **true** as turnips

1850 'It was as true...as turnips is.' (p. 308)
The Personal History of David Copperfield. 1850. The Oxford Illustrated Dickens, Vol. II. Oxford: Oxford University Press, 1948.

To blow the **trumpet**

1836 I have blown the trumpet. (p. 156)
The Letters of Charles Dickens: Volume One: 1820-1839. Eds. Madeline House and Graham Storey. Oxford: The Clarendon Press, 1965.
URDANG, *IDIOMS* 1559.

Put your **trust** in God and keep your powder dry.

1841 'Put your trust in the Lord, and keep this powder dry!' (p. 231)
Complete Plays and Selected Poems of Charles Dickens. London: Vision Press, 1970.
1850 ...if he could only have put his trust in Providence, and kept his paper damp—for printing.... (p. 137)
"A Paper-Mill." [with Mark Lemon]. *Charles Dickens' Uncollected Writings from Household Words 1850-1859*, 2 vols. Ed. Harry Stone. Bloomington: Indiana University Press, 1968.
ODEP 842; CODP 231; MP 646; DAP 478.

As **trustworthy** as the Bank of England [Cf. Safe.]

1857 'And is as trustworthy as the Bank of England.' (p. 101)
Little Dorrit. 1857. The Oxford Illustrated Dickens, Vol. XIV. Oxford: Oxford University Press, 1953.
ODEP 691; MP 30.

It is the honest **truth**.

1866 ...it is the honest truth. (p. 460)
The Letters of Charles Dickens, ed. Walter Dexter. Vol. III: 1858-1870. The Nonesuch Dickens. London: The Nonesuch Press, 1938.

The **truth** will out.

1852 Whatever is true, will assert itself. (p. 615)
The Letters of Charles Dickens: Volume Six: 1850-1852. Eds. Madeline House, Graham Storey, and Kathleen Tillotson. Oxford: The Clarendon Press, 1988.
APP 384; ODEP 845; EAP 456; CODP 231; MP 649; DAP 616.

To tell the **truth**, the whole truth, and nothing but the truth

1853 ...'I speak the truth, the whole truth, and nothing but the truth, so—' (p. 544)

Bleak House. 1853. The Oxford Illustrated Dickens, Vol. III. Oxford: Oxford University Press, 1948.
ODEP 845; EAP 456; MP 649.

Truth is mighty and will prevail.

1844 '...we had the presumption to console ourselves with the remark that Truth would in the end prevail, and Virtue be triumphant....' (p. 159)
The Life and Adventures of Martin Chuzzlewit. 1844. The Oxford Illustrated Dickens, Vol. IX. Oxford: Oxford University Press, 1951.
ODEP 844; EAP 455; DAP 617.

Truth is sacred.

1860 Truth is sacred.... (p. 200)
The Uncommercial Traveller and Reprinted Pieces Etc. 1850-1860. The Oxford Illustrated Dickens, Vol. XXI. Oxford: Oxford University Press, 1958.

Truth lies at the bottom of the well.

1844 "Beutiful Truth!" exclaimed the Chorus, looking upward. "How is your name profaned by vicious persons! You don't live in a well, my holy principle, but on the lips of false mankind." (p. 668)
The Life and Adventures of Martin Chuzzlewit. 1844. The Oxford Illustrated Dickens, Vol. IX. Oxford: Oxford University Press, 1951.
APP 384; ODEP 844; EAP 456; CODP 231; MP 648; DAP 617.

To change one's **tune**

1844 He...changed his tune, and whistled a little louder. (p. 215)
The Life and Adventures of Martin Chuzzlewit. 1844. The Oxford Illustrated Dickens, Vol. IX. Oxford: Oxford University Press, 1951.
APP 385; ODEP 736; EAP 457; MP 650.

To bring up with a round **turn**

1854 ...that brought him up with a round turn, as we say at sea. (p. 453)
The Letters of Charles Dickens: Volume Seven: 1853-1855. Eds. Graham Storey, Kathleen Tillotson, and Angus Easson. Oxford: The Clarendon Press, 1993.
URDANG, *IDIOMS* 1563.

To have a heavy **turn**

1836 ...I fear I shall have a heavy turn. (p. 138)

The Letters of Charles Dickens: Volume One: 1820-1839. Eds. Madeline House and Graham Storey. Oxford: The Clarendon Press, 1965.

Turn and turn about; one off, one on.

1844 'Turn and turn about; one off, one on.' (p. 779)
The Life and Adventures of Martin Chuzzlewit. 1844. The Oxford Illustrated Dickens, Vol. IX. Oxford: Oxford University Press, 1951.
URDANG, IDIOMS 1563.

Two can live as cheaply as one.

1839 '...it's nearly as cheap to keep two as it is to keep one....' (p. 322)
The Life and Adventures of Nicholas Nickleby. 1839. The Oxford Illustrated Dickens, Vol. VI. Oxford: Oxford University Press, 1950.
MP 654; DAP 620.

Two can play at that game.

1846 ...there are two parties to any such game. (p. 684)
The Letters of Charles Dickens: Volume Four: 1844-1846. Ed. Kathleen Tillotson. Oxford: The Clarendon Press, 1977.
APP 389; ODEP 295; EAP 460; MP 654.

Not to care **twopence**

1847 ...I don't care twopence for being behindhand.... (p. 59)
The Letters of Charles Dickens: Volume Five: 1847-1849. Eds. Graham Storey and K. J. Fielding. Oxford: The Clarendon Press, 1981.
MP 655.

U

Uncle Sam

1837 ...I have looked over Uncle Sam.... (p. 247)
1837 One of the accompanying parcels contains "Uncle Sam...." (p. 247)
The Letters of Charles Dickens: Volume One: 1820-1839. Eds. Madeline House and Graham Storey. Oxford: The Clarendon Press, 1965.
URDANG, *IDIOMS* 1572; STEVENSON 61:7.

It's **unekal**.

1837 '"It's unekal," as my father used to say wen his grog warn't made half-and-half....' (p. 576)

The Posthumous Papers of the Pickwick Club. 1837. The Oxford Illustrated Dickens, Vol. I. Oxford: Oxford University Press, 1948.

DOW 144.

Up and down

1841 '...as long as our people go backwards and forwards, to and fro, up and down....' (p. 186)

Barnaby Rudge: A Tale of the Riots of 'Eighty. 1841. The Oxford Illustrated Dickens, Vol. XV. Oxford: Oxford University Press, 1954.

1841 I was up and down—here and there.... (p. 372)

The Letters of Charles Dickens: Volume Two: 1840-1841. Eds. Madeline House and Graham Storey. Oxford: The Clarendon Press, 1969.

1842 ...I...set in for two hours of hard walking up and down. (p. 130)

American Notes and Pictures from Italy. 1842, 1846. The Oxford Illustrated Dickens, Vol. XIX. Oxford: Oxford University Press, 1957.

1856 ...I walked up and down there.... (p. 136)

Christmas Stories. 1871. The Oxford Illustrated Dickens, Vol. XI. Oxford: Oxford University Press, 1956.

1860 To and fro, up and down, aboard and ashore, swarming here there and everywhere, my Emigrants. (p. 222)

The Uncommercial Traveller and Reprinted Pieces Etc. 1850-1860. The Oxford Illustrated Dickens, Vol. XXI. Oxford: Oxford University Press, 1958.

URDANG, *IDIOMS* 1588.

Ups and downs

1852-54 ...here were greater ups and downs than ever. (p. 336)

1852-54 There were even greater ups and downs than these.... (p. 336)

Master Humphrey's Clock and A Child's History of England. 1840-41, 1852-54. The Oxford Illustrated Dickens, Vol. XX. Oxford: Oxford University Press, 1958.

APP 219; ODEP 856; EAP 461; MP 657.

Use and necessity are good teachers.

1841 'Use and necessity are good teachers, as I have heard....' (p. 343)

Barnaby Rudge: A Tale of the Riots of 'Eighty. 1841. The Oxford Illustrated Dickens, Vol. XV. Oxford: Oxford University Press, 1954.

DAP 425.

V

We live in a **vale** of tears.

1841 ...steering her course through this vale of tears.... (p. 170)
Barnaby Rudge: A Tale of the Riots of 'Eighty. 1841. The Oxford Illustrated Dickens, Vol. XV. Oxford: Oxford University Press, 1954.
1841 'Ah! what a vale of tears we live in.' (p. 367)
The Old Curiosity Shop. 1841. The Oxford Illustrated Dickens, Vol. VIII. Oxford: Oxford University Press, 1951.
URDANG, *IDIOMS* 1599.

Vanity of vanities, all is vanity.

1852 ...all is vanity! (p. 412)
"First Fruits." [with George Augustus Sala]. *Charles Dickens' Uncollected Writings from Household Words 1850-1859*, 2 vols. Ed. Harry Stone. Bloomington: Indiana University Press, 1968.
1861 ...Mr. Traveller thought..."Vanity, vanity, vanity! Verily, all is vanity!" (p. 295)
Christmas Stories. 1871. The Oxford Illustrated Dickens, Vol. XI. Oxford: Oxford University Press, 1956.
EAP 7; MP 9; DAP 630; STEVENSON 2415:3.

Verba sapientium sicut stimuli.

1840 Meantime verbum sap. (p. 77)
The Letters of Charles Dickens: Volume Two: 1840-1841. Eds. Madeline House and Graham Storey. Oxford: The Clarendon Press, 1969.
STEVENSON 2599:9. Ecclesiastes 12:11

He's the **victim** of connubiality.

1837 '...I think he's the wictim o' connubiality, as Blue Beard's domestic chaplain said, with a tear of pity, ven he buried him.' (p. 273)
The Posthumous Papers of the Pickwick Club. 1837. The Oxford Illustrated Dickens, Vol. I. Oxford: Oxford University Press, 1948.
DOW 145.

I claim my **Victim.**

1848 And, as the Demon says at the Surrey, "I claim my Victim. Ha! Ha! Ha!" (p. 334)
The Letters of Charles Dickens: Volume Five: 1847-1849. Eds. Graham Storey and K. J. Fielding. Oxford: The Clarendon Press, 1981.

One thing worse than a great **victory** is a great defeat.

1869 ...there was only one thing worse than a great victory, and that was a great defeat. (p. 564)
Toast to the crews of the International University Boat Race, Sydenham, 30 Aug. 1869. *The Works of Charles Dickens: The Speeches.* Ed. Richard H. Shepherd. New National Edition, Vol. II. New York: Hearst's International Library Company, n. d.
BARTLETT 371:7.

As **vigorous** as Julius Caesar

1840 "...as wiggerous as Julius Caesar, my grandfather was." (p. 599)
Sketches by Boz. 1833-40. The Oxford Illustrated Dickens, Vol. XII. Oxford: Oxford University Press, 1957.

To be double-dyed **villain**

1844 '...he is a double-dyed and most intolerable villain!' (p. 493)
The Life and Adventures of Martin Chuzzlewit. 1844. The Oxford Illustrated Dickens, Vol. IX. Oxford: Oxford University Press, 1951.
URDANG, *IDIOMS* 1603.

To nurse a **viper** at one's bosom

1839 ...she should ever have nourished in her bosom such a snake, adder, viper, serpent, and base crocodile.... (p. 690)
The Life and Adventures of Nicholas Nickleby. 1839. The Oxford Illustrated Dickens, Vol. VI. Oxford: Oxford University Press, 1950.
ODEP 747; EAP 464; MP 659.

Virtue is its own reward.

1844 ...a good action was its own reward.... (p. 140)
The Life and Adventures of Martin Chuzzlewit. 1844. The Oxford Illustrated Dickens, Vol. IX. Oxford: Oxford University Press, 1951.
APP 392; ODEP 861; EAP 466; CODP 238; MP 659; DAP 634.

Dum vivimus vivamus.

1839 *Dum vivimus*—live while we may— (p. 542)
The Letters of Charles Dickens: Volume One: 1820-1839. Eds. Madeline House and Graham Storey. Oxford: The Clarendon Press, 1965.
STEVENSON 1413:1.

W

A fair day's **wages** for a fair day's work.

1865 'A fair day's wages for a fair day's work is ever my partner's motto.' (p. 165)
Our Mutual Friend. 1865. The Oxford Illustrated Dickens, Vol. X. Oxford: Oxford University Press, 1952.
STEVENSON 2439:11.

Wait and see.

1833-36 The tailor...bid them wait and see what happened. (p. 66)
Sketches by Boz. 1833-40. The Oxford Illustrated Dickens, Vol. XII. Oxford: Oxford University Press, 1957.
1839 'Never mind; wait and see.' (p. 808)
The Life and Adventures of Nicholas Nickleby. 1839. The Oxford Illustrated Dickens, Vol. VI. Oxford: Oxford University Press, 1950.
ODEP 863; EAP 468; MP 661.

He **wants** you in particklar.

1837 'He wants you particklar; and no one else'll do, as the Devil's private secretary said ven he fetched away Doctor Faustus,' replied Mr. Weller. (p. 193)
The Posthumous Papers of the Pickwick Club. 1837. The Oxford Illustrated Dickens, Vol. I. Oxford: Oxford University Press, 1948.
DOW 147.

When **war** begins, then hell opens.

1854 That war is...a most dreadful and deplorable calamity, we need no proverb to tell us.... (p. 454)
Address to the Commercial Travellers, London, 30 Dec. 1854. *The Works of Charles Dickens: The Speeches.* Ed. Richard H. Shepherd. New National Edition, Vol. II. New York: Hearst's International Library Company, n. d.
ODEP 866.

As **warm** as a toast

1841 '...the room's as warm as any toast in a tankard.' (p. 96)
Barnaby Rudge: A Tale of the Riots of 'Eighty. 1841. The Oxford Illustrated Dickens, Vol. XV. Oxford: Oxford University Press, 1954.
APP 376; ODEP 827; MP 633.

It **was** to be—and was.

1837 '...it wos to be—and wos, as the old lady said arter she'd married the footman.' (p. 730)
The Posthumous Papers of the Pickwick Club. 1837. The Oxford Illustrated Dickens, Vol. I. Oxford: Oxford University Press, 1948.
DOW 6.

To be in hot **water**

1850-56 We have the glorious privilege of being always in hot water if we like. (p. 574)
The Uncommercial Traveller and Reprinted Pieces Etc. 1850-1860. The Oxford Illustrated Dickens, Vol. XXI. Oxford: Oxford University Press, 1958.
APP 395; EAP 472; MP 667.

To be of the first **water**

1842 All of which phrases...are pure Americanisms of the first water. (p. 90)
The Letters of Charles Dickens: Volume Three: 1842-1843. Eds. Madeline House, Graham Storey, and Kathleen Tillotson. Oxford: The Clarendon Press, 1974.
WILKINSON 99.

The **way** of the world

1849 'Which is the way the world goes?' (p. 345)
Christmas Books. 1843-49. The Oxford Illustrated Dickens, Vol. XVI. Oxford: Oxford University Press, 1954.
APP 396; EAP 475; MP 672; STEVENSON 2466:5.

The **way** to a man's heart is through his stomach.

1850 Indeed, it has become a kind of proverb that the way to Court often lies through the Old Lady's apartments.... (p. 127)
"The Old Lady in Threadneedle Street." [with W. H. Wills]. *Charles Dickens' Uncollected Writings from* Household Words *1850-1859*, 2 vols. Ed. Harry Stone. Bloomington: Indiana University Press, 1968.
APP 179; ODEP 871; CODP 242; MP 673; DAP 564.

It's a great deal more in your **way** than mine.

1837 'It's a great deal more in your way than mine, as the gen'l'm'n on the right side o' the garden vall said to the man on the wrong 'un, ven the mad bull wos a comin' up the lane.' (p. 524)

The Posthumous Papers of the Pickwick Club. 1837. The Oxford Illustrated Dickens, Vol.
I. Oxford: Oxford University Press, 1948.
DOW 147.

To go the **way** of all flesh

1837 "...he went the way of all flesh." (p. 443)
Sketches by Boz. 1833-40. The Oxford Illustrated Dickens, Vol. XII. Oxford: Oxford
University Press, 1957.
1859 ...I have made up my mind...to go...the way of all flesh. (p. 106)
The Letters of Charles Dickens, ed. Walter Dexter. Vol. III: 1858-1870. The Nonesuch
Dickens. London: The Nonesuch Press, 1938.
APP 396; ODEP 871; EAP 474; MP 671.

There are no two **ways** about it.

1842 "...that's a fact, and no two ways about it." (p. 84)
American Notes and Pictures from Italy. 1842, 1846. The Oxford Illustrated Dickens, Vol.
XIX. Oxford: Oxford University Press, 1957.
APP 397; MP 671.

Ways and means

1848 '...he has been devising ways and means....' (p. 745)
Dealings with the Firm of Dombey and Son. 1848. The Oxford Illustrated Dickens, Vol.
VII. Oxford: Oxford University Press, 1950.
1865 Casting about for ways and means of dissolving his connexion....
(p. 501)
Our Mutual Friend. 1865. The Oxford Illustrated Dickens, Vol. X. Oxford: Oxford
University Press, 1952.
URDANG, *IDIOMS* 1622.

As **weak** as a reed

1841 '...you were not as weak as a reed....' (p. 25)
The Old Curiosity Shop. 1841. The Oxford Illustrated Dickens, Vol. VIII. Oxford: Oxford
University Press, 1951.
EAP 359; MP 529.

As **weak** as flesh

1844 '...there's a wooden leg...which...was quite as weak as flesh, if not
weaker.' (p. 625)
The Life and Adventures of Martin Chuzzlewit. 1844. The Oxford Illustrated Dickens, Vol.
IX. Oxford: Oxford University Press, 1951.
ODEP 268.

It's an amiable **weakness**.

1837 'You know what the counsel said, Sammy, as defended the gen'l'm'n as beat his wife with a poker, venever he got jolly. "And arter all, my Lord," says he, "it's a amable weakness."' (p. 314)
The Posthumous Papers of the Pickwick Club. 1837. The Oxford Illustrated Dickens, Vol. I. Oxford: Oxford University Press, 1948.
DOW 148.

To be the worse for **wear**

1839 ...one was...a suit of clothes...much the worse for wear.... (p. 8)
The Life and Adventures of Nicholas Nickleby. 1839. The Oxford Illustrated Dickens, Vol. VI. Oxford: Oxford University Press, 1950.
1846 ...I am the worse for the wear.... (p. 638)
The Letters of Charles Dickens: Volume Four: 1844-1846. Ed. Kathleen Tillotson. Oxford: The Clarendon Press, 1977.
1857 His black was the worse for wear.... (p. 684)
Christmas Stories. 1871. The Oxford Illustrated Dickens, Vol. XI. Oxford: Oxford University Press, 1956.
APP 415; ODEP 232; EAP 502; MP 705.

Wear and tear

1844 But wear and tear of law is my consideration. (p. 26)
The Letters of Charles Dickens: Volume Four: 1844-1846. Ed. Kathleen Tillotson. Oxford: The Clarendon Press, 1977.
1848 ...traces were discernible among this finery, of wear and tear.... (p. 755)
Dealings with the Firm of Dombey and Son. 1848. The Oxford Illustrated Dickens, Vol. VII. Oxford: Oxford University Press, 1950.
1850 '...the rounds of that ladder must be made of stuff to stand wear and tear....' (p. 606)
The Personal History of David Copperfield. 1850. The Oxford Illustrated Dickens, Vol. II. Oxford: Oxford University Press, 1948.
1865 ...withdraw from the wear and tear of busy like is my expression. (p. 419)
1866 ..."Why go through this wear and tear...?" (p. 470)
1867 ...its wear and tear is reduced.... (p. 514)
The Letters of Charles Dickens, ed. Walter Dexter. Vol. III: 1858-1870. The Nonesuch Dickens. London: The Nonesuch Press, 1938.
URDANG, *IDIOMS* 1623; STEVENSON 2473:11.

It it fine **weather** for ducks.

1855 "...to say 'fine weather for the ducks,' as, truly, it is...!" (p. 534)
"By Rail to Parnassus." [with Henry Morley]. *Charles Dickens' Uncollected Writings from Household Words 1850-1859*, 2 vols. Ed. Harry Stone. Bloomington: Indiana University Press, 1968.
MP 674.

To keep one's **weather eye** open

1840-41 'Keep your vether eye open, my friend....' (p. 97)
Master Humphrey's Clock and A Child's History of England. 1840-41, 1852-54. The Oxford Illustrated Dickens, Vol. XX. Oxford: Oxford University Press, 1958.
1859 I wouldn't...shiver my ould timbers and rouse me up with a monkey's tail (man-of-war metaphor), not to chuck a biscuit into Davy Jones's weather eye.... (p. 123)
The Letters of Charles Dickens, ed. Walter Dexter. Vol. III: 1858-1870. The Nonesuch Dickens. London: The Nonesuch Press, 1938.
1865 'Keep your weather eye awake....' (p. 282)
Our Mutual Friend. 1865. The Oxford Illustrated Dickens, Vol. X. Oxford: Oxford University Press, 1952.
ODEP 419; WILKINSON 70.

One **wedding** makes many.

1848 ...the cook says at breakfast-time that one wedding makes many.... (p. 437)
Dealings with the Firm of Dombey and Son. 1848. The Oxford Illustrated Dickens, Vol. VII. Oxford: Oxford University Press, 1950.
APP 398; ODEP 875; EAP 477; CODP 243; MP 675; DAP 647.

Ill **weeds** are sure to thrive.

1841 '...ill weeds were sure to thrive.' (pp. 30-31)
The Old Curiosity Shop. 1841. The Oxford Illustrated Dickens, Vol. VIII. Oxford: Oxford University Press, 1951.
ODEP 401; EAP 478; CODP 120; DAP 648.

To get under **weigh**

1842 I wake...when we get under weigh.... (p. 129)
American Notes and Pictures from Italy. 1842, 1846. The Oxford Illustrated Dickens, Vol. XIX. Oxford: Oxford University Press, 1957.
PARTRIDGE 943.

To be worth one's **weight** in gold

1850 'A Suffolk Punch...is worth his weight in gold.' (p. 283)

The Personal History of David Copperfield. 1850. The Oxford Illustrated Dickens, Vol. II. Oxford: Oxford University Press, 1948.

1853 'She's worth her weight in gold,' says the trooper. (p. 478)

1853 'And he is worth...thrice his weight in gold,' said Richard. (p. 521)

Bleak House. 1853. The Oxford Illustrated Dickens, Vol. III. Oxford: Oxford University Press, 1948.

APP 398; ODEP 922; EAP 478; MP 676.

As **welcome** as coals at Christmas

1841 'He's as welcome as flowers in May, or coals at Christmas.' (p. 357)

The Old Curiosity Shop. 1841. The Oxford Illustrated Dickens, Vol. VIII. Oxford: Oxford University Press, 1951.

As **welcome** as the flowers in May

1841 'He's as welcome as flowers in May, or coals at Christmas.' (p. 357)

The Old Curiosity Shop. 1841. The Oxford Illustrated Dickens, Vol. VIII. Oxford: Oxford University Press, 1951.

1848 'Welcome to all as knowed you, as the flowers in May!' (p. 687)

Dealings with the Firm of Dombey and Son. 1848. The Oxford Illustrated Dickens, Vol. VII. Oxford: Oxford University Press, 1950.

1866 You will be as welcome as the flowers in May.... (p. 457)

The Letters of Charles Dickens, ed. Walter Dexter. Vol. III: 1858-1870. The Nonesuch Dickens. London: The Nonesuch Press, 1938.

ODEP 270; MP 233.

To be **well through** something

1841 I...wish you "well through it"—as the monthly nurses say.... (p. 433)

The Letters of Charles Dickens: Volume Two: 1840-1841. Eds. Madeline House and Graham Storey. Oxford: The Clarendon Press, 1969.

PARTRIDGE 1466.

As **wet** as a sop

1854 'As wet as a sop.' (p. 15)

Hard Times for These Times. 1854. The Oxford Illustrated Dickens, Vol. XVII. Oxford: Oxford University Press, 1955.

WILKINSON 348.

Whatever is, is right.

1837 'Wotever is, is right, as the young nobleman sveetly remarked wen they put him down in the pension list 'cos his mother's uncle's vife's grandfather vunce lit the king's pipe vith a portable tinder-box.' (p. 714)
The Posthumous Papers of the Pickwick Club. 1837. The Oxford Illustrated Dickens, Vol. I. Oxford: Oxford University Press, 1948.
1859 ...the Old Bailey...was a choice illustration of the precept, that 'Whatever is is right....' (p. 56)
A Tale of Two Cities. 1859. The Oxford Illustrated Dickens, Vol. IV. Oxford: Oxford University Press, 1948.
STEVENSON 1989:14.

What's-his-name

1846 '...little what's-her-name...makes her fantastic Pic-Nic here....' (p. 188)
Christmas Books. 1843-49. The Oxford Illustrated Dickens, Vol. XVI. Oxford: Oxford University Press, 1954.
1848 'In my desire to save young what's-his-name from being kicked out of this place, neck and crop....' (p. 467)
Dealings with the Firm of Dombey and Son. 1848. The Oxford Illustrated Dickens, Vol. VII. Oxford: Oxford University Press, 1950.
1850 'Oh my stars and what's-their-names!' she went on.... (p. 328)
The Personal History of David Copperfield. 1850. The Oxford Illustrated Dickens, Vol. II. Oxford: Oxford University Press, 1948.
PARTRIDGE 948.

The **wheel** of fortune is forever in motion.

1860 "But the wheel goes round, and round, and round; and because it goes round—so I am told by the politest authorities—it goes well." (p. 210)
The Uncommercial Traveller and Reprinted Pieces Etc. 1850-1860. The Oxford Illustrated Dickens, Vol. XXI. Oxford: Oxford University Press, 1958.
APP 144; EAP 165; MP 678; DAP 650.

There are **wheels** within wheels.

1867 ...a very remarkable book...for it suggestion of wheels within wheels.... (p. 567)
The Letters of Charles Dickens, ed. Walter Dexter. Vol. III: 1858-1870. The Nonesuch Dickens. London: The Nonesuch Press, 1938.
APP 400; ODEP 882; EAP 479; MP 678.

Say **when!**

1847 Say when! (p. 137)
The Letters of Charles Dickens: Volume Five: 1847-1849. Eds. Graham Storey and K. J. Fielding. Oxford: The Clarendon Press, 1981.
PARTRIDGE 949.

(Not) to know **where** to have [=find] someone

1839 ...he was considering, as the saying goes, where to have him. (p. 93)
The Life and Adventures of Nicholas Nickleby. 1839. The Oxford Illustrated Dickens, Vol. VI. Oxford: Oxford University Press, 1950.

To **whistle** for something

1852 ...I might as well whistle to the sea. (p. 765)
The Letters of Charles Dickens: Volume Six: 1850-1852. Eds. Madeline House, Graham Storey, and Kathleen Tillotson. Oxford: The Clarendon Press, 1988.
APP 401; ODEP 884; EAP 481; MP 681.

To wet one's **whistle**

1850 '...the wine shall be kept to wet your whistle....' (p. 93)
The Personal History of David Copperfield. 1850. The Oxford Illustrated Dickens, Vol. II. Oxford: Oxford University Press, 1948.
APP 401; ODEP 881; EAP 481; MP 680.

As **white** as a spectre

1859 'All covered with dust, white as a spectre, tall as a spectre!' (p. 109)
A Tale of Two Cities. 1859. The Oxford Illustrated Dickens, Vol. IV. Oxford: Oxford University Press, 1948.
APP 151.

As **white** as chalk

1844 'He's as white as chalk!' (p. 750)
The Life and Adventures of Martin Chuzzlewit. 1844. The Oxford Illustrated Dickens, Vol. IX. Oxford: Oxford University Press, 1951.
EAP 65; MP 104.

As **white** as marble

1841 ...she sat...as rigid, and almost as white and cold, as marble. (p. 453)
Barnaby Rudge: A Tale of the Riots of 'Eighty. 1841. The Oxford Illustrated Dickens, Vol. XV. Oxford: Oxford University Press, 1954.
APP 237; EAP 282; MP 403.

As white as milk; milk-white

1855 And on a milk-white courser...a glorious figure springs into the square. (p. 533)
"By Rail to Parnassus." [with Henry Morley]. *Charles Dickens' Uncollected Writings from Household Words 1850-1859*, 2 vols. Ed. Harry Stone. Bloomington: Indiana University Press, 1968.
1860 ...every horse was milk-white.... (p. 150)
1860 ...all the milk-white horses in the stables broke their halters.... (p. 152)
The Uncommercial Traveller and Reprinted Pieces Etc. 1850-1860. The Oxford Illustrated Dickens, Vol. XXI. Oxford: Oxford University Press, 1958.
APP 243; EAP 289; MP 410.

As white as snow

1844 ...she sits, at a little table, white as driven snow.... (p. 332)
The Life and Adventures of Martin Chuzzlewit. 1844. The Oxford Illustrated Dickens, Vol. IX. Oxford: Oxford University Press, 1951.
1851 "...the white satins...came up as white as driven snow." (p. 231)
"Spitalfields." [with W. H. Wills]. *Charles Dickens' Uncollected Writings from* Household Words 1850-1859, 2 vols. Ed. Harry Stone. Bloomington: Indiana University Press, 1968.
APP 342; EAP 403; MP 579.

To tell white lies

1862 ...look at...the lies (white, I hope) that are forced upon us! (p. 321)
Christmas Stories. 1871. The Oxford Illustrated Dickens, Vol. XI. Oxford: Oxford University Press, 1956.
URDANG, IDIOMS 1638.

A Whitechapel shave

1860 ...smoothness of cheek...is imparted by what is termed in Albion a "Whitechapel shave" (and which is, in fact, whitening, judiciously applied to the jaws with the palm of the hand).... (p. 278)
The Uncommercial Traveller and Reprinted Pieces Etc. 1850-1860. The Oxford Illustrated Dickens, Vol. XXI. Oxford: Oxford University Press, 1958.
PARTRIDGE 955.

Why and wherefore

1840 *...you know the why and wherefore....* (p. 60)
The Letters of Charles Dickens: Volume Two: 1840-1841. Eds. Madeline House and Graham Storey. Oxford: The Clarendon Press, 1969.
APP 401; ODEP 886; EAP 481; MP 682; DAP 652.

To go on a **wild-goose chase**

1841 'He...will have gone away upon some wild-goose errand....' (p. 37)
1841 'It was a wild-goose chase.' (p. 319)
Barnaby Rudge: A Tale of the Riots of 'Eighty. 1841. The Oxford Illustrated Dickens, Vol. XV. Oxford: Oxford University Press, 1954.
1844 '...how...does the woman come to be on board ship on such a wild-goose venture!' cried Martin. (p. 249)
The Life and Adventures of Martin Chuzzlewit. 1844. The Oxford Illustrated Dickens, Vol. IX. Oxford: Oxford University Press, 1951.
1860 ...the disappointed coachmaker had sent me on a wild-goose errand.... (p. 246)
The Uncommercial Traveller and Reprinted Pieces Etc. 1850-1860. The Oxford Illustrated Dickens, Vol. XXI. Oxford: Oxford University Press, 1958.
APP 65; ODEP 889; EAP 67; MP 106.

To sow one's **wild oats**

1839 '...he must sow his wild oats....' (p. 814)
The Life and Adventures of Nicholas Nickleby. 1839. The Oxford Illustrated Dickens, Vol. VI. Oxford: Oxford University Press, 1950.
1854 ...he is sowing his wild oats. (p. 505)
"On Her Majesty's Service." [with E. C. Grenville Murray]. *Charles Dickens' Uncollected Writings from* Household Words *1850-1859*, 2 vols. Ed. Harry Stone. Bloomington: Indiana University Press, 1968.
APP 268; ODEP 889; EAP 320; MP 459.

To spread like **wildfire**

1846 It...is going still, like Wildfire. (p. 464)
The Letters of Charles Dickens: Volume Four: 1844-1846. Ed. Kathleen Tillotson. Oxford: The Clarendon Press, 1977.
1852 ...it...goes "like wildfire", as Mr. Tonson says. (p. 748)
The Letters of Charles Dickens: Volume Six: 1850-1852. Eds. Madeline House, Graham Storey, and Kathleen Tillotson. Oxford: The Clarendon Press, 1988.
APP 402; EAP 483; MP 683.

To take the **will** for the deed

1841 Take the will for the deed.... (p. 356)
The Letters of Charles Dickens: Volume Two: 1840-1841. Eds. Madeline House and Graham Storey. Oxford: The Clarendon Press, 1969.
1842 ...you will take the will for the deed. (p. 242)
The Letters of Charles Dickens: Volume Three: 1842-1843. Eds. Madeline House, Graham Storey, and Kathleen Tillotson. Oxford: The Clarendon Press, 1974.
1850 ...you will take the will for the deed. (p. 118)
The Letters of Charles Dickens: Volume Six: 1850-1852. Eds. Madeline House, Graham Storey, and Kathleen Tillotson. Oxford: The Clarendon Press, 1988.
1854 ...take the will for the deed. (p. 289)
The Letters of Charles Dickens: Volume Seven: 1853-1855. Eds. Graham Storey, Kathleen Tillotson, and Angus Easson. Oxford: The Clarendon Press, 1993.
1861 'I'll accept the will for the deed,' said Wemmick. (p. 248)
Great Expectations. 1861. The Oxford Illustrated Dickens, Vol. XIII. Oxford: Oxford University Press, 1953.
APP 402; ODEP 890; EAP 483; MP 683.

Where there's a **will**, there's a way.

1839 'Where there's a will, there's a way, you know.' (p. 157)
1839 'Where there's a will, there's a way.' (p. 272)
The Life and Adventures of Nicholas Nickleby. 1839. The Oxford Illustrated Dickens, Vol. VI. Oxford: Oxford University Press, 1950.
1850 ...there must surely be a flaw in the old adage, and that where there was a will (and a great many wills) there was no way at all.... (p. 175)
"The Doom of English Wills: Cathedral Number Two." [with W. H. Wills]. *Charles Dickens' Uncollected Writings from* Household Words *1850-1859*, 2 vols. Ed. Harry Stone. Bloomington: Indiana University Press, 1968.
APP 402; ODEP 891; CODP 245; MP 683; DAP 655.

It is an ill **wind** that blows no good.

1838 '...evil winds blow nobody any good....' (p. 289)
The Adventures of Oliver Twist. 1838. The Oxford Illustrated Dickens, Vol. V. Oxford: Oxford University Press, 1948.
1839 'But it's a ill wind as blows no good to nobody....' (p. 740)
The Life and Adventures of Nicholas Nickleby. 1839. The Oxford Illustrated Dickens, Vol. VI. Oxford: Oxford University Press, 1950.
1850 ...'what wind blows you here? Not an ill wind, I hope?' (p. 220)
The Personal History of David Copperfield. 1850. The Oxford Illustrated Dickens, Vol. II. Oxford: Oxford University Press, 1948.
1860 ...ingenious gentlemen...to whom it is an ill wind that blows no good.... (p. 52)

The Uncommercial Traveller and Reprinted Pieces Etc. 1850-1860. The Oxford Illustrated
Dickens, Vol. XXI. Oxford: Oxford University Press, 1958.
APP 403; ODEP 401; EAP 486; CODP 120; MP 685; DAP 656.

Sow the **wind**; reap the whirlwind.

1857 Chapter XXVI: Reaping the Whirlwind (p. 711)
Little Dorrit. 1857. The Oxford Illustrated Dickens, Vol. XIV. Oxford: Oxford University
Press, 1953.
APP 404; ODEP 757; CODP 208; MP 687; DAP 656.

To get **wind** of something

1844 'Anthony Chuzzlewit and his son have got wind of it....' (p. 50)
The Life and Adventures of Martin Chuzzlewit. 1844. The Oxford Illustrated Dickens, Vol.
IX. Oxford: Oxford University Press, 1951.
1857 ...he might have even got wind of some Collegiate joke.... (p. 475)
Little Dorrit. 1857. The Oxford Illustrated Dickens, Vol. XIV. Oxford: Oxford University
Press, 1953.
1861 '...you had got wind of it.' (p. 392)
Great Expectations. 1861. The Oxford Illustrated Dickens, Vol. XIII. Oxford: Oxford
University Press, 1953.
APP 403; EAP 486; MP 686.

To throw something to the four **winds**

1843 ...I disposed of them to the four Winds. (p. 445)
The Letters of Charles Dickens: Volume Three: 1842-1843. Eds. Madeline House, Graham
Storey, and Kathleen Tillotson. Oxford: The Clarendon Press, 1974.
1849 ...their senses...were scattered to the four winds.... (p. 497)
1849 ...throwing all ceremony to the four winds...I would have come....
(p. 636)
The Letters of Charles Dickens: Volume Five: 1847-1849. Eds. Graham Storey and K. J.
Fielding. Oxford: The Clarendon Press, 1981.
1854 ...he gave everything to the four winds.... (p. 75)
Hard Times for These Times. 1854. The Oxford Illustrated Dickens, Vol. XVII. Oxford:
Oxford University Press, 1955.
APP 405; MP 686.

Wine in, truth out.

1839 'Oh, ho!...wine in, truth out.' (p. 349)
The Life and Adventures of Nicholas Nickleby. 1839. The Oxford Illustrated Dickens, Vol.
VI. Oxford: Oxford University Press, 1950.
APP 406; ODEP 895; EAP 448; MP 688.

Wisely and slow; they stumble that run fast.

1847 ...I made a run...and...you will, I hope, give me the benefit of the old proverb. (p. 38)
The Letters of Charles Dickens: Volume Five: 1847-1849. Eds. Graham Storey and K. J. Fielding. Oxford: The Clarendon Press, 1981.
STEVENSON 2142:7.

To be at one's **wits' end**

1846 ...I am driven to my wits' end.... (p. 684)
The Letters of Charles Dickens: Volume Four: 1844-1846. Ed. Kathleen Tillotson. Oxford: The Clarendon Press, 1977.
1851 ...your registered letter...drives me to my wits' end. (p. 472)
The Letters of Charles Dickens: Volume Six: 1850-1852. Eds. Madeline House, Graham Storey, and Kathleen Tillotson. Oxford: The Clarendon Press, 1988.
1852-54 ...he was at his wit's end.... (p. 248)
Master Humphrey's Clock and A Child's History of England. 1840-41, 1852-54. The Oxford Illustrated Dickens, Vol. XX. Oxford: Oxford University Press, 1958.
1867 ...we are at our wits' end.... (p. 572)
The Letters of Charles Dickens, ed. Walter Dexter. Vol. III: 1858-1870. The Nonesuch Dickens. London: The Nonesuch Press, 1938.
ODEP 905; EAP 490; MP 691.

Keep the **wolf** from the door

1843 ...he should find it hard for a season even to keep the wolf—hunger—from his door.... (p. 391)
Address at the Manchester Athenaeum, 5 Oct. 1843. *The Works of Charles Dickens: The Speeches*. Ed. Richard H. Shepherd. New National Edition, Vol. II. New York: Hearst's International Library Company, n. d.
1844 'We must keep the Wolf from the door, as the proverb says.' (p. 453)
The Life and Adventures of Martin Chuzzlewit. 1844. The Oxford Illustrated Dickens, Vol. IX. Oxford: Oxford University Press, 1951.
1853 '...she is...the wolf of the old saying. It is so very difficult to keep her from the door.' (p. 56)
Bleak House. 1853. The Oxford Illustrated Dickens, Vol. III. Oxford: Oxford University Press, 1948.
APP 408; ODEP 418; EAP 492; MP 692; DAP 665.

All **women** are good.

1837 'All women are angels, they say,' murmured the lady.... (p. 97)
The Posthumous Papers of the Pickwick Club. 1837. The Oxford Illustrated Dickens, Vol. I. Oxford: Oxford University Press, 1948.

ODEP 11.

Women are curious.

1841 'But curiosity you know is the curse of our sex....' (p. 342)
The Old Curiosity Shop. 1841. The Oxford Illustrated Dickens, Vol. VIII. Oxford: Oxford University Press, 1951.
EAP 494.

Women are fickle.

1842 "It has rendered you so fickle, and so given to change, that your inconstancy has passed into a proverb...." (p. 245)
American Notes and Pictures from Italy. 1842, 1846. The Oxford Illustrated Dickens, Vol. XIX. Oxford: Oxford University Press, 1957.
APP 410; MP 694; DAP 669.

Women are volatile.

1862 To say that Henrietta was volatile is but to say that she was a woman. (p. 353)
Christmas Stories. 1871. The Oxford Illustrated Dickens, Vol. XI. Oxford: Oxford University Press, 1956.

Do not halloo until you are out of the **wood**.

1851 One of the speakers this evening his [*sic*] referred to Lord Castlereagh's caution 'not to halloo until they were out of the wood.' (p. 433)
1851 ...they ought not to halloo until they are out of the Woods and Forests. (p. 433)
Toast at a banquet of the Metropolitan Sanitary Association, London, 10 May 1851. *The Works of Charles Dickens: The Speeches*. Ed. Richard H. Shepherd. New National Edition, Vol. II. New York: Hearst's International Library Company, n. d.
APP 411; ODEP 345; EAP 495; CODP 105; MP 696; DAP 670.

A **word** in earnest is as good as a speech.

1853 'A word in earnest is as good as a speech.' (p. 63)
Bleak House. 1853. The Oxford Illustrated Dickens, Vol. III. Oxford: Oxford University Press, 1948.
STEVENSON 2603:1 (CITING DICKENS).

A **word** to the wise is sufficient.

1841 '...a word to the wise is sufficient for them....' (p. 17)
The Old Curiosity Shop. 1841. The Oxford Illustrated Dickens, Vol. VIII. Oxford: Oxford University Press, 1951.
APP 412; ODEP 914; EAP 498; CODP 250; MP 701; DAP 672.

Never use a hard **word** when an easy one will serve your turn.

1843 ...never use a hard word, when an easy one will serve your turn. (p. 535)
The Letters of Charles Dickens: Volume Three: 1842-1843. Eds. Madeline House, Graham Storey, and Kathleen Tillotson. Oxford: The Clarendon Press, 1974.
STEVENSON 2606:5.

One **word** is as good as a thousand.

1851 One word, in certain cases, is not only "as good as a thousand"— but much better. (p. 292)
The Letters of Charles Dickens: Volume Six: 1850-1852. Eds. Madeline House, Graham Storey, and Kathleen Tillotson. Oxford: The Clarendon Press, 1988.
Psalms 84:10.

One's **word** is as good as his bond.

1841 '...you have my promise, my word, my sealed bond (for a verbal pledge with is quite as good)....' (p. 215)
Barnaby Rudge: A Tale of the Riots of 'Eighty. 1841. The Oxford Illustrated Dickens, Vol. XV. Oxford: Oxford University Press, 1954.
APP 413; ODEP 380; EAP 497; MP 699; DAP 672.

Word and deed

1844 ...principles which are practiced in word and deed in Polytechnic Institutions.... (p. 401)
Address to the Liverpool Mechanics' Institution, 26 Feb. 1844. *The Works of Charles Dickens: The Speeches*. Ed. Richard H. Shepherd. New National Edition, Vol. II. New York: Hearst's International Library Company, n. d.
URDANG, *IDIOMS* 1668; STEVENSON 2615:5.

Kind **words** and winning looks

1833 "Kind words and winning looks" have done much with me.... (p. 24)
The Letters of Charles Dickens: Volume One: 1820-1839. Eds. Madeline House and Graham Storey. Oxford: The Clarendon Press, 1965.

To be easy in the **words** of an acting part

1850 You are further requested to be "easy in the words" of Mrs. Kitely.... (p. 189)
The Letters of Charles Dickens: Volume Six: 1850-1852. Eds. Madeline House, Graham Storey, and Kathleen Tillotson. Oxford: The Clarendon Press, 1988.

All **work** and no play make Jack a dull boy.

1838 ...it was all play and no work. (p. 11)
The Adventures of Oliver Twist. 1838. The Oxford Illustrated Dickens, Vol. V. Oxford: Oxford University Press, 1948.
1838 All work and no play makes Jack a dull boy. (p. 353)
The Letters of Charles Dickens: Volume One: 1820-1839. Eds. Madeline House and Graham Storey. Oxford: The Clarendon Press, 1965.
1842 ...that young man...was always at work, and never at play; he was a dull dog at last. (p. 128)
The Letters of Charles Dickens: Volume Three: 1842-1843. Eds. Madeline House, Graham Storey, and Kathleen Tillotson. Oxford: The Clarendon Press, 1974.
1848 All work and no play makes Jack (Leech) a dull boy— (p. 442)
The Letters of Charles Dickens: Volume Five: 1847-1849. Eds. Graham Storey and K. J. Fielding. Oxford: The Clarendon Press, 1981.
1850 ...I fear the old spelling-book would "come true", and Jack would be but a dull boy. (p. 124)
The Letters of Charles Dickens: Volume Six: 1850-1852. Eds. Madeline House, Graham Storey, and Kathleen Tillotson. Oxford: The Clarendon Press, 1988.
1853 All work and no play may make Peter a dull boy as well as Jack. (p. 102)
The Letters of Charles Dickens: Volume Seven: 1853-1855. Eds. Graham Storey, Kathleen Tillotson, and Angus Easson. Oxford: The Clarendon Press, 1993.
APP 413; ODEP 916; EAP 499; CODP 250; MP 701; DAP 674.

To have one's **work** cut out

1856 ...I had my work cut out for me.... (p. 133)
Christmas Stories. 1871. The Oxford Illustrated Dickens, Vol. XI. Oxford: Oxford University Press, 1956.
WILKINSON 23; STEVENSON 2622:4.

All the **world** and his wife

1848 'All the world and his wife too, as the saying is,' returned the delighted Captain. (p. 234)
Dealings with the Firm of Dombey and Son. 1848. The Oxford Illustrated Dickens, Vol. VII. Oxford: Oxford University Press, 1950.
APP 414; ODEP 918; EAP 501; MP 703; DAP 678.

All the **world**'s a stage.

1851 ...all the world was a stage gas-lighted in a double sense.... (p. 339)
The Letters of Charles Dickens: Volume Six: 1850-1852. Eds. Madeline House, Graham Storey, and Kathleen Tillotson. Oxford: The Clarendon Press, 1988.
ODEP 918; DAP 677; STEVENSON 2627:1.

It is a small **world**.

1867 WILDING: Mr. Obenreizer says, 'The world is so small....' (*No Thoroughfare*, II, ii, p. 197)
Complete Plays and Selected Poems of Charles Dickens. London: Vision Press, 1970.
ODEP 918; MP 703; DAP 677.

(Not) to be long for this **world**

1838 TOM: I ain't long for this world. (*The Lamplighter*, I, iii, p. 138)
Complete Plays and Selected Poems of Charles Dickens. London: Vision Press, 1970.

This is a wicked **world**.

1851 SUSAN: What a wicked world this is, to be sure! (*Mr. Nightingale's Diary*, I, i, p. 162)
Complete Plays and Selected Poems of Charles Dickens. London: Vision Press, 1970.
APP 414; ODEP 887; EAP 500; MP 703.

To do one a **world** of good

1841 It will do you a world of good. (p. 353)
The Letters of Charles Dickens: Volume Two: 1840-1841. Eds. Madeline House and Graham Storey. Oxford: The Clarendon Press, 1969.
1846 A bottle of hock...did me a world of good.... (p. 638)
The Letters of Charles Dickens: Volume Four: 1844-1846. Ed. Kathleen Tillotson. Oxford: The Clarendon Press, 1977.
1867 ...it has done a world of good.... (p. 545)
Address to the Railway Benevolent Society, London, 5 June 1867. *The Works of Charles Dickens: The Speeches*. Ed. Richard H. Shepherd. New National Edition, Vol. II. New York: Hearst's International Library Company, n. d.
1868 It...did me a world of good. (p. 604)
The Letters of Charles Dickens, ed. Walter Dexter. Vol. III: 1858-1870. The Nonesuch Dickens. London: The Nonesuch Press, 1938.
URDANG, *IDIOMS* 1673.

A **worm** will turn if trodden upon.

1846 ...the worm would turn if trodden on.... (p. 231)
Christmas Books. 1843-49. The Oxford Illustrated Dickens, Vol. XVI. Oxford: Oxford University Press, 1954.
1851 TIP: The worm will turn if it's trod upon. (*Mr. Nightingale's Diary*, I, i, p. 143)
Complete Plays and Selected Poems of Charles Dickens. London: Vision Press, 1970.
APP 414; ODEP 837; EAP 501; CODP 251; MP 705; DAP 679.

To get **worse** before getting better

1845 ...who, in the ordinary rustic phrase, is likely to be worse before she is better. (p. 357)
The Letters of Charles Dickens: Volume Four: 1844-1846. Ed. Kathleen Tillotson. Oxford: The Clarendon Press, 1977.
ODEP 811.

If the **worst** come to the worst....

1837 ...I can easily obtain it elsewhere, if "the worst come to the worst"— (p. 239)
The Letters of Charles Dickens: Volume One: 1820-1839. Eds. Madeline House and Graham Storey. Oxford: The Clarendon Press, 1965.
1850 If the worst came to the worst.... (p. 186)
The Letters of Charles Dickens: Volume Six: 1850-1852. Eds. Madeline House, Graham Storey, and Kathleen Tillotson. Oxford: The Clarendon Press, 1988.
1850 ...'when the worst comes to the worst, no man is without a friend.... (p. 261)
The Personal History of David Copperfield. 1850. The Oxford Illustrated Dickens, Vol. II. Oxford: Oxford University Press, 1948.
1863 "...if the worst was to come to the worst?" said the Major. (p. 380)
Christmas Stories. 1871. The Oxford Illustrated Dickens, Vol. XI. Oxford: Oxford University Press, 1956.
URDANG, *IDIOMS* 1674; STEVENSON 2637:14.

Prepare for the **worst** and hope for the best.

1860 ...a few shadowy Englishmen prepared for the worst and pretending not to expect it. (p. 181)
The Uncommercial Traveller and Reprinted Pieces Etc. 1850-1860. The Oxford Illustrated Dickens, Vol. XXI. Oxford: Oxford University Press, 1958.
ODEP 250; EAP 502; CODP 114; MP 705; DAP 680.

The **worth** of a thing is best known by the want of it.

1865 We are all of us in the habit of saying in our every-day life [*sic*], that 'We never know the value of anything until we lose it.' (p. 523)
Address to the Newsvendors' Benevolent and Provident Association, London, 9 May 1865. *The Works of Charles Dickens: The Speeches*. Ed. Richard H. Shepherd. New National Edition, Vol. II. New York: Hearst's International Library Company, n. d.
ODEP 922; EAP 469; DAP 680.

To see the **writing** on the wall

1844 '...what is plain enough to them as needn't look through mill-stones...to find out wot is wrote upon the wall behind.' (p. 704)
The Life and Adventures of Martin Chuzzlewit. 1844. The Oxford Illustrated Dickens, Vol. IX. Oxford: Oxford University Press, 1951.
1850 ...I saw it start forth like the old writing on the wall. (p. 295)
The Personal History of David Copperfield. 1850. The Oxford Illustrated Dickens, Vol. II. Oxford: Oxford University Press, 1948.
ODEP 923; MP 706.

X

X Y Z

1850 This is the place for X. Y. Z. to hear something of advantage in. (p. 133)
"The Old Lady in Threadneedle Street." [with W. H. Wills]. *Charles Dickens' Uncollected Writings from* Household Words *1850-1859*, 2 vols. Ed. Harry Stone. Bloomington: Indiana University Press, 1968.
BREWER 1169.

Y

As **yellow** as a November fog

1844 ...the window-blinds, as yellow a November fog, were drawn.... (p. 316)
The Life and Adventures of Martin Chuzzlewit. 1844. The Oxford Illustrated Dickens, Vol. IX. Oxford: Oxford University Press, 1951.

As **young** as the flowers of spring
1857 '...you look young and fresh as the flowers of Spring!' (p. 547)
Little Dorrit. 1857. The Oxford Illustrated Dickens, Vol. XIV. Oxford: Oxford University Press, 1953.

Not to be as **young** as one was

1844 'I am not as young as I was, sir.' (p. 627)
The Life and Adventures of Martin Chuzzlewit. 1844. The Oxford Illustrated Dickens, Vol. IX. Oxford: Oxford University Press, 1951.
STEVENSON 2663:9.

To be a **young Turk**

1840-41 'There is vun young Turk, mum,' said Mr. Weller.... (p. 102)
Master Humphrey's Clock and A Child's History of England. 1840-41, 1852-54. The Oxford Illustrated Dickens, Vol. XX. Oxford: Oxford University Press, 1958.
URDANG, *IDIOMS* 1686.

Z

Zigzag

1846 Gradually down, by zig-zag roads.... (p. 349)
American Notes and Pictures from Italy. 1842, 1846. The Oxford Illustrated Dickens, Vol. XIX. Oxford: Oxford University Press, 1957.
1854 ...it quivered and zigzagged on the iron tracks. (p. 213)
Hard Times for These Times. 1854. The Oxford Illustrated Dickens, Vol. XVII. Oxford: Oxford University Press, 1955.
1857 New zig-zags sprung into the cruel pattern sometimes. (p. 291)
1857 ...and so the work of form-filling...crosswise, and zig-zag, recommenced. (p. 517)
1857 ...the reflected marks...of the zig-zag iron...faded away. (p. 650)
Little Dorrit. 1857. The Oxford Illustrated Dickens, Vol. XIV. Oxford: Oxford University Press, 1953.
1866 ...I placed my foot on the first notch of the zigzag.... (p. 529)
Christmas Stories. 1871. The Oxford Illustrated Dickens, Vol. XI. Oxford: Oxford University Press, 1956.
APP 418; EAP 506.